THE GREAT EXPLORERS SERIES

WEST AND BY NORTH

THE GREAT EXPLORERS SERIES

CONCEIVED BY
Vilhjalmur Stefansson

GENERAL EDITOR
Evelyn Stefansson Nef

BOOKS ALREADY PUBLISHED

BEYOND THE PILLARS OF HERACLES
The Classical World, *by Rhys Carpenter*

SOUTH FROM THE SPANISH MAIN
South America, *by Earl Parker Hanson*

SILKS, SPICES AND EMPIRE
Asia, *by Owen and Eleanor Lattimore*

WEST AND BY NORTH
North America—Sea
by Louis B. Wright and Elaine W. Fowler

BOOKS IN PREPARATION

THE MOVING FRONTIER
North America—Land
by Louis B. Wright and Elaine W. Fowler

NORTH AMERICA SEEN THROUGH THE EYES
OF ITS SEAFARING DISCOVERERS

West and By
North

Edited, annotated, and introduced by
LOUIS B. WRIGHT AND ELAINE W. FOWLER

DELACORTE PRESS / NEW YORK

973.1
W

Contents

81921

List of Maps

Preface

WHEN Vilhjalmur Stefansson first said "a land may be said to be discovered the first time a white man, preferably an Englishman, sets foot on it," it was funnier because it was truer. British leadership in exploration reached its peak early in this century at the time of the Scott and Shackleton expeditions in the Antarctic, and has declined since. But the marrow of the joke contains a valid message that like disagreeable truths generally is seldom dwelt upon.

We do not like to remember that the discoverer who set foot on great new lands of our earth found a native there to welcome him. With the exception of Antarctica, every continent in the world was inhabited when it was "discovered," and what we must deal with in history and this Great Explorer Series is *re*discovery. The real heroes of the exploration sagas were nameless Stone and Bronze Age men who, armed mainly with their intelligence, primitive weapons and boats, found not only all the large land areas, but, even more remarkable, the tiny, terrifyingly isolated Pacific island groups. We can only speculate about how they did it. Archeology, as it becomes more sophisticated and widespread, offers us pieces of the puzzle marked *solved,* but in relation to the whole these areas of light are still depressingly small.

One cannot help mourning the absence of some kind of record, whether artistic, runic or alphabetical, which might have captured something of the first real discovery of North America across Bering Strait, whether man came afoot or in a skin boat. On second thought, a tape recording of the event, even if it were miraculously possible to have one, would be anticlimactic. For the concept of discovering a new land and claiming ownership of it is a relatively recent, civilized idea. It would never occur, for instance, to a Stone Age Eskimo to discover a place he saw for the first time; the idea that a person could own land would be laughable. So if we mourn at all let it be for all the records, letters, logs and journals that *were* written down, but which were lost through fire, flood, prejudice, war, ignorant grandchildren and uninformed librarians.

We must deal then with what does remain, and happily this is a great deal. If one essays the role of a geographical Sherlock Holmes, learning what to look for and how to enjoy it when found, like insects trapped in amber, the firsthand narratives in *West and By North* offer useful information and aesthetic pleasure. The most interesting nuggets are those revealing psychological information about the writers—presenting opportunity for endless, delicious speculation.

All novelists and most writers know that however hard we try it is impossible to conceal our secrets. By the choice of subject, word and image a writer reveals himself unconsciously as well as consciously, especially to a trained detective. The case of Henry James comes to mind immediately. Like other masters of the English language, he tried to bury certain aspects of his private life, but his gifted biographer, Leon Edel, by patiently and carefully reconstructing every detail, proved how futile was the attempt.

Psychologists tell us that we see what we are expecting to see, and the conclusions we often draw about what we see are those we bring ready-made to the encounter. When one of our explorers sees a uniped, cyclops or a mermaid (Columbus reported seeing one of the latter), you may be sure he was expecting to see one. When he mistakes iron pyrites for gold, as Frobisher did, or reports the existence of pearls and precious stones in an area where none exist, he is confirming the psychologists. When he tastes salt in a fresh river we may conclude that he is in search of a salty sea that will lead him to Cathay, fame and riches. As we become expert at reading between the lines and can safely jump to certain conclusions about the writer, we, too, become discoverers, and this may explain our pleasure in reading these narratives. We also find, alas, that not all of our explorers are genuine heroes. They are good and bad, greedy and generous (albeit they tend to be the former more often than the latter), callous and tender, noble and base—in other words, human, like us, and therein lies their charm. We are won not by their perfections but by the flaws which permit us imperfect creatures to identify with them.

One of the threats most of us feel deeply in our present culture is that of being dominated and run by computer and machine. We like to remind ourselves of men, performing heroic, almost impossible, deeds successfully. We need to be reminded of the success of a single human fighting against great odds. Columbus' success becomes ours; we journey with Drake; and we vicariously feel the success or pathos of our explorers.

My favorite armchair explorer, Stephen Leacock, expressed this sense of identification perfectly in his introduction to Stefansson's *Unsolved Mysteries of the Arctic*. Sitting before the comfortable fire in his Côte des Neiges study-library, with a hot toddy handily near, he says:

> I have been with Franklin on that famous journey to the Coppermine that was the prelude to his last and fatal adventure. I remember no more thrilling episode in my life than when Franklin and I—with Richardson and Back (later the Admiral) to support us—crossed the freezing Coppermine, running heavy with ice, in a craft made of willow sticks. Several times I had to stop reading and warm up.

In current slang Leacock and we are *with it* as we read.

Further fulfilling the prophecies of the psychologists it is amusing to notice among the early explorers national and cultural traits that still exist today. Each reflects his own portrait. Our French discoverers describe with respect, interest and enthusiasm the food and wit of the Indians they encounter. The British comment on their gentlemanly manners, the Spanish on their cruelty and gentleness. I was reminded of young Winston Churchill's first African journey when he remarked that today he passed the most beautiful country encountered thus far, "quite like England."

We learn also from this volume of Dr. Wright's that one of the uses of the then brand-new tobacco was that it curbs the appetite. Raleigh's account of the germ warfare which the white man waged against the Indians, nondeliberate to be sure, but just as deadly, moves us as it has all who have read it since it was written. There is a timelessness in the demonstration of earlier man's effortless ability to believe in Christianity while enslaving the Indians. This parallels our own thinking about black people's problems. We see what we expect to see, we find what we want to find, we recognize familiar things, even if they aren't there; and we believe those things we have a need to believe, preferring those ideas which keep us comfortable. *Plus ça change, plus c'est la même chose.*

A dividend of this particular volume, number four of the Great Explorer Series, is that for the first time we are dealing with men, events and places that are relatively familiar because they deal with home territory, North America. This time we are more or less familiar with the geography of the arena, with names of many of the leaders and the rough outlines of their deeds. There is a cheerful, homely immediacy about the material we are dealing with, absent in previous volumes.

The Delacorte Press is fortunate and I am proud to have as editors of *West and By North,* and its forthcoming companion volume, which will deal with the *land* discovery of the continent, a formidable team. Dr. Louis Wright is the distinguished historian who directed the great Folger Shakespeare Library in Washington, D.C., for more than two decades. He has an enviable reputation for combining accuracy with liveliness in his scholarship, and he has accumulated more honorary degrees than anyone I know—in excess of twenty-five! With his longtime researcher and collaborator Elaine W. Fowler, he has produced a book that is enlightening and fascinating.

—Evelyn Stefansson Nef

A Note on the Sources

A S THE annotations will indicate, we have tried to utilize, wherever possible, the original printings of documents and narratives. Anyone dealing with early voyages inevitably incurs a debt to the magnificent series of narratives of exploration published by the Hakluyt Society. We have expressed our indebtedness to the Hakluyt Society in specific references in the text. Another series, the *Original Narratives of Early American History*, has also been of great value.

For all aspects of Columbus' career the mose useful book is still Samuel E. Morison, *Admiral of the Ocean Sea: A Life of Christopher Columbus* (Boston, 1949). One of the most readable accounts of French exploration in North America is Francis Parkman, *Pioneers of France in the New World*, in many editions. A succinct and accurate account of early English activities in the Caribbean will be found in James A. Williamson, *Hawkins of Plymouth* (London, 1949). See also the same author's *Sir Francis Drake* (New York, 1962). For Captain John Smith see Philip L. Barbour, *The Three Worlds of Captain John Smith* (Boston, 1964).

For general information on various aspects of exploration of North America by sea, relevant chapters in the following books will be useful: *A Short History of British Expansion* (London, 1947); Louis B. Wright, *Middle-Class Culture in Elizabethan England* (Chapel Hill, N.C., 1935) and *Gold, Glory, and the Gospel* (New York, 1970); Boies Penrose, *Travel and Discovery in the Renaissance* (Cambridge, Mass., 1952), which contains a useful bibliography of works on exploration; John B. Brebner, *The Explorers of North America, 1492–1806* (London, 1933); Edward Heawood, *A History of Geographical*

Discovery in the Seventeenth and Eighteenth Centuries (Cambridge, 1912); J. H. Parry, *Europe and a Wider World, 1415–1715* (London, 1949) and *The Age of Reconnaissance* (London, 1963); David B. Quinn, *Raleigh and the British Empire* (London, 1947); and Justin Windsor, *Narrative and Critical History of America* (8 vols., Boston, 1884–89).

Note to the Reader

THIS volume attempts to provide a narrative of the principal voyages of discovery that revealed the outlines of North America. Naturally the emphasis is on early voyages beginning with the Norsemen and concentrating upon the probing voyages of the sixteenth and seventeenth centuries. One of the constant dreams of Europeans was the hope of finding a northern passage to Asia. Much exploration in the early seventeenth century was promoted by the effort to find the Northwest Passage to China, an effort that continued long afterward.

We have added a final chapter briefly describing the exploration of the coast of the Pacific Northwest. With the mapping of Cook and Vancouver and the discovery of the mouth of the Columbia River by Robert Gray, the main outlines of North America were made known to Europeans.

Not every voyage to North America in the early days was a voyage of discovery and exploration, and not even every genuine voyage of discovery can be described in the brief compass of one book. We have tried to include those voyages of great explorers that were the most significant for later developments. Some of the early expeditions were designed merely to land emigrants on these shores. For example, the voyage of the *Mayflower,* known to every school child, was distinctly not a voyage of discovery. Actually the *Mayflower* set out for Virginia, got lost and wound up in Plymouth harbor, where its passengers went ashore and settled. We have therefore not included the adventures of the *Mayflower* in our chronicle of explorations. We have also omitted discussions of the early settlements as such, for we have not wanted to repeat material easily available in Colonial histories.

All the explorers were fascinated by the native peoples they encountered and the natural products of the new land. The excitement over a few rocks and a bit of soil from the moon that astronauts have brought back in our time may suggest the much greater excitement caused by living people and exotic products that explorers of the New World found and carried back to Europe. Most of their chronicles devote much space to people and products. Even at the risk of some repetition we have included a number of passages on the Indians to indicate the interest this topic had for European observers and to suggest the importance these early contacts had for future relations with the aborigines.

The sixteenth and seventeenth centuries were devoted to finding out about the outlines of the great land mass that blocked man's access to the Pacific and the riches of Asia. Once these outlines were discovered, explorers turned, in the eighteenth and nineteenth centuries, to investigating the interior of this land mass and to exploring its resources. The inland journeys were made both by land and by water, on the great rivers of the continent. Documents on these explorations will form the basis of a further volume in the Great Explorers Series—the second volume on the discovery of North America by land.

In reprinting excerpts from original narratives, we have modernized spelling but have left obsolete words. We have also modernized capitalization and punctuation. Where proper names have known modern equivalents, we have given the modern versions. In cases where no modern equivalents of proper names are known, we have left them as in the original. We have left dates and degrees of latitude and longitude as written in the originals.

—L. B. W.
E. W. F.

February 10, 1970

THE GREAT EXPLORERS SERIES

WEST AND BY
NORTH

❧ I ❧

The Background of
the Age of Discovery

A PEASANT boy, driving his goats to pasture along the
banks of the Rio Tinto on the morning of August 3,
1492, would not have guessed that the three little ships making their way to sea from the harbor of Palos were about
to undertake a voyage that would change his world. Even the
learned friars in the monastery of La Rábida at the bend of the
river, those friars who had welcomed Columbus and encouraged
him in his great Enterprise of the Indies, little dreamed that
their world never would be the same after the return of the
Captain General from his discoveries in the West. Not even
Queen Isabella and King Ferdinand, whose marriage had
united the kingdoms of Castile and Aragon and made possible
the rise of modern Spain, were aware of the implications of
the voyage. They hoped that Columbus, the plausible and persistent Genoese navigator, would succeed in his promise to find
a westerly route to China and Japan; they hoped that he would
blaze a trail for trading ships that would bring profitable
cargoes to Spain, as Portugal's vessels were bringing gold, ivory
and slaves to her from newfound territory on the coast of Africa.
Already the Portuguese were talking of sailing to India around
the point of Africa which Bartholomeu Dias had rounded in
1487. Least of all did Columbus, for all of his theories, know
that he was about to double the extent of the known surface
of the earth and open the way for the expansion of Europe's
people into a whole New World. Columbus thought that the
Western Sea was reasonably narrow and that a few hundred
leagues west of the Canaries he would find Cipangu (Japan)

1

and that he would make an easy journey thence to Cathay (China). On the way perhaps he might discover new islands such as the Canaries which he could claim for their Catholic Majesties and which he might be allowed to govern. But his main intention was to establish a new route to the riches of the East. That had been the selling point with Isabella and Ferdinand. Spain was not willing to sit idly by and allow her neighbor Portugal to monopolize that lucrative trade.

The year of Columbus' departure on his first voyage of discovery was a crucial time in the history of Western man. If few knew or cared about the three little ships sailing out from Palos on that August day, many knew of other things that had recently happened, events that made them restless and uncertain and that were to alter the course of mankind in the Mediterranean basin and elsewhere in Europe. The spirit of change was beginning to affect many regions. Some changes had come with dramatic speed; others as yet were scarcely discernible. But everywhere tension was rising as new ideas and new concepts began to stir thoughtful men in all countries. Although conventional notions that prevailed for centuries would not give way suddenly, a tide had turned and a current was gathering force that eventually would sweep away most of the vestiges of medieval Europe. But as Columbus ordered sail set for the Western Sea on August 3, 1492, neither he nor his seamen nor most of the men then living realized that their civilization had reached a turning point from which there would be no going back to the ancient ways of their forefathers. On Columbus' vessels, the ship's company at sunset sang the ancient hymn "Salve Regina," as men had sung it for generations before them, secure in their faith that the Queen of Heaven would have a special care for a world that would remain as they had always known it.

Behind the men of 1492 lay centuries of confusion, turmoil, war and sometimes torpor—the centuries of the so-called Middle Ages. The Spain which Columbus now served had been a broken land of various kingdoms, Christian and Mohammedan. Italy, whence Columbus had come to Castile, was only a geographical expression without unity or coherence, a country of warring city-states where the Papacy exercised a dubious and varying influence upon some of the towns and local potentates. Wolves

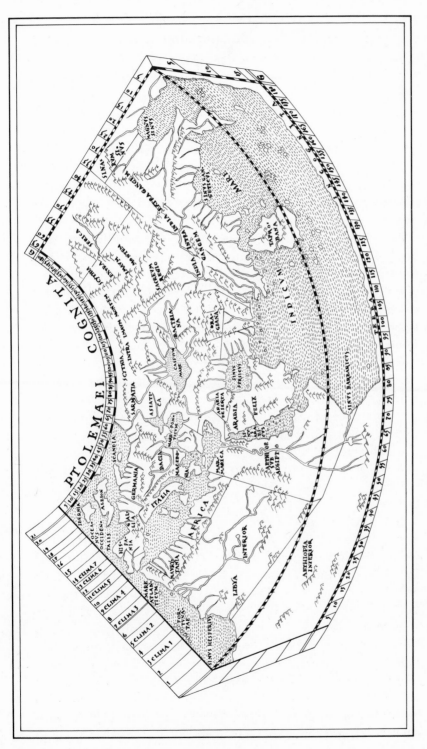

The pre-Columbian world as Europeans knew it. This map, often reproduced, first appeared in the work of the Greco-Egyptian geographer Ptolemy, ca. A.D. 150.

ranged the slopes of the Apennines, carrying off sheep and occasionally children of the hapless peasants. Condottieri, sometimes as savage as the wolves, sold their services to the highest bidder and kept Italy seething with internecine warfare. But a city on each coast of northern Italy built ships, developed seamen and grew prosperous and powerful. Genoa, the native city of Columbus, on the Ligurian coast to the west of the peninsula, was famous for the daring of its seamen, who were equally ready to fight the Islamic corsairs of North Africa or the galleys of its hated rival, Venice, which had made itself supreme in the Adriatic.

Elsewhere in Western Europe during the Middle Ages conditions were hardly any better than in Italy or Spain. The French king who reigned in Paris had constantly to dispute and often to fight with an English king who reigned in London for vast territories in France. Bordeaux, for example, was an English possession for longer than it had been a French city. Powerful French nobles also contended with the King in Paris for authority in their provinces. The dukes of Burgundy frequently exerted more power in international affairs than the kings of France. Germany, like Italy, was merely a geographical expression composed of multitudinous principalities, kingdoms, electorates, independent cities and other minor political divisions. The Emperor of the Holy Roman Empire—which someone said was not holy, nor Roman, nor an Empire—was in a persistent state of controversy and sometimes in a state of war with the Papacy.

Not until the age of Columbus could England call itself a united nation. During the Middle Ages the great barons had fought for influence and for the crown until they destroyed themselves in the Wars of the Roses between the rival houses of York and Lancaster. When Henry Tudor conquered the last Yorkist king, Richard III, in 1485, he took advantage of the weakened state of the barons to create a new nobility, subservient to the crown, and began the development of a unified state. England as a modern state with a centralized authority dates from the accession of Henry VII. This monarch was vaguely aware of new stirrings in the world and his seamen were beginning to probe the murky seas to the west. Indeed, some scholars believe that fishermen from Bristol or other ports of the west of England may have pushed beyond the mist-shrouded coasts of Iceland to anticipate Columbus' discovery of lands beyond. Henry VII, overly cautious and crafty, missed the opportunity of sponsoring Columbus' voyage of discovery, for the great explorer's brother Bartholomew appealed to him in vain for support of the Enterprise of the Indies. For Henry, like his fellow king Charles VIII of France a little later, declined to risk ships, money and men in an endeavor which his advisers declared visionary and fantastic. King John II of Portugal had also let his craftiness defeat him in dealing with Columbus. Only a few years would pass before both England and France would regret their lack of vision.

Although unaware of the significance of the crucial time, the men of 1492, all over Western Christendom, stood upon the divide between two worlds, the old and the new, the Middle Ages and the Modern. As yet they did not know it, but before them lay a new geographical world. But more significant was the new spiritual, intellectual, economic and political world about to rise on the ruins of the crumbling structure of medieval institutions.

Behind the men of 1492 lay an age of faith. This faith would not altogether disappear in the new world about to come into being, but it would be vastly and inexorably altered in the years to come. Indeed, religion, which had exerted such an enormous influence in medieval society, would continue to affect the course of history, but it would undergo many changes and would exert many differing influences, for good and for ill, in the life of Western man. In the later period religion would play a divisive rather than a unifying role.

During the Middle Ages, Western Christendom accepted the spiritual—and sometimes the temporal—authority of the Bishop of Rome as the supreme head of the Church. Strong popes at times might exercise great power, as for example, in January 1077 at Canossa, when Pope Gregory VII forced the Holy Roman Emperor, Henry IV, to stand barefoot in the snow for three days before he agreed to withdraw his excommunication and remove the papal interdict from his cities. Not many later popes had so much power, but despite feuds and wars between papal and antipapal political factions—and despite a few sporadic outbreaks of minor heresies—Western

Christendom throughout the Middle Ages remained a united spiritual force.

Indeed, the light of civilization was kept burning by consecrated monks in abbeys and monasteries throughout the reaches of Europe. The Benedictines were the earliest to establish houses, to promulgate rules of conduct for their order and to organize a system of religious work and instruction. A branch of the Benedictines, the monks of Cluny in France, exerted a great influence in the promotion of learning during the Dark Ages and in the establishment of the Peace of God—a church-inspired truce between warring secular factions. Another branch of the Benedictines, the Cistercians—called "White Monks"—spread over most of Europe and did more than most secular authorities to maintain established order, even to improve farming and to keep learning alive. Later came the Augustinians (to which order both Desiderius Erasmus and Martin Luther at one time belonged), the Dominicans, the Franciscans and other orders too numerous to mention. The Dominicans, known as the "Black Friars," were particularly enjoined to preach, to study and to promulgate the true doctrine of the Church. They had a particular responsibility for the administration of the Inquisition and the rooting out of heresy. The Franciscans, known as the "Gray Friars," though their habit is now characteristically brown, were diligent teachers and missionaries who would one day help to bring their form of Christianity to the heathen in a land that Columbus was on his way to discover in the autumn of 1492.

The faith that the preaching friars of the Middle Ages sought to inculcate discounted the worth of the temporal life and held out a hope of reward in heaven hereafter. It was an appealing doctrine for men who could see little amelioration of their lot here below. At least they might look forward to bliss in the world to come, a bliss that had evaded them on this earth. To insure that heavenly reward, they might engage in good works of sundry sorts, each according to his means and ability. The rich could endow abbeys; the poor could give of their time and their labor; and kings could organize crusades against the followers of Mohammed and seek to free the holy places from the rule of the infidels.

The threat of Saracen domination of Western Europe was

very great in the Middle Ages and it was eased in the year of Columbus' departure only by the surrender of the last stronghold of the Moors in Spain. The capitulation of Mohammed XI, better known as Boabdil, at Granada on January 2, 1492, tempered but did not end the threat of Moslem onslaughts on Christendom which had begun centuries before.

The age-old warfare between Christians and Moslems had brought about some of the conditions that made Columbus' voyage imperative. The Crusades, which began in 1095 with the exhortation of Pope Urban II for Christians to go forth and save the holy places from the Seljuk Turks, brought Western Europeans to the Levant and there into contact with the ancient civilizations and delectable wares of the East. In the course of the next few centuries these contacts resulted in an increase in the European appetite for Oriental luxuries: the silks and porcelains of China and fine cottons of Madras; gold filigree work of India, king's ransoms in rubies, emeralds and pearls; perfumes of Araby and bronze utensils, fine cutlery and drugs distilled from rhubarb; all the preservatives and condiments of the far Spice Islands—cloves and pepper, nutmeg, mace and cinnamon; and from fabled Ophir, the "ivory, and apes and peacocks" that had adorned the Biblical court of Solomon. All these treasures of Scheherazade's legends the Crusaders found materialized in the bazaars of the Near East and North Africa, terminal points for the long and arduous routes overland by caravan and over the seas—the Indian Ocean, Red, Caspian and Black Seas—by Arab dhow. Such luxuries had been known in Western Europe before the Crusades, of course, and in fact one materialistic motive that encouraged some Christians to don the cross of the Crusader was the desire for territorial expansion into the East and the accompanying hope of some Italian cities such as Venice and Genoa to increase their trade in Eastern products. Piety, as so often in history, was mixed with the hope of worldly pelf.

The establishment of the shaky Latin Kingdom with its capital in Jerusalem entailed a continuing struggle with Islam in the Near East, but it also assured an increase in prosperity for Italian cities with war galleys and trading ships. Venice prospered enormously and vastly increased its power and trade. Its merchants established entrepôts in the Near East, and its galleys returned loaded with luxuries for the insatiable markets of Europe. Not all voyages were successful, it is true, and many a galley fell into the hands of Moslem corsairs, but if one out of five got through, it was said, the profits were more than sufficient to offset the losses.

Unwittingly the Crusaders helped to further a process of Christian disintegration in the East that would have repercussions upon Columbus' age. In 1204 the leaders of the Fourth Crusade, influenced by the Venetians, turned aside from their proclaimed objective of conquering Egypt to capture Byzantium (Constantinople) and to overthrow the joint emperors Isaac II and Alexius IV. The Crusaders sacked the city. Its fabulous wealth—including the four bronze horses over the portico of St. Mark's—enriched them and their Venetian underwriters, but the pillage served to weaken the Eastern Empire and to undermine this ancient bulwark against Islam, a bulwark that fell to the Ottoman Turks in 1453.

A Venetian traveler who went to China and returned to tell of its wonders at the end of the thirteenth century did much to stimulate European curiosity about the Far East and to influence later explorations that began probing for a new route to the Indies around the Cape of Good Hope and across the western seas. This traveler—a certain Marco Polo—in 1271 set out from Venice with his father and uncle, who had already made a journey beyond the Crimea to touch the territories of the Mongol emperor of China, Kublai Khan. Polo and his companions were headed for the court of the Great Khan, and they arrived there (Peking) in 1275. Marco Polo found favor in the sight of the Khan, who employed him on business missions, gave him rule over a city and finally allowed him to return home, which he reached in 1295 after twenty years in the East. Finding Venice at war with Genoa, Polo volunteered his services and was captured by the Genoese, perhaps fortunately for posterity, because he dictated to a fellow prisoner the story of his travels, and this descriptive narrative telling of the wonders of Cathay was widely read by later generations. Columbus knew his Marco Polo well; his copiously annotated copy of Polo's work still exists. Indeed, Polo's errors in placing China and Japan much nearer Europe than they are helped to persuade Columbus that a sea crossing to those lands was feasible. This alluring error was compounded by a Florentine physician and scientist, Paolo Toscanelli, with whom Columbus corresponded. From Toscanelli he obtained assurance that Polo's description of the location of China and Japan (which Polo named Cipangu) was mathematically credible. That assurance kept the explorer encouraged through his long autumn voyage, and he maintained a belief, long after his first landfall, that the gold-roofed houses of Cipangu, mentioned by Polo, would soon appear on the horizon.

Marco Polo had told of the religious tolerance of Kublai Khan, grandson of the conqueror Chingis Khan, and had led his readers to believe that the Great Khan would welcome Christians. Promoters of explorations did not fail to suggest that God would prosper an enterprise that promised to carry the gospel message to the Khan, and that thought was not allowed to escape pious Queen Isabella. Unhappily, had Columbus reached the empire that he supposed a descendant of Kublai Khan still governed, he would have been grieved to discover that others who knew not Kublai now ruled: the Ming dynasty, whose first emperor, Chu Yüan-chang, had been a Buddhist monk, in the latter half of the fourteenth century had thrown out the Mongols and all their works. He had also discouraged the traffic with "foreign devils" that Mongol rulers had approved. Although Columbus was unaware of it, this change in the Far East had interposed another block in communications between East and West.

More obvious was the break in communications caused by the rise of the Ottoman Turks, who swept over much of Asia Minor and the Balkans in the fourteenth and fifteenth centuries, affecting directly and indirectly events that influenced Columbus and his age. They were ruthless and ferocious warriors with an excellent sense of military organization. By 1402 they were threatening Constantinople, but that city was saved as if by a miracle by an attack on the Ottomans' flank by another ruthless Asiatic conqueror, Tamerlane, descendant of Chingis Khan, who had his capital at Samarkand. The respite vouchsafed Constantinople was not long enough for the effete rulers of the Eastern Empire to gather strength to resist the Turks, and the city fell in 1453.

Constantinople, or Byzantium, had been for a thousand years

a center of Greek culture and its influence was widespread throughout Eastern Europe. From Byzantium had gone missionaries who carried Christianity and elements of Greek civilization as far as the steppes of Russia. But Constantinople's influence had also affected Western Europe, and for a century before its fall to the Turks, Greeks had been filtering into Italy, bringing with them manuscripts and stimulating a revival of interest in Greek literature and learning. Before the fourteenth century much of the learning of the ancient world, particularly Greek scientific ideas, had found its way into Europe from Arabian sources.

The fall of Constantinople merely stimulated a movement that was already underway, a movement that came to be called the "Renaissance," the revival or rebirth of learning, with its emphasis upon the study of the Greek language as well as Greek literature. Coincidental with the new interest in learning came a revival of interest in painting and sculpture, partly inspired by classical models from Greece and Rome.

One of the characteristics of the Italian Renaissance was its concern with the present world and its goodness. Medieval preachers had taught that mankind was placed in this vale of tears to prepare for a better life to come and that the sooner one managed to get through the earthly existence, the sooner one would inherit the rewards of heaven—provided, of course, that one had led a life that would permit an ascent into heaven after a proper cleansing in Purgatory.

The great discovery of the Italian Renaissance was the infinite pleasure that the present world might confer, joys to be had without waiting—and without too much worry about the consequences. The world was good. The sun shone, the birds sang, women were beautiful and love was not to be denied. We should make the most of our opportunities, and philosophers set about proving the rightness of this view. They read Aristotle and Plato and the Bible, and they tried to reconcile Greek and Christian ethics. Sometimes they succeeded to their entire satisfaction. Gradually, as the impetus of new ideas grew, the Italian Renaissance became more and more pagan, and preachers of the older, medieval type looked upon it as wicked. But the more "enlightened" clergy, those with rich benefices, those whose concern was more with Plato than with the books of Moses, adopted new fashions, wrote poetry, encouraged painters who saw life realistically and lived with pleasure and gaiety to match any secular lord.

The later years of the fifteenth century—the years when Columbus was learning the rudiments of navigation at Genoa—saw a climax of secularization in Italy. Eight days after Columbus set sail into the Western Sea an event occurred that vividly dramatized the change from an age of faith to one of secular rationalization. On August 11, 1492, Rodrigo Borja, or Borgia, Cardinal of Valencia, Vice-Chancellor of the Church, Bishop of Oporto and Abbot of Subiaco, was elected pope and took the name of Alexander VI. In the previous January, when news of the fall of Granada reached the Cardinal of Valencia in Rome, he had staged a spectacular bullfight in a public square by way of celebrating God's victory over the infidels. If these festivities of thanksgiving are not sufficient to symbolize the shift from the piety of an earlier age to the secular activities of the Renaissance, Pope Alexander VI provided many other evidences of the change.

Not all of Pope Alexander VI's predecessors had been models of Christian asceticism, but none had so openly flaunted their extravagance, their worldliness and their lust for women as did this Spanish servant of the servants of God. Others might allude to their "nephews." Alexander exhibited with pride his children and enjoyed having them visible on ceremonial occasions. Juan, Cesare and Lucrezia Borgia each had a role to play in history, and they, like their father, have gone down in the annals of the Renaissance as the epitome of all that was wicked in the age. Yet none of them, not even Cesare, was probably so black as he was painted. Cesare so impressed Machiavelli that he became the model for that political writer's concept of the efficient if dictatorial ruler, the ideal prince. Alexander, ruthless and greedy though he was, brought a certain amount of order into the papacy and displayed more statesmanship than most of his immediate predecessors. His reign exemplified a growing efficiency in worldly materialism, a hint of things to come in the brave new world then springing to life.

Alexander's unspiritual behavior was merely symptomatic of the direction that the Italian Renaissance had taken in the preceding decades. His conduct was not untypical of some others in his age, and his death would not end the paganism of Rome. Indeed, Pope Julius II and Pope Leo X were equally cynical in their conception of the obligations resting upon the Vicar of Christ.

The secularism that characterized the Italian Renaissance— in contrast to the pious symbols of the Middle Ages—had been increasing for several decades when Alexander's elevation to the papal throne gave dramatic emphasis to a tendency that would become a commonplace of the modern world. Nowhere was this secularism more manifest than in literature, sculpture and painting. A new day had dawned when men would rejoice to be alive, to savor the good things of the earth and to revel in the pleasure of all their senses.

Petrarch, sometimes called the first modern man, wrote his immortal *Trionfi* and *Canzoniere* to glorify secular love— his love for Laura. It makes little difference to us whether Laura was an actual woman or the creation of Petrarch's imagination. The important thing is that his songs are in glorification of an earthly woman and the great love that an earthly woman can inspire. Had Petrarch lived a century or two earlier, he might have written—if he had written at all—in praise of the Mother of God and of that heavenly love that good men must feel for the Virgin.

Lorenzo de' Medici, called "Il Magnifico," the patron of writers and artists, was no mean poet himself, but he lavished his best efforts not upon hymns and sacred songs, but upon gay and often ribald *canti carnascialeschi,* the carnival songs that rocked Florence with laughter in carnival time before Lent. Tellers of tales in verse and prose sought to amuse and to entertain, and they were not squeamish about their subjects and the manner of their treatment. Life was a great panorama, good to look upon and delightful to talk about. Writers might be gentlemen attached to one of the little courts where the arts flourished, like that at Urbino, for example, where Federico da Montefeltro, he of the broken nose, gathered men of letters and artists about him. Or they might be learned clerks in holy orders familiar with the workings of the Roman Curia. It made little difference. The gentleman from Urbino or the cleric from Rome might write with the same carefree abandon.

The most famous center of art in the period before 1492 was Florence, where the Medici in particular encouraged writers and artists. Cosimo de' Medici, called "the Elder" to distinguish him from later Cosimos of a collateral branch, a shrewd banker and politician, laid the foundation of Medicean prosperity and power. But mere wealth and power were not enough for Cosimo. He was the patron of Donatello, Brunelleschi, Ghiberti, Luca della Robbia and many another artist who was bringing reality and life into the arts. He encouraged Marsilio Ficino to translate Plato into Latin, and he died on August 1, 1464, listening to one of Plato's *Dialogues*.

Lorenzo de' Medici, "the Magnificent," grandson of Cosimo, outdid his ancestor in the patronage of the arts. Indeed, he made the palace of the Medici a veritable school for artists and he encouraged sculptors, painters and writers and made them his friends. Impressed by young Michelangelo, who was at work on a block of marble in the Medici garden, Lorenzo took him into the palace to live and to continue his sculpture and painting. In Lorenzo's household Luigi Pulci read aloud cantos from his burlesque heroic poem, *Il Morgante Maggiore*.

Not one of the greatest artists but one of the most typical of the secular trend was Filippo Lippi, called "Fra Lippo Lippi" (the subject of Browning's poem of that name). A waif brought up by the Carmelites, he did not take kindly to monastic life. Early the fathers discovered his talent for painting and set him to work on religious subjects, but Lippi managed to paint into his pictures the faces that he saw in the streets, sometimes to the scandal of the pious clergy who wanted their Virgins and saints to look otherworldly. Lippi was patronized by the Medici, and it was not for nothing that he gave lessons to Botticelli and Benozzo Gozzoli, who learned to look at the world around them and draw inspiration for paintings that are timeless.

The most versatile and brilliant of the Florentine artists at this time was a man who was to spend much of his later career elsewhere, often engaged in the practical problems of engineering. He was Leonardo da Vinci. He learned his craft in the workshop of Verrocchio in Florence, but his genius soon transcended the bounds of painting and sculpture and in 1482 he went on a mission to the court of Lodovico Sforza at Milan and there he remained as Lodovico's military engineer until 1499. Leonardo was painter, sculptor, writer, architect, engineer, scientist and inventor. His notebooks show that he was far in advance of his age in his speculations about many scientific problems. He made a design for a flying machine on such sound principles that, had he been able to provide power for his craft, there is no reason why it could not have flown successfully. Leonardo is the supreme representative of the Renaissance conception of the well-rounded man—the *uomo universale*—competent in many fields; but Leonardo surpassed all others of his day in his versatility. In a later age in a new world another great individual was to exemplify in other terms a similar versatility. That individual was Thomas Jefferson.

In the period before 1492 a development was taking place that would alter the thoughts of men more profoundly than anything else that had happened. That was the multiplication of printing presses and the distribution of books. Since Johann Gutenberg had printed the Bible at Mainz about 1456, printing from movable type had spread rapidly throughout Western Europe. Although presses were established in many places in Flanders, France, Switzerland and Germany, Italy was particularly noted for the development of printing and Venice became one of the major centers of the craft in the fifteenth century. Before 1500, books had appeared from more than 150 Venetian presses. The most famous of Venetian printers was Aldo Manuzio (Latinized to "Aldus Manutius"), who established a press at Venice in 1489. It was his contribution to begin the production of the first inexpensive books for the mass market. Manuzio realized that a great demand existed for Greek and Roman classics, but that most would-be readers of these works were unable to pay for handsome folios, the kind of books that graced the libraries of the great patrons of learning. So he began the publishing of small quartos, bearing on the title pages his well-known symbol, the anchor and dolphin. These books, which sold for a moderate price, reached large numbers of readers and helped to point the way to the use of the printing press as a means of mass communication.

Had Aldo Manuzio been living in the mid-twentieth century, he would have been a publisher of paperback classics.[1]

Another printer also pointed the way to influencing the masses of men. He was William Caxton, a prosperous English merchant who had been a member of the Merchants Adventurers in Bruges and had learned the craft of printing there. Caxton returned to England in 1476 and set up a printing shop in Westminster. He had the wisdom to realize that Englishmen particularly needed books, not in Latin and Greek, but in the vernacular, and he set about publishing translations into English of popular works—the lives of the saints, encyclopedias of general information, fiction and many other types of writing that the general public would want or need. Caxton died in 1491, but his apprentice, Wynkyn de Worde, had had the wit to marry his master's daughter, and the influence of Caxton's press continued. The year of Columbus' departure saw Wynkyn de Worde and other imitators of Caxton busily turning out books that any apprentice in London would find appealing. Only a few of the wisest perhaps realized that this instrument of communication would in time be one of the chief influences in overturning the established order and of stretching men's minds to comprehend the expanding world that lay before them.

A visitor in Florence, Rome, Venice, Genoa or almost any busy Italian city in 1492 would have been convinced that the old days of the Middle Ages were over, that a new sophisticated and cultivated society which smiled at the naïveté of their forefathers was there to stay. But if this visitor had probed more deeply, he might have discovered that not every man approved of this modern sophistication. To some, sophistication looked like cynicism or paganism.

One of those who found much in the new or "modern" society that offended him was Girolamo Savonarola, a Dominican friar, whose flaming rage at the vanities of his age would at length stir all Italy and—for a brief interval—shake Florence to its foundations. Savonarola spoke with a voice of repudiation of all things frivolous, extravagant, sensuous, all things that

[1] As a matter of fact, two present-day series of paperback reprints, published by Doubleday, are entitled "Anchor Books" and "Dolphin Books" to symbolize the intent to emulate Manuzio.

were prone to tempt men and women from the straight and narrow path that led to heaven. His was the recurring voice of the reformer, who frequently makes no distinction between the things of this world that merely please the senses and those that corrode the soul. His was the recurring voice that in other times and places would be called "Puritanism." In the mid-Renaissance it was a particularly insistent and strident voice that made itself heard even in the palace of the Medici.

Savonarola was born of a wealthy family in Ferrara and knew at first hand the literati and the artists who frequented the court of the D'Este in that city. Outside the walls of the palace of the D'Este today stands a marble statue of the friar to attest to his origins in Ferrara. At the age of nineteen Savonarola fell in love with the beautiful daughter of one of the Strozzi, who had been driven from Florence by the Medici. His suit was scornfully rejected and he was told that no Strozzi could demean herself by marrying a Savonarola. This episode seared his soul and it may have determined the already serious youth to join the Dominican order. At any rate, he was soon serving his novitiate as a preaching friar, and in 1482, having become a full-fledged priest, he was sent to the Dominican monastery of San Marco in Florence.

Savonarola's first experience of Florence pleased him, but he soon perceived that Florence, like Ferrara, was a sink of sin. His early preaching at San Marco made little impression, however, and he went to San Gimignano, where he first attracted attention by his eloquent condemnation of iniquity. A little later, at Brescia, preaching in the old square, he stirred the Brescians to repentance. Pico della Mirandola, the philosopher-humanist and friend of Lorenzo de' Medici, heard him preach, was impressed with his earnestness, his learning and his message, and urged Lorenzo to ask for his recall to Florence. Lorenzo little realized the temper of the man. Returning to San Marco in 1490, Savonarola immediately became the sensation of Florence. In his fiery sermons he rebuked the citizens for their extravagance and laxity in morals and showed no fear even of the Medici, whose sins did not escape his notice and comment. When Lorenzo sent five of the most prominent citizens of Florence to remonstrate with him and to urge more temperate speech from his pulpit, Savonarola delivered yet more violent sermons, predicting imminent calamities upon the city, the invasion of Italy by the King of France, the down-fall of the Medici and other dire happenings.

Becoming Prior of San Marco in 1491, Savonarola's power over the city increased and his denunciations of wickedness grew ever more passionate. In the meantime, even as Savonarola was reported to have foretold, Lorenzo the Magnificent fell ill, so grievously ill that he and his doctors knew that the end was near. The time-serving clerics around the great man were no consolation. Lorenzo had heard them before and suspected that their voices might not reach to the gates of heaven. In this emergency, according to legend, he sent for the Prior of San Marco. Surely Savonarola could shrive him effectively and send his soul on its way. Savonarola came, but said he could absolve him only if Lorenzo would do three things. He must repent and give evidence of true faith in God's mercy. To this Lorenzo assented. He must give up his ill-gotten wealth. To this, with a groan, Lorenzo agreed. He must restore to Florence its ancient liberties. When Lorenzo turned his face to the wall and made no answer, Savonarola stamped out of the chamber and left him to die without his absolution. This episode illu-minates the characters of both Lorenzo and Savonarola. Lorenzo's death occurred on April 8, 1492.

Had Lorenzo lived a few years more, he would not have recognized his Florence, particularly in carnival time. Under the influence of the ascetic Prior of San Marco, everyone took to sober dress. Men gave up their mistresses—or sometimes their wives in place of their mistresses. Everybody turned out for sermons, especially for Savonarola's sermons. The Piazza Santa Maria Novella was packed with people on their way to church, on weekdays as well as on Sundays. Savonarola even organized small boys into a sort of sacred militia or the equivalent of pious Boy Scouts. When carnival time came around in 1496, Savonarola made it a religious observance instead of the gay and boisterous festival it had always been. The next year the *carnivale* was even more solemn and godly, and men and women brought pictures and books that they believed un-seemly and burned them in the Piazza della Signoria, in front of the Palazzo Vecchio. Botticelli brought some of his drawings and cast them into the flames. Savonarola was now unofficial dictator of Florence, and he used his opportunity to preach against the wickedness of Pope Alexander VI, who excommunicated the prior and placed an interdict upon the city.

Ascetic virtue, the virtue that theologians of the Middle Ages had commended, can hypnotize a people for a time, but at length the laws of nature reassert themselves and mankind falls from that state of grace to which puritanical preachers occasionally elevate it. So it was with Florence. Savonarola held the Florentines in thrall for an interval and then they turned upon him. They were tired of virtue, Savonarola's virtue and their own. And presently, on May 23, 1498, not far from the spot where Botticelli and others had burned their books and art, Savonarola and two of his fellows, condemned on a trumped-up charge of heresy and schism, were hanged and burned. Florence lapsed back into its paganism, its love of art and the sophistication that characterized the full life of the Renaissance. Italian society had tasted of the civilization of the classical and modern worlds and preferred it.

Perhaps the most significant difference between medieval civilization, coming to an end in 1492, and the modern society just beginning to emerge was the new emphasis placed upon business and commerce. Since the beginning of time, of course, men had traded, and ships had carried cargoes from the earliest period of recorded history, but in 1492 Western Europe was on the verge of new developments in commerce. As yet no one knew it, but Europe was at the beginning of an era of business civilization which is still with us. As the centuries passed, the emphasis upon commerce increased until it dominated all other influences in society. And the land that lay still unknown in the West would become the most powerful of all commercial societies. All of this lay yet hidden in the mists of the future.

But commerce was beginning to make its influence felt in new ways in the years immediately preceding Columbus' Enterprise of the Indies. His bold scheme itself was indicative of, and found motivation in, the new spirit abroad. Venice, it is true, had magnified commerce for centuries and had grown rich, powerful and arrogant on the profits of her Eastern trade. But always in the Middle Ages, even in Venice, there remained a niggling fear that riches obtained in any fashion must in some proportion—a tithe at least—be dedicated to God and His saints lest the owner in death burn in hellfire. The clergy, to be sure, had a vested interest in maintaining this doctrine of the danger of dying wealthy. Hence we see countless churches built and lavishly decorated as insurance against the last, the ultimate hazard of a business career. Rich merchants without number subsidized artists to paint pictures of the Virgin, or some of the saints, with the donor tucked into a corner piously adoring the subject of the picture. This phenomenon becomes less frequent as merchants begin to find other uses for their money from the late fifteenth century onward. One of these uses was capital investment with the hope of profit in this world rather than in the world to come. And other tradesmen than the merchants of Venice were beginning to have capital to invest.

As the ancient trade routes came under increasing pressure from chauvinistic Buddhism in the Far East and the Ottoman Empire in the Near East, Venice had been forced, or found it a good excuse, to increase her middleman's charges to cover the new risks. Not surprisingly, the Venetian monopoly became more unpopular than ever with her European customers. Portugal, recently emerged from Spanish domination and with her face toward the Western Sea, was in a peculiarly fortunate position to profit by the shifting balance of commercial power and to pluck some of the plums from the commercial pie that Venice had so long and greedily kept to herself. For Portugal had a rising bourgeoisie in her port towns, a merchant class relatively free of the restraints that feudal society imposed upon trade in other areas. And by great good fortune Portugal had an enlightened leader in the person of Prince Henry, third son of King John I and Philippa, daughter of English John of Gaunt. Prince Henry is known to English historians as Henry the Navigator. Born in 1394 and dying in 1460, Henry greatly influenced Portugal's first expansion overseas. He combined in his own personality some of the piety of the Middle Ages and much of the new spirit of adventure and commercial enterprise. His first success was the capture of a North African base at Ceuta, on the African side of the Strait of Gibraltar, which he wrested from the Moors in 1415. This campaign started as a religious crusade against the Moorish infidels, but it quickly acquired commercial overtones when the Portuguese realized the value of Ceuta in the newly developing African trade.

Prince Henry had a vision of Portugal's destiny as an expanding commercial power and at once set about creating the means of stimulating exploration and discovery. In 1416 he established himself at Sagres, which served as arsenal and naval base as well as a point of recruitment for skillful seamen and navigators. Maritime powers were already bidding for the services of skilled navigators and seamen with special knowledge, and these men now occupied a position somewhat like that of mercenary troops or the *condottieri* of Italy. They were free agents in international society. Prince Henry welcomed navigators and seamen from all nations to Sagres and enlisted them in the service of Portugal. Later, graduates from the Portuguese service entered the service of other nations. It should be remembered that Ferdinand Magellan, a Portuguese, made his epochal voyage around Cape Horn and sacrificed his life, not for Portugal, but in the service of Spain. Pilots in some of England's expeditions to the New World in later generations were Portuguese and Spaniards. Her first Atlantic venture, just four years after Columbus' first voyage, was the enterprise of John Cabot, born Giovanni Caboto in Genoa and later naturalized in Venice.

The Portuguese managed to maintain a nice balance in their consciences between piety and commerce in the early days of their expansion. Prince Henry himself was grand master of the knightly Order of Christ, the Portuguese successors to the Knights Templar, and the only surviving portrait shows him in the official garb of the order. As the capture of Ceuta was in the nature of a religious crusade against the infidel Moors, so the Portuguese maintained the fiction that as they expanded their trade along the coast of Africa they were also carrying a message of Christ to the heathen. When they brought African slaves back to Portugal, they salved such conscience as they had in the matter—as men were to do for centuries to come—with the assertion that they were bringing poor heathen souls under the beneficent influence of Christianity.

The Portuguese navigators were pushing down the coast of Africa during the middle years of the fifteenth century, but they made it a practice to withhold information about their voyages, insofar as they could, from other nations. They hoped to keep details of their oceanic ventures a trade secret of Portugal. But a Venetian in the employ of Prince Henry, Alvise da ca da Mosto (anglicized "Cadamosto"), who made voyages to the Canaries and Madeira and to the coast of Africa as far south as Gambia in 1455 and 1456, kept vivid notes of what he saw and left a description of an implausible beast called the hippopotamus. He also ate some roasted elephant, because no other Christian had ever eaten such meat.

By 1471 Fernando Po sailed to the mouth of the Niger River and found that Africa sloped away to the southeast. This discovery raised Portuguese hopes of reaching India by sailing around the continent. In the meantime, however, Portugal had laid claim to the throne of Castile and a war with Spain ensued, which Portugal lost. Queen Isabella was installed on the throne of Castile and in 1479 Spain signed the Treaty of Alcaçovas, which confirmed Portugal in its monopoly of trade and expansion in Africa and in the possession of all the Atlantic islands except the Canaries, which Spain had undertaken to conquer from the native Guanches. Portugal had lost the war but won the peace. Three years later King John II set about constructing a Portuguese base at Elmina, in the Bight of Benin. Henceforth, gold, slaves, malaguetta pepper, ivory and other African products flowed into Portuguese markets.

India, however, was still the dream of Portuguese navigators and India had so far eluded them. But in 1486–88 Bartholomeu Dias succeeded in sailing around the Cape of Good Hope, making a landing on the east coast of Africa at what is now Mossel Bay on the Indian Ocean, and returning to report that the way to India was assured. Columbus, in Lisbon when Dias docked, made technical notes concerning this voyage. Since the Portuguese had a monopoly of the route around the Cape of Good Hope, other nations would have to try another way, and Columbus also made note of that.

The ultimate success of the Portuguese came in 1497–99 when Vasco da Gama at last reached Calicut and paved the way for the establishment of a Portuguese empire in the East. In 1510 Affonso de Albuquerque seized Goa, which became the center of Portuguese activity in India and so remained until Nehru took it in 1961.

Spain was not unconscious of what the rival kingdom of Portugal was doing during its early years of commercial and geographical expansion, but Spain was preoccupied with the final phase of its age-old war against the Moors and could give little attention to new enterprises. In the spring and autumn of 1490 King Ferdinand laid waste the cultivated plains before Granada and once more demanded the surrender of the city, the last stronghold of the Moors. The siege of Granada was the culmination of a ten-year campaign. When King Boabdil refused, the Spaniards prepared for a long siege and, as part of the investing force, erected outside the walls of Granada a town of substantial proportions which they named Santa Fe. There at last on January 2, 1492, with pomp and ceremony, King Boabdil, El Chico, surrendered the keys of Granada to their Catholic majesties King Ferdinand and Queen Isabella of Aragon, Castile and Leon. These sovereigns, says a Spanish historian of the event, having completed "the glorious conquest . . . seemed to represent even more than their wonted majesty. Equal with each other, they were raised far above the rest of the world. They appeared, indeed, more than mortal, and as if sent by Heaven for the salvation of Spain." [2] Columbus was present at this ceremony, for he had come to Spain to lay his Enterprise of the Indies before these sovereigns who had been raised by Heaven for supernal events. The patience of the navigator was wearing thin, but still he waited for the great ones to make up their minds, and the great ones waited for wise men within the Church to sort through their learning and advise what should be done about Columbus. In the meantime, in faraway England, news of the victory over the Moors was received with joy, and King Henry VII ordered a procession of the nobility and prelates, together with the Lord Mayor and aldermen of London, to march to St. Paul's to hear a sermon from the Lord Chancellor, now Cardinal Morton. He let them know, says a contemporary chronicler, that "they were assembled in that consecrated place to sing unto God a new song." [3]

Ferdinand and Isabella, too, had other matters of moment

[2] *The Complete Works of William Hickling Prescott* (12 vols., London, 1896–97), I, 480–81.
[3] *Ibid.*, p. 483.

upon their minds. The piety of Queen Isabella moved her to make a special demonstration of gratitude to the God of Hosts who had given the Christian forces a final victory over the Moorish unbelievers. She agreed that the time had come to expel from Spain all Jews who refused to accept conversion. The edict of expulsion, following hard upon the surrender of Granada, was promulgated on March 30, 1492. The responsibility for enforcing the edict was left to Tomás de Torquemada, confessor to the sovereigns and Inquisitor-General of Castile and Aragon. This ruthless and fanatical director of the Inquisition lost no time in setting his agents to work to examine, frequently under torture, all converted Jews and to deport all Jews who would not give up the faith of their fathers.

The Jews of Spain were among the most learned and talented of the subjects of Ferdinand and Isabella. Through eight centuries of cold and hot war between Islam and Christendom they had been the go-betweens, the carriers of Arabian science and learning, the apostles of learning to Western Europe. They were the leaders in the professions of medicine, law and the arts generally. They had also shown great sagacity in developing banking and commerce. In short, they were the people who had done more than any others to provide Christian Spain with intellectual and economic leadership. Now, to satisfy the pious wishes of the sovereigns—and to comply with the Christian commands of their confessor and Inquisitor-General—these people were herded like cattle to the ports and shipped out of Spain, many to die in the deserts of North Africa. Some refugee Jews found asylum in Portugal, to the great benefit of that nation, but presently, under pressure from Queen Isabella, through her daughter who was queen in Lisbon, Portugal too had to close her doors to the Jews.

After the conquest of Granada, many Moslem craftsmen left Spain, taking with them skills which Spain sorely needed. Later, despite a promise made to respect the religion of Moors in Aragon, Emperor Charles V forcibly converted some and deported others. That the economic life of Spain could prosper after the loss of so many talented Jews and Moors is a miracle that the pious could attribute to St. James, though actually the gold brought back from America by the *conquistadores* had something to do with it. Be that as it may, the seeds of ultimate disaster for Spain—and the Spanish Empire about to be born—were sown at the start by the expulsion of some of the best intellects in the Iberian Peninsula.

Ferdinand and Isabella suffered an almost schizophrenic conflict of interest and desires: the domination of an old medieval type of piety, which had been accentuated by the excitement of war against the infidels, in opposition to new concepts of trade and expansion, which were powerfully stimulated by the example of neighboring Portugal. While the rulers of Spain concerned themselves with deep religious matters, Portugal was pushing her trade with Africa and preparing to monopolize India. In the meantime Columbus continued to talk persuasively of expansion westward to China and Japan.

When their Catholic majesties finally accepted Columbus' proposals and the details were completed for the voyage, the little town of Palos was chosen as the port of departure for various convenient reasons, including the fact that their majesties had recently imposed a fine upon the town requiring it to provide the use for a year of two caravels—vessels which Columbus now required. Furthermore, Cádiz, the port that one might think of first, was occupied in 1492. From Cádiz throughout that long and weary year the unhappy Jews of Spain were shipping out. Had they but known the ultimate results of Columbus' discoveries, they might have taken heart, but the fact that they would one day find freedom and prosperity in the New World was hidden from them.

Columbus included among the specialists taken on his first voyage a converted Jew, one Luis de Torres, a man skilled in languages, at least in Hebrew and Arabic. Columbus fondly believed that he would reach the land of the Great Khan and that de Torres would be able to communicate in Arabic with the occupant of the throne of Cathay.

The story of Columbus' first voyage is by now familiar to most Americans interested in the backgrounds of this nation. When the persistence and courage of the Genoese navigator were at last rewarded on October 12 by the landfall at San Salvador or Watlings Island in the Bahamas, he, of course, thought he had found some bit of land off the coast of Japan, and he confidently expected to find the rich country that Marco Polo had led him to believe lay somewhere thereabout.

In the meantime, he took note of the natives whom he encountered, observed that some were wearing gold nose plugs
and pearls, and determined to find the source of the gold
and the pearls. The search for gold, which was to be a will-o'-the-
wisp for thousands of Spaniards—and men of other nations
besides—had begun. Early in November, still in search of the
Great Khan, Columbus discovered Cuba, and a mission that he
sent inland reported men and women carrying firebrands in
their hands to light an herb, the leaves of which they made into
a roll and smoked. The Spaniards had had their first encounter
with tobacco, a commodity that one day would bring more
wealth to traders than all the gold of the Indies. Other herbs,
shrubs and trees Columbus noted with the comment that they
might have commercial value. The native people he also
observed to be gentle and suitable to provide tractable labor
for their masters. If these islands should turn out to be no part
of the dominion of Cipangu or Cathay, Columbus saw himself
the ruler under the crown of Spain of territories already popu-
lated with a convenient supply of labor. Not all the natives
would prove so tractable as those first encountered, but Columbus' premonition that they would be useful proved all too true.
Within a few years after Spanish occupation thousands of
Indians had died in mines and on plantations as slaves of heart-
less masters.

On Christmas Day 1492, while searching the Caribbean for
Cipangu, the heaviest of Columbus' ships, the *Santa Maria*,
ran aground and wrecked on the northern coast of what is now
Haiti. This island, which Columbus named "La Isla Española"
(Latinized to "Hispaniola"), was the site of the first attempt
to make a settlement in the New World. Because he could not
carry home all of the crew of the *Santa Maria*, he decided to
establish a fort at a spot not far from Cape Haitien, which in
commemoration of Christmas he called "La Navidad." The
natives of the region brought objects made of gold and bartered
them for hawks' bells. Furthermore, they told of much gold
not far away, so plentiful indeed that the inhabitants held it
"for naught." Proximity to so rich a mine, it seemed obvious,
was the proper place for a settlement. Though this first settlement ended disastrously, the gold fever had taken hold and
henceforth Spain would search until the collected hoards and

the mines were theirs. The motivation for expansion was clear, and Columbus, in all piety, had shown the way.

The difficult voyage home, the imminence of disaster from the winter storms in the Atlantic, the attempt at arrest by the Portuguese in the Azores and of assassination in Lisbon, the final arrival at Palos, the reception by the Spanish sovereigns in Barcelona, Columbus' three later voyages of discovery, his disappointments and humiliations—all these are a part of later history. The year 1492 ended, perhaps symbolically for Columbus, with the wreck of his flagship, the *Santa Maria,* on a coral reef near the source of gold. The Almighty in His inscrutable way had taken this method of showing His servant the proper place to establish Spanish dominion, Columbus believed, for he had a deep strain of medieval piety in his soul. In danger of shipwreck on the homeward voyage, he and his crew made numerous vows to the saints if they might be saved: to go on pilgrimage to famous shrines, to march to church like penitents clad only in their shirts. Mixed with his piety, however, was the new sense of commercial aggrandizement that was taking possession of men. Columbus had his share of the greed for gold and the lust for power that would dominate Spanish *conquistadores* for generations to come. He saw himself not only as the Admiral of the Ocean Sea, a title granted him by the Spanish Crown, but as viceroy, governor and lord of territories that would make him and his heirs rich forever. Not only would his discoveries give him wealth and prestige, but they would also enhance the glory of the sovereigns of Spain. As Columbus basked in the sun of royal favor at Barcelona in the late days of April 1493, he could contemplate a feat that had given the rulers of Spain the keys to a vast empire, the extent of which none yet knew. He can be forgiven his self-satisfaction and the pride that at times touched on arrogance.

Others were soon to reveal that Columbus had discovered a vast new world. It makes little difference that he himself continued to believe that the lands he had discovered lay just off the coast of China, that some undiscovered strait would lead to the fabled lands described by Marco Polo. The search for that passage through the new continent to the Great South Sea would consume the energies of explorers for two centuries more. Ironically a Florentine map maker, diligent letter writer and companion of explorers named Amerigo Vespucci, who himself never commanded an expedition but went along for the ride, gave his name to the whole of the new lands discovered by Columbus.

If none knew in 1492 that Columbus had in fact discovered a new world, at least the rulers of Spain and Portugal believed that on his new route to the Indies he had found rich new territories, perhaps the fabled Islands of Antillia, and that these islands contained gold. What other lands remained undiscovered beyond the Pillars of Heracles neither Spain nor Portugal knew, but they wanted an understanding of their respective rights in those unknown regions. Fortunately for Spain, the reigning pope was a Spanish Borgia, Alexander VI, who in a series of bulls confirmed Spain in her new possessions and in the second bull *Inter caetera*, dated May 4, 1493 accepted Ferdinand and Isabella's suggestion of a line of demarcation 100 leagues west of the Azores. All lands west of that line would belong to Spain regardless of the nationality of the discoverer. Portugal, which had rights to all lands east of the line, was not satisfied with this division and after a long series of negotiations signed the Treaty of Tordesillas on June 7, 1494, which moved the line 370 leagues west of the Cape Verde Islands, a line which gave Portugal possession of Brazil.

Although Christendom at the time recognized the right of the Holy See to decide such matters as the disposition of heathen lands, not all rulers were prepared to recognize the justice of this Spanish pope's decision. King Henry VII of England in 1497 sent John Cabot on an exploring expedition into the North Atlantic, which laid the foundation of England's claim to part of the New World. Somewhat later, when France was demanding a share of the wealth overseas, Francis I remarked sarcastically that he would like to read the will of his father Adam to see how he had disposed of his patrimony. Far away in the little German town of Eisleben lived a youth who was just nine and still learning his Latin declensions when Columbus made his landfall on San Salvador. That youth would one day stir such an upheaval in the world that the pretensions of the Holy See to dispose of the patrimony of Adam would no longer have any validity. That youth was Martin Luther, who, when he threw his inkpot at the devil, exploded the cohesive notion of one Church and one Christendom. The political fission that ensued required a new and expanding world. Had there not been the New World, the Old might well have destroyed itself.

Doubtless, others would have crossed the fearful, unknown Atlantic if Columbus had not, but their timing might not have been so propitious. He was the first to have the courage, the skill and the good fortune to point the way and open the door that led to the expansion of the modern world. Because of Christopher Columbus 1492 is the most significant date in the history of Western man.

Pre-Columbian Voyages Across the Atlantic

ALTHOUGH Columbus made the first effective discovery of the New World in the sense that the discovery led to permanent settlements and development of the country, others had preceded him. Legends tell of voyages by Irish, Welsh, Norse and other explorers, but we have convincing evidence only of the Norse voyages.

Ancient Irish stories describe voyages of Saint Brandon (or Brendon), a great traveler, who visited mysterious islands in the Atlantic and named one after himself. Enthusiastic Irishmen have attempted to prove that the Irish discovered America, and one such enthusiast found a potato cellar in Massachusetts which he believed had been built by pre-Columbian settlers. As yet, no credible evidence points to Irishmen in the New World before Columbus.

Another legend asserts that a Welsh prince, Madoc by name, sailed from Wales in 1170 with ten ships and landed in what is now the state of Alabama. This story was known to the Elizabethans, and Dr. John Dee, on making a list in 1578 of English claims to North America, mentioned Madoc's discovery of the new land. Richard Hakluyt cited Welsh sailors who claimed that they had conversed in the Welsh language with North American Indians and had been understood. The legend of the Welsh Indians was so persistent that finally the Smithsonian Institution investigated the possibility and reported that no single Indian word could be found that corresponded to a Welsh word. But belief in Madoc has lingered, and the Daughters of the American Revolution are responsible for a historical marker at Fort Morgan, Mobile Bay, Alabama, which reads: "In memory of Prince Madoc, a Welsh explorer, who landed on the shores of Mobile Bay and left behind, with the Indians, the Welsh language." [1]

The Icelandic Sagas give an account of Norsemen who crossed the Atlantic and found a land which they called "Vinland the Good." Recently a map, purporting to date from about 1440, published by the Yale University Press, shows Vinland as a large island in the North Atlantic. This "Vinland Map" would suggest that some pre-Columbian cartographer had heard about the Viking voyages and had incorporated the Norse discovery on his map.[2] The Norsemen themselves were not map makers and did not depend upon maps and charts in their navigation.

Archaeological explorations in northern Newfoundland at L'Anse aux Meadows have uncovered Scandinavian housesites dating from very early in the eleventh century. Among other objects discovered was a Norse spindle whorl, which indicated the presence of women to spin wool into thread. These excavations provide tangible proof that the Vikings made voyages to the New World and established settlements, as the Sagas relate.

The location of Vinland the Good has been a matter of controversy. Some scholars have placed Vinland in Labrador, others in the region around Cape Cod and still others as far south as Rhode Island and Connecticut. The recent excavations make the Newfoundland locale plausible. In this region grow many types of berries, which the Norsemen may have confused with grapes since grapes did not grow in their native land. Scholars have been puzzled by allusions in the Sagas to grapes' being taken as part of the cargo of ships loaded in late winter or early spring. Nowhere would wild grapes hang on the vines that long. The latest scholarship indicates that some other type of berry must have been confused with grapes.[3] The suggestion has also been made that "Vinland" does not

---

[1] Richard Deacon, *Madoc and the Discovery of America* (London, 1967), p. 10.
[2] R. S. Skelton, *et al.*, *The Vinland Map and the Tartar Relation* (New Haven, Conn., 1965).
[3] Helge Ingstad, *Westward to Vinland* (New York, 1969), p. 73.

mean "Wineland" but "Grassland," from a similar Scandinavian word meaning "grass." This would be analogous to the naming of another part of the coast "Markland," or "Woodland."

The Sagas also tell of the Norsemen's encounters with natives whom they called "Skraelings" (sometimes "Skrellings"). These were either Indians or Eskimos. The most recent scholarship on the subject suggests that the Norse discoverers probably encountered both Indians and Eskimos and made no distinction between them.

The Icelandic Sagas telling the discovery of North America were written down in the fourteenth and fifteenth centuries, but like all the Sagas and much poetry, they had been composed centuries earlier and recited widely. Although the Sagas contain many contradictions and illustrate the poetic license of fiction writers, a core of fact can be discerned and corroborated from other sources. From the evidence available a fairly plausible story of the Norse discoveries can be worked out. From their base in Iceland, Norsemen, led by Eric the Red, colonized Greenland in the decade after 986. Eric had previously explored the country and had named it "Greenland," "because," he said, "men would be the more readily persuaded thither if the land had a good name." He established his own base and home at Brattahlid, just west of Cape Farewell.

About the time that Eric was settling his colony in Greenland, another Norseman, Bjarni Herjolfsson, after being blown off course, observed hitherto unknown lands to the west. He would not permit his men to go ashore but brought back stories of the pleasant well-wooded country observed from the sea. In the year 1000 Eric the Red's son, Leif Ericsson, bought a ship from Bjarni and set out to find the territory that Bjarni had failed to explore. Starting in the north, he sighted a region of flat rocks and glaciers, of no promise, which he named "Helluland" ("Flat-Rock Land"). This was possibly Baffin Island. Leif next made a landfall on a wooded region which he called "Markland," perhaps Labrador. His next discovery was a grassy and pleasant country that he called "Vinland," which Helge Ingstad in *Westward to Vinland* identifies with northern Newfoundland. Leif and his crew spent the winter in Vinland and returned to Greenland in the spring. On the way back they rescued 15 shipwrecked mariners from a reef. Because of his own good fortune, Leif earned the name of "Leif the Lucky."

Leif's report of the fertility of Vinland prompted other voyages. His brother Thorvald explored the country but was killed by the Skraelings. Another brother, Thorstein, in the year 1008 tried without success to reach Vinland. In 1020 an Icelander, Thorfinn Karlsefni, led an expedition that retraced Leif's route, but after two winters in the west he returned to Greenland.

An expedition consisting of 95 men and five women that went out to Vinland the year after Karlsefni's return to Greenland ended in disaster when Leif Ericsson's sister, Freydis, one of the party, induced her husband to slaughter the rival leaders. Freydis herself killed the other women with an axe. Although the Norsemen showed considerable interest in Vinland in the early years of the eleventh century, no enduring settlements were established.

Brief extracts from Eric the Red's Saga follow:

The Saga of Eric the Red [4]

Eric was married to a woman named Thorhild, and had two sons; one of these was named Thorstein and the other Leif. They were both promising men. Thorstein lived at home with his father, and there was not at that time a man in Greenland who was accounted of so great promise as he. Leif had sailed to Norway, where he was at the court of King Olaf Tryggvason. . . . He was well received by the king, who felt that he could see that Leif was a man of great accomplishments. Upon one occasion the king came to speech with Leif, and asks him: "Is it thy purpose to sail to Greenland in the summer?" "It is my purpose," said Leif, "if it be your will." "I believe it will be well," answers the king, "and thither thou shalt go upon my errand, to proclaim Christianity there." . . .

[4] "The Saga of Eric the Red" is based on texts of two manuscripts in "Hauk's Book" Nos. 544 and 557 in the Arne-Magnaean Collection, Copenhagen. Long excerpts will be found in *The Northmen, Columbus, and Cabot, 985–1503*, edited by Julius E. Olson and Edward G. Bourne, Original Narratives of Early American History (New York, 1906).

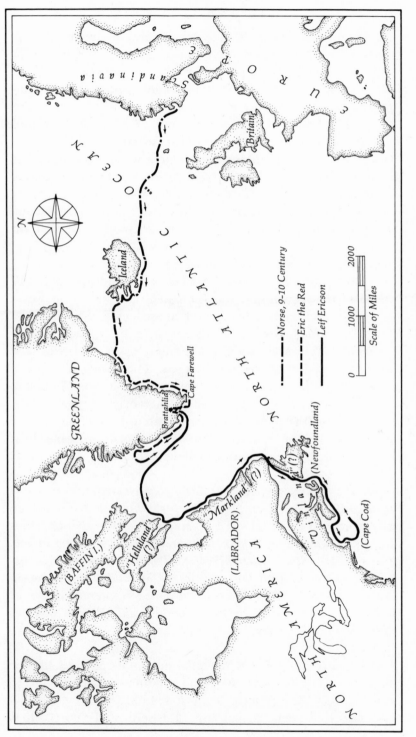

Voyages of Norsemen before Columbus

Leif put to sea when his ship was ready for the voyage. For a long time he was tossed about upon the ocean, and came upon lands of which he had previously had no knowledge. There were self-sown wheat [wild grain] fields and vines growing there. There were also those trees there which are called "mausur" [thought to be maple], and of all these they took specimens. Some of the timbers were so large that they were used in building. Leif found men upon a wreck, and took them home with him, and procured quarters for them all during the winter. In this wise he showed his nobleness and goodness, since he introduced Christianity into the country [Greenland] and saved men from the wreck; and he was called Leif the Lucky ever after. . . .

At this time there began to be much talk about a voyage of exploration to that country which Leif had discovered. The leader of this expedition was Thorstein Ericsson, who was a good man and an intelligent and blessed with many friends. . . . They sailed cheerily out of Ericsfirth in high spirits over their plan. They were long tossed about upon the ocean, and could not lay the course they wished. They came in sight of Iceland, and likewise saw birds from the Irish coast. Their ship was, in sooth, driven hither and thither over the sea. In the autumn they turned back, worn out by toil, and exposure to the elements, and exhausted by their labors, and arrived at Ericsfirth at the very beginning of winter. . . .

[*In the following autumn Thorstein marries Gudrid, a beautiful and intelligent woman for whom a distinguished future has been foretold. That winter Thorstein sickens and dies, and Gudrid lives under the protection of her father-in-law, Eric the Red. Some time thereafter Thorfinn Karlsefni, a successful trader and well born, comes to Greenland on a trading voyage and is invited by Eric to make winter quarters at Brattahlid, his home. Karlsefni seeks the hand of Gudrid and at Yuletide they are married.*]

About this time there began to be much talk at Brattahlid to the effect that Wineland the Good should be explored, for, it was said, that country must be possessed of many goodly qualities. And so it came to pass that Karlsefni and Snorri fitted out their ship for the purpose of going in search of that country in the spring. . . .

They had in all one hundred and sixty men when they sailed to the Western Settlement [of Greenland], and thence to Bear Island [an unidentified island to the southeast, off the coast of Markland]. Thence they bore away to the southward two *doegr* [twelve hours' sailing, estimated to have been about 100 miles; it is thought that the "two" in the text was a clerical error for "seven"]. Then they saw land and launched a boat and explored the land, and found there large flat stones; and many of these were 12 ells [a measure varying from 25 to 48 inches] wide. There were many Arctic foxes there. They gave a name to the country and called it Helluland [Land of Flat Stones]. Then they sailed with northerly winds two *doegr,* and land then lay before them, and upon it was a great wood and many wild beasts. An island lay off the land to the southeast, and there they found a bear, and they called this Biarney [Bear Island], while the land where the wood was they called Markland [Forest Land]. Thence they sailed southward along the land for a long time, and came to a cape. The land lay upon the starboard; there were long strands and sandy banks there. They rowed to the land and found upon the cape there the keel of a ship, and they called it there Kialarnes [Keelness. A promontory somewhere northeast of Vinland]. They also called the strands Furdustrandir [Wonderstrands], because they were so long to sail by. Then the country became indented with bays, and they steered their ships into a bay.

It was when Leif was with King Olaf Tryggvason, and he bade him proclaim Christianity to Greenland, that the king gave him two Gaels; the man's name was Haki, and the woman's, Haekia. The king advised Leif to have recourse to these people if he should stand in need of fleetness, for they were swifter than deer. Eric and Leif had tendered Karlsefni the services of this couple. Now when they had sailed past Wonderstrands they put the Gaels ashore, and directed them to run to the southward and investigate the nature of the country and return again before the end of the third half-day. . . . Karlsefni and his companions cast anchor and lay there during their absence. And when they came again, one of them carried a bunch of grapes, and the other an ear of new-sown wheat.

They went on board the ship, whereupon Karlsefni and his followers held on their way until they came to where the coast was indented with bays. They stood into a bay with their ships. There was an island out at the mouth of the bay, about which there were strong currents, wherefore they called it Straumey [Stream Isle]. There were so many birds there that it was scarcely possible to step between the eggs. They sailed through the firth and called it Straumfiord [Streamfirth], and carried their cargoes ashore from the ships, and established themselves there. They had brought with them all kinds of livestock. It was a fine country there. There were mountains thereabouts. They occupied themselves exclusively with the exploration of the country. They remained there during the winter, and they had taken no thought for this during the summer. The fishing began to fail, and they began to fall short of food. . . .

It is now to be told of Karlsefni that he cruised southward off the coast, with Snorri and Biarni and their people. They sailed for a long time and until they came at last to a river, which flowed down from the land into a lake and so into the sea. There were great bars at the mouth of the river, so that it could only be entered at the height of the flood tide. Karlsefni and his men sailed into the mouth of the river and called it there Hop [small land-locked bay]. They found self-sown wheat fields on the land there, wherever there were hollows, and wherever there was hilly ground there were vines. Every brook there was full of fish. They dug pits on the shore where the tide rose highest, and when the tide fell, there were halibut in the pits. There were great numbers of wild animals of all kinds in the woods. They remained there half a month and enjoyed themselves and kept no watch. They had their livestock with them.

Now one morning early, when they looked about them, they saw a great number of skin canoes [whether kayaks or bark canoes is uncertain], and staves [double-edged paddles] were brandished from the boats with a noise like flails, and they were revolved in the same direction in which the sun moves. Then said Karlsefni: "What may this betoken?" Snorri, Thorbrand's son, answers him: "It may be that this is a signal of peace, wherefore let us take a white shield and display it." And thus they did. Thereupon the strangers rowed toward them, and went upon the land, marveling at those whom they saw before them. They were swarthy men and ill-looking, and the hair of their heads was ugly. They had great eyes and were broad of cheek. They tarried there for a time looking curiously at the people they saw before them, and then rowed away and to the southward around the point.

Karlsefni and his followers had built their huts above the lake, some of their dwellings being near the lake, and others farther away. Now they remained there that winter. No snow came there, and all of their livestock lived by grazing. And when spring opened, they discovered early one morning a great number of skin canoes rowing from the south past the cape, so numerous that it looked as if coals had been scattered broadcast out before the bay; and on every boat staves were waved. Thereupon Karlsefni and his people displayed their shields, and when they came together, they began to barter with each other. Especially did the strangers wish to buy red cloth, for which they offered in exchange peltries [furs] and [other] quite gray skins. They also desired to buy swords and spears, but Karlsefni and Snorri forbade this. In exchange for perfect unsullied skins, the Skrellings [aborigines: Indians or Eskimos] would take red stuff a span in length, which they would bind around their heads. So their trade went on for a time until Karlsefni and his people began to grow short of cloth, when they divided it into such narrow pieces that it was not more than a finger's breadth wide; but the Skrellings still continued to give just as much for this as before, or more.

It so happened that a bull, which belonged to Karlsefni and his people, ran out from the woods bellowing loudly. This so terrified the Skrellings that they sped out to their canoes and then rowed away to the southward along the coast. For three entire weeks nothing more was seen of them. At the end of this time, however, a great multitude of Skrelling boats was discovered approaching from the south, as if a stream were pouring down, and all of their staves were waved in a direction contrary to the course of the sun, and the Skrellings were all uttering loud cries. Thereupon Karlsefni and his men took red shields and displayed them. The Skrellings sprang from their boats, and they met then and fought together. There was a fierce shower of missiles, for the Skrellings had war slings.

Karlsefni and Snorri observed that the Skrellings raised up on a pole a great ball-shaped body, almost the size of a sheep's belly and nearly black in color, and this they hurled from the pole up on the land above Karlsefni's followers, and it made a frightful noise where it fell. Whereat a great fear seized upon Karlsefni and all his men, so that they could think of nought but flight and of making their escape up along the river bank. For it seemed to them that the troop of the Skrellings was rushing toward them from every side, and they did not pause until they came to certain jutting crags, where they offered a stout resistance. . . .

Two of Karlsefni's men had fallen and a great number of the Skrellings. Karlsefni's party had been overpowered by dint of superior numbers. They now returned to their dwellings, and bound up their wounds, and weighed carefully what throng of men that could have been which had seemed to descend upon them from the land. It now seemed to them that there could have been but the one party, that which came from the boats, and that the other troop must have been an ocular delusion. . . .

It now seemed clear to Karlsefni and his people that, although the country thereabouts was attractive, their life would be one of constant dread and turmoil by reason of the inhabitants of the country. So they forthwith prepared to leave, and determined to return to their own country.

❧ III ❧

Columbus Reports on His Voyage of Discovery

IN THE long years after the Northmen sent their dragon-prowed vessels plunging into the waves of the North Atlantic, Europeans learned much about the Ocean Sea, but it took centuries for explorers to make an effective landing in the New World. Christopher Columbus' momentous voyage of 1492 marked the culmination of much speculation and probing and opened the way for an era of exploration the like of which the world had never seen. Most of what we know about the voyage is contained in a journal that Columbus kept.

According to Samuel Eliot Morison, author of the best biography of the discoverer, Columbus' own journal is "the source of about 98 percent of our information about the actual discovery of America." [1] Columbus' manuscript version has long since disappeared, but excerpts made in his own lifetime have been preserved, and one long version, made by Bartolomé de Las Casas from a copy of the original in his possession, has survived and is the basis of the best versions of the journal now available.

The journal opens with a prologue addressed to the sovereigns of Spain, King Ferdinand and Queen Isabella, which Las Casas was careful to reprint verbatim. In the rest of the journal he abbreviated passages, switched from first to third person, and omitted some nautical details, which Morison says "we should wish to have," but he also quoted directly passages that Columbus had written. Though incomplete, the journal, in Morison's

[1] Samuel E. Morison, *Admiral of the Ocean Sea: A Life of Christopher Columbus* (Boston, 1949), p. 155.

39

opinion, is "the most interesting and the most entrancing sea journal of any voyage in history."

Excerpts follow:

Columbus' Journal of the First Voyage [2]

In the name of our Lord Jesus Christ

Because, O most Christian, and very high, very excellent, and puissant Princes, King and Queen of the Spains and of the islands of the Sea, our Lords, in this present year of 1492, after Your Highnesses had given an end to the war with the Moors who reigned in Europe and had finished it in the very great city of Granada, where in this present year, on the second day of the month of January, by force of arms, I saw the royal banners of Your Highnesses placed on the towers of Alfambra [the Alhambra], which is the fortress of that city, and I saw the Moorish King come forth from the gates of the city and kiss the royal hands of Your Highnesses . . . ; and presently in that same month, acting on the information that I had given to Your Highnesses touching the lands of India and respecting a prince who is called Gran Can [Great Khan] . . . : Your Highnesses, as Catholic Christians and princes who love the holy Christian faith and the propagation of it, and who are enemies to the sect of Mahoma [Mohammed] and to all idolatries and heresies, resolved to send me, Cristóbal Colón, to the said parts of India to see the said princes . . . with a view that they might be converted to our holy faith. And ordered that I should not go by land to the eastward, as had been customary, but that I should go by way of the west, whither up to this day we do not know for certain that anyone has gone.

Thus, after having turned out all the Jews from all your kingdoms and lordships in the same month of January, Your

[2] A translation of Las Casas' version of Columbus' journal was made by Sir Clements R. Markham and published by the Hakluyt Society in 1893: *The Journal of Christopher Columbus . . . and Documents Relating to the Voyages of John Cabot and Gaspar Corte Real* (London, 1893). Long excerpts are reprinted in *The Northmen, Columbus, and Cabot . . .* , Original Narratives of Early American History (New York, 1906).

Highnesses gave orders to me that with a sufficient fleet I should go to the said parts of India, and for this they made great concessions to me and ennobled me, so that henceforthward I should be called Don, and should be chief admiral of the Ocean Sea, perpetual viceroy and governor of all the islands and continents that I should discover and gain, and that I might hereafter discover and gain in the Ocean Sea, and that my eldest son should succeed, and so on from generation to generation forever.

I left the city of Granada on the 12th day of May in the same year of 1492, being Saturday, and came to the town of Palos, which is a seaport; where I equipped three vessels well suited for such service, and departed from that port, well supplied with provisions and with many sailors, on the 3d day of August of the same year, being Friday, half an hour before sunrise, taking the route to the islands of Canaria [the Canaries], belonging to Your Highnesses, which are in the said Ocean Sea, that I might thence take my departure for navigating until I should arrive at the Indies and give the letters of Your Highnesses to those princes, so as to comply with my orders. As part of my duty I thought it well to write an account of all the voyage very punctually, noting from day to day all that I should do and see, and that should happen, as will be seen further on. Also, Lords Princes, I resolved to describe each night what passed in the day, and to note each day how I navigated at night. . . . Above all, I shall have accomplished much, for I shall forget sleep and shall work at the business of navigation, that so the service may be performed; all which will entail great labor.

Friday, 3d of August

We departed on Friday, the 3d of August, in the year 1492, from the bar of Saltés at eight o'clock, and proceeded with a strong sea breeze until sunset toward the south for 60 miles, equal to 15 leagues [four Italian miles make a league]; afterward southwest and west-southwest, which was the course for the Canaries.

. . . .

Monday, 6th of August

The rudder of the caravel *Pinta* became unshipped, and Martín Alonso Pinzón, who was in command, believed or suspected that it was by contrivance of Gomes Rascon and Cristóbal Quintero, to whom the caravel belonged, for they dreaded to go on that voyage. The admiral says that, before they sailed, these men had been displaying a certain backwardness, so to speak. The admiral was much disturbed at not being able to help the said caravel without danger, and he says that he was eased of some anxiety when he reflected that Martín Alonso Pinzón was a man of energy and ingenuity. They made, during the day and night, 29 leagues.

Tuesday, 7th of August

The rudder of the *Pinta* was shipped and secured, and they proceeded on a course for the island of Lanzarote, one of the Canaries. They made, during the day and night, 25 leagues.

Wednesday, 8th of August

Opinions respecting their position varied among the pilots of the three caravels; but that of the admiral proved to be nearer the truth. He wished to go to Gran Canaria, to leave the caravel *Pinta* because she was disabled by the faulty hanging of her rudder and was making water. He intended to obtain another there if one could be found. They could not reach the place that day.

Thursday, 9th of August

The admiral was not able to reach Gomera until the night of Sunday, while Martín Alonso remained on that coast of Gran Canaria by order of the admiral, because his vessel could not be navigated. Afterward the admiral took her to Canaria, and they repaired the *Pinta* very thoroughly through the pains and labor of the admiral, of Martín Alonso, and of the rest. Finally they came to Gomera. They saw a great fire issue from the mountain of the island of Tenerife, which is of great height.

They rigged the *Pinta* with square sails, for she was lateen rigged; and the admiral reached Gomera on Sunday, the 2d of September, with the *Pinta* repaired. . . . Having taken in water, wood, and meat, and all else that the men had who were left at Gomera by the admiral when he went to the island of Canaria to repair the caravel *Pinta,* he finally made sail from the said island of Gomera with his three caravels on Thursday, the 6th day of September.

. . . .

Sunday, 9th of September

This day the admiral made 19 leagues, and he arranged to reckon less than the number run because, if the voyage was of long duration, the people would not be so terrified and disheartened. In the night he made 120 miles, at the rate of 12 miles an hour, which are 30 leagues. The sailors steered badly, letting the ship fall off to northeast and even more, respecting which the admiral complained many times.

Monday, 10th of September

In this day and night he made 60 leagues, at the rate of ten miles an hour, which are two and a half leagues [an hour]. But he only counted 48 leagues, that the people might not be alarmed if the voyage should be long.

. . . .

Monday, 17th of September

They proceeded on their west course and made over 50 leagues in the day and night, but the admiral only counted 47. They were aided by the current. They saw much very fine grass and herbs from rocks, which came from the west. They therefore considered that they were near land. The pilots observed the north point and found that the needles turned a full point to the west of north. So the mariners were alarmed and dejected, and did not give their reason. But the admiral knew and ordered that the north should be again observed at dawn. They then found that the needles were true. The cause was that the star makes the movement, and not the needles.

. . . .

Friday, 21st of September

Most of the day it was calm, and later there was a little wind. During the day and night they did not make good more than 13 leagues. At dawn they saw so much weed that the sea appeared to be covered with it, and it came from the west. A booby was seen. The sea was very smooth, like a river, and the air the best in the world. They saw a whale, which is a sign that they were near land, because they always keep near the shore.

Saturday, 22d of September

They shaped a course west-northwest more or less, her head turning from one to the other point, and made 30 leagues. Scarcely any weed was seen. They saw some sandpipers and another bird. Here the admiral says: "This contrary wind was very necessary for me, because my people were much excited at the thought that in these seas no wind ever blew in the direction of Spain." Part of the day there was no weed, and later it was very thick.

. . . .

Monday, 1st of October

Course west, and 25 leagues made good, counted for the crew as 20 leagues. There was a heavy shower of rain. At dawn the admiral's pilot made the distance from Hierro 578 leagues to the west. The reduced reckoning which the admiral showed to the crew made it 584 leagues. But the truth which the admiral observed and kept secret was 707.

. . . .

Wednesday, 10th of October

The course was west-southwest, and they went at the rate of ten miles an hour, occasionally 12 miles, and sometimes seven.

During the day and night they made 59 leagues, counted as no more than 44. Here the people could endure no longer. They complained of the length of the voyage. But the admiral cheered them up in the best way he could, giving them good hopes of the advantages they might gain from it. He added that, however much they might complain, he had to go to the Indies, and that he would go on until he found them, with the help of our Lord.

Thursday, 11th of October

The course was west-southwest, and there was more sea than there had been during the whole of the voyage. They saw sandpipers and a green reed near the ship. Those of the caravel *Pinta* saw a cane and a pole, and they took up another small pole, which appeared to have been worked with iron; also another bit of cane, a land plant, and a small board. The crew of the caravel *Niña* also saw signs of land, and a small branch covered with berries. Everyone breathed afresh and rejoiced at these signs. The run until sunset was 27 leagues.

After sunset the admiral returned to his original west course, and they went along at the rate of 12 miles an hour. Up to two hours after midnight they had gone 90 miles, equal to 22½ leagues. As the caravel *Pinta* was a better sailer and went ahead of the admiral, she found the land, and made the signals ordered by the admiral. The land was first seen by a sailor named Rodrigo de Triana. But the admiral, at ten o'clock, being on the castle of the poop, saw a light, though it was so uncertain that he could not affirm it was land. He called Pedro Gutiérrez, a gentleman of the King's bedchamber, and said that there seemed to be a light, and that he should look at it. He did so and saw it. . . . After the admiral had spoken he saw the light once or twice, and it was like a wax candle rising and falling. It seemed to few to be an indication of land, but the admiral made certain that land was close.

When they said the "Salve," which all the sailors were accustomed to sing in their way, the admiral asked and admonished the men to keep a good lookout on the forecastle and to watch well for land; and to him who should first cry out that he saw land, he would give a silk doublet, besides the other

rewards promised by the Sovereigns—which were 10,000 mara-
vedis [about $67.50; the maravedi was worth less than 7/10 of
a cent] to him who should first see it [Columbus received the
award]. At two hours after midnight the land was sighted at a
distance of two leagues. They shortened sail and lay by under
the mainsail without the bonnets.

Friday, 12th of October

The vessels were hove to, waiting for daylight. And on
Friday they arrived at a small island of the Lucayos [Bahamas]
called, in the language of the Indians, Guanahani [Watling
Island]. Presently they saw naked people. The admiral went
on shore in the armed boat, and Martín Alonso Pinzón and
Vicente Yáñez, his brother, who was captain of the *Niña*.
The admiral took the royal standard, and the captains went
with two banners of the green cross, which the admiral took in
all the ships as a sign, with an F and a Y [for "Fernando" and
"Ysabel"] and a crown over each letter, one on one side of the
cross and the other on the other.

Having landed, they saw trees very green and much water
and fruits of diverse kinds. The admiral called to the two
captains and to the others who leaped on shore and to Rodrigo
de Escobedo, secretary of the whole fleet, and to Rodrigo Sánchez
of Segovia [the royal inspector], and said that they should bear
faithful testimony that he, in presence of all, had taken, as he
now took, possession of the said island for the King and for
the Queen his Lords, making the declarations that are required,
as is now largely set forth in the testimonies which were then
made in writing.

Presently many inhabitants of the island assembled. What
follows is in the actual words of the admiral in his book of the
first navigation and discovery of the Indies: "I," he says, "that
we might form great friendship, for I knew that they were a
people who could be more easily freed and converted to our
holy faith by love than by force, gave to some of them red
caps, and glass beads to put round their necks, and many other
things of little value, which gave them great pleasure and made
them so much our friends that it was a marvel to see. They after-

wards came to the ship's boats where we were, swimming and bringing us parrots, cotton threads in skeins, darts, and many other things. And we exchanged them for other things that we gave them, such as glass beads and small bells. In fine, they took all and gave what they had with good will.

"It appeared to me to be a race of people very poor in everything. They go as naked as when their mothers bore them, and so do the women, although I did not see more than one young girl. All I saw were youths, none more than thirty years of age. They are very well made, with very handsome bodies and very good countenances. Their hair is short and coarse, almost like the hairs of a horse's tail. They wear the hairs brought down to the eyebrows, except a few locks behind which they wear long and never cut. They paint themselves black, and they are the color of the Canarians, neither black nor white. Some paint themselves white, others red, and others of what color they find. Some paint their faces, others the whole body, some only round the eyes, others only on the nose. They neither carry nor know anything of arms, for I showed them swords, and they took them by the blade and cut themselves through ignorance. . . . They should be good servants and intelligent, for I observed that they quickly took in what was said to them, and I believe that they would easily be made Christians, as it appeared to me that they had no religion.

"I, our Lord being pleased, will take hence, at the time of my departure, six natives for Your Highnesses, that they may learn to speak. I saw no beast of any kind, except parrots, on this island." The above is in the words of the admiral.

. . . .

Sunday, 21st of October

". . . According as I obtain tidings of gold or spices I shall settle what should be done. I am still resolved to go to the mainland and the city of Guisay [the Quinsay of Marco Polo], and to deliver the letters of Your Highnesses to the Gran Can, requesting a reply and returning with it."

. . . .

Wednesday, 24th of October

"At midnight I weighed the anchors and left the anchorage
. . . in the island of Isabella [settlement on north coast of
Hispaniola] . . . to go to the island of Cuba, where I heard
of the people who were very great, and had gold, spices, merchandise, and large ships. They showed me that the course
thither would be west-southwest, and so I hold. For I believe
that it is so, as all the Indians of these islands, as well as those I
brought with me in the ships, told me by signs. I cannot understand their language, but I believe that it is of the island of
Cipango that they recount these wonders. On the spheres I
saw, and on the delineations of the map of the world, Cipango
is in this region. . . ."

. . . .

Sunday, 28th of October

. . . [The admiral] says that this island [Cuba] is the most
beautiful that eyes have seen, full of good harbors and deep
rivers, and the sea appeared as if it never rose. . . . He says
that the island is full of very beautiful mountains, although
they are not very extensive as regards length, but high; and
all the country is high like Sicily. . . . The Indians say that in
this island there are gold mines and pearls, and the admiral
saw a likely place for them and mussel shells, which are signs
of them. He understood that large ships of the Gran Can
came here, and that from here to the mainland was a voyage
of ten days. The admiral called this river and harbor San
Salvador [Bahía Bariay, Oriente Province, Cuba].

. . . .

Friday, 2d of November

The admiral decided upon sending two Spaniards, one named
Rodrigo de Jerez, who lived in Ayamonte, and the other Luis
de Torres, who had served in the household of the Adelantado
of Murcia, and had been a Jew, knowing Hebrew, Chaldee,
and even some Arabic. With these men he sent two Indians,

one from among those he had brought from Guanahani and another a native of the houses by the riverside. He gave them strings of beads with which to buy food if they should be in need, and ordered them to return in six days. He gave them specimens of spices to see if any were to be found. Their instructions were to ask for the king of that land, and they were told what to say on the part of the Sovereigns of Castile, how they had sent the admiral, with letters and a present, to inquire after his health and establish friendship, favoring him in what he might desire from them. They were to collect information respecting certain provinces, ports, and rivers of which the admiral had notice, and to ascertain their distances from where he was.

This night the admiral took an altitude with a quadrant and found that the distance from the equinoctial line was 42 degrees. . . . He still believes that he has reached the mainland [of China].

. . . .

Tuesday, 6th of November

Yesterday at night, says the admiral, the two men came back who had been sent to explore the interior. . . . Finding that they [the Indians] had no information respecting cities, the Spaniards returned; and if they had desired to take those who wished to accompany them, more than 500 men and women would have come, because they thought the Spaniards were returning to heaven. . . . The two Christians met with many people on the road going home, men and women, with a half-burnt weed in their hands, being the herbs they are accustomed to smoke. [This is the earliest recorded reference to smoking tobacco.] . . .

. . . .

Tuesday, 25th of December. Christmas.

. . . It pleased our Lord that, at twelve o'clock at night, when the admiral had retired to rest and when all had fallen asleep, seeing that it was a dead calm and the sea like glass, the tiller being in the hands of a boy, the current carried the ship

on one of the sandbanks. If it had not been night, the bank
could have been seen, and the surf on it could be heard for a
good league. But the ship ran upon it so gently that it could
scarcely be felt. The boy, who felt the helm and heard the
rush of the sea, cried out. The admiral at once came up, and
so quickly that no one had felt that the ship was aground.
Presently the master of the ship, whose watch it was, came on
deck. The admiral ordered him and others to launch the boat,
which was on the poop, and lay out an anchor astern. The
master, with several others, got into the boat, and the admiral
thought that they did so with the object of obeying his orders.
But they did so in order to take refuge with the caravel, which
was half a league to leeward. The caravel would not allow them
to come on board, acting judiciously, and they therefore returned to the ship, but the caravel's boat arrived first. When
the admiral saw that his own people fled in this way, the water
rising and the ship being across the sea, seeing no other course,
he ordered the masts to be cut away and the ship to be lightened
as much as possible, to see if she would come off. But, as the
water continued to rise, nothing more could be done. Her side
fell over across the sea, but it was nearly calm. Then the
timbers opened and the ship was lost. . . .

. . . .

Friday, 15th of March

Yesterday, after sunset, she went on her course with little
wind and at sunrise she was off Saltés. At noon, with the tide
rising, they crossed the bar of Saltés and reached the port
which they had left on the 3d of August of the year before.
The admiral says that so ends this journal, unless it becomes
necessary to go to Barcelona by sea, having received news that
their Highnesses are in that city, to give an account of all his
voyage which our Lord permitted him to make, and saw fit to
set forth in him.

Columbus' Letter Concerning the First Voyage [3]

[*Before Columbus reached Europe after the discoveries made on his first voyage, he sat down in his cabin aboard ship and composed a letter which he proposed to send by some messenger from his first landfall in case anything should happen to him before his arrival in Spain. Actually, he carried the letter to Spain himself. It was enclosed with one addressed to the sovereigns, which has been lost.*

[*When this open letter to the public reached the sovereigns, they had several copies made. One was addressed to Luis de Santangel, keeper of the privy purse, who had advanced at least half the cost of the voyage. A copy of this letter was printed at Barcelona in the summer of 1493. A Latin translation of the letter, printed in Rome, Paris, Basle, and Antwerp, went through nine editions between 1493 and 1494. This Latin version served to herald to the world Columbus' achievement.*

[*The letter, endorsed to Santangel, follows:*]

SIR: As I know that you will have pleasure from the great victory which our Lord hath given me in my voyage, I write you this, by which you shall know that in 33 days I passed over to the Indies with the fleet which the most illustrious King and Queen, our Lords, gave me; where I found very many islands peopled with inhabitants beyond number. And, of them all, I have taken possession for their Highnesses, with proclamation and the royal standard displayed; and I was not gainsaid. To the first which I found, I gave the name San Salvador, in commemoration of His High Majesty, who marvelously hath given all this. . . .

When I reached Juana [Cuba], I followed its coast westwardly, and found it so large that I thought it might be mainland, the province of Cathay. And as I did not thus find any towns and villages on the seacoast, save small hamlets with the people whereof I could not get speech, because they all fled away forthwith, I went on further in the same direction, think-

---

[3] This letter has been often reprinted in the original Spanish and in translation. This version is taken from *The Northmen, Columbus, and Cabot, op. cit.*

ing I should not miss of great cities or towns. And at the end of many leagues, seeing that there was no change, and that the coast was bearing me northwards, whereunto my desire was contrary, since the winter was already confronting us, I formed the purpose of making from thence to the south, and as the wind also blew against me, I determined not to wait for other weather and turned back as far as a port agreed upon; from which I sent two men into the country to learn if there were a king, or any great cities. They traveled for three days, and found innumerable small villages and a numberless population, but nought of ruling authority; wherefore they returned. I understood sufficiently from other Indians whom I had already taken, that this land, in its continuousness, was an island. And so I followed its coast eastwardly for a hundred and seven leagues as far as where it terminated; from which headland I saw another island to the east, eighteen leagues distant from this, to which I at once gave the name La Spañola [Hispaniola].

And I proceeded thither, and followed the northern coast, as with La Juana, eastwardly for 188 great leagues in a direct easterly course, as with La Juana. The which, and all the others, are most fertile to an excessive degree, and this extremely so. In it there are many havens on the seacoast, incomparable with any others that I know in Christendom, and plenty of rivers so good and great that it is a marvel. The lands thereof are high, and in it are very many ranges of hills, and most lofty mountains incomparably beyond the island of Tenerife, all most beautiful in a thousand shapes, and all accessible, and full of trees of a thousand kinds, so lofty that they seem to reach the sky. And I am assured that they never lose their foliage, as may be imagined, since I saw them as green and as beautiful as they are in Spain during May. And some of them were in flower, some in fruit, some in another stage according to their kind. And the nightingale was singing, and other birds of a thousand sorts, in the month of November, there where I was going. There are palm trees of six or eight species, wondrous to see for their beautiful variety; but so are the other trees, and fruits, and plants therein. There are wonderful pine groves, and very large plains of verdure, and there is honey, and many kinds of birds, and many various fruits. In the earth there are many mines of metals; and there is a population of incalculable number. Española is a marvel; the mountains and hills, and plains, and fields, and the soil, so beautiful and rich for planting and sowing, for breeding cattle of all sorts, for building of towns and villages. There could be no believing, without seeing, such harbors as are here, as well as the many and great rivers and excellent waters, most of which contain gold. In the trees and fruits and plants there are great diversities from those of Juana. In this, there are many spiceries, and great mines of gold and other metals.

The people of this island, and of all the others that I have found and seen, or not seen, all go naked, men and women, just as their mothers bring them forth; although some women cover a single place with the leaf of a plant, or a cotton something which they make for that purpose. They have no iron or steel, nor any weapons. Nor are they fit thereunto, not because they be not a well-formed people and of fair stature, but that they are most wondrously timorous. They have no other weapons than the stems of reeds in their seeding state, on the end of which they fix little sharpened stakes. Even these they dare not use. For many times has it happened that I sent two or three men ashore to some village to parley, and countless numbers of them sallied forth; but as soon as they saw those approach, they fled away in such wise that even a father would not wait for his son. And this was not because any hurt had ever been done to any of them:—on the contrary, at every headland where I have gone and been able to hold speech with them, I gave them of everything which I had, as well cloth as many other things, without accepting aught therefor;—but such they are, incurably timid. It is true that since they have become more assured, and are losing that terror, they are artless and generous with what they have, to such a degree as no one would believe but him who had seen it. Of anything they have, if it be asked for, they never say no, but do rather invite the person to accept it, and show as much lovingness as though they would give their hearts. And whether it be a thing of value or one of little worth, they are straightways content with whatsoever trifle of whatsoever kind may be given them in return for it. I forbade that anything so worthless as fragments of broken platters, and pieces of broken glass, and strap buckles should be given them. Although when they were able to get such things, they seemed to think they had the best jewel in the world, for it was the hap of a sailor to get, in exchange for a strap, gold to the weight of two and a half castellanos [one castellano equals 1/6 ounce of gold], and others much more for other things of far less value. . . . They took even pieces of broken barrel hoops, and gave whatever they had, like senseless brutes, insomuch that it seemed to me bad. I forbade it, and I gave gratuitously a thousand useful things that I carried, in order that they may conceive affection, and furthermore may become Christians. For they are inclined to the love and service of their Highnesses and of all the Castilian nation, and they strive to combine in giving us things which they have in abundance, and of which we are in need. And they knew no sect, nor idolatry, save that they all believe that power and goodness are in the sky. And they believed very firmly that I, with these ships and crews, came from the sky. And in such opinion they received me at every place where I landed, after they had lost their terror. And this comes not because they are ignorant—on the contrary, they are men of very subtle wit, who navigate all those seas, and who give a marvelously good account of everything—but because they never saw men wearing clothes, nor the like of our ships. And as soon as I arrived in the Indies, in the first island that I found, I took some of them by force, to the intent that they should learn [our speech] and give me information of what there was in those parts. And so it was that very soon they understood [us] and we them, what by speech or what by signs; and those [Indians] have been of much service. To this day I carry them [with me] who are still of the opinion that I come from Heaven [as appears] from much conversation which they have had with me. And they were the first to proclaim it wherever I arrived. And the others went running from house to house and to the neighboring villages, with loud cries of "Come! come to see the people from Heaven!" Then, as soon as their minds were reassured about us, everyone came, men as well as women, so that there remained none behind, big or little; and they all brought something to eat and drink, which they gave with wondrous lovingness.

They have in all the islands very many *canoas,* after the manner of rowing galleys, some larger, some smaller; and a good many are larger than a galley of eighteen benches. They are not so wide, because they are made of a single log of timber, but a galley could not keep up with them in rowing, for their motion is a thing beyond belief. And with these they navigate through all those islands, which are numberless, and ply their traffic. I have seen some of those *canoas* with 70 and 80 men in them, each one with his oar.

In all those islands, I saw not much diversity in the looks of the people, nor in their manners and language. But they all understand each other, which is a thing of singular advantage for what I hope their Highnesses will decide upon for converting them to our holy faith, unto which they are well disposed. I have already told how I had gone 107 leagues, in a straight line from west to east, along the seacoast of the island of Juana, according to which itinerary, I can declare that that island is larger than England and Scotland combined. . . . This other, Española, has a greater circumference than the whole of Spain from Col[ibre in Catal]unya, by the seacoast, as far as Fuente Ravia in Biscay; since, along one of its four sides, I went for 188 great leagues in a straight line from west to east. This is [a land] to be desired,—and once seen, never to be relinquished —in which (although, indeed, I have taken possession of them all for their Highnesses, and all are more richly endowed than I have skill and power to say, and I hold them all in the name of their Highnesses who can dispose thereof as much and as completely as of the kingdoms of Castile) in this Española, in the place most suitable and best for its proximity to the gold mines, and for traffic with the mainland both on this side [i.e., Europe] and with that over there belonging to the Great Can (where there will be great commerce and profit), I took possession of a large town which I named the city of Navidad. And I have made fortification there, and a fort (which by this time will have been completely finished) and I have left therein men enough for such a purpose, with arms and artillery, and provisions for more than a year, and a boat, and a master of all seacraft for making others; and great friendship with the king of that land, to such a degree that he prided himself on calling and holding me as his brother. And even though his mind might change toward attacking those men, neither he nor his people know what arms are, and go naked. As I have already said, they are the most timorous creatures there are in the world, so that the men who remain there are alone sufficient to destroy all that land, and the island is without personal danger for them if they know how to behave themselves.

It seems to me that in all those islands, the men are all content with a single wife; and to their chief or king they give as many as 20. The women, it appears to me, do more work than the men. Nor have I been able to learn whether they held personal property, for it seemed to me that whatever one had, they all took share of, especially of eatable things. Down to the present, I have not found in those islands any monstrous men, as many expected, but on the contrary all the people are very comely. Nor are they black like those in Guinea, but have flowing hair. And they are not begotten where there is an excessive violence of the rays of the sun. It is true that the sun is there very strong, although it is 26 degrees distant from the equinoctial line. In those islands, where there are lofty mountains, the cold was very keen there this winter; but they endure it by being accustomed thereto, and by the help of the meats which they eat with many and inordinately hot spices. Thus I have not found, nor had any information of monsters, except of an island which is here the second in the approach to the Indies, which is inhabited by a people whom, in all the islands, they regard as very ferocious, who eat human flesh. These have many canoes with which they run through all the islands of India and plunder and take as much as they can. They are no more ill-shapen than the others, but have the custom of wearing their hair long, like women; and they use bows and arrows of the same reed stems, with a point of wood at the top, for lack of iron which they have not. Amongst those other tribes who are excessively cowardly, these are ferocious; but I hold them as nothing more than the others. These are they who have to do with the women of Matinino [perhaps Martinique]—which is the first island that is encountered in the passage from Spain to the Indies—in which there are no men. Those women practice no female usages, but have bows and arrows of reed such as above mentioned, and they arm and cover themselves with plates of copper of which they have much. In another island, which they assure me is larger than Española, the people have no hair. In this there is incalculable gold; and concerning these and the rest I bring Indians with me as witnesses.

And in conclusion, to speak only of what has been done in this voyage, which has been so hastily performed, their Highnesses may see that I shall give them as much gold as they may need, with very little aid which their Highnesses will give me; spices and cotton at once, as much as their Highnesses will order to be shipped; and as much as they shall order to be shipped of mastic [resin from small evergreen tree; used in varnish]—which till now has never been found except in Greece, in the island of Xio [Chios], and the Seigniory [of Genoa, which owned Chios at that time] sells it for what it likes; and aloe wood, as much as they shall order to be shipped; and slaves, as many as they shall order to be shipped—and these shall be from idolators. And I believe that I have discovered rhubarb and cinnamon, and I shall find that the men whom I am leaving there will have discovered a thousand other things of value (as I made no delay at any point, so long as the wind gave me an opportunity of sailing, except only in the town of Navidad, till I had left things safely arranged and well established). And in truth I should have done much more if the ships had served me as well as might reasonably have been expected.

This is enough. And [thanks to] Eternal God our Lord who gives to all those who walk His way victory over things which seem impossible—and this was signally one such, for although men have talked or written of those lands, it was all by conjecture, without confirmation from eyesight, amounting only to this much: that the hearers for the most part listened and judged that there was more fable in it than anything actual, however trifling. Since thus our Redeemer has given to our most illustrious King and Queen and to their famous kingdoms this victory in so high a matter, Christendom should have rejoicing therein and make great festivals and give solemn thanks to the Holy Trinity for the great exaltation they shall have by the conversion of so many peoples to our holy faith; and next for the temporal benefit which will bring hither refreshment and profit, not only to Spain, but to all Christians. This briefly, in accordance with the facts. Dated, on the caravel, off the Canary Islands, the 15 February of the year 1493.

At your command,
THE ADMIRAL

Postscript which came within the letter

After having written this letter, and being in the sea of Castile, there rose upon me so much wind, south and south-east, that it has caused me to lighten the vessels. However, I ran hither today into this port of Lisbon, which was the greatest wonder in the world, where I decided to write to their Highnesses. I have always found the seasons like May in all the Indies, whither I passed in thirty-three days, and returned in twenty-eight, but that these storms have delayed me twenty-three days running about this sea. All the seamen say here that there never has been so bad a winter, nor so many shipwrecks.

Dated the 14th of March.

✤ IV ✤

Rights of Discovery and Early Claims to the New World

PORTUGAL and Spain had taken the initiative in searching for new sea routes to the East. Portugal had found a way around Africa to India and had made Lisbon an entrepôt for Eastern goods, including highly prized pepper and spices. Columbus had found islands in the western Atlantic and further discoveries would soon reveal new continents there. King John of Portugal, encouraged by his mariners, hoped to find lands in the South Atlantic that would be richer than any that Columbus had found in the West. Furthermore, he wanted to preserve Portuguese rights to heathen lands in the Indies and was fearful lest Spanish explorers sailing westward would land on these eastern islands and claim them. Ferdinand and Isabella, on their part, were eager to prevent Portuguese navigators from claiming any part of the new discoveries that Columbus had made or that other Spanish explorers in the West would make.

In this situation, the Spanish sovereigns in 1493 applied to the pope in Rome to settle the question of rights to the new discoveries. At this time the pope was that Spaniard of the Borgia family known by the name of Alexander VI. According to European tradition, the pope, as the spiritual head of Christendom, had the right to decide upon the sovereignty of heathen lands not already occupied by any Christian prince. Accordingly, Ferdinand and Isabella appealed to Pope Alexander VI to issue a bull to secure their possession of lands discovered by Columbus. Before the matter was settled, the pope had issued four bulls. The second of these called *Inter caetera*, issued on

May 4, 1493, drew a demarcation line 100 leagues west of the Azores and Cape Verde Islands and gave Spain possession of lands west of this line; lands to the east, not in the possession of any Christian prince, he allotted to Portugal.

Because Portugal was unsatisfied with the papal dispensation, King John began direct negotiations with Ferdinand and Isabella for a more favorable disposition of the new territories. Since Portugal had a powerful navy and much naval experience, and might be strong enough to dispute Spanish claims in the New World if the controversy deteriorated into armed conflict, the Spanish sovereigns concluded the Treaty of Tordesillas on June 7, 1494, by which the line of demarcation was moved 370 leagues west of the Cape Verde Islands. This line cut through the hump of Brazil and gave Portugal everything east and Spain everything west of the line. Because no one knew precisely how to determine longitude, the exact location of the line remained vague, but the treaty served to make at least a rough division of the world between these two maritime powers. Other powers would presently question the pope's right to dispose of all the new discoveries to these two nations, and, in the end, neither Spain nor Portugal could prevent other nations from encroaching on their nominal domains.

The Papal Bull, *Inter Caetera*, May 4, 1493 [1]

Alexander, bishop, servant of the servants of God, to the illustrious sovereigns, our very dear son in Christ, Ferdinand, King, and our very dear daughter in Christ, Isabella, Queen, of Castile, Leon, Aragon, Sicily, and Granada, health and apostolic benediction. . . .

We have indeed learned that you, who for a long time had intended to seek out and discover certain islands and mainlands remote and unknown and not hitherto discovered by others . . . having been up to the present time greatly engaged in the siege and recovery of the kingdom itself of Granada, were unable to accomplish this holy and praiseworthy purpose. But, the said

[1] Translation in *European Treaties Bearing on the History of the United States and Its Dependencies to 1648*, ed. by F. G. Davenport (Washington, D.C., 1917–1934), I, 7–78.

kingdom having at length been regained, as was pleasing to the Lord, you, with the wish to fulfill your desire, chose our beloved son, Christopher Columbus . . . whom you furnished with ships and men equipped for like designs. . . . And they at length, with divine aid and with the utmost diligence sailing in the ocean sea, discovered certain very remote islands and even mainlands that hitherto had not been discovered by others; wherein dwell very many peoples living in peace, and, as reported, going unclothed and not eating any flesh. . . .

In the islands and countries already discovered are found gold, spices, and very many other precious things of divers kinds and qualities. Wherefore, as becomes Catholic kings and princes . . . you have purposed with the favor of divine clemency to bring under your sway the said mainlands and islands. . . . We, of our own accord, not at your instance nor the request of anyone else in your regard, but of our own sole largess and certain knowledge and out of the fullness of our apostolic power . . . do by tenor of these presents . . . give, grant, and assign to you and your heirs and successors, kings of Castile and Leon, forever . . . all islands and mainlands found and to be found . . . toward the west and south, by drawing and establishing a line from the Arctic pole, namely the north, to the Antarctic pole, namely the south, no matter whether the said mainlands and islands are found and to be found in the direction of India or toward any other quarter, the said line to be distant one hundred leagues toward the west and south from any of the islands commonly known as the Azores and Cape Verde. With this proviso, however, that none of the islands and mainlands, found and to be found . . . beyond that said line toward the west and south, be in the actual possession of any Christian king or prince up to the birthday of our Lord Jesus Christ just past, from which the present year one thousand four hundred and ninety-three begins. . . .

Furthermore, under penalty of excommunication . . . we strictly forbid all persons of whatsoever rank, even imperial and royal, to dare, without your special permit or that of your aforesaid heirs and successors, to go for the purpose of trade or any other reason to the island or mainlands, found and to be found, toward the west and south . . . other decrees whatsoever to the contrary notwithstanding. . . .

Let no one, therefore, infringe, or with rash boldness con-
travene, this our recommendation, . . . mandate, prohibition,
and will. Should anyone presume to attempt this, be it known to
him that he will incur the wrath of Almighty God and of the
blessed apostles Peter and Paul. Given at Rome, at St. Peter's,
in the year of the incarnation of our Lord one thousand four
hundred and ninety-three, the fourth of May, and the first year
of our pontificate.

Gratis by order of our most holy lord, the Pope. . . .

The Treaty of Tordesillas, June 7, 1494 [2]

Don Ferdinand and Doña Isabella, by the grace of God King
and Queen of Castile, Leon, Aragon, Sicily, Granada . . . by
. . . members of our council it was treated, adjusted, and agreed
for us and in our name . . . with the most serene Dom John,
by the grace of God King of Portugal and of the Algarves on
this side and beyond the sea in Africa, Lord of Guinea, our
very dear and very beloved brother . . . as follows:

That, whereas a certain controversy exists between the said
lords . . . as to what lands, of all those discovered in the ocean
sea up to the present day, the date of this treaty, pertain to each
one of the said parts respectively . . . their said representatives
. . . covenanted and agreed that a boundary or straight line
be determined and drawn north and south, from pole to pole,
on the said ocean sea, from the Arctic to the Antarctic pole.
This boundary or line shall be drawn straight, as aforesaid,
at a distance of three hundred and seventy leagues west of the
Cape Verde Islands, being calculated by degrees. . . . And all
lands, both islands and mainlands, found and discovered already,
or to be found and discovered hereafter, by the said King of
Portugal and by his vessels on this side of the said line and
bound determined as above, toward the east, in either north or
south latitude, on the eastern side of the said bound . . . shall
belong to, and remain in the possession of, and pertain forever
to the said King of Portugal and his successors. And all other
lands, both islands and mainlands, found or to be found here-

[2] Translation, *ibid.*, pp. 93–96.

after, discovered or to be discovered . . . by the said King and Queen of Castile, Aragon, etc. and by their vessels, on the western side of the said bound . . . shall belong to and remain in the possession of and pertain forever to the said King and Queen. . . .

Item, . . . from this date no ships shall be dispatched . . . [of] the said King and Queen of Castile . . . on this side the said bound, which pertains to the said King of Portugal and the Algarves, etc.; nor the said King of Portugal to the other part of the said bound, which pertains to the said King and Queen of Castile . . . for the purpose of discovering and seeking any mainlands or islands, or for the purpose of trade, barter, or conquest of any kind.

Item, in order that the said line or bound of the said division may be made straight and as nearly as possible the said distance of three hundred and seventy leagues west of the Cape Verde Islands, . . . within the ten months immediately following the date of this treaty their said constituent lords shall dispatch two or four caravels, namely, one or two by each one of them. . . . These vessels shall meet at the Grand Canary Island during this time, and each one of the said parties shall send certain persons in them, to wit: pilots, astrologers, sailors, and any others they may deem desirable. But there must be as many on one side as on the other, and certain of the said pilots, astrologers, sailors, and others of those sent by the said King and Queen of Castile, Aragon, etc., and who are experienced, shall embark in the ships of the said King of Portugal and the Algarves; in like manner certain of the said persons sent by the said King of Portugal shall embark in the ship or ships of the said King and Queen of Castile. . . .

The English Stake a Claim to North America

Before Columbus had finally gained the support of Ferdinand and Isabella for his Enterprise of the Indies, he had sent his brother Bartholomew to England to appeal to King Henry VII, but that economical monarch could not be persuaded to invest in the voyage. Thus England lost the opportunity of gaining lands that Spain acquired. After the news of Columbus' success,

Henry realized that he had made a mistake and soon took more interest in the exploration of the western ocean.

Englishmen had already shown their initiative in probing the northern seas, for fishermen and traders from Bristol were accustomed to sail as far as Iceland. They regularly fished in Icelandic waters and traded for Icelandic products. Some scholars believe that Bristol seamen may have gone as far as Newfoundland even before Columbus' first voyage, though definite proof is lacking. Evidence set forth by James A. Williamson indicates that as early as 1494 two Bristol men, Robert Thorne and Hugh Elyot, made a voyage to the west and discovered Newfoundland.[3] Undoubtedly in the last decade of the fifteenth century interest in exploration ran high in Bristol.

About this time a certain John Cabot appears on the scene, and it is to John Cabot that England owed its later claims to a portion of the New World. This man was born in Genoa and later was naturalized in Venice. Italian records show his name as Zuan Caboto, "Zuan" being the Venetian dialectical form of "Giovanni" (in English, "John"). A merchant who had been to Alexandria in Venetian galleys and had learned about the spice trade, Cabot was reported to have gone into Arabia as far as Mecca. At any rate, he knew the value of the trade with the Near East. By 1495 he was in England with a project similar to Columbus': he would find a route to Cathay by sailing northwest. We should remember that Columbus had come back convinced that he had reached outlying islands off the coast of Asia, but it was evident to Cabot that he had seen none of the civilized parts of the East where riches were to be found. The source of Eastern commodities was Cabot's goal.

This time Henry VII showed more interest, and on March 5, 1496, he granted to John Cabot and his three sons, Luigi, Sebastian, and Sancio, letters patent authorizing them to sail in five ships of any tonnage, at their own costs, to any parts of the "eastern, western, and northern sea" and to explore "whatsoever islands, countries, regions or provinces of heathens and infidels in whatsoever part of the world placed, which before this time were unknown to all Christians." [4]

[3] James A. Williamson, *The Cabot Voyages and Bristol Discovery under Henry VII* (Cambridge: The Hakluyt Society, 1962), pp. 26–32.
[4] *Ibid.*, p. 51.

In this fashion did Henry VII plan to circumvent Spain. He recognized Spain's right to lands already discovered, but he asserted the right of explorers flying his flag to investigate and claim lands unknown to any Christian.

The Cabots were granted the privilege of occupying lands in the king's name. One-fifth of any profits made were to be paid to the king. They also were to be exempt from paying duty on goods imported into England from their new possessions and were to use the port of Bristol exclusively. King Henry did not supply the Cabots with money for their exploration or with ships; that responsibility lay with the Bristol merchants.

But these businessmen, for all of their concern over exploration, did not open their pocketbooks very wide. Evidence now indicates that John Cabot managed to launch an expedition in 1496 that ran into bad weather, had trouble with the crew and had to turn back.[5] The next year Cabot tried again, this time in a small ship of about 50 tons, named the *Matthew,* with 18 or 20 men. His son Sebastian, then aged about fifteen, may or may not have gone along. The expedition left sometime in May and was back in Bristol by August 6. Precisely where Cabot made a landfall in North America is a matter for argument among geographers: perhaps it was Cape Breton Island, perhaps somewhere on the coast of Maine, but no doubt exists of his exploration of the northern coast. A map made by Juan de La Cosa dating from 1500 shows little English flags on the North American coast, though these may indicate discoveries made after 1497. In December King Henry awarded Cabot an annual pension of £20.

By early 1498 Cabot was making ready to sail on another exploring expedition. From the landfall previously made in North America he planned to work south in the hope of reaching the settled parts of Asia, where he could set up a center of trade. On this expedition he had one ship equipped and victualed by the king, accompanied by four small ships supplied by the Bristol merchants. These carried trade goods which the merchants hoped to exchange for Asiatic products.

The expedition set out from Bristol in May, but what happened to the five ships is shrouded in mystery. A manuscript of a Latin history of England written by an Italian, Polydore

[5] *Ibid.,* p. 54.

Vergil, has a passage saying that John Cabot's ship was lost. Whether all five ships were lost or whether one or more came home to report discoveries along the American coast, perhaps as far south as the Caribbean, remains in the realm of conjecture.[6] The memory of John Cabot soon died out, and since his son Sebastian gained some note as an explorer and as pilot major in Spain, Sebastian was given credit by European writers for the discoveries made by his father in 1497 and perhaps in 1498.

The return of John Cabot in 1497, however, created some excitement among foreign observers in London. Merchants and ambassadors took note of this venture of the English in search of the riches of Asia and wrote home about it. Several of the letters follow:

Lorenzo Pasqualigo Writes to His Brothers in Venice [7]

The Venetian, our countryman, who went with a ship from Bristol to find new islands, has returned, and says that 700 leagues hence he discovered mainland, the territory of the Grand Cham [Great Khan]. He coasted for 300 leagues and landed. He did not see any person, but he has brought hither to the king certain snares which had been set to catch game, and a needle for making nets. He also found some cut trees, wherefore he supposed there were inhabitants. Being in doubt he returned to his ship.

He was three months on the voyage, and this is certain; and on his return he saw two islands but would not land, so as not to lose time, as he was short of provisions. The king is much pleased with this. He says that the tides are slack and do not flow as they do here.

The king has promised that in the spring our countryman shall have ten ships; armed to his order, and at his request has conceded him all the prisoners, except traitors, to go with him as he has requested. The king has also given him money wherewith to amuse himself till then, and he is now at Bristol

---

[6] *Ibid.*, pp. 95–115, for a discussion of the problem.

[7] This letter was received in Venice on September 23, 1497. It is here reprinted from the version in *The Northmen, Columbus, and Cabot*, Original Narratives of Early American History (New York, 1906), pp. 423–424.

with his wife, who is also Venetian, and with his sons. His name is Zuam Talbot [*sic*], and he is styled the great admiral. Vast honor is paid him. He dresses in silk, and these English run after him like mad people, so that he can enlist as many of them as he pleases, and a number of our own rogues besides.

The discoverer of these things planted on his new-found land a large cross, with one flag of England and another of Saint Mark, by reason of his being a Venetian, so that our banner has floated very far afield.

London, 23 August, 1497.

Report to the Duke of Milan, Lodovico Sforza, Il Moro [8]

[*Raimondo de Soncino, agent of Lodovico Sforza, known as Il Moro, Duke of Milan, wrote to his master soon after Cabot's return from the voyage of 1497 as follows:*]

. . . Some months ago His Majesty sent out a Venetian, who is a very good mariner and has good skill in discovering new islands, and he has returned safe, and has found two very large and fertile new islands; having likewise discovered the Seven Cities [legendary cities located on the legendary island of Antilia, in the Atlantic] 400 leagues from England on the western passage. This next spring His Majesty means to send him with fifteen or twenty ships.

[*Raimondo de Soncino followed this note with a longer letter to the Duke, dated from London, December 18, 1497:*]

Most Illustrious and Excellent My Lord:—

Perhaps among Your Excellency's many occupations, it may not displease you to learn how His Majesty here has won a part of Asia without a stroke of the sword. There is in this kingdom a Venetian fellow, Master John Caboto by name, of fine mind, greatly skilled in navigation, who, seeing that those most serene kings, first he of Portugal and then the one of Spain, have occupied unknown islands, determined to make a

[8] Letters reprinted *ibid.*, pp. 424–429.

like acquisition for His Majesty aforesaid. And having obtained
royal grants that he should have the usufruct of all that he
should discover, provided that the ownership of the same is
reserved to the Crown, with a small ship and eighteen persons
he committed himself to fortune. And having set out from
Bristol, a western port of this kingdom, and passed the western
limits of Ireland, and then, standing to the northward, he began
to sail toward the Oriental regions, leaving (after a few days)
the North Star on his right hand. And, having wandered about
considerably, at last he struck mainland, where, having planted
the royal banner and taken possession on behalf of this king, and
taken certain tokens, he has returned thence. The said Master
John, as being foreign-born and poor, would not be believed
if his comrades, who are almost all Englishmen and from
Bristol, did not testify that what he says is true. This Master
John has the description of the world in a chart, and also in a
solid globe which he has made; and he shows where he landed,
and that going toward the east he passed considerably beyond
the country of the Tanais. ["Tanais" was the Latin name for the
river Don. Marco Polo wrote of a kingdom of Tana in western
India. It is not certain which of these Soncino intended.] And
they say that it is a very good and temperate country, and they
think that brazilwood and silk grow there. And they affirm that
that sea is covered with fishes, which are caught not only with
the net but with baskets, a stone being tied to them in order
that the baskets may sink in the water. And this I heard the said
Master John relate.

And the aforesaid Englishmen, his comrades, say that they
will bring so many fishes that this kingdom will no longer have
need of Iceland, from which country there comes a very great
store of fish which are called stockfish [dried cod or haddock].
But Master John has set his mind on something greater. For he
expects to go farther on toward the East from that place
already occupied, constantly hugging the shore, until he shall
be over against an island, by him called Cipango, situated in
the equinoctial region, where he thinks all the spices of the
world, and also the precious stones, originate. And he says that
in former times he was at Mecca, whither spices are brought
by caravans from distant countries, and that those who brought

them, on being asked where the said spices grow, answered that they do not know, but that other caravans come to their homes with this merchandise from distant countries, and these again say that they are brought to them from other remote regions. And he argues thus: that if the Orientals affirmed to the Southerners that these things come from a distance from them, and so from hand to hand, presupposing the rotundity of the earth, it must be that the last ones get them at the north toward the west. And he said it in such a way that, having nothing to gain or lose by it, I too believe it. And what is more, the king here, who is wise and not lavish, likewise puts some faith in him; for ever since his return he has made good provision for him, as the same Master John tells me. And it is said that, in the spring, His Majesty aforenamed will fit out some ships, and will besides give him all the convicts, and they will go to that country to make a colony, by means of which they hope to establish in London a greater emporium of spices than there is in Alexandria. And the chief men of the enterprise are of Bristol—great sailors who, now that they know where to go, say that it is not a voyage of more than 15 days; nor do they ever have storms after they get away from Hibernia.

I have also talked with a Burgundian, a comrade of Master John's, who confirms everything, and wishes to return thither because the admiral (for so Master John already entitles himself) has given him an island. And he has given another one to a barber of his from Castiglione-of-Genoa; and both of them regard themselves as counts, nor does my lord the admiral esteem himself anything less than a prince. I think that with this expedition there will go several poor Italian monks who have all been promised bishoprics. And, as I have become a friend of the admiral's, if I wished to go thither I should get an archbishopric. But I have thought that the benefices which Your Excellency has in store for me are a surer thing; and therefore I beg that if these should fall vacant in my absence, you will cause possession to be given to me, taking measures to do this rather where it is needed, in order that they be not taken from me by others who, because they are present, can be more diligent than I, who in this country have been brought to the pass of eating ten or twelve dishes at every meal and

sitting at table three hours at a time twice a day for the sake
of Your Excellency, to whom I humbly commend myself.

Your Excellency's
Very humble servant,
RAIMONDO

A Spanish Envoy Informs Ferdinand and Isabella [9]

[*Spain would naturally be concerned about English explorations in the Atlantic, but since Ferdinand and Isabella were
eager to curry favor with Henry VII, in the hope of winning
him to their side in a contest with the French in Italy, they
took no overt action to protest. The junior ambassador in
England, Pedro de Ayala, wrote to their Majesties, however,
on July 25, 1498, to inform them of the continuing interest of
the English king in explorations. His letter follows:*]

I think Your Majesties have already heard that the king
of England has equipped a fleet in order to discover certain
islands and mainland which, he was informed, some people
from Bristol (who manned a few ships for the same purpose
last year) had found. I have seen the map which the discoverer
has made, who is another Genoese like Colón [Columbus], who
has been in Seville and in Lisbon asking assistance for this discovery.

The people of Bristol have, for the last seven years, sent out
every year two, three, or four light ships [*caravelas*] in search
of the island of Brazil [mythical island in Atlantic] and the
Seven Cities [supposed to have been settled somewhere in
Atlantic by seven bishops] according to the fancy of this Genoese.
The king determined to send out [ships] because, the year
before, they brought certain news that they had found land.
The fleet consisted of five vessels, which carried provisions
for one year. It is said that one of them, in which another Fai
Buil [*sic;* there was a Friar Buil on Columbus' second voyage]
went, has returned to Ireland in great distress, the ship being
much damaged. The Genoese continued his voyage.

I, having seen the route which they took and the distance
they sailed, find that what they have found, or what they are

9 *Ibid.,* pp. 429–430.

in search of, is what Your Highnesses already possess since it is, in fine, what fell to Your Highnesses by the treaty with Portugal. It is expected that they will be back in the month of September.

I inform Your Highnesses in regard to it. The king of England has often spoken to me on this subject. He hoped to derive great advantage from it. I think it is not further distant than four hundred leagues. I told him that, in my opinion, the land was already in the possession of Your Majesties; but, though I gave him my reasons, he did not like it. Because I believe that Your Highnesses will presently receive information in regard to all this matter, and the chart or map which this man has made, I do not now send it. It is here and it, according to my opinion, is false, in order to make it appear that they are not the said islands.

Report to the King by Giovanni da Verrazano

[The French, like the English, did not intend to be excluded from the New World. King Francis I had querulously commented that he would like to see the will of Father Adam to learn how he had disposed of his patrimony. Obviously Francis I did not intend for Spain to gobble up the whole of this "inheritance."

[Since the Emperor Charles V, who was also King of Spain, was his bitter enemy, Francis sought every way possible to thwart him. One way was to find a route to the Spice Islands that would cut into the revenue of his rival. The French king found that the seamen of Dieppe were interested in explorations, and the silk merchants of Lyons were eager to gain access to the products of Asia. They were in contact with Florentine bankers and merchants, who were also anxious to develop new trade connections with the East.

[Taking advantage of their Italian connections, the French enlisted a Florentine, Giovanni da Verrazano, to lead an exploring expedition that sailed from Rouen in 1524. Verrazano reached the coast of what is now North Carolina; beyond the sandspits he saw the waters of Pamlico Sound, which he took to

*be the Pacific Ocean, separated from the Atlantic by only a nar-
row neck of land. This body of water appeared on maps for some
time thereafter as the "Sea of Verrazano" and led other navigators to believe that an opening to Asia might be nearby.*

*[Verrazano continued to explore the coastline of North Amer-
ica as he sailed south and again north. Though he missed Chesapeake Bay, he did enter the mouth of the Hudson River. His
discovery of New York harbor is commemorated today by a New
York bridge that bears his name. Upon Verrazano's discoveries,
combined with the explorations of later French navigators,
France laid claim to part of North America.*

*[Verrazano returned to France in the summer of 1524, reach-
ing Dieppe in July. Immediately he made a report to Francis I.
That report follows* ¹⁰*:]*

The relation of John Verrazanus, a Florentine, of the land
by him discovered in the name of His Majesty, written in
Dieppe the eighth of July, 1524.

I wrote not to Your Majesty (most Christian king), since the
time we suffered the tempest in the north parts, of the success
of the four ships which Your Majesty sent forth to discover new
lands by the Ocean, thinking Your Majesty had been already
duly informed thereof. Now, by these presents, I will give
Your Majesty to understand how, by the violence of the winds,
we were forced with the two ships—the *Norman* and the
Dolphin [actually *La Dauphine*] in such evil case as they were
—to land in Britaine [Brittany]. Where, after we had repaired
them in all points as was needful and armed them very well,
we took our course along by the coast of Spain. Afterward, with
the *Dolphin* alone, we determined to make discovery of new
countries to prosecute the navigation we had already begun,
which I purpose at this present to recount unto Your Majesty to
make manifest the whole proceeding of the matter.

The 17 of January, the year 1524, by the grace of God we
departed from the dishabited Rock [one of the Deserta islands]
by the isle of Madeira, appertaining to the king of Portingal,
with fifty men, with victuals, weapon, and other ship munition

¹⁰ Text modernized from the version printed by Richard Hakluyt, *Divers Voyages*
(1582).

very well provided and furnished for eight months. And, sailing westward with a fair easterly wind, in 25 days we ran 500 leagues. And the 20 of February we were overtaken with as sharp and terrible a tempest as ever any sailors suffered; whereof, with the divine help and merciful assistance of almighty God and the goodness of our ship, accompanied with the good hap of her fortunate name, we were delivered, and with a prosperous wind followed our course west and by north. And in other 25 days we made above 400 leagues more, where we discovered a new land [probably the vicinity of Charleston, South Carolina] never before seen of any man, either ancient or modern. And at the first sight it seemed somewhat low but, being within a quarter of a league of it, we perceived by the great fires that we saw by the seacoast that it was inhabited, and saw that the land stretched to the southward.

In seeking some convenient harbor whereby to come aland and have knowledge of the place, we sailed 50 leagues in vain; and, seeing the land to run still to the southward, we resolved to return back again toward the north, where we found ourselves troubled with the like difficulty. At length, being in despair to find any port, we cast anchor upon the coast and sent our boat to shore, where we saw great store of people which came to the seaside; and seeing us to approach, they fled away, and sometimes would stand still and look back, beholding us with great admiration. But afterward, being animated and assured with signs that we made them, some of them came hard to the seaside, seeming to rejoice very much at the sight of us and, marveling greatly at our apparel, shape, and whiteness, showed us by sundry signs where we might most commodiously come aland with our boat, offering us also of their victuals to eat.

Now I will briefly declare to Your Majesty their life and manners, as far as we could have notice thereof: These people go altogether naked, except only that they cover their privy parts with certain skins of beasts like unto martens, which they fasten unto a narrow girdle made of grass, very artificially [skillfully] wrought, hanged about with tails of divers other beasts, which round about their bodies hang dangling down to their knees. Some of them wear garlands of birds' feathers. The people are of color russet, and not much unlike the Saracens, their hair black, thick, and not very long, which they tie together in a knot behind and wear it like a tail. They are well featured in their limbs, of mean [medium] stature, and commonly somewhat bigger than we; broad breasted, strong arms, their legs and other parts of their bodies well fashioned, and they are disfigured in nothing saving that they have somewhat broad visages, and yet not all of them; for we saw many of them well favored, having black and great eyes with a cheerful and steady look, not strong of body yet sharp-witted, nimble, and great runners, as far as we could learn by experience. And in those two last qualities they are like to the people of the East parts of the world, and especially to them of the uttermost parts of China. We could not learn of this people their manner of living nor their particular customs by reason of the short abode we made on the shore—our company being but small and our ship riding far off in the sea. And not far from these we found another people, whose living we think to be like unto theirs (as hereafter I will declare unto Your Majesty), showing at this present the situation and nature of the foresaid land.

The shore is all covered with small sand, and so ascendeth upward for the space of 15 feet, rising in form of little hills about 50 paces broad. And sailing forward, we found certain small rivers and arms of the sea that enter at certain creeks, washing the shore on both sides as the coast lyeth. And beyond this we saw the open country rising in height above the sandy shore, with many fair fields and plains, full of mighty great woods, some very thick and some thin, replenished with divers sorts of trees, as pleasant and delectable to behold as is possible to imagine. And Your Majesty may not think that these are like the woods of Hercynia [a forest in ancient Germany of which the Black Forest was a part], or the wild deserts of Tartary, and the northern coasts full of fruitless trees; but full of palm trees, bay trees, and high cypress trees, and many other sorts of trees unknown in Europe which yield most sweet savors far from the shore; the property whereof we could not learn for the cause aforesaid and not for any difficulty to pass through the woods, seeing they are not so thick but that a man may pass through them. Neither do we think that they, partaking of the East world round about them, are altogether void of drugs or spicery and other riches of gold, seeing the color of the land doth so much argue it. And the land is full of many beasts, as stags, deer, and hares. . . .

This land is in latitude 34 d[egrees], with good and wholesome air, temperate between hot and cold; no vehement winds do blow in those regions, and those that do commonly reign in those coasts are the northwest and west winds in the summer season (in the beginning whereof we were there), the sky clear and fair with very little rain. And if at any time the air be cloudy and misty with the southern wind, immediately it is dissolved, and waxeth clear and fair again. The sea is calm, not boisterous, the waves gentle, and, although all the shore be somewhat low and without harbor, yet it is not dangerous to the sailers [sailing ships], being free from rocks and deep, so that within four or five feet of the shore there is 20-foot deep of water without ebb or flood, the depth still increasing in such uniform proportion. There is very good riding at sea; for any ship being shaken in a tempest can never perish there by breaking of her cables, which we have proved by experience. For in the beginning of March (as is usual in all regions), being in the sea oppressed with northern winds, and riding there, we found our anchor broken before the earth failed or moved at all.

We departed from this place, still running along the coast which we found to trend toward the east, and we saw everywhere very great fires by reason of the multitude of the inhabitants. While we rode on that coast, partly because it had no harbor and for that we wanted water, we sent our boat ashore with 25 men; where, by reason of great and continual waves that beat against the shore—being an open coast—without succor none of our men could possibly go ashore without losing our boat. We saw there many people, which came unto the shore making divers signs of friendship and showing that they were content we should come aland, and by trial we found them to be very courteous and gentle, as Your Majesty shall understand by the success.

To the intent we might send them of our things which the Indians commonly desire and esteem, as sheets of paper, glasses, bells, and suchlike trifles, we sent a young man, one of our mariners, ashore; who, swimming toward them and being within three or four yards off the shore, not trusting them, cast the things upon the shore. Seeking afterward to return, he was with such violence of the waves beaten upon the shore that he was so bruised that he lay there almost dead; which the Indians perceiving, [they] ran to catch him and, drawing him out, they carried him a little way off from the sea. The young man, perceiving they carried him [and] being at the first dismayed, began then greatly to fear and cried out piteously. Likewise did the Indians which did accompany him, going about to cheer him and give him courage; and then, setting him on the ground at the foot of a little hill, against the sun, began to behold him with great admiration, marveling at the whiteness of his flesh. And, putting off his clothes, they made him warm at a great fire, not without our great fear which remained in the boat that they would have roasted him at that fire and have eaten him. The young man, having recovered his strength and having stayed awhile with them, showed them by signs that he was desirous to return to the ship. And they, with great love clapping him fast about with many embracings, accompanying him unto the sea and, to put him in more assurance, leaving him alone, they went unto a high ground and stood there beholding him until he was entered into the boat. This young man observed, as we did also, that these are of color inclining to black, as the other were, with their flesh very shining; of mean stature, handsome visage, and delicate limbs, and of very little strength, but of prompt wit; farther we observed not.

Departing from hence, following the shore, which trended somewhat toward the north, in 50 leagues' space we came to another land, which showed much more fair and full of woods, being very great, where we rode at anchor. And that we might have some knowledge thereof we sent 20 men aland, which entered into the country about two leagues; and they found that the people were fled to the woods for fear. They saw only one old woman with a young maid of eighteen or twenty years old, which, seeing our company, hid themselves in the grass for fear. The old woman carried two infants on her shoulders and behind her neck a child of eight years old. The young woman was laden likewise with as many. But when our men came unto them, the women cried out; the old woman made signs that the men were fled unto the woods as soon as they saw us. To quiet them and to win their favor, our men gave them such victuals as they had with them to eat, which the old woman received thankfully. But the young woman disdained them all and threw them disdainfully on the ground. They took a child from the old woman to bring into France, and, going about to take the young woman, which was very beautiful and of tall stature, they could not possibly, for the great outcries that she made, bring her to the sea; and especially having great woods to pass through, and being far from the ship, we purposed to leave her behind, bearing away the child only.

We found those folks to be more white than those that we found before, being clad with certain leaves that hang on boughs of trees, which they sew together with threads of wild hemp. Their heads were trussed up after the same manner as the former were. Their ordinary food is of pulse [porridge of meal], whereof they have great store, differing in color and taste from ours, of good and pleasant taste. Moreover they live by fishing and fowling, which they take with gins [snares] and bows made of hard wood, the arrows of canes being headed with the bones of fish and other beasts. The beasts in these parts are much wilder than in our Europe by reason they are continually chased and hunted.

We saw many of their boats, made of one tree, 20 feet long and four feet broad, which are not made with iron, or stone, or any other kind of metal (because that in all this country, for the space of 200 leagues which we ran, we never saw one stone of any sort). They help themselves with fire, burning so much of the tree as is sufficient for the hollowness of the boat; the like they do in making the stern and the forepart, until it be fit to sail upon the sea. The land is, in situation, goodness, and fairness, like the other: it hath woods like the other, thin and full of divers sorts of trees, but not so sweet because the country is more northerly and cold.

We saw in this country many vines growing naturally, which growing up take hold of the trees as they do in Lombardy; which, if by husbandmen they were dressed in good order, without all doubt they would yield excellent wines; for we having oftentimes seen the fruit thereof dried, which was sweet and pleasant and not differing from ours. We do think that they do esteem the same, because that in every place where they grow they take away the under branches growing round about, that the fruit thereof may ripen the better.

We found also roses, violets, lilies, and many sorts of herbs, and sweet and odoriferous flowers different from ours. We knew not their dwellings because they were far up in the land, and we judge by many signs that we saw that they are of wood and of trees framed together.

We do believe also, by many conjectures and signs, that many of them, sleeping in the fields, have no other cover than the open sky. Further knowledge have we not of them. We think that all the rest whose countries we passed live all after one manner.

Having our abode three days in this country, riding on the coast for want of harbors, we concluded to depart from thence, trending along the shore between the north and the east, sailing only in the daytime and riding at anchor by night. In the space of 100 leagues' sailing we found a very pleasant place situated amongst certain little steep hills, from amidst the which hills there ran down into the sea a great stream of water, which within the mouth was very deep; and from the sea to the mouth of same [probably the mouth of the Hudson River], with the tide, which we found to rise eight feet, any great vessel laden may pass up.

But because we rode at anchor in a place well fenced from the wind, we would not venture ourselves without knowledge of the place; and we passed up with our boat only into the said river, and saw the country very well peopled. The people are almost like unto the others, and clad with the feathers of fowls of divers colors. They came toward us very cheerfully, making great shouts of admiration, showing us where we might come to land most safely with our boat. We entered up the said river into the land about half a league, where it made a most pleasant lake about three leagues in compass; on the which they rowed from the one side to the other to the number of 30 of their small boats, wherein were many people, which passed from one shore to the other to come and see us. And behold, upon the sudden (as it is wont to fall out in sailing), a contrary flaw [sudden gust] of wind coming from the sea, we were enforced to return to our ship, leaving this land to our great discontentment, for the great commodity and pleasantness thereof, which we suppose is not without some riches, all the hills showing mineral matters in them.

We weighed anchor and sailed toward the east, for so the coast trended, and so always for 50 leagues, being in the sight thereof. We discovered an island in the form of a triangle, distant from the mainland three leagues, about the bigness of the island of Rhodes. It was full of hills, covered with trees, well peopled for we saw fires all along the coast. We gave the name of it of Your Majesty's mother [i.e., Luisa, probably the island now known as Block Island], not staying there by reason of the weather being contrary.

And we came to another land, being 15 leagues distant from the island, where we found a passing good haven; wherein, being entered, we found about 20 small boats of the people, which, with divers cries and wonderings, came about our ship. Coming no nearer than 50 paces toward us, they stayed and beheld the artificialness [skillful construction] of our ship, our shape and apparel. Then they all made a loud shout together, declaring that they rejoiced. When we had something [that] animated them (using their gests [judging by their gestures]), they came so near us that we cast them certain bells and glasses and many toys, which, when they had received, they looked on them with laughing and came without fear aboard our ship. There were amongst these people two kings of so goodly stature and shape as is possible to declare. The eldest was about forty years of age; the second was a young man of twenty years old. Their apparel was on this manner: the elder had upon his naked body a hart's skin, wrought artificially with divers branches like damask; his head was bare, with the hair tied up behind with divers knots; about his neck he had a large chain garnished with divers stones of sundry colors. The young man was almost appareled after the same manner. This is the goodliest people, and of the fairest conditions, that we have found in this our voyage. They exceed us in bigness, they are of the color of brass, some of them incline more to whiteness. Others are of yellow color, of comely visage, with long and black hair which they are very careful to trim and deck up. They are black- and quick-eyed. I write not to Your Majesty of the other part of their body, having all such proportion as appertaineth to any handsome man. The women are of the like conformity and beauty, very handsome and well favored. They are as well mannered and continent as any women of good education. They are all naked save their privy parts, which they cover with a deer's skin, branched or embroidered, as the men use. There are also of them which wear on their arms very rich skins of leopards. They adorn their heads with divers ornaments made of their own hair, which hang down before on both sides their breasts. Others use other kind of dressing themselves, like unto the women of Egypt and Syria; these are of the elder sort. And when they are married they wear divers toys, according to the usage of the people of the East, as well men as women.

Among whom we saw many plates of wrought copper, which they esteem more than gold, which for the color they make no account of for that among all other it is counted the basest; they make most account of azure and red. The things that they esteemed most of all those which we gave them were bells, crystal of azure color, and other toys to hang at their ears or about their neck. They did not desire cloth of silk or of gold, much less of any other sort. Neither cared they for things made of steel and iron, which we often showed them in our armor, which they made no wonder at, and, in beholding them, they only asked the art of making them. The like they did at our glasses, which, when they beheld, they suddenly laughed and gave them us again. They are very liberal, for they give that which they have.

We became great friends with these, and one day we entered into the haven with our ship, whereas before we rode a league off at sea by reason of the contrary weather. They came in great companies of their small boats unto the ship, with their faces all bepainted with divers colors showing us that it was a sign of joy, bringing us of their victuals. They made signs unto us where we might safest ride in the haven for the safeguard of our ship, keeping still our company. And after we were come to an anchor, we bestowed 15 days in providing ourselves many necessary things, whither every day the people repaired to see our ship, bringing their wives with them whereof they are very jealous. And they, themselves entering aboard the ship and staying there a good space, caused their wives to stay in their boats; and for all the entreaty we could make, offering to give them divers things, we could never obtain that they would suffer them to come aboard our ship.

And oftentimes one of the two kings coming, with his queen and many gentlemen for their pleasure, to see us, they all stayed on the shore 200 paces from us, sending a small boat to give us intelligence of their coming, saying they would come to see our ship. This they did in token of safety. And as soon as they had answer from us they came immediately; and, having stayed a while to behold it, they wondered at hearing the cries and noise of the mariners. The queen and her maids stayed in a very light boat at an island a quarter of a league off while the king abode a long space in our ship, uttering divers conceits with gestures, viewing with great admiration all the furniture of the ship, demanding the property of everything particularly. He took likewise great pleasure in beholding our apparel, and in tasting our meats, and so, courteously taking his leave, departed. And sometimes, our men staying for two or three days on a little island near the ship for divers necessaries (as it is the use of seamen), he returned with seven or eight of his gentlemen to see what we did, and asked of us ofttimes if we meant to make any long abode there, offering us of their provision. Then the king, drawing his bow and running up and down with his gentlemen, made much sport to gratify our men.

We were oftentimes within the land five or six leagues, which we found as pleasant as is possible to declare, very apt for any kind of husbandry of corn, wine, and oil, for that there are plains 25 or 30 leagues broad, open and without any impediment of trees, of such fruitfulness that any seed being sown therein will bring forth most excellent fruit. We entered afterward into the woods, which we found so great and thick that any army, were it never so great, might have hid itself therein, the trees whereof are oaks, cypress trees, and other sorts unknown in Europe. We found *Pomi appii* [a kind of apple], damson trees, and nut trees, and many other sorts of fruits differing from ours. There are beasts in great abundance—as harts, deers, leopards, and other kinds—which they take with their nets and bows, which are their chief weapons. The arrows which they use are made with great cunning, and instead of iron, they head them with smeriglio [emery], with jasper stone, and hard marble and other sharp stones; which they use instead of iron to cut trees and make their boats of one whole piece of wood, making it hollow with great and wonderful art, wherein ten or twelve men may be [seated] commodiously. Their oars are short and broad at the end, and they use them in the sea without any danger and by main force of arms, with as great speediness as they list themselves.

We saw their houses, made in circular or round form ten or twelve feet in compass, made with half circles of timber, separate one from another without any order of building, covered with mats of straw wrought cunningly together which save them from the wind and rain. And if they had the order of building and perfect skill of workmanship as we have, there were no doubt but that they would also make eftsoons great and stately buildings. For all the seacoasts are full of clear and glistering stones and alabaster, and therefore it is full of good havens and harbors for ships. They move the foresaid houses from one place to another, according to the commodity of the place and season wherein they will make their abode; and only taking off the cover they have other houses builded incontinent [at once]. The father and the whole family dwell together in one house in great number; in some of them we saw 25 or 30 persons. They feed as the other do aforesaid, of pulse, which do grow in that country with better order of husbandry than in the others.

They observe in their sowing the course of the moon and the rising of certain stars, and divers other customs spoken of by antiquity. Moreover they live by hunting and fishing. They live long and are seldom sick; and if they chance to fall sick at any time, they heal themselves with fire, without any physician; and they say that they die for very age. They are very pitiful and charitable toward their neighbors. They make great lamentations in their adversity, and in their misery the kindred reckon up all their felicity. At their departure out of life they use mourning mixed with singing, which continueth for a long space. This is as much as we could learn of them.

This land is situated in the parallel of Rome, in 41 degrees and two tierces [thirds]; but somewhat more cold, by accidental cause and not of nature (as I will declare unto Your Highness elsewhere). Describing at this present the situation of the foresaid country, which lieth east and west, I say that the mouth of the haven lieth open to the south half a league broad; and, being entered within it, between the east and the north it stretcheth 12 leagues, where it waxeth broader and broader and maketh a gulf about 20 leagues in compass; wherein are five small islands, very fruitful and pleasant, full of high and broad trees; among the which islands any great navy may ride safe without any fear of tempest or other danger. Afterward, turning toward the south and in the entering into the haven, on both sides there are the most pleasant hills, with many rivers of most clear water falling into the sea. In the midst of this entrance there is a rock of freestone, growing by nature, apt to build any castle or fortress there for the keeping of the haven [probably Narragansett Bay].

The 5th of May, being furnished with all things necessary, we departed from the said coast, keeping along in the sight thereof. And we sailed 150 leagues finding it always after one manner, but the land somewhat higher with certain mountains, all which bear a show of mineral matter. We sought not to land there in any place because the weather served our turn for sailing. But we suppose that it was like to the former. The coast ran eastward for the space of 50 leagues. And trending afterward [to] the north, we found another land: high, full of thick woods, the trees whereof were firs, cypresses, and suchlike as are wont to grow in cold countries [probably New Hampshire or southern Maine]. The people differ much from the other; and look how much the former seemed to be courteous and gentle, so much were these full of rudeness and ill manners, and so barbarous that by no signs that ever we could make we could have any kind of traffic with them. They clothe themselves in bearskins and leopards' and seals' and other beasts' skins. Their food, as far as we could perceive [by their] repairing often unto their dwellings, we suppose to be by hunting and fishing, and of certain fruits which are a kind of roots which the earth yieldeth of her own accord. They have no grain, neither saw we any kind or sign of tillage; neither is the land, for the barrenness thereof, apt to bear fruit or seed.

If at any time we desired by exchange to have any of their commodities, they used to come to the seashore upon certain craggy rocks, and, we standing in our boats, they let down with a rope what it pleased them to give us, crying continually that we should not approach to the land, demanding immediately the exchange, taking nothing but knives, fishhooks, and tools to cut withal; neither did they make any account of our courtesy. And when we had nothing left to exchange with them, when we departed from them, the people showed all signs of discourtesy and disdain as was possible for any creature to invent. We were, in despite of them, two or three leagues within the land, being in number 25 armed men of us. And when we went on shore they shot at us with their bows, making great outcries, and afterward fled into the woods.

We found not in this land anything notable or of importance, saving very great woods and certain hills. They may have some mineral matter in them because we saw many of them have beadstones of copper hanging at their ears. We departed from thence, keeping our course northeast along the coast, which we found more pleasant champion and without woods, with high mountains within the land. Continuing directly along the coast for the space of 50 leagues, we discovered 32 islands [probably in Penobscot Bay, Maine] lying all near the land, being small and pleasant to the view, high, and having many turnings and windings between them, making many fair harbors and channels as they do in the gulf of Venice, in Slavonia, and Dalmatia. We had no knowledge or acquaintance with the people; we suppose they are of the same manners and nature that the others are.

Sailing northeast for the space of 150 leagues, we approached to the land that in times past was discovered by the Britons, which is in fifty degrees [Newfoundland]. Having now spent all our provision and victuals, and having discovered about 700 leagues and more of new countries, and being furnished with water and wood, we concluded to return into France.

Touching the religion of this people which we have found: for want of their language we could not understand, neither by signs nor gesture, that they had any religion or law at all, or that they did acknowledge any First Cause or Mover; neither that they worship the heaven or stars, the sun or moon or other planets, and, much less, whether they be idolators. Neither could we learn whether that they used any kind of sacrifices or other adorations; neither in their villages have they any temples or houses of prayer. We suppose that they have no religion at all, and that they live at their own liberty. And that all this proceedeth of ignorance, for that they are very easy to be persuaded, and all that they see us Christians do in our divine service they did the same, with the like imitation as they saw us to do it.

Naming America

[*The name "America" derives from the name of an Italian merchant, Amerigo Vespucci, who claimed to have made four voyages of discovery to the west and to have reached a mainland in the New World (the coast of South America) on June 16, 1497, earlier than John Cabot's landfall in the North Atlantic on June 24, 1497. He set forth his claims in two letters, one written to Lorenzo Piero Francesco de' Medici and the other to Piero Soderini. Both letters were several times published.*

[*The two letters were read and reprinted by Martin Waldsee-müller, a cartographer of St. Dié in Lorraine, in* Cosmographiae Introductio *(1507), which explained two maps of the world included in this work. Waldseemüller gave the name "America" to the southern portion of the New World. A translation of his explanation was published by Justin Winsor in* A Narrative and Critical History of America *(Boston, 1886), Volume II, pp. 147–148. A pertinent excerpt from the translation follows:*]

And the fourth part of the world having been discovered by Americus, it may be called Amerige, that is, the land of Americus or America.

. . . Now truly, as these regions are more widely explored, and another fourth part is discovered, by Americus Vesputius, as may be learned from the following letters, I do not see why anyone may justly forbid it to be named Amerige, that is, Americ's Land, from Americus the discoverer, a man of sagacious mind, or America, since both Europe and Asia derived their names from women.

V

Jacques Cartier of Saint-Malo
Explores Canada

TEN years after Giovanni da Verrazano made the first reconnaissance of North America for Francis I of France, another French expedition went out to make a more intensive investigation of the region that Verrazano had discovered. The leader was Jacques Cartier, a mariner of Saint-Malo, a town that bred hardy seamen. In the years to come, many French corsairs would sail from Saint-Malo to prey on Spanish galleons wallowing home with gold from Mexico and Peru.

On April 20, 1534, Cartier sailed from Saint-Malo in two ships on his first voyage of discovery in the New World. Setting a course for the northwest, he reached Newfoundland by May 10 and continued on through the Strait of Belle Isle. Crossing the Gulf of Saint Lawrence, he landed at Gaspé, set up a cross and hung upon it a shield bearing the arms of France, thus claiming the land for Francis I. After kidnapping two Indians and sailing along the east coast of Anticosti Island, the expedition held a council and decided that since the stormy season was about to begin, they should return to France, which they reached on September 5. The voyage had shown that well-wooded and fertile land lay within easy sailing distance from France. But land for settlement was not at the moment uppermost in Cartier's mind. Like Verrazano and Cabot, he was hoping for a quick route to Cathay, and he believed that the Gulf of Saint Lawrence (as yet unnamed) might provide the way.

The Admiral of France, Philippe de Brion-Chabot, encouraged by the reports that Cartier brought back, soon issued

to him a commission to organize another expedition, this time
with three well-equipped ships, the largest of 120 tons burden,
the smallest being a light bark. By the middle of May 1535 the
vessels were fitted out; on May 16 the captain and crew took
communion in the Cathedral of Saint-Malo and received the
bishop's blessing; three days later they hoisted sail and were
off on a much longer voyage than the previous one.

Although the little fleet parted company in a storm soon
after its departure, they all managed to meet at the Strait of
Belle Isle. After sailing along the Canadian coast of what is now
Labrador and Quebec, they anchored off Anticosti Island. This
body of water Cartier now named the Bay (later Gulf) of Saint
Lawrence. The Saint Lawrence River was called by Cartier
"The River of Hochelaga" and sometimes "the great river of
Canada." Cartier had brought back the two kidnapped Indians,
who now served as guides as he attempted to navigate the great
river into the interior of the land he had entered. Passing
the site of Quebec, then called "Stadaconé," he explored a
tributary of the Saint Lawrence that now bears his name and
left his two largest vessels at anchor. With the bark and two
longboats he continued up the Saint Lawrence to the present
site of Montreal, which the Indians called "Hochelaga," a
name attached also to the river.

Cartier encountered many Indians but his contacts were
peaceful. At the site of Quebec, a chief named Donnacona with
swarms of his followers turned out to see the newcomers.
Donnacona made a long unintelligible speech and tried to no
avail to discourage Cartier from going farther up the river.
On his arrival at the site of Montreal, more Indians, dancing
and chanting, swarmed around the Frenchmen; they brought
gifts of fish and Indian corn. The explorers visited the Indians,
a branch of the Iroquois as it turned out, and marveled at the
"long houses" often described by later travelers.

After further explorations at Montreal, Cartier and his
company turned back and rejoined the party left with the two
ships at Saint Croix, near Quebec. There they built a stockade
and went into winter quarters. At first the Indians frequented
the camp and brought gifts of food, but by December their
visits ended. About this time scurvy broke out and took a
terrible toll; after many had died, Cartier learned from an

Indian how to make a concoction from spruce needles that provided the vitamins needed to cure the disease.

With the coming of warm weather, Cartier made preparations to sail. He had heard tales of a land of gold and rubies somewhere in the interior, but other than these vague stories of hidden riches he had little to show for his winter in Canada. Since the chief, Donnacona, had reported many marvels of the country beyond the point of his own explorations, Cartier decided to take him to France to tell the king in person of these wonders. Luring Donnacona and four of his lesser chiefs into an ambuscade, he sailed away with his captives and reached Saint-Malo on July 16, 1536. Cartier had planted the cross and the fleur-de-lis at strategic points claiming the new land for France.

The possibility of creating a New France overseas aroused the imagination of a French nobleman, Jean François de la Roque, Sieur de Roberval, who received from Francis I a sequence of grandiose titles to the new country and prepared to organize a colonizing expedition. Cartier was named to the post of captain general. The king announced that he had resolved to send Roberval to the lands of "Canada and Hochelaga, which form the extremity of Asia toward the west." The conviction still persisted that the New World, which explorers were probing, was merely an outlying region of Asia.

Because Roberval experienced difficulties getting sufficient supplies, munitions and colonists, Cartier was ordered to sail without him. Departing from Saint-Malo on May 23, 1541, with five ships, he lingered in Newfoundland waiting for Roberval and finally went on without him, reaching the old camp site at Saint Croix on August 23, 1541. When Indians came out inquiring about Donnacona and the four other chiefs whom Cartier had taken to France on the pretext that they would come back enriched by the French king, the captain general reported that Donnacona had died but that the other four had married French women and were living like great lords. Actually they, too, had died, but he dared not confess it.

The expedition landed this time a few miles up the river from Saint Croix at a place they named Charlesbourg Royal and made themselves huts. A nobleman, the Vicomte de Beaupré, took command of the colony, and Cartier went exploring. After another dismal Canadian winter, the discouraged group went aboard their ships and sailed for home. In June of 1542, at Saint John's Harbor, Newfoundland, they met Roberval's colonists, 200 souls in three ships; after many delays they had sailed from Rochelle two months earlier. Although Roberval demanded that Cartier return to Canada, the captain general declined and sailed for home. Roberval continued on his journey, anchored off Cap Rouge in the Saint Lawrence and settled his colony there. But quarrels, disease and hunger discouraged them, and in the summer of 1543 Cartier, on command of the king, sailed to Canada and brought home the remnant of Roberval's colony. Thus ended the first episode in the French attempt at the colonization of New France. Cartier lived out the rest of his life as a respected counselor on explorations. The king in the meantime had made him lord of a manor called Limoilou near Saint-Malo, and there he died on September 1, 1557. Excerpts from his account of his second voyage to Canada follow:

Cartier Explores the Saint Lawrence [1]

A short and brief narration of the navigation made by the commandment of the King of France to the islands of Canada, Hochelaga [Montreal], Saguenay [Indian kingdom west of Montreal], and divers others which now are called New France, with the particular customs and manners of the inhabitants therein.

In the year of our Lord 1535, upon Whitsunday, being the 16 of May, by the commandment of our captain, James Cartier, and with a common accord, in the Cathedral Church of Saint-Malo we devoutly each one confessed ourselves and received the Sacrament. And, all entering into the choir of the said church, we presented ourselves before the Reverend Father in Christ, the Lord Bishop of Saint-Malo [Bishop Bohier], who blessed us all, being in his bishop's robes. The Wednesday following, being the 19 of May, there arose a good gale of wind,

[1] Modernized from Richard Hakluyt's version in *The Principal Navigations* (1598–1600).

and therefore we hoisted sail with three ships, that is to say, the *Great Hermina,* being in burden about 100 or 120 tons, wherein the foresaid Captain James Cartier was General . . . ; the *Little Hermina,* being of threescore tons burden, . . . [and] the *Hermerillon,* being of 40 tons in burden. . . .

So we sailed with a good and prosperous wind until the 20 of the said month, at which time the weather turned into storms and tempests, the which with contrary winds and darkness endured so long that our ships, being without any rest, suffered as much as any ships that ever went on seas; so that the 25 of June, by reason of that foul and foggy weather, all our ships lost sight one of another again till we came to Newfoundland, where we had appointed to meet. . . .

Upon the 8th of the said month [July] we sailed further, and, with a prosperous weather, came to the port called the Port of White Sands [Blanc Sablon, Quebec, at Newfoundland border] that is in the bay called the Bay of Castles [Strait of Belle Isle] where we had purposed to meet and stay together the 15 of the said month. In this place therefore we looked for our fellows, that is to say the other two ships, till the 26 of the month, on which day both came together. So soon as our fellows were come, we set our ships in a readiness, taking both water, wood, and other necessaries. And then on the 29 of the said month early in the morning we hoisted sail to pass on further. . . .

The 7th of August being Sunday . . . we hoisted sail and came toward land on the south side toward Cape Rabast [Cow Point, on the island of Anticosti], distant from the said haven about 20 leagues north-northeast and south-southwest. But the next day there rose a stormy and contrary wind, and because we could find no haven there toward the south, thence we went coasting along toward the north beyond the above-said haven about ten leagues, where we found a goodly great gulf full of islands, passages, and entrances toward what wind soever you please to bend. For the knowledge of this gulf, there is a great island that is like to a cape of land, stretching somewhat further forth than the others; and about two leagues within the land there is a hill fashioned as it were a heap of corn [Mount Saint Genevieve]. We named the said gulf Saint Lawrence, his bay [Pillage Bay].

The 12th of the said month we went from the said Saint Lawrence his bay, or gulf, sailing westward, and discovered a cape of land toward the south [North Cape, on Anticosti Island] that runneth west and by south, distant from the said Saint Lawrence his bay about five and 20 leagues. And of the two wild men which we took in our former voyage, it was told us that this was part of the southern coast, and that there was an island on the southerly part of which is the way to go from Honguedo [Gaspé] (where the year before we had taken them) to Canada, and that two days' journey from the said cape and island began the kingdom of Saguenay. On the north shore extending toward Canada, and about three leagues athwart the said cape, there is above 100 fathom water. Moreover, I believe that there were never so many whales seen as we saw that day about the said cape.

The next day after, being Our Lady's day of August, the fifteenth of the month [the feast of the Assumption of the Virgin Mary], having passed the strait we had notice of certain lands that we left toward the south, which lands are full of very great and high hills, and this cape we named the Island of the Assumption [Anticosti]. And one cape of the said high countries lieth east-northeast and west-southwest, the distance between which is about five and 20 leagues. The countries lying north may plainly be perceived to be higher than the southerly, more than 30 leagues in length. We trended the said lands about toward the south. . . .

There is between the southerly lands and the northerly about 30 leagues' distance and more than 200 fathom depth. The said men did moreover certify unto us that there was the way and beginning of the great river of Hochelaga [the Saint Lawrence] and ready way to Canada, which river the further it went the narrower it came, even unto Canada; and that then there was fresh water which went so far upward that they had never heard of any man who had gone to the head of it, and that there is no other passage but with small boats. Our captain, hearing their talk and how they did affirm no other passage to be there, would not at that time proceed any further till he had seen and noted the other lands and coast toward the north, which he had omitted to see from Saint Lawrence his gulf because he would know if between the lands toward the north any passage might be discovered [i.e., the northwest passage to the Indies].

CHAPTER 2

How our captain caused the ships to return back again, only to know if in Saint Lawrence Gulf there were any passage toward the north.

Upon the 18 of August being Wednesday, our captain caused his ships to wind back and bend toward the other shore, so that we trended the said northerly coast which runneth northeast and southwest, being fashioned like unto half a bow and is a very high land, but yet not so high as that on the south parts. The Thursday following we came to seven very high islands, which we named the Round Islands [the Seven Islands]. These islands are distant from the south shore about 40 leagues and stretch out into the sea about three or four leagues. Against these there are goodly low grounds to be seen, full of goodly trees, which we the Friday following with our boats compassed about. Overthwart these lands there are divers sandy shelves more than two leagues into the sea, very dangerous, which at a low water remain almost dry. At the furthest bounds of these low lands that contain about ten leagues, there is a river of fresh water [Trout River], that with such swiftness runneth into the sea that for the space of one league within it the water is as fresh as any fountain water. We with our boats entered in the said river, at the entrance of which we found about one fathom and a half of water. There are in this river many fishes shaped like horses [walrus], which, as our wild men told us, all the day long lie in the water and the night on land, of which we saw therein a great number. . . .

Upon the 1st of September we departed out of the said haven, purposing to go toward Canada; and about 15 leagues from it toward the west and west-southwest, amidst the river, there are three islands over against the which there is a river which runneth swift and is of a great depth, and it is that which leadeth and runneth into the country and kingdom of Saguenay, as by the two wild men of Canada it was told us. This river passeth and runneth along very high and steep hills of bare stone where very little earth is, and not withstanding there is a great quantity of sundry sorts of trees that grow in the said bare stones, even as upon good and fertile ground, in such sort that we have seen some so great as well would suffice to make a mast for a ship of 30 ton burden, and as green as possibly can be, growing in a stony rock without any earth at all. At the entrance of the said river we met with four boats full of wild men, which, as far as we could perceive, very fearfully came toward us so that some of them went back again, and the other came as near us as easily they might hear and understand one of our wild men, who told them his name and then took acquaintance of them, upon whose word they came to us.

The next day, being the 2 of September, we came out of the said river to go to Canada; and by reason of the seas flowing, the tide was very swift and dangerous, for that on the south part of it there lie two islands, about which, more than three leagues' compass, lie many rocks and great stones, and but two fathom water; and the flowing amidst those islands is very unconstant and doubtful, so that if it had not been for our boats, we had been in great danger to lose our pinnace; and coasting along the said dry sands there is more than 30 fathom water.

About five leagues beyond the river of Saguenay southwest there is another island [Hare Island] on the north side, wherein are certain high lands; and thereabouts we thought to have cast anchor on purpose to stay the next tide, but we could sound no ground in a 120 fathom within a flight shoot from shore, so that we were constrained to wind back to the said island, where we sounded again and found 35 fathom. The next morning we hoisted sail and went thence, sailing further on where we had notice of a certain kind of fish never before of any man seen or known. They are about the bigness of a porpoise, yet nothing like them, of body very well proportioned, headed like grey-hounds, altogether as white as snow without any spot, within which river there is great quantity of them. They do live altogether between the sea and the fresh water. These people of the country call them *adhothuys* [the narwhal]. They told us that they be very savory and good to be eaten. Moreover, they affirm none to be found elsewhere but in the mouth of that river.

The 6th of the month, the weather being calm and fair, we went about 15 leagues more upward into the river and there lighted on an island that looketh northward, and it maketh a little haven or creek wherein are many and innumerable great tortoises continually lying about that island. There are likewise great quantity of the said *adhothuys* taken by the inhabitors of the country, and there is as great a current in that place as is at Bordeaux in France at every tide. This island is in length about three leagues and in breadth two, and is a goodly and fertile plot of ground, replenished with many goodly and great trees of many sorts. Among the rest there are many filbert [hazelnut] trees, which we found hanging full of them, somewhat bigger and better in savor than ours, but somewhat harder, and therefore we called it the Land of Filberts. . . .

After we had cast anchor between the said great island [Isle of Orleans] and the northerly coast, we went on land and took our two wild men with us, meeting with many of these country people, who would not at all approach unto us but rather fled from us, until our two men began to speak unto them, telling them that they were Taignoagny and Domagaia, who, so soon as they had taken acquaintance of them, began greatly to rejoice, dancing and showing many sorts of ceremonies; and many of the chiefest of them came to our boats and brought many eels and other sorts of fishes, with two or three burdens of great millet wherewith they make their bread, and many great muskmelons [pumpkins]. The same day came also many other boats full of those countrymen and women to see and take acquaintance of our two men, all which were as courteously received and friendly entertained of our captain as possibly could be. And, to have them the better acquainted with him and make them his friends, he gave them many small gifts, but of small value; nevertheless they were greatly contented with them. The next day following, the Lord of Canada (whose proper name was Donnacona, but by the name of lord they call him Agouhanna) with 12 boats came to our ships, accompanied with many people who, causing ten of his boats to go back with the other two, approached unto us with 16 men. Then began the said Agouhanna over against the smallest of our ships, according to their manner and fashion, to frame a long oration, moving all his body and members after a strange fashion, which thing is a ceremony and sign of gladness and security among them; and then, coming to the general's ship, where Taignoagny and Domagaia were, he spake with them and they with him, where they began to tell and show unto him what they had seen in France, and what good entertainment they had had. Hearing which things the said lord seemed to be very glad thereof, and prayed our captain to reach him his arm that he might kiss it, which thing he did; their lord taking it, laid it about his neck, for so they use to do when they will make much of one. Then our captain entered into Agouhanna's boat, causing bread and wine to be brought to make the said lord and his company to eat and drink, which thing they did and were greatly thereby contented and satisfied. Our captain for that time gave them nothing, because he looked for a fitter opportunity. These things being done, each one took leave of others, and the said lord went with his boats again to his place of abode.

Our captain then caused our boats to be set in order, that with the next tide he might go up higher into the river to find some safe harbor for our ships. And we passed up the river against the stream about ten leagues, coasting the said island at the end whereof we found a goodly and pleasant sound where is a little river and haven, where, by reason of the flood, there is about three fathom water. This place seemed to us very fit and commodious to harbor our ships therein, and so we did very safely. We named it the Holy Cross [Saint Charles], for on that day [September 14] we came thither. Near unto it there is a village whereof Donnacona is lord, and there he keepeth his abode. It is called Stadacona [or Stadaconé, present site of Quebec], as goodly a plot of ground as possibly may be seen and therewithal very fruitful, full of goodly trees even as in France, as oaks, elms, ashes, walnut trees, maple trees, cedars, vines, and whitethorns that bring forth fruit as big as any damsons, and many other sorts of trees under which grows as fair tall hemp as any in France, without any seed or any man's work or labor at all.

Having considered the place, and finding it fit for our purpose, our captain withdrew himself on purpose to return to our ships; but behold, as we were coming out of the river we met coming against us one of the lords of the said village of Stadacona, accompanied with many others, as men, women, and children, who, after the fashion of their country, in sign of mirth and joy began to make a long oration, the women still singing and dancing up to the knees in water. Our captain, knowing their good will and kindness toward us, caused the boat wherein they were to come unto him, and gave them certain trifles, as knives and beads of glass, whereat they were marvelous glad, for, being gone about [?] leagues from them, for the pleasure they conceived of our coming we might hear them sing, and see them dance for all they were so far.

. . . .

CHAPTER 5

How our captain with all his gentlemen and 50 mariners departed with our pinnace and the two boats from Canada to go to Hochelaga; and also there is described what was seen by the way upon the said river.

The next day being the 19 of September, we hoisted sail and with our pinnace and two boats departed to go up the river with the flood, where on both shores of it we began to see as goodly a country as possibly can with eye be seen, all replenished with very goodly trees and vines laden as full of grapes as could be all along the river, which rather seemed to have been planted by man's hand than otherwise. True it is that, because they are not dressed and wrought as they should be, their bunches of grapes are not so great nor sweet as ours. Also we saw all along the river many houses inhabited of fishers which take all kinds of fishes, and they came with as great familiarity and kindness unto us as if we had been their countrymen, and brought us great store of fish with other such things as they had, which we exchanged with them for other wares; who, lifting up their hands toward heaven, gave many signs of joy.

We stayed at a place called Hochelai [Hochelaga; i.e., Montreal], about five and 20 leagues from Canada, where the river waxeth very narrow and runneth very swift, wherefore it is very dangerous, not only for that, but also for certain great stones that are therein. Many boats and barks came unto us, in one of which came one of the chief lords of the country, making a long discourse, who, being come near us, did by evident signs and gestures show us that the higher the river went, the more dangerous it was, and bade us take heed of ourselves. The said lord presented and gave unto our captain two of his own children, of which our captain took one being a wench of seven or eight years old; the man-child he gave him again because it was too young, for it was but two or three years old. Our captain as friendly and as courteously as he could did entertain and receive the said lord and his company, giving them certain small trifles, and so they departed toward the shore again. Afterward the said lord and his wife came unto Canada to visit his daughter, bringing unto our captain certain small presents.

From the 19th until the 28th of September we sailed up along the said river, never losing one hour of time, all which time we saw as goodly and pleasant a country as possibly can be wished for, full (as we have said before) of all sorts of goodly trees, that is to say, oaks, elms, walnut trees, cedars, firs, ash, box, willows, and great store of vines, all as full of grapes as could be, so that if any of our fellows went on shore, they came home laden with them. There are likewise many cranes, swans, geese, ducks, pheasants, partridges, thrushes, blackbirds, turtles, finches, redbreasts, nightingales, sparrows of divers kinds, with many other sorts of birds, even as in France, and great plenty and store. . . .

. . . .

CHAPTER 10

The manner how the people of that country live, and of certain conditions; of their faith, manners, and customs.

This people believe no whit in God, but in one whom they call Cudruaigni. They say that often he speaketh with them and telleth them what weather shall follow, whether good or bad. Moreover they say that when he is angry with them, he casteth dust into their eyes. They believe that when they die they go into the stars, and thence by little and little descend down into the horizon, even as the stars do, and that then they go into certain green fields full of goodly, fair, and precious trees, flowers, and fruits. After that they had given us these things to understand, we showed them their error and told [them] that their Cudruaigni did but deceive them, for he is but a devil and an evil spirit; affirming unto them that there is but one only God, who is in heaven and who giveth us all necessaries, being the Creator of all Himself, and that only we must believe in Him; moreover, that it is necessary for us to be baptized; otherwise we are damned into hell. These and many other things concerning our faith and religion we showed them, all which they did easily believe, calling their Cudruaigni, Agouiada, that is to say, nought, so that very earnestly they desired and prayed our captain that he would cause them to be baptized; and their lord, and Taignoagny, Domagaia, and all the people of the town came unto us, hoping to be baptized. But because we did not thoroughly know their mind, and that there was nobody could teach them our belief and religion, we excused ourselves, desiring Taignoagny and Domagaia to tell the rest of their countrymen that [we] would come again another time and bring priests and chrisom with us, for without them they could not be baptized; which they did easily believe, for Domagaia and Taignoagny had seen many children baptized in Britain [Brittany] whiles they were there. Which promise when they heard they seemed to be very glad.

They live in common together, and of such commodities as their country yieldeth they are indifferently well stored. The inhabitants of the country clothe themselves with the skins of certain wild beasts, but very miserably. In winter they wear hose and shoes made of wild beasts' skins, and in summer they go barefooted. They keep and observe the rites of matrimony, saving that everyone weddeth two or three wives, which (their husbands being dead) do never marry again but for the death of their husbands wear a certain black weed all the days of their life, besmearing all their faces with coal dust and grease mingled together as thick as the back of a knife, and by that they are known to be widows. They have a filthy and detestable use in marrying of their maidens, and that is this: they put them all (after they are of lawful age to marry) in a common place as harlots, free for every man that will have to do with them, until such time as they find a match. This I say because

I have seen by experience many houses full of those damsels even as our schools are full of children in France to learn to read. Moreover, the misrule and riot that they keep in those houses is very great, for very wantonly they sport and dally together, showing whatsoever God hath sent them.

They are no men of great labor. They dig their grounds with certain pieces of wood as big as half a sword, on which ground groweth their corn, which they call *offici* [maize]. It is as big as our small peas; there is great quantity of it growing in Brazil. They have also great store of muskmelons, pompions [pumpkins], gourds, cucumbers, peas, and beans of every color, yet differing from ours. There groweth also a certain kind of herb whereof in summer they make great provision for all the year, making great account of it; and only men use of it; and first they cause it to be dried in the sun, then wear it about their necks wrapped in a little beast's skin made like a little bag, with a hollow piece of stone or wood like a pipe. Then when they please they make powder of it and then put it in one of the ends of the said cornet or pipe, and laying a coal of fire upon it, at the other end suck so long that they fill their bodies full of smoke till that it cometh out of their mouth and nostrils, even as out of the tunnel of a chimney. They say that this doth keep them warm and in health; they never go without some of it about them. We ourselves have tried the same smoke, and having put it in our mouths, it seemed almost as hot as pepper.

The women of that country do labor much more than the men, as well in fishing (whereto they are greatly given) as in tilling and husbanding their grounds, and other things; as well the men as women and children are very much more able to resist cold than savage beasts, for we with our own eyes have seen some of them when it was coldest (which cold was extreme raw and bitter) come to our ships stark naked, going upon snow and ice, which thing seemeth incredible to them that have not seen it. When as the snow and ice lyeth on the ground, they take great store of wild beasts, as fawns, stags, bears, martens, hares, and foxes, with divers other sorts, whose flesh they eat raw, having first dried it in the sun or smoke, and so they do their fish. As far forth as we could perceive and understand by these people, it were a very easy thing to bring them to some

familiarity and civility and make them learn what one would.
The Lord God for his mercy's sake set thereunto his helping
hand when he seeth cause. Amen.

CHAPTER 11

Of the greatness and depth of the said river, and of the
sorts of beasts, birds, fishes, and other things that we have seen,
with the situation of the place.

The said river beginneth beyond the Island of the Assumption [Anticosti], over against the high mountains of Hognedo
[i.e., Honguedo, the Notre-Dame Mountains in Gaspé] and of
the seven islands. The distance over from one side to the other
is about 35 or 40 leagues. In the midst it is above 200 fathom
deep. The surest way to sail upon it is on the south side. And
toward the north, that is to say from the said seven islands, from
side to side there is seven leagues' distance, where are also two
great rivers that come down from the hills of Saguenay [Moisie
and Saint Margaret] and make divers very dangerous shelves
in the sea. At the entrance of those two rivers we saw many and
great store of whales and sea horses. Overthwart the said islands
there is another little river that runneth along those marish
[marshy] grounds about three or four leagues, wherein there
is great store of waterfowls. From the entrance of that river to
Hochelaga there is about 300 leagues' distance; the original beginning of it is in the river that cometh from Saguenay, which
riseth and springeth among high and steep hills. It entereth
into that river before it cometh to the province of Canada on
the north side. That river is very deep, high, and strait,
wherefore it is very dangerous for any vessel to go upon it.

After that river followeth the province of Canada, wherein
are many people dwelling in open boroughs and villages. There
are also in the circuit and territory of Canada, along and within
the said river, many other islands, some great and some small,
among which there is one that containeth above ten leagues
in length, full of goodly and high trees and also many vines.
You may go into it from both sides, but yet the surest passage
is on the south side. On the shore or bank of that river westward there is a goodly, fair, and delectable bay or creek con-

venient and fit for to harbor ships. Hard by there is in that river one place very narrow, deep, and swift-running, but it is not passing the third part of a league, over against the which there is a goodly high piece of land with a town therein; and the country about it is very well tilled and wrought and as good as possibly can be seen. That is the place and abode of Donnacona and of our two men we took in our first voyage. It is called Stadacona [Quebec]. But before we come to it, there are four other peopled towns, that is to say, Ayraste [or Ajoaste], Starnatan, Tailla (which standeth upon a hill), Scitadin [four small tribes and villages, unidentifiable today], and then Stadacona, under which town toward the north the river and port of the Holy Cross [St. Charles] is, where we stayed from the 15 of September until the 16 of May, 1536, and there our ships remained dry, as we have said before. . . .

CHAPTER 12

Of certain advertisements and notes given unto us by those countrymen after our return from Hochelaga.

After our return from Hochelaga, we dealt, trafficked, and with great familiarity and love were conversant with those that dwelt nearest unto our ships, except that sometimes we had strife and contention with certain naughty people, full sore against the will of the others. We understood of Donnacona and of others that the said river is called the river of Saguenay, and goeth to Saguenay, being somewhat more than a league farther west-northwest, and that eight or nine days' journey beyond it will bear but small boats. But the right and ready way to Saguenay is up that river to Hochelaga, and then into another that cometh from Saguenay and then entereth into the foresaid river, and that there is yet one month's sailing thither. Moreover, they told us and gave us to understand that there are people clad with cloth as we are, very honest, and many inhabited towns, and that they have great store of gold and red copper; and that about the land beyond the said first river to Hochelaga and Saguenay is an island environed round about with that and other rivers, and that beyond Saguenay the said river entereth into two or three great lakes, and that there is a sea of fresh water [possibly Lake Ontario] found; and as they have heard say of those of Saguenay, there was never man heard of that found out the end thereof. For, as they told us, they themselves were never there. Moreover, they told us that where we had left our pinnace when we went to Hochelaga, there is a river [the Richelieu] that goeth southwest, from whence there is a whole month's sailing to go to a certain land where there is neither ice nor snow seen, where the inhabitants do continually war one against another, where there is great store of oranges, almonds, nuts, and apples, with many other sorts of fruits; and that the men and women are clad with beasts' skins even as they. We asked them if there were any gold or red copper; they answered no. I take this place to be toward Florida [early name for most of Atlantic coast as far as Maine], as far as I could perceive and understand by their signs and tokens.

CHAPTER 13

Of a strange and cruel disease that came to the people of Stadacona, wherewith, because we did haunt their company, we were so infected that there died 25 of our company.

In the month of December we understood that the pestilence was come among the people of Stadacona, in such sort that before we knew of it, according to their confession, there were dead above 50; whereupon we charged them neither to come near our fort, nor about our ships, or us. And albeit we had driven them from us, the said unknown sickness [scurvy] began to spread itself amongst us after the strangest sort that ever was either heard of or seen, insomuch as some did lose all their strength and could not stand on their feet; then did their legs swell, their sinews shrink as black as any coal. Others also had all their skins spotted with spots of blood of a purple color; then did it ascend up to their ankles, knees, thighs, shoulders, arms, and neck; their mouth became stinking, their gums so rotten that all the flesh did fall off, even to the roots of the teeth, which did also almost all fall out.

With such infection did this sickness spread itself in our three ships that about the middle of February, of 110 persons that we were, there were not ten whole, so that one could not help the other—a most horrible and pitiful case, considering the place we were in, forsomuch as the people of the country would daily come before our fort and saw but few of us. There were already eight dead and more than 50 sick and, as we thought, past all hope of recovery. Our captain, seeing this our misery and that the sickness was gone so far, ordained and commanded that every one should devoutly prepare himself to prayer, and, in remembrance of Christ, caused his image to be set upon a tree about a flight shot from the fort amidst the ice and snow, giving all men to understand that on the Sunday following, service should be said there, and that whosoever could go, sick or whole, should go thither in procession singing the seven Psalmes of David, with other litanies, praying most heartily that it would please the said our Christ to have compassion upon us. Service being done and as well celebrated as we could, our captain there made a vow that if it would please God to give him leave to return into France, he would go on pilgrimage to our Lady of Rocquemado. That day Philip Rougemont, born in Amboise, died, being twenty-two years old; and, because the sickness was to us unknown, our Captain caused him to be ripped to see if by any means possible we might know what it was, and so seek means to save and preserve the rest of the company; he was found to have his heart white but rotten and more than a quart of red water about it; his liver was indifferent fair, but his lungs black and mortified; his blood was altogether shrunk about the heart so that, when he was opened, great quantity of rotten blood issued out from about his heart; his milt [spleen] toward the back was somewhat perished [deteriorated], rough as [if] it had been rubbed against a stone. Moreover, because one of his thighs was very black without, it was opened, but within it was whole and sound; that done as well as we could, he was buried.

In such sort did the sickness continue and increase that there were not above three sound men in the ships, and none was able to go under hatches to draw drink for himself nor for his fellows. Sometimes we were constrained to bury some of the dead under the snow because we were not able to dig any graves for them, the ground was so hard frozen and we so weak. Besides this, we did greatly fear that the people of the country would perceive our weakness and misery, which to hide, our captain, whom it pleased God always to keep in health, would go out with two or three of the company, some sick and some whole, whom when he saw out of the fort, he would throw stones at them and chide them, feigning that so soon as he came again he would beat them, and then with signs showed the people of the country that he caused all his men to work and labor in the ships, some in calking them, some in beating of chalk, some in one thing and some in another, and that he would not have them come forth till their work was done. And to make his tale seem true and likely, he would make all his men whole and sound to make a great noise with knocking sticks, stones, hammers, and other things together; at which time we were so oppressed and grieved with that sickness that we had lost all hope ever to see France again, if God, of His infinite goodness and mercy, had not with His pitiful eye looked upon us and revealed a singular and excellent remedy against all diseases unto us, the best that ever was found upon earth, as hereafter shall follow.

CHAPTER 14

How long we stayed in the port of the Holy Cross amidst the snow and ice, and how many died of the said disease from the beginning of it to the midst of March.

From the midst of November until the midst of March we were kept in amidst the ice above two fathoms thick and snow above four feet high and more, higher than the sides of our ships, which lasted till that time in such sort that all our drinks were frozen in the vessels, and the ice through all the ships was above a hand-breadth thick, as well above hatches as beneath; and so much of the river as was fresh, even to Hochelaga, was frozen; in which space there died 25 of our best and chiefest men, and all the rest were so sick that we thought they should never recover again, only three or four excepted. Then it pleased God to cast His pitiful eye upon us, and sent us the knowledge of remedy of our healths and recovery in such manner as in the next chapter shall be showed.

CHAPTER 15

How by the grace of God we had notice of a certain tree
whereby we all recovered our health, and the manner how to
use it.

Our captain, considering our estate (and how that sickness
was increased and hot amongst us), one day went forth of the
fort and, walking upon the ice, he saw a troupe of those countrymen coming from Stadacona, among which was Domagaia,
who, not passing ten or 12 days afore, had been very sick
with that disease and had his knees swollen as big as a child of
two years old, all his sinews shrunk together, his teeth spoiled,
his gums rotten and stinking. Our captain, seeing him whole
and sound, was thereat marvelous glad, hoping to understand
and know of him how he had healed himself, to the end he
might ease and help his men. So soon as they were come near
him, he asked Domagaia how he had done to heal himself; he
answered that he had taken the juice and sap of the leaves of
a certain tree and therewith had healed himself, for it is a
singular remedy against that disease. Then our captain asked
of him if any were to be had thereabout, desiring him to show
him for to heal a servant of his who, whilst he was in Canada
with Donnacona, was stricken with that disease. That he did
because he would not show the number of his sick men.
Domagaia straight sent two women to fetch some of it, which
brought ten or 12 branches of it and therewithal showed the
way how to use it, and that is thus: to take the bark and leaves
of the said tree and boil them together, then to drink of the
said decoction every other day and to put the dregs of it upon
his legs that is sick; moreover, they told us that the virtue of
that tree was to heal any other disease. The tree is in their
language called *ameda* or *hanneda;* this is thought to be the
sassafras tree. Our captain presently caused some of that drink
to be made for his men to drink of it, but there was none durst
taste of it except one or two who ventured the drinking of it
only to taste and prove it. The others, seeing that, did the like
and presently recovered their health and were delivered of that
sickness and what other disease soever, in such sort that there

were some had been diseased and troubled with the French pox [syphilis] four or five years and with this drink were clean healed. After this medicine was found and proved to be true, there was such strife about it who should be first to take it that they were ready to kill one another, so that a tree as big as any oak in France was spoiled and lopped bare and occupied all in five or six days; and it wrought so well that if all the physicians of Montpellier and Louvain had been there with all the drugs of Alexandria, they would not have done so much in one year as that tree did in six days; for it did so prevail that as many as used of it by the grace of God recovered their health.

VI

John Hawkins Scouts the
Caribbean and Appraises Florida

THE English, like the French, were unwilling to admit that the pope had any temporal jurisdiction over newly discovered lands. During the reign of Elizabeth, Sir William Cecil (later, Lord Burghley) informed the Spanish ambassador that England did not recognize such authority. But England did admit that effective occupation gave a nation the right to lands thus settled. Hence, England recognized Spanish rights in the West Indies and on "the Main" where Spanish settlements were established. That, however, did not prevent efforts by English traders, freebooters and buccaneers to poach on the Spanish possessions. The Spanish Empire, though legally protected, was virtually undefended, and hostile French and English raiders frequently pillaged Spanish settlements.

The enterprise of English seamen, legitimate and otherwise, caused untold worry to both the Portuguese and the Spanish throughout the sixteenth century. Among the early pioneers in overseas adventures were members of the Hawkins family of Plymouth. During the reign of Henry VIII, William Hawkins, a substantial citizen and member of Parliament, had a famous ship, the *Paul of Plymouth,* which traded on the coast of Africa in the region of modern Liberia and continued on to Brazil. How Hawkins' ship evaded the Portuguese is not known, but the vessel brought back to England Brazilian dyewood, African ivory and other exotic products.

English seamen continued to find African voyages profitable in spite of Portuguese opposition. They brought back sugar and dates from Morocco and, beginning in 1553, they began to

poach on the territory claimed by the Portuguese in Lower
Guinea, where they bought gold and sometimes slaves. Queen
Elizabeth early in her reign refused to forbid this trade, on the
ground that the Portuguese had not effectively occupied Africa
and hence it was open to traders of any nation.

William Hawkins' son John, later to be knighted, early realized that a profitable trade might be developed between Africa
and the Spanish possessions in America if he could circumvent
the Spanish prohibition against unlicensed traders. He knew
that African slaves were in great demand in the Spanish settlements where the supply of Indian labor had run short. Nobody
in this period looked upon the enslavement of heathen as wicked.
Indeed, many a pious religionist preached the doctrine that a
heathen made a good bargain by exchanging his temporal liberty
for the hope of salvation in the next world. Slave owners were
enjoined to convert their bondsmen to Christianity. Certainly
John Hawkins and his contemporaries felt no qualms about
buying or seizing slaves from African kings on the Guinea
coast; for untold centuries human slaves had been a principal
commodity of African tribes, which made incessant war for the
purpose of acquiring them. Hawkins' main problem was to
dispose of them in Spanish America without incurring the
wrath of the Spanish authorities. His first efforts were encourag-
ing.

Enlisting the interest of a syndicate in London that included
officials of the royal navy, Hawkins in 1562 organized an expedition of three, and possibly four, ships that sailed from
Plymouth for Africa in October. The records of the voyage are
confusing and in some instances contradictory, for the Portuguese later claimed that Hawkins seized six of their ships on
the African coast between Liberia and Sierra Leone with some
900 slaves. Hawkins claimed to have bought or captured 300
slaves, whom he took to Spanish America. The Spaniards later
claimed that he brought 400, which J. A. Williamson, who has
written in detail of this episode, thinks may be about right.[1]
At any rate, Hawkins acquired profitable cargoes of slaves and
conveyed them to Hispaniola, where he managed to dispose of
them. The authorities made a token effort to stop the trading,
but Hawkins bought them off. Through a Spanish trader in the

[1] James A. Williamson, *Hawkins of Plymouth* (London, 1949), pp. 50–51.

Canaries he had made contacts with useful men in Hispaniola. He even hoped to gain a license that would make his trade legitimate.

Pleased with his success to date, Hawkins loaded his vessels with hides, sugar and other products of the West Indies and sailed for England. Two vessels he loaded with hides and sent to Spain; one was a Spanish hulk that he chartered in the islands and another was a Portuguese ship that he had taken in Guinea. Hawkins believed that his connections with Spanish traders would insure the safety of the cargoes, but, alas, his luck ran out. One ship was seized in Lisbon, the other, in Seville. Nevertheless, the cargoes that his ships brought back to England proved sufficiently profitable to stimulate investors to plan a second expedition to Africa and America.

Hawkins had hopes of getting the Spanish government to recognize him as a legitimate trader and give him a license. The trade in slaves looked like commerce of mutual benefit to both buyers and sellers. The Spaniards in the colonies needed labor and Hawkins had demonstrated his ability to deliver the goods. In his behalf Queen Elizabeth sent a letter to the English ambassador in Spain and even wrote to Philip II himself. One should remember that England and Spain at this time were not yet openly hostile, and commerce between the two countries was profitable. The queen and her ministers obviously wanted to encourage the trade that Hawkins was pioneering.

By 1564, when Hawkins was preparing his second expedition, conditions were changing. Refugee French Huguenots had designs on Florida and the English government had given them encouragement, even to planning an Anglo-French colony under the French explorer Jean Ribaut. Through the treachery of the English collaborator in the enterprise, Thomas Stukeley, the joint scheme failed to materialize, and the French Huguenots were left to settle without English help. Nevertheless, the Florida project excited Hawkins' interest, and an investigation of the region was one of his objectives. Florida, thought to be a land of riches, was believed to be beyond the jurisdiction of Spain.

Hawkins' second expedition got under way on October 18, 1564. This time the queen herself provided the largest ship, the old *Jesus of Lübeck* of 700 tons. The three other ships, the

Solomon of 130 tons and two small barks, the *Tiger* and the *Swallow*, were supplied by the Hawkins family. Investors in the voyage again included officials of the royal navy and at least three members of the queen's Privy Council. The queen authorized Hawkins to sail under the royal ensign as an officer of the Crown and to announce himself as such. Clearly Queen Elizabeth had some objective other than a mere trading venture. Williamson believes that she hoped to use Hawkins to demonstrate to the Spaniards the value of maintaining the old Spanish-English alliance, which was beginning to wear thin because of religious differences. France, though predominantly Catholic, was hostile to Spain, and Elizabeth apparently believed that Philip II might prefer to have as an ally a heretic who could help protect his colonies and supply them with needed commodities than to suffer continued attacks from French marauders.[2] If this is what she and Hawkins contemplated, subsequent events proved them wrong. When news of Hawkins' voyage reached Philip, he sent orders to the colonies to refuse to trade with the Englishmen; he also instructed his ambassador in London to make a protest to the queen.

On the coast of Africa, principally in the region of Sierra Leone, Hawkins gathered a cargo of slaves, ivory and gold. Apparently the Portuguese aided him in his trade and later made a complaint to their own government to cover the illegality of their dealings with Hawkins. Their depositions claimed that Hawkins took 16 or 17 Portuguese ships and 600 slaves by force of arms.[3] Whatever may have been the manner of his dealings, he sailed away to the Spanish Main with 400 or 500 slaves.

King Philip's warning to the Spanish colonies not to trade with Hawkins had merely served to announce his coming. The planters and miners were eager for slaves, and, though the authorities might make some token resistance, Hawkins found little difficulty in marketing his human cargo. In fact, on at least one occasion he declared, "I am a great servitor of the majesty of King Philip, whom I served when he was King of England" (when Philip was the husband of Elizabeth's sister,

[2] *Ibid.*, pp. 63–67.
[3] *Ibid.*, p. 74.

Mary Tudor).[4] Now he was sailing as an officer of the queen of England, the fleet he commanded belonged to the queen, and his purpose was peaceful trade. The Spaniards were naturally puzzled, and they found it easy to rationalize their own desire to traffic with Hawkins. At Borburata in April Hawkins won the gratitude of the Spaniards by preventing a French raider from pillaging the town, and received from the governor of that town a certificate of good conduct, which he exhibited elsewhere.

Hawkins' technique in dealing with the Spaniards is illustrated by an episode at Rio de la Hacha, where, after he had explained his peaceful purposes, the Spaniards themselves suggested he threaten to burn down the town unless they permitted trade; this threat would give them an excuse for the royal authorities from Spain if they complained. After a bogus threat, Hawkins' trade went merrily forward to the mutual satisfaction of all. Hawkins sold slaves and other goods that he brought: ship biscuit, cloth, wine, caps and cloaks. Furthermore, he took orders for both slaves and English wares which he promised to deliver on subsequent voyages, for he believed this expedition merely the opening wedge for a continuing trade.

After selling all his slaves and goods he loaded £2,000 worth of cowhides, at that time one of the most useful products of the Spanish possessions, and prepared to sail for home via the Florida Channel. In July 1565 he touched the Florida coast at Fort Caroline, near the Saint Johns river, then called the River of May, where René de Laudonnière had settled 200 French Huguenots in the previous year. The French were short of supplies and discouraged, but declined Hawkins' offer to take them back home. To give them some aid, he sold them a small vessel and a small quantity of foodstuffs. The fleet finally arrived in England in September 1565, with a comfortable profit for everyone. Hawkins regarded the expedition as a success, with a promise of continued profits from this triangular trade between England, Africa and the Spanish colonies.

John Sparke, one of the gentleman adventurers with Hawkins, wrote a valuable narrative of the expedition, which Hakluyt

[4] *Ibid.*, p. 77.

published in *The Principal Navigations* (1589). Excerpts from this narrative, with spelling modernized, follow:

Sparke's Narrative

Master John Hawkins with the *Jesus of Lübeck,* a ship of 700, and the *Solomon,* a ship of sevenscore, the *Tiger,* a bark of 50, and the *Swallow* of 30 tons, being all well furnished with men to the number of 170, as also with ordnance and victual requisite for such a voyage, departed out of Plymouth the eighteenth day of October in the year of our Lord 1564, with a prosperous wind. . . .

The 14th day [of July] the ship and barks came to the *Jesus* . . . to the rejoicing of the captain and the whole company. And so then all together they kept on their way along the coast of Florida, and the fifteenth day come to an anchor, and so from 26 degrees to 30½ degrees, where the Frenchmen are, ranging all the coast along, seeking for fresh water, anchoring every night, because we would overshoot no place of fresh water; and in the daytime the captain in the ship's pinnace sailed along the shore, went into every creek, speaking with divers of the Floridians, because he would understand where the Frenchmen inhabited; and not finding them in 28 degrees, as it was declared unto him, marveled thereat and never left sailing along the coast till he found them, who inhabited in a river by them called the River of May [the Saint Johns] and standing in 30 degrees and better.

In ranging this coast along, the captain found it to be all an island, and therefore it is all lowland and very scant of fresh water, but the country was marvelously sweet, with both marsh and meadow ground and goodly woods among. There they found sorrel to grow as abundantly as grass and, where their houses were, great store of maize and mill [millet], and grapes of great bigness but of taste much like our English grapes. Also deer great plenty, which came upon the sands before them.

Their houses are not many together, for in one house an hundred of them do lodge; they being made much like a great

barn and in strength not inferior to ours, for they have stan-
chions and rafters of whole trees and are covered with palmetto
leaves, having no place divided but one small room for their
king and queen. In the midst of this house is a hearth, where
they make great fires all night, and they sleep upon certain pieces
of wood, hewn in for the bowing of their backs and another
place made high for their heads, which they put one by another
all along the walls on both sides. In their houses they remain
only in the nights, and in the day they desire the fields, where
they dress their meat and make provision for victuals, which
they provide only for a meal from hand to mouth. There is one
thing to be marveled at, for the making of their fire, and not
only they but also the Negroes do the same; which is made
only by two sticks, rubbing them one against another; and this
they may do in any place they come where they find sticks
sufficient for the purpose.

In their apparel the men only use deerskins, wherewith some
only cover their privy members, othersome use the same as
garments to cover them before and behind; which skins are
painted, some yellow and red, some black and russet, and every
man according to his own fancy. They do not omit to paint
their bodies also with curious knots or antic [bizarre] work,
as every man in his own fancy deviseth, which painting, to
make it to continue the better, they use with a thorn to prick
their flesh and dent in the same, whereby the painting may have
better hold. In their wars they use a sleighter [more skillful]
color of painting their faces, thereby to make themselves show
the more fierce, which, after their wars ended, they wash away
again.

In their wars they use bows and arrows, whereof their bows
are made of a kind of yew, but blacker than ours, and for the
most part passing the strength of the Negroes' or Indians', for it
is not greatly inferior to ours. Their arrows are also of a great
length but yet of reeds like other Indians', but varying in two
points, both in length and also for nocks [notches, for the bow-
string] and feathers, which the other lack, whereby they shoot
very steady. The heads of the same are vipers' teeth, bones of
fishes, flintstones, piked points of knives, which they, having
gotten of the Frenchmen, broke the same, and put the points
of them in their arrows' heads. Some of them have their heads

of silver, othersome, that have want of these, put in a kind of hard wood, notched, which pierces as far as any of the rest.

In their fight, being in the woods, they use a marvelous policy for their own safeguard, which is by clasping a tree in their arms and yet shooting notwithstanding; this policy they used with the Frenchmen in their fight, whereby it appeareth that they are people of some policy; and although they are called by the Spaniards *gente triste,* that is to say, "sad people," meaning thereby that they are not men of capacity, yet have the Frenchmen found them so witty in their answers that, by the captain's own report, a councilor with us could not give a more profound reason.

The women also for their apparel use painted skins, but most of them gowns of [Spanish] moss, somewhat longer than our moss, which they sew together artificially and make the same surplice-wise, wearing their hair down to their shoulders like the Indians.

In this River of May aforesaid, the captain, entering with his pinnace, found a French ship of fourscore ton and two pinnaces of 15 ton apiece by her, and, speaking with the keepers thereof, they told him of a fort two leagues up which they had built, in which their captain, Monsieur Laudonnière, was, with certain soldiers therein. To whom our captain, sending to understand of a watering place where he might conveniently take it in and to have license for the same, he straight (because there was no convenient place but up the river five leagues, where the water was fresh) did send him a pilot for the more expedition thereof, to bring in one of his barks; which, going in with other boats provided for the same purpose, anchored before the fort, into the which our captain went; where he was by the general, with other captains and soldiers, very gently entertained; who [Laudonnière] declared unto him the time of their being there, which was 14 months, with the extremity they were driven to for want of victuals, having brought very little with them. In which place they [the French], being 200 men at their first coming, had in short space eaten all the maize they could buy of the inhabitants about them and therefore were driven, certain of them, to serve a king of the Floridians against other his enemies for mill and other victuals; which, having gotten, could not serve them, being so many, so long a time, but want came upon them in such sort that they were fain to gather acorns, which, being stamped small and often washed to take away the bitterness of them, they did use for bread, eating withal sundry times roots, whereof they found many good and wholesome and such as serve rather for medicines than for meats alone.

But this hardness not contenting some of them, who would not take the pains so much as to fish in the river before their doors but would have all things put in their mouths, they did rebel against the captain, taking away first his armor and afterward imprisoning him; and so, to the number of fourscore of them, departed with a bark and a pinnace, spoiling their store of victual and taking away a great part thereof with them, and so went to the islands of Hispaniola and Jamaica a-roving, where they spoiled and pilled [pillaged] the Spaniards; and, having taken two caravels laden with wine and cassava, which is a bread made of roots, and much other victuals and treasure, had not the grace to depart therewith but were of such haughty stomachs that they thought their force to be such that no man durst meddle with them, and so kept harbor in Jamaica, going daily ashore at their pleasure. But God, which would not suffer such evildoers unpunished, did indurate [harden] their hearts in such sort that they lingered the time so long that a ship and galleass, being made out of Santo Domingo, came thither into the harbor and took 20 of them, whereof the most part were hanged and the rest carried into Spain; and some (to the number of 25) escaped in the pinnace and came to Florida, where at their landing they were put in prison, and, incontinent [at once], four of the chiefest, being condemned at the request of the soldiers, did pass the harquebusiers and then were hanged upon a gibbet.

This lack of threescore men was a great discourage[ment] and weakening to the rest, for they were the best soldiers that they had; for they had now made the inhabitants weary of them by their daily craving of maize, having no wares left to content them withal, and therefore were enforced to rob them and to take away their victual perforce. Which was the occasion that the Floridians (not well contented therewith) did take certain of their company in the woods and slew them, whereby there grew great wars betwixt them and the Frenchmen. And therefore they, being but a few in number, durst not venture abroad but at such time as they were enforced thereunto for want of food to do the same; and, going 20 harquebusiers in a company, were set upon by 18 kings, having 700 or 800 men, which with one of their bows slew one of their men and hurt a dozen and drove them all down to their boats. Whose policy in fight was to be marveled at, for, having shot at divers of their bodies which were armed and perceiving that their arrows did not prevail against the same, they shot at their faces and legs, which were the places that the Frenchmen were hurt in. Thus the Frenchmen returned, being in ill case by the hurt of their men, having not above 40 soldiers left unhurt, whereby they might ill make any more invasions upon the Floridians and keep their fort withal, which they must have been driven unto had not God sent us thither for their succor, for they had not above ten days' victual left before we came. In which perplexity our captain seeing them, [he] spared them out of his ship 20 barrels of meal and four pipes [casks] of beans, with divers other victuals and necessaries which he might conveniently spare; and to help them the better homeward, whither they were bound before our coming, at their request we spared them one of our barks of fifty ton.

Notwithstanding the great want that the Frenchmen had, the ground doth yield victuals sufficient, if they would have taken pains to get the same; but they, being soldiers, desired to live by the sweat of other men's brows, for while they had peace with the Floridians they had fish sufficient, by weirs which they made to catch the same; but when they grew to wars the Floridians took away the same again, and then would not the Frenchmen take the pains to make any more.

The ground yieldeth naturally grapes in great store, for in the time that the Frenchmen were there they made 20 hogsheads of wine. Also it yieldeth roots passing good, deer marvelous store, with divers other beasts and fowl serviceable to the use of man. These be things wherewith a man may live, having corn or maize wherewith to make bread, for maize maketh good savory bread and cakes as fine as flour. Also it maketh good meal, beaten and sodden [boiled] with water, and eateth like pap wherewith we feed children. It maketh also good beverage, sodden in water, and nourishable, which the Frenchmen did

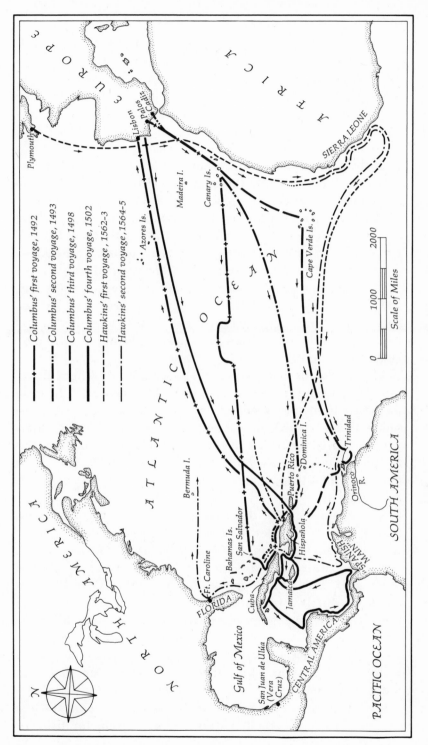

Voyages of Columbus and John Hawkins

use to drink of in the morning, and it assuageth their thirst so that they had no need to drink all the day after. And this maize was the greatest lack they had, because they had no laborers to sow the same, and therefore to them that should inhabit the land it were requisite to have laborers to till and sow the ground; for they, having victuals of their own, whereby they neither rob nor spoil the inhabitants, may live not only quietly with them, who naturally are more desirous of peace than of wars, but also shall have abundance of victuals proffered them for nothing; for it is with them as it is with one of us: when we see another man ever taking away from us, although we have enough besides, yet then we think all too little for ourselves. For surely we have heard the Frenchmen report, and I know it by the Indians, that a very little contenteth them; for the Indians with the head of maize roasted will travel a whole day, and when they are at the Spaniards' finding [fed by the Spaniards], they give them nothing but sodden herbs and maize, and in this order I saw threescore of them feed, who were laden with wares and came fifty leagues off.

The Floridians when they travel have a kind of herb dried, who, with a cane and an earthen cup in the end, with fire and the dried herbs put together, do suck through the cane the smoke thereof, which smoke satisfieth their hunger and therewith they live four or five days without meat or drink. And this all the Frenchmen used for this purpose; yet do they hold opinion withal that it causeth water and phlegm to void from their stomachs.

The commodities of this land are more than are yet known to any man, for besides the land itself, whereof there is more than any king Christian is able to inhabit, it flourisheth with meadow, pasture ground, with woods of cedar and cypress and other sorts, as better cannot be in the world. They have for apothecary herbs, trees, roots, and gums great store, as storax liquida, turpentine, gum, myrrh, and frankincense, with many others whereof I know not the names. Colors both red, black, yellow, and russet, very perfect, wherewith they so paint their bodies and deerskins which they wear about them that with water it neither fadeth away nor altereth color.

Gold and silver they want not; for at the Frenchmen's first coming thither they had the same offered them for little or nothing, for they received for a hatchet two pound weight of gold because they knew not the estimation thereof; but the soldiers, being greedy of the same, did take it from them, giving them nothing for it, the which they, perceiving that both the Frenchmen did greatly esteem it and also did rigorously deal with them by taking the same away from them, at last would not be known they had any more, neither durst they wear the same for fear of being taken away; so that, saving at their first coming, they could get none of them. And how they came by this gold and silver the Frenchmen know not as yet but by guess, who, having traveled to the southwest of the cape, having found the same dangerous by means of sundry banks, as we also have found the same, and there finding masts which were wrecks of Spaniards coming from Mexico, judged that they had gotten treasure by them. For it is most true that divers wrecks have been made of Spaniards having much treasure; for the Frenchmen, having traveled to the capeward 150 miles, did find two Spaniards with the Floridians, which they brought afterward to their fort, whereof one was in a caravel coming from the Indies which was cast away 14 years ago and the other 12 years, of whose fellows some escaped, othersome were slain by the inhabitants. It seemeth they had estimation of [valued] their gold and silver, for it is wrought flat and graven, which they wear about their necks; othersome made round like a pancake, with a hole in the midst, to bolster up their breasts withal, because they think it a deformity to have great breasts. As for mines, either of gold or silver, the Frenchmen can hear of none they have upon the island but of copper, whereof as yet also they have not made the proof because they were but few men; but it is not unlike but that in the main where are high hills may be gold and silver as well as in Mexico, because it is all one main.

The Frenchmen obtained pearls of them of great bigness, but they were black by means of roasting of them, for they do not fish for them as the Spaniards do but for their meat; for the Spaniards used to keep daily a-fishing some 200 or 300 Indians, some of them that be of choice, a thousand; and their order is to go in canoes, or rather great pinnaces, with 30 men in a piece, whereof the one half or most part be divers, the rest do open the same for the pearls; for it is not suffered that they should use dragging, for that would bring them out of estimation [bring down the price] and mar the beds of them. The oysters which have the smallest sort of pearls are found in seven or eight fathom water but the greatest in 11 or 12 fathom.

The Floridians have pieces of unicorns' horns which they wear about their necks, whereof the Frenchmen obtained many pieces. Of those unicorns they have many, for that they do affirm it to be a beast with one horn, which, coming to the river to drink, putteth the same into the water before he drinketh. Of this unicorns' horn there are [some] of our company that, having gotten the same of the Frenchmen, brought home thereof to show. It is therefore to be presupposed that there are more commodities as well as that, which for want of time and people sufficient to inhabit the same cannot yet come to light; but I trust God will reveal the same before it be long, to the great profit of them that shall take it in hand.

Of beasts in this country besides deer, foxes, hares, polecats, conies [rabbits], ounces [probably lynxes], and leopards, I am not able certainly to say; but it is thought that there are lions and tigers as well as unicorns, lions especially, if it be true that is said of the enmity between them and the unicorns, for there is no beast but hath his enemy, as the cony the polecat, a sheep the wolf, the elephant the rhinoceros, and so of other beasts the like, insomuch that whereas [where] the one is, the other cannot be missing. And seeing I have made mention of the beasts of this country, it shall not be from my purpose to speak also of the venomous beasts, as crocodiles, whereof there is great abundance, adders of great bigness, whereof our men killed some of a yard and a half long. Also I heard a miracle of one of these adders, upon the which a falcon seizing, the said adder did clasp her tail about her; which the French captain seeing, came to the rescue of the falcon and took her, slaying the adder; and this falcon being wild, he did reclaim her and kept her for the space of two months, at which time for very want of meat he was fain to cast her off. On these adders the Frenchmen did feed, to no little admiration of us, and affirmed the same to be a delicate meat. And the captain of the Frenchmen saw also a serpent with three heads and four feet, of the bigness of a great spaniel, which for want of a harquebus he durst not attempt to slay.

Of fish also they have in the river pike, rock, salmon, trout, and divers other small fishes, and of great fish some of the length of a man and longer, being of bigness accordingly, having a snout much like a sword of a yard long. There be also of sea fishes which we saw coming along the coast flying, which are of the bigness of a smelt, the biggest sort whereof have four wings but the other have but two; of these we saw coming out of Guinea 100 in a company, which, being chased by the giltheads, otherwise called the bonitos, do to avoid them the better take their flight out of the water; but yet are they not able to fly far because of the drying of their wings, which serve them not to fly but when they are moist, and therefore when they can fly no further they fall into the water and, having wet their wings, take a new flight again. These bonitos be of bigness like a carp and in color like a mackerel, but it is the swiftest fish in swimming that is, and followeth her prey very fiercely, not only in the water but also out of the water; for as the flying fish taketh her flight, so does this bonito leap after them and taketh them sometimes above the water. There were some of those bonitos which, being galled by a fishgig [fish spear], did follow our ship coming out of Guinea 500 leagues. There is a seafowl also that chaseth this flying fish as well as the bonito; for as the flying fish taketh her flight, so doth this fowl pursue to take her, which to behold is a greater pleasure than hawking, for both the flights are as pleasant, and also more often than 100 times; for the fowl can fly no way but one or other lighteth in her paws, the number of them are so abundant. There is an innumerable young fry of these flying fishes, which commonly keep about the ship and are not so big as butterflies and yet by flying do avoid the unsatiableness of the bonito. Of the bigger sort of these fishes we took many which both night and day flew into the sails of our ship, and there was not one of them which was not worth a bonito; for, being put upon a hook drabbling in the water, the bonito would leap thereat and so was taken. Also, we took many with a white cloth made fast to a hook, which being tied so short in the water that it might leap out and in, the greedy bonito, thinking it to be a flying fish, leapeth thereat and so is deceived. We took also dolphins, which are of very goodly color and proportion to behold and no less delicate in taste.

Fowls also there be many, both upon land and upon sea; but, concerning them on the land, I am not able to name them because my abode was there so short. But for the fowl of the fresh rivers, these two I noted to be the chief: whereof the flamingo is one, having all red feathers and long red legs like a heron, a neck, according to the bill, red, whereof the upper neb hangeth an inch over the nether; and an egret, which is all white as the swan, with legs like to an heronshaw [heron] and of bigness accordingly, but it hath in her tail feathers of so fine a plume that it passeth the ostrich his feather. Of the seafowl, above all other not common in England I noted the pelican, which is feigned to be the lovingest bird that is; which, rather than her young should want, will spare her heartblood out of her belly; but for all this lovingness she is very deformed to behold, for she is of color russet, notwithstanding in Guinea I have seen of them as white as a swan, having legs like the same and a body like a heron, with a long neck and a thick, long beak, from the nether jaw whereof down to the breast passeth a skin of such a bigness as is able to receive a fish as big as one's thigh, and this her big throat and long bill doth make her seem so ugly.

Here I have declared the estate of Florida and the commodities therein to this day known; which although it may seem unto some, by the means that the plenty of gold and silver is not so abundant as in other places, that the cost bestowed upon the same will not be able to quit the charges; yet am I of the opinion that, by that which I have seen in other islands of the Indians, where such increase of cattle hath been that of 12 head of beasts in 25 years did in the hides of them raise £1,000 profit yearly, that the increase of cattle only would raise profit sufficient for the same; for we may consider, if so small a portion did raise so much gains in such short time, what would a greater do in many years? And surely I may this affirm, that the ground of the Indians for the breed of cattle is not in any point to be compared to this of Florida, which all the year long is so green as any time in the summer with us; which surely is not to be marveled at, seeing the country standeth in so watery a climate, for once a day without fail they have a shower of rain which, by means of the country itself, which is dry and more fervent hot than ours, doth make all things to flourish therein. And because there is not the thing we all seek for, being rather desirous of present gains, I do therefore affirm the attempt thereof to be more requisite for a prince, who is of power able to go through with the same, rather than for any subject. . . .

VII

Hawkins and Drake Become
Inveterate Enemies of Spain

HAWKINS' second voyage to Africa and America had proved profitable enough to the syndicate and to the queen to warrant another effort. While John Hawkins was planning an expedition that he himself would lead, the Hawkins brothers in 1566 dispatched four ships under the command of Captain John Lovell. He took along as one of his officers young Francis Drake, who was thus to gain experience in the Caribbean that would later prove useful. Lovell's expedition followed the usual practice of collecting slaves on the coast of Africa and transporting them to the Spanish Main, but Lovell lacked the acumen of John Hawkins and allowed the Spaniards at Rio de la Hacha to trick him out of some 90 slaves.

By the autumn of 1567 Hawkins was ready with his own expedition, which was destined to have a profound influence on the future attitude of English seamen toward Spain. Investors included the queen, Sir William Cecil, members of the navy board and many prominent courtiers and citizens. The queen once more contributed the largest ship, the old and somewhat decrepit *Jesus of Lübeck*. The next ship in size was another naval vessel, the *Minion* of 300 tons. Hawkins had four other, smaller vessels, the *William and John,* the *Swallow,* the *Judith* and the *Angel.* The crews of the six ships consisted of some 400 men, of whom only a few would survive. On October 2, 1567, the flotilla sailed out of Plymouth, bound for Africa.

This time Hawkins encountered genuine difficulties with the Portuguese, who showed less willingness to trade. By the time he reached Sierra Leone, he had collected only 150 slaves and was debating whether to continue to the Gold Coast when he discovered that the king of Sierra Leone desperately needed help in conquering an enemy holed up in a town of some 8,000 souls. Hawkins offered to help capture the town on the promise of enough slaves to fill his ships. After the capture, Hawkins' allies slaughtered most of the inhabitants and held a cannibal feast in the smouldering ruins of the town. But they considerately left him 260 captives, enough to fill out his quota and make the voyage to the Spanish Main worthwhile. On February 7, 1568, he weighed anchor for the Caribbean.

Although the Spanish authorities were a bit stiffer to deal with this time, by diplomacy, bluff or force Hawkins contrived to sell at a profit all of his slaves and English goods and was ready to sail for home when heavy weather further damaged the old *Jesus,* which now would have to be careened in some safe harbor and patched. She was leaking badly. Rotten planks on each side of the sternposts "did open and shut with every sea . . . the leaks so big as the thickness of a man's arm [that] the living fish did swim upon the ballast as in the sea." [1]

Sailing up the Mexican coast, Hawkins found only one spot suitable for his repairs, the barren little port of San Juan de Ulúa, on the site of modern Vera Cruz. The chief importance of San Juan de Ulúa was that it served as the port of entry for Mexico City. Here each year the plate fleet loaded the treasure collected in Mexico to take back to Spain. When Hawkins anchored at San Juan on September 16, he learned that the plate fleet from Spain was expected at the end of the month, but he thought he could make his repairs and get away before that time. Unhappily the fleet had made unusual speed on the westward voyage and arrived the next morning.

Hawkins' cannon commanded the mouth of the harbor. He could keep the Spanish vessels out of the harbor in the open roadstead, where they would be in constant danger of shipwreck from high winds then prevailing. This action would have been considered hostile, and he dared not risk the anger of Queen Elizabeth at such provocation. Furthermore, the plate fleet had aboard a new viceroy of Mexico and other grandees. Hawkins decided to negotiate. The upshot was a solemn

---

[1] Quoted in James A. Williamson, *Hawkins of Plymouth* (London, 1949), p. 133.

pledge by the viceroy that the Spanish fleet would cause no harm to the Englishmen if they were permitted to come to anchor at San Juan. With this promise, and the exchange of ten hostages, Hawkins allowed the Spaniards to enter.

Immediately the Spanish viceroy began treacherously planning the capture of the English ships, and on the morning of September 23 the attack began. From ten in the morning until four in the afternoon, the English struggled against overpowering numbers. At last Hawkins made his way out of the harbor in the *Minion* with 200 men; Drake escaped in the *Judith* and sailed away. His precipitate departure was criticized at the time, but apparently his action did not permanently mar his relations with Hawkins, with whom he later sailed again.

Although Hawkins had salvaged most of the gold stored in the *Jesus,* he had been able to load very little food. The 200 men aboard the damaged and unsupplied vessel had little hope of reaching England. In this desperate situation Hawkins called for volunteers to remain behind and take their chances with Indians or Spaniards. One account says 96 and another says 114 men agreed to go ashore, and the commander landed them on the desolate Mexican coast at 23½ degrees latitude, some distance north of the present city of Tampico. As the party plodded southward the first day, Indians set upon them, killed eight and robbed them of a little cloth that Hawkins had left with them for trading purposes. Twenty-three men decided to turn north and take their chances with the unknown rather than face Spaniards in Mexico. Three of these survived the long march north, all the way to Cape Breton, Nova Scotia, they claimed, and were taken back to England by a French fishing vessel. An account of this trek by one of the three, David Ingram, was printed by Richard Hakluyt in the 1589 edition of *The Principal Navigations* but was omitted in subsequent editions because of certain "incredibilities."

The rest of the marooned sailors, 78 in number, after making contact with Spaniards at Tampico and surrendering, were sent under guard to Mexico. A few died on the way but most survived. After a year in prison they were permitted to find jobs. A few were sent to Spain but most remained to work out their fate in Mexico. After 1571, however, they again suffered misfortune, for they were all haled before the Inquisition and tried for heresy. Those who were too young to have received Catholic instruction in their youth got off with light sentences, but the older men were severely punished by as much as 200 lashes and ten years in the galleys. A few suffered death at the stake. The Inquisition records of about half of the victims survive and provide an illuminating record of the views of Englishmen of this class in the sixteenth century.

On October 16, 1568, with the 100 men who had elected to try to reach England in the *Minion,* Hawkins sailed from the Mexican coast. The voyage was difficult and the men were near starvation. For days on end their only food consisted of cowhides from the cargo, which they boiled until soft enough to chew. At last, on December 31, they reached the northwest corner of Spain and entered the harbor of Vigo, bought food and escaped without capture. Unhappily, sudden abundance was too much for the starved sailors and 45 died. Hawkins managed to recruit 12 men from an English ship and made it to Mount's Bay on the Cornish coast by January 25, 1569. Five days earlier Drake with a small number of men in the *Judith* had sailed into Plymouth Harbor. Hawkins had to wait at Mount's Bay for the arrival of a fresh crew sent by his brother to take the *Minion* into Plymouth. A report to Madrid from the Spanish ambassador asserted that only 15 men of the 100 who had sailed reached England.

The third and "troublesome" voyage of John Hawkins is important for the history of the English exploitation of North America because it marked a turning point in Anglo-Spanish relations. The old Spanish-English alliance was now ended forever. Hawkins and Drake became inveterate enemies of Spain and their future forays against the Spanish empire in America would have a lasting effect upon the relations of the two countries and upon efforts to found English settlements overseas.

The religious animosities between Protestants and Catholics were increasing, and the punishment of Hawkins' men in Mexico by the Inquisition exacerbated English feelings against Spain. The English had also watched with concern the efforts of the French Huguenots to establish colonies in Florida in the face of Spanish opposition. In 1565 Pedro Menéndez de Avilés had taken out 500 colonists and troops to Florida and planted

a colony at Saint Augustine. This colony was designed to check-
mate the French at Fort Caroline, about 35 miles to the north.
As Menéndez was settling his colony at Saint Augustine, Jean
Ribaut returned to the Florida coast with aid for Fort Caroline.
He set out to attack Menéndez' new settlement and wipe out
that danger. Unhappily a storm dispersed and wrecked his
ships, leaving his men stranded in the Florida swamps. In the
autumn of 1565, Menéndez took the offensive, marched overland
to Fort Caroline and captured and massacred most of the settlers.
Some he hanged and placed above them an inscription reading:
"I do this, not as to Frenchmen, but as to Lutherans." [2] He also
captured and slaughtered Ribaut and his sailors after he had led
them to believe that they could expect mercy. Englishmen
who sympathized with the unfortunate Huguenots, and with
the prisoners in Spanish hands in Mexico, henceforth looked
forward to the time when they could wreak vengeance upon
the Spaniards, occupy a portion of North America and block
further advance of Spain in the New World.

French hatred of the Spaniards equaled that of the English,
and in the spring of 1568 a French sea captain, Dominique de
Gourgues, avenged Menéndez' massacre of his countrymen in
Florida. Gourgues had reason to hate the Spaniards, for they had
captured him during the French and Spanish wars in Italy
and had kept him chained to an oar in one of their galleys
until its capture by the Knights of Malta. With three small
ships and 180 men he secretly sailed for Florida; but, like
Hawkins, he went by way of the African coast. Outwardly the
voyage looked like another slaving and trading expedition. Once
past Cuba, Gourgues revealed his real intentions to his men.
His immediate objective was the site of Fort Caroline, which
the Spaniards had fortified and renamed San Mateo. Arriving
off the coast, he discovered that the Indians were in an uproar
over the cruelties of the Spaniards. With an army of Indian
allies he laid siege to San Mateo, captured it and slaughtered all
the defenders except a few whom he saved to hang from the
same trees that Menéndez had used to hang Frenchmen.
Paraphrasing Menéndez, Gourgues nailed a board above these
victims with an inscription reading: "I do not this as unto

[2] Quoted in Francis Parkman, *Pioneers of New France in the New World*
(Boston, 1907), p. 128.

Spaniards, nor as unto mariners, but as unto traitors, robbers, and murderers." [3]

With the approval of the government, Hawkins wrote a brief account of his voyage which was published as a pamphlet in 1569. Hakluyt, in the 1589 edition of *The Principal Navigations,* reprinted the document under the title below. Excerpts follow:

The Third Troublesome Voyage Made . . . in the Years 1567 and 1568 by M. John Hawkins

The ships departed from Plymouth the second day of October, *anno* 1567, and had reasonable weather until the seventh day, at which time, 40 leagues north from Cape Finisterre, there arose an extreme storm, which continued four days in such sort that the fleet was dispersed and all our great boats lost and the *Jesus,* our chief ship, in such case as not thought able to serve the voyage. Whereupon, in the same storm we set our course homeward, determining to give over the voyage. But the eleventh day of the same month the wind changed with fair weather, whereby we were animated to follow our enterprise and so did, directing our course with the islands of the Canaries, where, according to an order before prescribed, all our ships, before dispersed, met at one of those islands called Gomera, where we took water and departed from thence the 4th day of November toward the coast of Guinea and arrived at Cape Verde the 18th of November, where we landed 150 men, hoping to obtain some Negroes; where we got but few and those with great hurt and damage to our men, which chiefly proceeded of their envenomed arrows, and although in the beginning they seemed to be but small hurts, yet there hardly escaped any that had blood drawn of them but died in strange sort, with their mouth shut [from tetanus?] some ten days before they died and after their wounds were whole; where I myself had one of the greatest wounds yet, thanks be to God, escaped.

From thence we passed the time upon the coast of Guinea, searching with all diligence the rivers from Rio Grande unto

[3] Quoted in René de Laudonnière, *A Notable Historie* (1587), translated by Richard Hakluyt, sig. Q 4 verso.

Sierra Leone till the twelfth of January, in which time we had
not gotten together 150 Negroes. Yet, notwithstanding, the
sickness of our men and the late time of the year commanded
us away. And thus, having nothing wherewith to seek the coast
of the West Indies, I was with the rest of our company in consultation to go to the coast of the Mine [the Gold Coast], hoping
there to have obtained some gold for our wares and thereby to
have defrayed our charge. But even in that present instant
there came to us a Negro, sent from a king oppressed by other
kings, his neighbors, desiring our aid, with promise that as
many Negroes as by these wars might be obtained, as well of his
part as of ours, should be at our pleasure. Whereupon we concluded to give aid and sent 120 of our men, which the 15th
of January assaulted a town of the Negroes of our ally's adver-
saries, which had in it 8,000 inhabitants, being very strongly
impaled and fenced after their manner. But it was so well
defended that our men prevailed not but lost six men and 40
hurt, so that our men sent forthwith to me for more help.
Whereupon, considering that the good success of this enterprise might highly further the commodity of our voyage, I went
myself and with the help of the king of our side assaulted the
town, both by land and sea, and very hardly with fire (their
houses being covered with dry palm leaves) obtained the town
and put the inhabitants to flight, where we took 250 persons,
men, women, and children. And by our friend the king of our
side there were taken 600 prisoners, whereof we hoped to have
had our choice; but the Negro (in which nation is seldom or
never found truth) meant nothing less, for that night he removed his camp and prisoners so that we were fain to content
us with those few which we had gotten ourselves.

Now had we obtained between 400 and 500 Negroes, wherewith we thought it somewhat reasonable to seek the coast of the
West Indies; and there for our Negroes and other our merchandise we hoped to obtain whereof to countervail our charges
with some gains, whereunto we proceeded with all diligence,
furnished our watering, took fuel, and departed the coast of
Guinea the 3rd of February, continuing at the sea with a passage
more hard than before hath been accustomed till the 27th day
of March, which day we had sight of an island called Dominica

upon the coast of the West Indies, in 14 degrees. From thence we coasted from place to place, making our traffic with the Spaniards as we might, somewhat hardly, because the king had straitly commanded all his governors in those parts by no means to suffer any trade to be made with us. Notwithstanding, we had reasonable trade and courteous entertainment from the isle of Margarita unto Cartagena, without anything greatly worth the noting saving at Capo de la Vela [Cabo de la Vela, Colombia], in a town called Rio de la Hacha [Riohacha, Colombia], from whence come all the pearls, the treasurer who had the charge there would by no means agree to any trade or suffer us to take water. He had fortified his town with divers bulwarks in all places where it might be entered and furnished himself with an hundred harquebusiers, so that he thought by famine to have enforced us to have put aland our Negroes; of which purpose he had not greatly failed unless we had by force entered the town, which (after we could by no means obtain his favor) we were enforced to do, and so with 200 men broke in upon their bulwarks and entered the town with the loss only of two men of our parts and no hurt done to the Spaniards, because after their volley of shot discharged they all fled.

Thus, having the town with some circumstance [advantage], as partly by the Spaniards' desire of Negroes and partly by friendship of the treasurer, we obtained a secret trade whereupon the Spaniards resorted to us by night and bought of us to the number of 200 Negroes. In all other places where we traded the Spaniard inhabitants were glad of us and traded willingly.

At Cartagena, the last town we thought to have seen on the coast, we could by no means obtain to deal with any Spaniard, the governor was so strait. And because our trade was so near finished, we thought not good either to adventure any landing or to detract [delay] further time but in peace departed from thence the 24th of July, hoping to have escaped the time of their storms, which then soon after began to rain, the which they called *furicanos*. But, passing by the west end of Cuba toward the coast of Florida, there happened to us the 12th day of August an extreme storm which continued by the space of four days, which so beat the *Jesus* that we cut down all her higher buildings; her rudder also was sore shaken and withal was in so extreme a leak that we were rather upon the point to leave her than to keep her any longer. Yet, hoping to bring all to good pass, we sought the coast of Florida, where we found no place nor haven for our ships because of the shallowness of the coast. Thus, being in greater despair and taken with a new storm which continued over three days, we were enforced to take for our succor the port which serves the city of Mexico, called San Juan de Ulúa, which stands in 19 degrees; in seeking of which port we took in our way three ships which carried passengers to the number of 100, which passengers we hoped should be a mean to us the better to obtain victuals for our money and a quiet place for the repairing of our fleet.

Shortly after this, the 16th of September, we entered the port of San Juan de Ulúa, and, in our entry, the Spaniards thinking us to be the fleet of Spain, the chief officers of the country came aboard us; which, being deceived of their expectation, were greatly dismayed, but immediately when they saw our demand was nothing but victuals were recomforted. I found also in the same port 12 ships which had in them, by report, £200,000 in gold and silver, all which (being in my possession, with the king's island, as also the passengers before in my way thither-ward stayed) I set at liberty, without the taking from them the weight of a groat. Only, because I would not be delayed of my dispatch, I stayed two men of estimation and sent post immediately to Mexico, which was 200 miles from us, to the presidents and council there, showing them of our arrival there by the force of weather and the necessity of the repair of our ships and victuals, which wants we required as friends to King Philip to be furnished of for our money, and that the presidents and council there should with all convenient speed take order that at the arrival of the Spanish fleet, which was daily looked for, there might no cause of quarrel rise between us and them, but for the better maintenance of amity their commandment might be had in that behalf.

This message, being sent away the 16th day of September at night, being the very day of our arrival, in the next morning, which was the 17th day of the same month, we saw open of the haven 13 great ships, and, understanding them to be the fleet of Spain, I sent immediately to advertise the general of the fleet of my being there, doing him to understand that before I would

suffer them to enter the port there should some order of conditions pass between us for our safe being there and maintenance of peace.

Now it is to be understood that this port is made by a little
island of stones not three feet above the water in the highest
place and but a bowshot of length any way; this island standeth
from the mainland two bowshots or more. Also it is to be
understood that there is not in all this coast any other place
for ships to arrive in safety, because the north wind hath there
such violence that unless the ships be very safely moored with
their anchors fastened upon this island there is no remedy for
these north winds but death. Also the place of the haven was so
little that of necessity the ships must ride one aboard the
other, so that we could not give place to them nor they to
us; and here I began to bewail that which after followed. For
now, said I, I am in two dangers and forced to receive the one
of them. That was, either I must have kept out the fleet from
entering the port, the which with God's help I was very well able
to do, or else suffer them to enter in with their accustomed
treason, which they never fail to execute where they may have
opportunity to compass it by any means. If I had kept them
out, then had there been present shipwreck of all the fleet, which
amounted in value to six millions, which was in value of our
money £1,800,000, which I considered I was not able to answer,
fearing the Queen's Majesty's indignation in so weighty a
matter. Thus with myself revolving the doubts, I thought rather
better to abide the jut [thrust] of the uncertainty than the
certainty. The uncertain doubt I account was their treason,
which by good policy I hoped might be prevented, and therefore, as choosing the least mischief, I proceeded to conditions.

Now was our first messenger come and returned from the
fleet with report of the arrival of a viceroy, so that he had
authority, both in all this province of Mexico (otherwise called
Nueva España) and in the sea, who sent us word that we should
send our conditions, which of his part should (for the better maintenance of amity between the princes) be both favorably granted
and faithfully performed, with many fair words how, passing the
coast of the Indies, he had understood of our honest behavior
toward the inhabitants where we had to do, as well elsewhere
as in the same port, the which I let pass. Thus following our

demand, we required victuals for our money and license to sell as much ware as might furnish our wants, and that there might be of either part 12 gentlemen as hostages for the maintenance of peace; and that the island for our better safety might be in our own possession during our abode there, and such ordnance as was planted in the same island, which were 11 pieces of brass; and that no Spaniard might land in the island with any kind of weapon.

These conditions at the first he somewhat misliked, chiefly the guard of the island to be in our own keeping, which if they had had, we had soon known our fare, for with the first north wind they had cut our cables and our ships had gone ashore. But in the end he concluded to our request, bringing the 12 hostages to ten, which with all speed of either part were received, with a writing from the viceroy signed with his hand and sealed with his seal of all the conditions concluded, and forthwith a trumpet blown with commandment that none of either part should bemean to violate the peace upon pain of death; and further it was concluded that the two generals of the fleets should meet and give faith each to other for the performance of the premises, which was so done.

Thus, at the end of three days all was concluded and the fleet entered the port, saluting one another as the manner of the sea doth require. Thus, as I said before, Thursday we entered the port, Friday we saw the fleet, and on Monday at night they entered the port. Then we labored two days placing the English ships by themselves and the Spanish ships by themselves, the captains of each part and inferior men of their parts promising great amity of all sides; which even as with all fidelity it was meant on our part, so the Spaniards meant nothing less on their parts, but from the mainland had furnished themselves with a supply of men to the number of one thousand and meant the next Thursday, being the 23rd of September, at dinnertime, to set upon us on all sides.

The same Thursday in the morning, the treason being at hand, some appearance showed, as shifting of weapon from ship to ship, planting and bending of ordnance from the ship to the island where our men warded, passing to and fro of companies of men more than required for their necessary business, and many other ill likelihoods, which caused us to have a vehement

suspicion and therewithal sent to the viceroy to inquire what
was meant by it; which sent immediately strait commandment
to unplant all things suspicious, and also sent word that he in
the faith of a viceroy would be our defense from all villainies.
Yet we, being not satisfied with this answer, because we suspected a great number of men to be hid in a great ship of
900 tons which was moored next unto the *Minion,* sent again
to the viceroy the master of the *Jesus,* which had the Spanish
tongue, and required to be satisfied if any such thing were or
not. The viceroy, now seeing that the treason must be
discovered, forthwith stayed our master, blew the trumpet, and
of all sides set upon us. Our men which warded ashore, being
stricken with sudden fear, gave place, fled, and sought to recover succor of the ships. The Spaniards, being before provided
for the purpose, landed in all places in multitudes from their
ships, which they might easily do without boats, and slew all
our men ashore without mercy; a few of them escaped aboard
the *Jesus.* The great ship, which had by the estimation 300
men placed in her secretly, immediately fell aboard the *Minion,*
but by God's appointment in the time of suspicion we had,
which was only one half hour, the *Minion* was made ready
to avoid; and so leesing [unfastening] her head-fasts and haling
[hauling] away by the stern-fasts, she was gotten out. Thus with
God's help she defended the violence of the first brunt of these
300 men.

The *Minion* being passed, they came aboard the *Jesus,* which
also, with very much ado and the loss of many of our men,
was defended and kept out. Then there were also two other
ships that assaulted the *Jesus* at the same instant, so that she
had hard getting loose, but yet witn some time we had cut
our head-fasts and gotten out by the stern-fasts. Now when the
Jesus and the *Minion* were gotten about two ships' length from
the Spanish fleet, the fight began so hot on all sides that within
one hour the admiral of the Spaniards was supposed to be sunk,
their vice-admiral burned, and one other of their principal
ships supposed to be sunk, so that the ships were little able to
annoy us.

Then it is to be understood that all the ordnance upon the
island was in the Spaniards' hands, which did us so great
annoyance that it cut all the masts and yards of the *Jesus,* in

such sort that there was no hope to carry her away; also it sunk our small ships, whereupon we determined to place the *Jesus* on that side of the *Minion* that she might abide all the battery from the land and so to be a defense for the *Minion* till night, and then to take such relief of victual and other necessaries from the *Jesus* as the time would suffer us and to leave her. As we were thus determining and had placed the *Minion* from the shot of the land, suddenly the Spaniards had fired two great ships, which were coming directly with us, and, having no means to avoid the fire, it bred among our men a marvelous fear, so that some said, "Let us depart with the *Minion*"; others said, "Let us see whether the wind will carry the fire from us." But, to be short, the *Minion*'s men, which had always their sails in a readiness, thought to make sure work, and so, without either consent of the captain or master, cut their sail, so that very hardly I was received into the *Minion*.

The most part of the men that were left alive in the *Jesus* made shift and followed the *Minion* in a small boat; the rest, which the little boat was not able to receive, were enforced to abide the mercy of the Spaniards (which I doubt was very little). So with the *Minion* only and the *Judith* (a small bark of 50 ton) we escaped, which bark the same night forsook us in our great misery. We were now removed with the *Minion* from the Spanish ships two bowshots and there rode all that night. The next morning we recovered an island a mile from the Spaniards, where there took us a north wind and, being left only with two anchors and two cables (for in this conflict we lost three cables and two anchors), we thought always upon death, which ever was present, but God preserved us to a longer time.

The weather waxed reasonable, and the Saturday we set sail and, having a great number of men and little victuals, our hope of life waxed less and less. Some desired to yield to the Spaniards, some rather desired to obtain a place where they might give themselves to the infidels, and some had rather abide with a little pittance the mercy of God at sea. So thus, with many sorrowful hearts, we wandered in an unknown sea by the space of 14 days, till hunger enforced us to seek the land, for hides were thought very good meat; rats, cats, mice, and dogs, none escaped that might be gotten. Parrots and monkeys, that were had in great price, were thought there very profitable if they served the turn one dinner. Thus in the end the 8th day of October we came to the land in the bottom of the same Bay of Mexico in 23½ degrees, where we hoped to have found inhabitants of the Spaniards, relief of victuals, and place for the repair of our ship, which was so sore beaten with shot from our enemies and bruised with shooting off our own ordnance that our weary and weak arms were scarce able to defend and keep out water. But all things happened to the contrary, for we found neither people, victual, nor haven of relief, but a place where, having fair weather, with some peril we might land a boat. Our people, being forced with hunger, desired to be set on land, whereunto I consented.

And such as were willing to land I put them apart, and such as were desirous to go homewards I put apart, so that they were indifferently parted 100 of one side and 100 of the other side. These 100 men we set aland with all diligence in this little place beforesaid, which, being landed, we determined there to take in fresh water and so with our little remain of victuals to take the sea.

The next day, having aland with me 50 of our 100 men that remained for the speedier preparing of our water aboard, there arose an extreme storm, so that in three days we could by no means repair aboard our ship; the ship also was in such peril that every hour we looked for shipwreck.

But yet God again had mercy on us and sent fair weather. We had aboard our water and departed the 16th day of October, after which day we had fair and prosperous weather till the 16th day of November, which day, God be praised, we were clear from the coast of the Indies and out of the channel and gulf of Bahama, which is between the cape of Florida and the islands of Lucayo [early Spanish name for the Bahamas]. After this, growing near to the cold country, our men, being oppressed with famine, died continually, and they that were left grew into such weakness that we were scantly able to manage our ship, and, the wind being always ill for us to recover England, we determined to go with Galicia in Spain with intent there to relieve our company and other extreme wants. And being arrived the last day of December in a place near unto Vigo called Pontevedra, our men with excess of fresh meat grew into miserable diseases and died, a great part of them.

This matter was borne out as long as it might be, but in the end, although there were none of our men suffered to go aland, yet, by access of the Spaniards, our feebleness was known to them. Whereupon they ceased not to seek by all means to betray us, but with all speed possible we departed to Vigo, where we had some help of certain English ships and 12 fresh men, wherewith we repaired our wants as we might and, departing the 20th day of January 1568 [1569 new style], arrived in Mounts Bay in Cornwall the 25th of the same month, praised be God therefor.

If all the miseries and troublesome affairs of this sorrowful voyage should be perfectly and thoroughly written, there should need a painful [painstaking] man with his pen and as great a time as he had that wrote the lives and deaths of the martyrs [i.e., John Foxe, whose *Acts and Monuments* (1563) was generally called *The Book of Martyrs*].

David Ingram's "Incredible" Narrative

[*Three men left by Hawkins on the coast of Mexico survived the long journey northward and were picked up by a French fishing vessel and brought home to England. They were David Ingram, Richard Browne and Richard Twide. According to Ingram, the French vessel picked them up near Cape Breton, but the place of their rescue may have been much farther south. A report made by Ingram in 1582 to Sir Francis Walsingham and others concerned with exploration of North America was published by Hakluyt in the 1589 edition of* The Principal Navigations *but omitted from later editions. Samuel Purchas asserted that the omission was the result of Hakluyt's skepticism about the accuracy of the report and "certain incredibilities." Excerpts from Hakluyt's version follow:*]

The relation of David Ingram of Barking, in the county of Essex, sailor, of sundry things which he with others did see, in traveling by land from the most northerly parts of the Bay of Mexico (where he with many others were set on shore by Master Hawkins) through a great part of America, until he came within 50 leagues or thereabouts of Cape Breton.

About the beginning of October, *anno* 1568, David Ingram with the rest of his company, being 100 persons in all, were set on land by Master John Hawkins about six leagues to the west of the river La Mina, or Rio de Minas, which standeth about 140 leagues west and by north from the cape of Florida; who, traveling toward Cape Breton, spent about 12 months in the whole, and about seven months thereof in those countries which lie toward the north of the River of May [St. Johns River]; in which time (as the said Ingram thinketh) he traveled by land 2,000 miles at the least and never continued in any one place above three or four days, saving only at the city of Balma, where he stayed six or seven days.

There are in those parts (saith he) very many kings, commonly within 100 or 120 miles one from another, who are at continual wars together. The first king that they came before dwelt in a country called Giricka, who caused them to be stripped naked and, wondering greatly at the whiteness of their skins, let them depart without further harm.

The kings in those countries are clothed with painted or colored garments, and thereby you may know them. And they wear great precious stones, which commonly are rubies, being four inches long and two inches broad. And if the same be taken from them, either by force or sleight, they are presently deprived of their kingdoms.

When they mean to speak with any person publicly they are always carried by men in a sumptuous chair of silver or crystal garnished with divers sorts of precious stones. . . .

There is in some of those countries great abundance of pearl, for in every cottage be found pearl: in some houses a quart, in some a pottle [half gallon], in some a peck, more or less, where he did see some as great as a bean. . . .

All the people generally do wear manilios, or bracelets, as big as a man's finger upon each of their arms, and the like on the small of each of their legs, whereof commonly one is gold and two silver. And many of the women also do wear plates of gold, covering their bodies in manner of a pair of curiets [breastplates], and many bracelets and chains of great pearl. The people commonly are of good favor, feature, and shape of body; of growth above five foot high, somewhat thick, with their faces and skins of color like an olive, and toward the north somewhat tawny, but some of them are painted with divers colors. They are very swift of foot; the hair of their heads is shaven in sundry spots, and the rest of their head is traced [braided]. In the south parts of these countries they go all naked, saving that the noblemen's privities are covered with the neck of a gourd and the women's privities with the hair or leaf of the palm tree. But in the north parts they are clothed with beasts' skins, the hairy side being next to their bodies in winter.

They are so brutish and beastly that they will not forbear the use of their wives in open presence. They are naturally very courteous if you do not abuse them, either in their persons or goods, but use them courteously. The killing or taking of their beasts, birds, fishes, or fruits cannot offend them, except it be of their cattle which they keep about their houses, as kine, guinea hens, or suchlike. If any of them do hold up both their hands at length together and kiss the backs of them on both sides, then you may undoubtedly trust them, for it is the greatest token of friendship that may be. . . .

If you will bargain for ware with them, leave the thing that you will sell upon the ground and go from it a pretty way off; then will they come and take it and set down such wares as they will give for it in the place. And if you think it not sufficient, leave the wares with signs that you like it not and they will bring more, until either they or you be satisfied or will give no more. Otherwise you may hang your wares upon a long pole's end and so put more or less on it until you have agreed on the bargain. . . .

The people in those countries are professed enemies to the cannibals or men-eaters. The cannibals do most inhabit between Norumbega and Bariniah [the territory north of Florida]. They have teeth like dogs' teeth, and thereby you may know them. In the wars they do pitch their camp as near as they may into some wood of palm trees, which yield them meat, drink, and present remedy against poisonous arrows.

Their buildings are weak and of small force. Their houses are made round like dovehouses, and they do dwell together in towns and villages. And some of them have banqueting houses in the top of them, made like the louver of a hall, builded with pillars of massy silver and crystal, framed square. Whereof many of them are as big as a boy's leg of fifteen years of age, and some less. . . .

They have in every house scoops, buckets, and divers other vessels of massy silver, wherewith they do throw out water and dust, and otherwise do employ them to their necessary uses in their houses. All which this Ingram did see common and usual in some of these countries, especially where he found the great pearls.

There are also great rivers, at the heads whereof this Ingram and his companions did find sundry pieces of gold, some as big as a man's fist, the earth being washed away with the water. And in other places they did see great rocks of crystal, which grew at the heads of great and many rivers, being in quantity to load ships. There are also in those parts plenty of fine furs unknown to this Ingram, dressed after the manner of the country.

The people there do burn a kind of white turf or earth, which they dig out of the marishes [marshes], a fathom deep in the ground. It burneth very clear and smelleth as sweet as musk, and that earth is as wholesome, sweet, and comfortable to smell unto as any pomander. They do make their fire of this earth for the sweetness thereof, having great abundance of wood. When they want fire they take briers and rub them very hard together between their fists, and so with hard and often rubbing they kindle and make fire.

They have great plenty of iron, and there is also great plenty of mineral salt in the marish ground, which looketh reddish, a thing necessary for the great fishings near the seashore, which are there abundant and the fish very large and huge.

The ground and country is most excellent, fertile and pleasant, and specially toward the River of May. For the grass of the rest is not so green as it is in these parts, for the other is burnt away with the heat of the sun. And as all the country is good and most delicate, having great plains, as large and as fair in many places as may be seen, being as plain as a board. And then great and huge woods of sundry kind of trees, as cedar, lignum vitae, Bombax [silk-cotton tree], plants and bushes, bark that biteth like pepper (of which kind young Master Winter brought home part from the Straits of Magellan), with the fruitful palm tree and great plenty of other sweet trees to this Ingram unknown. And after that plains again and in other places great closes of pasture environed with most delicate trees instead of hedges, they being as it were set by the hands of men. Yet the best grass for the most part is in the high countries, somewhat far from the seaside and great rivers, by reason that the low grounds there be so rank that the grass groweth faster than it can be eaten, whereby the old grass lieth withered thick and the new grass growing through it. Whereas in the upper parts the grass and ground is most excellent and green, the ground not being overcharged with any old withered grass, as is afore specified.

The palm tree aforesaid carrieth hairs on the leaves thereof, which reach to the ground, whereof the Indians do make ropes and cords for their cotton beds and do use the same to many other purposes. The which tree, if you pick with your knife about two foot from the root, it will yield a wine in color like whey but in taste strong and somewhat like bastard [a sweet Spanish wine], which is most excellent drink. But it will distemper both your head and body if you drink too much thereof, as our strong wines will do in these parts. The branches of the top of the tree are most excellent meat raw, after you have pared away the bark. Also there is a red oil that cometh out of the root of this tree, which is most excellent against poisoned arrows and weapons, for by it they do recover themselves of their poisoned wounds.

There is a tree called a plantain, with a fruit growing on it like a pudding [i.e., sausage], which is most excellent meat raw.

They have also a red berry like a peasecod [pea pod] called buyathos, two or three inches long, which groweth on short bushes full of pricks like the sloe- or thorn-tree; and the fruit eateth like a green raisin but sharper somewhat. They stamp this berry and make wine thereof, which they keep in vessels made of wood.

They have also in many places vines which bear grapes as big as a man's thumb.

There is also great plenty of herbs and of all kinds of flowers, as roses and gillyflowers, like ours in England, and many others which he knew not.

Also, they have a kind of grain the ear whereof is as big as the wrist of a man's arm; the grain is like a flat pea; it maketh very good bread and white.

They do also make bread of the root called cassava, which they do dry and beat it as small as they can and temper it with water, and so bake it in cakes on a stone.

There is also great plenty of buffs [buffalo], bears, horses, kine, wolves, foxes, deer, goats, sheep, hares, and conies. Also other cattle like ours, [and other] to this examinate unknown, the most part being wild; the hides and skins of them are good merchandise. There is very great store of those buffs, which are beasts as big as two oxen, in length almost 20 foot, having long ears like a bloodhound, with long hairs about their ears. Their horns be crooked like rams' horns, their eyes black, their hairs long, black, rough, and shagged as a goat. The hides of these beasts are sold very dear. This beast doth keep company only by couples, male and female, and doth always fight with others of the same kind when they do meet.

There is also great plenty of deer, both red, white, and speckled. This last sort this examinate knoweth not.

There is also great plenty of another kind of sheep which carry a kind of coarse wool. This sheep is very good meat, although the flesh be very red. They are exceeding fat and of nature loath to rise when they are laid, which is always from five o'clock at night until five o'clock in the morning, between which time you may easily kill them; but after they be on foot they are very wild and rest not in one place but live together in herds, in some 500, as it happeneth, more or less. And these red sheep are most about the Bay of Saint Marie [probably mouth of St. Mary's River, Florida-Georgia border], as this examinate guesseth.

There are bears both black and white. There are wolves. The foxes have their skins more grizzled than ours in England. There are conies both white and red and gray, in every place great plenty.

This examinate did also see in those countries a monstrous beast twice as big as an horse and in proportion like to an horse, both in mane, hoof and hair, and neighing, saving it was small toward the lower parts like a greyhound. These beasts hath two teeth or horns of a foot long growing straight forth by their nostrils; they are natural enemies to the horse.

He did also see in that country both elephants and ounces [leopards]. He did also see one other strange beast bigger than a bear; he had neither head nor neck; his eyes and mouth were in his breast. This beast is very ugly to behold and cowardly of kind. It beareth a very fine skin like a rat, full of silver hairs [probably a sea lion].

There are in those countries abundance of russet parrots, but very few green. There are also birds of all sorts as we have, and many strange birds to this examinate unknown. There are great plenty of guinea hens, which are tame birds and proper to the inhabitants, as big as geese, very black of color, having feathers like down. There is also a bird called a flamingo, whose feathers are very red, and is bigger than a goose, billed like a shovel, and is very good meat.

There is also another kind of fowl in that country which hunteth the rivers near unto the islands. They are of the shape and bigness of a goose but their wings are covered with small yellow feathers and cannot fly. You may drive them before you like sheep. They are exceeding fat and very delicate meat. They have white heads, and therefore the countrymen call them penguins [really auks] (which seemeth to be a Welsh name, and they have also in use divers other Welsh words, a matter worthy the noting).

There is also a very strange bird thrice as big as an eagle, very beautiful to behold; his feathers are more orient [lustrous] than a peacock's feathers, his eyes are glittering as an hawk's eyes but as great as a man's eyes, his head and thigh as big as a man's head and thigh. It hath a crest and tuft of feathers of sundry colors on the top of the head like a lapwing hanging backward, his beak and talons in proportion like eagles but very huge and large.

Touching tempests and other strange monstrous things in those parts, this examinate saith that he hath seen it lighten [lightning] and thunder in summer season by the space of four-and-twenty hours together, the cause whereof he judgeth to be the heat of the climate.

He farther saith that there is a cloud sometime of the year seen in the air which commonly turneth to great tempests. And that sometimes of the year there are great winds in manner of whirlwinds. . . .

He saith further that he and his two fellows, namely, Richard Browne and Richard Twide, went into a poor man's house and there they did see the said Colluchio or devil with very great eyes like a black calf. Upon the sight whereof Browne said, "There is the Devil," and thereupon he blessed himself in the name of the Father, and of the Son, and of the Holy Ghost. And Twide said very vehemently, "I defy thee and all thy works." And presently the Colluchio shrank away in a stealing manner forth of the doors and was seen no more unto them.

Also they passed over many great rivers in those countries in canoes or boats. Some four, some six, some eight, some ten miles over, whereof one was so large that they could scarce cross the same in four-and-twenty hours.

Also he saith that in the same country the people have instruments of music made of a piece of a cane almost a foot long, being open at both ends, which, sitting down, they smite upon their thighs and one of their hands, making a pleasant kind of sound. And they do use another kind of instrument like a tabor, covered with a white skin somewhat like parchment. This examinate can very well describe their gestures, dancing, and songs.

After long travail, the aforesaid David Ingram with his two companions, Browne and Twide, came to the head of a river called Garinda [or Guinda] which is 60 leagues west from Cape Breton, where they understood by the people of that country of the arrival of a Christian. Whereupon they made their repair to the seaside and there found a French captain named Monsieur Champagne, who took them into his ship and brought them unto Newhaven [possibly Nijerhaven or Nieupoort in Flanders] and from thence they were transported into England, *anno Domini* 1569.

This Monsieur Champagne, with divers of his company, was brought into that village of Bariniah about 20 miles up into the country of the said examinate and his two companions, by whose means he had a trade with the people of divers sorts of fine furs and of great red leaves of trees almost a yard long and about a foot broad, which he thinketh are good for dyeing.

Also the said Monsieur Champagne had there, for exchange of trifling wares, a good quantity of rude and wrought silver.

He saith further that divers of the said Frenchmen which

were in the said ship called the *Gargarine* are yet living in Honfleur upon the coast of France, as he thinketh, for he did speak with some of them within these three years.

About a fortnight after their coming from Newhaven into England, this said examinate and his two companions came to Master John Hawkins, who had set them on shore upon the Bay of Mexico, and unto each of them he gave a reward.

Richard Browne, his companion, was slain about five years past in the *Elizabeth* of Master Cockins of London; and Richard Twide, his other companion, died at Ratcliff in John Sherwood's house there, about three years past. . . .

Also the said David Ingram, traveling toward the north, found the main sea upon the north side of America and traveled in the sight thereof the space of two whole days, where the people signified unto him that they had seen ships on that coast and did draw upon the ground the shape and figure of ships and of their sails and flags. Which thing especially proveth the passage of the northwest and is agreeable to the experience of Vásquez de Coronado, which found a ship of China or Cataia upon the northwest of America.

Also the said examinate saith that there is an island called Corrafau [Curaçao], and there are in it 5,000 or 6,000 Indians at the least, and all those are governed by one only Negro, who is but a slave to a Spaniard. And moreover, the Spaniards will send but one of their slaves with 100 or 200 of the Indians when they go to gather gold in the rivers descending from the mountains. And when they shall be absent by the space of 20 or 30 days at the least, every one of the Indians will nevertheless obey all the slave's commandments with as great reverence as if he were their natural king, although there be never a Christian near them by the space of 100 or 200 miles; which argueth the great obedience of those people and how easily they may be governed when they be once conquered.

French Reports of the Florida Tragedy

[*René de Laudonnière, a leader in the French effort to establish colonies in Florida in the 1560s, was one of the few Frenchmen to escape the massacre by Menéndez' Spanish soldiers*

*in September and October of 1565. Taken to England, he
eventually got back to France, found himself discredited and
wrote an account of the Florida venture as a defense of his
own actions. The manuscript was lost for nearly 20 years, until
Richard Hakluyt found it while he was serving with the English
ambassador in Paris. He persuaded a Frenchman, Martin
Basanier, to edit it for publication and he himself made an
English translation, with a dedication to Sir Walter Raleigh,
printed in London in 1587. Hakluyt thought Laudonnière's
work contained information that might be useful to future
English colonizers in North America. At the end of Laudonnière's account of Florida, the editor, Basanier, tacked on a
brief account of Dominique de Gourgues' punitive expedition
against the Spaniards in Florida. This Hakluyt also included
in his translation. Excerpts from Hakluyt follow:]*

The third voyage of the Frenchmen made by Captain John
Ribaut unto Florida.

As I was thus occupied in these conferences, the wind and
the tide served well to set sail, which was the eight-and-twentieth
of August [1565], at which instant Captain Vasseur, which
commanded in one of my ships, and Captain Verdier, which
was chief in the other, now ready to go forth began to descry
certain sails at sea, whereof they advertised me with diligence.
Whereupon I appointed to arm forth a boat in good order to
go to descry and know what they were. I sent also to the sentinels, which I caused to be kept on a little knap [knoll], to cause
certain men to climb up to the top of the highest trees the
better to discover them. They descried the great boat of the
ships, which as yet they could not perfectly discern, which as
far as they could judge seemed to chase my boat, which by this
time was past the bar of the river; so that we could not
possibly judge whether they were enemies which would have
carried her away with them. . . . Upon this doubt I put my
men in order and in such array as though they had been enemies.
And indeed I had great occasion to mistrust the same: for my
boat came unto their ship about two of the clock in the
afternoon, and sent me no news all that day long to put me out
of doubt who they should be.

The next day in the morning, about eight or nine of the

clock, I saw seven boats (among which mine own was one) full of soldiers enter into the river, having every man his harquebus, and morion [helmet] on his head, which marched all in battle along the cliffs where my sentinels were, to whom they would make no kind of answer, notwithstanding all the demands that were made unto them; insomuch as one of my soldiers was constrained to bestow a shot at them, without doing hurt nevertheless to any of them by reason of the distance between him and the boats. The report hereof being made unto me, I placed each of my men in his quarter, with full deliberation to defend ourselves if they had been enemies, as in truth we thought them to have been. Likewise I caused the two small field pieces which I had left me to be trimmed, in such sort as, if in approaching to the fort they had not cried that it was Captain Ribaut, I had not failed to have discharged the same upon them. Afterward I understood that the cause why they entered in this manner proceeded of the false reports which had been made unto my Lord Admiral by those which were returned into France in the first ships. For they had put in his head that I played the lord and king, and that I would hardly suffer that any other save myself should enter in thither to govern there. . . .

Being therefore advertised that it was Captain Ribaut, I went forth of the fort to go to meet him; and to do him all the honor I could by any means, I caused him to be welcomed with the artillery and a gentle volley of my shot, whereunto he answered with his. Afterward being come on shore and received honorably with joy, I brought him to my lodging, rejoicing not a little because that in this company I knew a good number of my friends, which I entreated in the best sort that I was able with such victuals as I could get in the country and that small store which I had left me, with that which I had of the English general [John Hawkins]. . . .

The next day the Indians came in from all parts to know what people these were; to whom I signified that this was he which in the year 1562 arrived in this country and erected the pillar which stood at the entry of the river. Some of them knew him; for in truth he was easy to be known by reason of the great beard which he wore. He received many presents of them which were of the villages near adjoining, among whom there were some that he had not yet forgotten. . . . I advertised them that he was sent thither by the king of France to remain in my room, and that I was sent for. . . . About the time of these conferences, comings and goings of the kings of the country, being weakened with my former travail and fallen into a melancholy upon the false reports that had been made of me, I fell into a great continual fever which held me eight or nine days. During which time Captain Ribaut caused his victuals to be brought on shore, and bestowed the most part thereof in the house which my lieutenant had built about 200 paces without the fort; which he did to the end they might be the better defended from the weather, and likewise to the intent that the meal might be nearer to the bakehouse, which I had built of purpose in that place the better to avoid the danger of the fire, as I said before. But lo, how oftentimes misfortune doth search and pursue us, even then when we think to be at rest! Lo, see what happened after that Captain Ribaut had brought up three of his small ships into the river, which was the fourth of September!

Six great Spanish ships arrived in the road where four of our greatest ships remained, which cast anchor, assuring our men of good amity. They asked how the chief captain of the enterprise did, and called them all by their names and surnames. I report me to you if it could be otherwise but these men before they went out of Spain must needs be informed of the enterprise and of those that were to execute the same. About the break of day they began to make toward our men. But our men, which trusted them never a deal, had hoisted their sails by night, being ready to cut the strings that tied them. Wherefore, perceiving that this making toward our men of the Spaniards was not to do them any pleasure, and knowing well that their furniture was too small to make head against them because that the most part of their men were on shore, they cut their cables, left their anchors, and set sail.

The Spaniards, seeing themselves discovered, lent them certain volleys of their great ordnance, made sail after them, and chased them all day long; but our men got way of them still toward the sea. And the Spaniards, seeing they could not reach them, by reason that the French ships were better of sail than theirs and also because they would not leave the coast, turned back and went on shore in the River Seloy [Seloy was an Indian village near St. Augustine harbor] which we call the River of Dolphins [St. Augustine harbor], eight or ten leagues distant from the place where we were. Our men therefore, finding themselves better of sail than they, followed them to descry what they did, which after they had done, they returned unto the River of May [St. Johns River] where Captain Ribaut, having descried them, embarked himself in a great boat to know what news they had. Being at the entry of the river, he met with the boat of Captain Couset's ship, wherein there was a good number of men which made relation unto him of all the Spaniards' doings and how the great ship named the *Trinity* had kept the sea and she was not returned with them. They told him moreover that they had seen three Spanish ships enter into the River of Dolphins, and the other three remained in the road; farther, that they had put their soldiers, their victuals, and munition on land.

After he understood these news he returned to the fortress and came to my chamber where I was sick. And there in the presence of the captains . . . he propounded that it was necessary for the king's service to embark himself with all his forces and, with the three ships that were in the road, to seek the Spanish fleet; whereupon he asked our advice. I first replied and showed unto him the consequence of such an enterprise, advertising him among other things of the perilous flaws of winds that rise on this coast, and that if it chanced that he were driven from the shore it would be very hard for him to recover it again; that in the meanwhile they which should stay in the fort should be in fear and danger. [Two of] the captains . . . declared unto him farther that they thought it not good to put any such enterprise in execution, that it was far better to keep the land and do their best endeavor to fortify themselves; and that after that the *Trinity* (which was the principal ship) were returned there would be much more likelihood to enterprise this voyage. This notwithstanding, he resolved to undertake it; and that which more is, after[ward] he understood by King Emola, one of our neighbors which arrived upon the handling of these matters, that the Spaniards in great numbers were gone on shore, which had taken possession of the houses of Seloy, in the most part whereof they had placed their Negroes which they had brought to labor, and also lodged themselves and had cast divers trenches about them.

Thus for the considerations which he had, and doubting [suspecting] (as he might well do) that the Spaniards would encamp themselves there to molest us and in the end to chase us out of the country, he resolved and continued in his embarkment, caused a proclamation to be made that all soldiers that were under his charge should presently with their weapons embark them, and that his two ensigns should march; which was put in execution. He came into my chamber and prayed me to lend him my lieutenant, mine ensign, and my sergeant, and to let all my good soldiers which I had go with him, which I denied him, because, myself being sick, there was no man to stay in the fort. . . . Then he told me that he could do no less than to continue this enterprise, and that in the letter which he had received from my Lord Admiral there was a postscript, which he showed me written in these words: "Captain John Ribaut: As I was enclosing up this letter I received certain advice that Don Pedro Melendes [Menéndez] departeth from Spain to go to the coast of New France; see that you suffer him not to encroach upon you, no more than he would that you should encroach upon him." "You see," quoth he, "the charge that I have, and I leave it unto yourself to judge if you could do any less in this case, considering the certain advertisement that we have that they are already on land and will invade us." This stopped my mouth. Thus therefore confirmed, or rather obstinate, in this enterprise . . . he embarked himself the eight of September and took mine ensign and eight-and-thirty of my men away with him. . . .

The very day that he departed, which was the tenth of September, there rose so great a tempest, accompanied with such storms, that the Indians themselves assured me that it was the worst weather that ever was seen on the coast. Whereupon two or three days after, fearing lest our ships might be in some distress, I sent for Monsieur du Luys unto me to take order to assemble the rest of our people to declare unto them what need we had to fortify ourselves. . . . And if any misfortune were fallen unto our men which were at sea, we ought to make a full account with ourselves that we were to endure many great miseries, being in so small number and so many ways afflicted as we were. Thus everyone promised me to take pains. And therefore considering that their proportion of victuals was small, and that so continuing they would not be able to do any great work, I augmented their allowance, although . . . I was so far from having means to do so that the Captain himself took two of my boats wherein the rest of the meal was which was left me of the biscuits which I caused to be made to return into France; so that if I should say that I received more favor at the hands of the Englishmen, being strangers unto me, I should say but a truth.

We began therefore to fortify ourselves and to repair . . . the palissado with the planks which I caused to be taken off the ship which I had builded. Nevertheless, notwithstanding all our diligence and travail, we were never able fully to repair it by reason of the storms which commonly did us so great annoy that we could not finish our enclosure. Perceiving myself in such extremity, I took a muster of the men which Captain Ribaut had left me, to see if there were any that wanted weapon; I found nine or ten of them wherof not past two or three had ever drawn sword out of a scabbard, as I think. . . . Of the nine there were four but young striplings which served Captain Ribaut and kept his dogs; the fifth was a cook; among those that were without the fort, and which were of the foresaid company of Captain Ribaut, there was a carpenter of threescore years old, one a beer-brewer, one old crossbow maker, two shoemakers, and four or five men that had their wives, a player on the virginals, two servants of Monsieur du Luys, one of Monsieur de Beauhaire, one of Monsieur de la Grange, and about fourscore and five or six in all, counting as well lackeys as women and children. . . .

The night between the 19th and 20th of September La Vigne kept watch with his company, wherein he used all endeavor although it rained without ceasing. When the day was therefore come, and that he saw that it rained still worse than it did before, he pitied the sentinels so too moiled and wet; and thinking the Spaniards would not have come in such a strange time, he let them depart, and, to say the truth, he went himself unto his lodging. In the meanwhile one which had something to do without the fort, and my trumpet, which went up unto the rampart, perceived a troop of Spaniards which came down from a little knap [knoll]. Where incontinently they began to cry alarm, and the trumpeter also. Which as soon as ever I understood, forthwith I issued out with my target [shield] and sword in my hand and got me into the midst of the court, where I began to cry upon my soldiers. Some of them which were of the forward sort went toward the breach, which was on the south side and where the munitions of the artillery lay, where they were repulsed and slain. By the selfsame place two [Spanish] ensigns entered, which immediately were planted on the walls. Two other ensigns also entered on the other side toward the west where there was another breach; and those which were lodged in this quarter, and which showed themselves, were likewise defeated. As I went to succor them which were defending the breach on the southwest side, I encountered by chance a great company of Spaniards, which had already repulsed our men and were now entered, which drave me back unto the court of the fort. Being there I espied with them one called Francis Jean, which was one of the mariners which stole away my barks and had guided and conducted the Spaniards thither. As soon as he saw me he began to say, "This is the captain."

This troop was led by a captain whose name, as I think, was Don Pedro Melendes; these made certain pushes at me with their pikes which landed on my target. But perceiving that I was not able to withstand so great a company, and that the court was already won and their ensigns planted on the ramparts, and that I had never a man about me saving one only whose name was Bartholomew, I entered into the yard of my lodging, into which they followed me; and had it not been for a tent that was set up, I had been taken. But the Spaniards which followed me were occupied in cutting of the cords of the tent, and in the meanwhile I saved myself by the breach which was on the west side near unto my lieutenant's lodging and got away into the woods, where I found certain of my men which were escaped, of which number there were three or four which were sore hurt. . . . Some would needs go to a little village which was in the woods; the rest followed me through the reeds in the water, where, being able to go no farther by reason of my sickness which I had, I sent two of my men which were with me, which could swim well, unto the ships to advertise them of that which had happened and to send them word to come and help me. They were not able that day to get unto the ships . . . so I was constrained to stand in the water up to the shoulders all that night long, with one of my men which would never forsake me. . . .

After I was come into the ship called the *Greyhound*, Captain James Ribaut and Captain Valvot came to see me; and there we concluded to return into France. . . . And because I lacked a pilot, I prayed James Ribaut that he would grant me one of the four men that he had in his ship, which I should name unto him, to serve me for a pilot. He promised to give me them, which nevertheless he did not at the instant when we were ready to depart . . . declaring that it was for the King's service. I was constrained to leave the ship behind me which I had bought of the English captain [Hawkins] because I wanted [needed] men to bring her away. . . .

The 25 of September we set sails to return into France, and Captain James Ribaut and I kept company all that day and the next until three or four a clock in the afternoon; but because his ship was better at bowline than ours, he kept him to the wind and left us the same day. Thus we continued our voyage, wherein we had marvelous flaws [gusts] of wind. . . .

I will plainly say one thing: that the long delay that Captain John [*sic*] Ribaut used in his embarking and the 15 days that he spent in roving along the coast of Florida before he came to our Fort Caroline were the cause of the loss that we sustained. For he discovered the coast the 14 of August, and spent the time in going from river to river which had been sufficient for him to have discharged his ships in and for me to have embarked myself to return into France. I wot well that all that he did was upon a good intent; yet in mine opinion he should have had more regard unto his charge than to the devices of his own brain, which sometimes he printed in his head so deeply that it was very hard to put them out. Which also turned to his utter undoing: for he was no sooner departed from us but a tempest took him which in fine wracked him upon the coast, where all his ships were cast away, and he with much ado escaped drowning to fall into their hands which cruelly massacred him and all his company.

The Fourth Voyage of the Frenchmen into Florida, under
the Conduct of Captain Gourgues, in the Year 1567.

Captain Gourgues, a gentleman born in the country near
unto Bordeaux, incited with a desire of revenge to repair the
honor of his nation, borrowed of his friends and sold part of
his own goods to set forth and furnish three ships of indifferent
burden with all things necessary, having in them 150 soldiers
and fourscore chosen mariners. . . . He set forth the 22 of
August 1567. And having endured contrary winds and storms
for a season, at length he arrived and went on shore in the
isle of Cuba. From thence he passed to the Cape of Saint
Anthony at the end of the isle of Cuba, about 200 leagues
distant from Florida, where the captain disclosed unto them
his intention, which hitherto he had concealed from them,
praying and exhorting them not to leave him being so near
the enemy, so well furnished, and in such a cause. Which they
all sware unto him, and that with such courage that they would
not stay the full moon to pass the channel of Bahama, but
speedily discovered Florida, where the Spaniards saluted them
with two cannon shot from their fort, supposing that they had
been of their nation. And Gourgues saluted them again to
entertain them in this error that he might surprise them at
more advantage, yet sailing by them and making as though he
went to some other place until he had sailed out of sight of
the place. So that, about evening, he landed 15 leagues from
the fort at the mouth of the River Tacatacouru, which the
Frenchmen called Seine [St. Mary's Sound, border of Florida
and Georgia] because they thought it to be like Seine in France.
    Afterward perceiving the shore to be covered with savages
with their bows and arrows . . . he sent his trumpeter to assure them that they were come thither for none other end
but to renew the amity and ancient league of the French with
them. The trumpeter did his message so well (by reason he
had been there before under Laudonnière) that he brought back
from King Satouriova, the greatest of all the other kings, a kid
and other meat to refresh us, besides the offer of his friendship
and amity. Afterward they retired, dancing in sign of joy,
to advertise all the king's, Satouriova's, kinsmen to repair

thither the next day to make a league of amity with the Frenchmen. . . .

Satouriova, going to meet him, caused him to sit on his right hand in a seat of wood of lentiscus [mastic] covered with moss made of purpose like unto his own. Then two of the eldest of the company pulled up the brambles and other weeds which were before them, and after they had made the place very clean they all sat round about them on the ground.

Afterward, Gourgues being about to speak, Satouriova prevented him, declaring at large unto him the incredible wrongs and continual outrages that all the savages, their wives and children, had received of the Spaniards since their coming into the country and massacring of the Frenchmen, with their continual desire if we would assist them thoroughly to revenge so shameful a treason, as well as their own particular griefs, for the firm good will they always had borne unto the Frenchmen. . . .

In the meantime, Gourgues very narrowly examined Peter de Bré, born in Newhaven, which being but a young stripling escaped out of the fort into the woods while the Spaniards murdered the rest of the French and was afterward brought up with Satouriova, which at that time bestowed him on our General; whose [de Bré's] advice stood him in great stead. Whereupon he sent to discover the fort and the estate of the enemies by certain of his men, being guided by Olotacara, Satouriova's nephew, which he had given him for this purpose. . . .

Now he had learned that the Spaniards were 400 strong, divided into three forts builded and flanked and well fortified upon the River of May, the great fort especially, begun by the French and afterward repaired by them; upon the most dangerous and principal landing place whereof, two leagues lower and nearer toward the river's mouth, they had made two smaller forts, which were defended . . . with six score soldiers, good store of artillery, and other munition which they had in the same. . . .

With a French courage they prepared themselves to the assault on the Sunday eve next after Easter day, in April, 1568. . . . Being descried as they came, holding down their heads, within 200 paces from the fort, the gunner being upon the terrace of the fort, after he had cried, "Arm! Arm! These be Frenchmen!", discharged twice upon them a culverin [type of cannon] whereon the arms of France were graven, which had been taken from Laudonnière. But as he went about to charge it the third time, Olotocara, which had not learned to keep his rank, or rather moved with rage, leapt on the platform and thrust him through the body with his pike and slew him. Whereupon Gourgues advanced forward . . . and so hemmed them in between him and his lieutenant that, of threescore, there escaped not a man saving only 15 reserved unto the same death which they had put the French unto. The Spaniards of the other fort in the meanwhile ceased not to play with their ordnance, which much annoyed the assailants; although to answer them they had by this [time] placed and oftentimes pointed the four pieces found in the first fort. . . .

To conclude, they all there ended their days saving 15 of those which were reserved to be executed for the example of others. Whereupon Captain Gourgues, having caused all that he found in the second fort to be transported unto the first, where he meant to strengthen himself to take resolution against the great fort, the state whereof he did not understand: in fine, a sergeant of a band, one of the prisoners, assured him that they might be there very near 300 well furnished under a brave governor, which had fortified there, attending further succors. Thus having obtained [learned] of him the platform, the height, the fortification, and passages unto it, and having prepared eight good ladders, and raised all the country against the Spaniard that he neither might have news nor succors, nor retract on any side, he determined to march forward. . . .

The fort, when it was taken, was found well provided of all necessaries. . . . The rest of the Spaniards, being led away prisoners with the others, after that the General had showed them the wrong which they had done without occasion to all the French nation, were all hanged on the boughs of the same trees whereon the French hung; of which number five were hanged by one Spaniard, which, perceiving himself in the like miserable estate, confessed his fault and the just judgment which God had brought upon him. But instead of the writing which Pedro Melendes had hanged over them, importing these words in Spanish: "I do not this as unto Frenchmen, but as unto Lutherans," Gourgues caused to be imprinted with a searing iron in a table of firewood: "I do not this as unto Spaniards, nor as unto mariners, but as unto traitors, robbers, and murderers." . . .

The 3rd of May, 1568 all things were made ready, the rendezvous appointed, and the anchors weighed to set sail—so prosperously that in 17 days they ran 1,100 leagues; continuing which course they arrived at Rochelle the 6th of June, the four-and-thirtieth day after their departure from the River of May, having lost but a small pinnace and eight men in it, with a few gentlemen and others which were slain in the assaulting of the forts. After the cheer and good entertainment which he received of those of Rochelle, he sailed to Bordeaux to inform Monsieur Monluc of the things above mentioned. . . . The Catholic king, being afterward informed that Gourgues could not easily be taken, offered a great sum of money to him that could bring him his head, praying moreover King Charles to do justice on him as of the author of so bloody an act contrary to their alliance and good league of friendship. Insomuch as, coming to Paris to present himself unto the King to signify unto him the success of his voyage and the means which he had to subdue this whole country unto his obedience (wherein he offered to employ his life and all his goods), he found his entertainment and answer so contrary to his expectation that, in fine, he was constrained to hide himself a long space in the court of Roanne [Rouen] about the year 1570.

VIII

Drake Sails Around the World
and Discovers California

THE disaster at San Juan de Ulúa in 1568 left both Hawkins and Drake bitter and determined to seek revenge against the Spaniards. Hawkins proposed a voyage of reprisal to recoup his losses, but the queen would not let him sail. The political situation between Spain and England had worsened, and in case of overt hostilities in the English Channel, Hawkins would be needed at home. But Francis Drake, a young man in his late twenties who had not yet won such a reputation that his services were deemed essential, sailed in late 1570 on a voyage of reconnaissance to the Isthmus of Panama. It was common knowledge that the Spaniards transported the treasure of Peru by mule train across the isthmus from Panama City to the Atlantic port of Nombre de Dios. Drake also knew that runaway Negro slaves called "Cimaroons" inhabited the hills of the isthmus. These Cimaroons, Drake believed, some 2,000 or 3,000 in number, might be potential allies against the Spaniards if he could make contact with them.

With one little ship, the *Swan* of 25 tons, and a handful of stout young sailors, Drake explored the Panamanian coastline, found a secret harbor called Port Pheasant, where he buried supplies against his return, captured some Spanish shipping and held talks with the Cimaroons. From captured Spaniards and from the Cimaroons he learned the schedules of the treasure shipments and acquired detailed plans of the port of Nombre de Dios. Having gained a thorough knowledge of the treasure traffic, he returned to England in 1571 determined to organize an expedition strong enough to capture Nombre de Dios and the gold and silver of Peru.

Drake, like Hawkins, planned his ventures with care. Utilizing information gathered on the Isthmus of Panama, he spent the winter of 1571 organizing another expedition, this time for action rather than reconnaissance. In the spring of 1572 he sailed from Plymouth with two vessels, the *Swan* and the *Pasco* of 70 tons. His crew of 73 men, nearly all under thirty, included his two brothers, John and Joseph. Eager, hardy, well trained and courageous, these young sailors could be expected to give a good account of themselves against any enemy they might encounter.

Drake's immediate destination was the secret harbor of Port Pheasant, where he assembled three pinnaces, timbers for which he had brought with him. With these light vessels, drawing little water, his men could row to attack a becalmed ship or approach a town in the night without being discovered. An attack on Nombre de Dios, which soon followed, proved a disappointment, for Drake was wounded in the leg and his men carried him back to the pinnaces without pillaging the town, though they observed stacks of silver bars. The surprise attack had failed and Drake had to employ his men elsewhere. For the next year he sailed up and down the coast from one secret anchorage to another, capturing an occasional Spanish ship. After two unsuccessful efforts to surprise the mule trains bringing treasure to Nombre de Dios, Drake had to wait for the Spaniards to become less watchful. Finally in the summer of 1573, with the aid of a French corsair who had joined the party, they captured a treasure train and divided the spoils equally between the English and the French; each group received gold and silver worth something like £500,000 in modern money. Drake's venture had paid off, but he had lost both of his brothers, one by fever and the other from battle wounds. On Sunday, August 9, 1573, he reached Plymouth, and the news of his exploit brought him instant fame. Henceforth Francis Drake was a name cherished by the English and feared by the Spaniards. This latest foray against Spain, however, was an embarrassment to Queen Elizabeth's government, for she was trying to make peace with Philip II. Consequently Drake had to lie low for a time and could not immediately capitalize upon his reputation as a skilled adversary of the Spaniards in the Caribbean.

But by 1577 the political climate was again changing. The anti-Spanish party in the government was gaining influence, and the queen was ready to take a bolder stand against Philip. A group around the queen that included the Earl of Leicester, Sir Humphrey Gilbert, Sir Walter Raleigh and Sir Francis Walsingham believed that England must prevent Spain's monopolizing all of the New World. A few already were talking of the desirability of establishing colonies overseas and of seizing bases that could threaten Spain's communications with her overseas colonies. Richard Hakluyt, the lawyer, and his nephew Richard Hakluyt, the preacher, were constantly urging activity overseas as a check to Spanish domination. The younger Hakluyt, the preacher, made overseas expansion his religion, and his great compilation of voyages was designed to further this enterprise.

Francis Drake came to the notice of Sir Francis Walsingham, principal secretary to the queen, and Walsingham arranged for Drake to see Her Majesty. Drake had a plan that appealed to both Walsingham and Queen Elizabeth, but the precise details of his scheme are still a matter of debate. Later Drake asserted that the queen told him: "I would gladly be revenged on the King of Spain for divers injuries that I have received." [1] Obviously Queen Elizabeth, Drake and Walsingham agreed upon some secret strategy, for Drake also declared that she warned him that "of all men my Lord Treasurer [Lord Burghley] is not to know it." [2] Burghley opposed overt action against Spain that might bring on war, and clearly Drake's proposed expedition was such that Burghley might regard it as dangerous to peace. Drake planned to sail to the coast of South America, reconnoiter that coastline to the Strait of Magellan, sail through the Strait and explore the region beyond. At this point controversy begins about his ultimate purposes because his surviving instructions are ambiguous, and contemporary statements are subject to different interpretations. Drake's objectives, as set forth by various writers, may be summarized as follows: a voyage of reprisal authorized by the queen against Spanish

[1] Quoted in James A. Williamson, *Sir Francis Drake* (New York, 1962), p. 43.
[2] *Ibid.*, p. 44.

shipping on the west coast of America; a trading voyage to the
Spice Islands and probably to China; a voyage to explore the
Pacific coast of America with a view to colonization; an exploration of the continent of *Terra Australis,* believed to exist in the
South Sea; the discovery of the Strait of Anian, believed to lead
from the Pacific to the Northwest Passage from the Atlantic.
The most recent essay on Drake's purposes suggests that the
promoters did not intend a circumnavigation of the globe, but
that they expected him to explore the "coast of South America
from the Plate River round to that part of the coast of Chile
where Spanish occupation petered out." He was to make
contact with the American Indians "but a long-term purpose
to settle and even perhaps to conquer Spanish Peru cannot be
ruled out." [3] As in all such expeditions, the commander was
left with considerable discretion and perhaps alternate plans
in case his first did not work out.

Whatever may have been his secret instructions, Drake did
circumnavigate the world, pillage the Spaniards of wealth on
the west coast of South America, search for the Strait of Anian
to no avail, discover and claim California for the Queen of
England, trade in the Spice Islands and come home with
enormous wealth and a reputation that won him a knight-
hood.

As preparation for the voyage began, the story was given out
that Drake was to lead an expedition to Alexandria to open
the spice trade with the Turks. Five ships were fitted out: the
Pelican (later renamed the *Golden Hind*) of perhaps 120 tons;
the *Elizabeth* of some 80 tons; the *Marigold,* a smaller vessel; the
Swan, a store ship (not the one that Drake had used on an
earlier voyage); and a pinnace named the *Benedict.* After a
severe storm had turned them back for repairs, the fleet finally
cleared Plymouth on December 13, 1577. Only when they were
well out to sea did the sailors learn that Alexandria was not
their destination.

Off the African coast Drake captured two Portuguese ships
and left the pinnace *Benedict* in place of one of these vessels.
More valuable than the wine and food in the captured ships

---

[3] K. R. Andrews, "The Aims of Drake's Expedition of 1577–1580," *American
Historical Review,* LXXIII (1968), pp. 724–741. Andrews gives a useful summary
in the beginning of his essay on the various views of Drake's intentions.

was a pilot, Nuño da Silva, whom Drake took along after putting the other Portuguese ashore on the island of La Brava.

On the long voyage across the Atlantic, one of the gentlemen who had come along, Thomas Doughty, incurred Drake's suspicion that he was attempting to sabotage the expedition. Reports of Doughty's mutinous talk confirmed Drake's suspicions, and on reaching Port St. Julian, north of the Strait of Magellan, he had Doughty tried and beheaded. Before the execution, Drake ate dinner with his prisoner and took Communion with him. One curious element in Doughty's case was the belief among the mariners that he was a necromancer who could cast spells to determine the weather. On one occasion Drake forbade him to have any books except those in English, for books of magic were in Latin. He was ordered also not to write anything. The evidence suggests that Drake feared that Doughty would detach a ship, return to England and betray to Burghley the plans for the expedition.

The story of Drake's struggle to get through the Strait of Magellan and his subsequent voyage has been often told. When finally he was out in the Pacific and clear of the rocky shores of the strait, Drake found himself with only the *Pelican,* now renamed the *Golden Hind.* He had abandoned the supply ships, but the *Marigold* and the *Elizabeth,* both well armed, he hoped to take with him. The *Marigold* was lost in the stormy seas, but the *Elizabeth* under Captain John Winter sailed back through the strait and returned to England. His men had refused to sail any farther into the Pacific.

Drake made his way up the coast of Chile and Peru, taking unarmed Spanish ships and plundering towns as it pleased him. The Spaniards, convinced that no enemy could threaten them on the west coast, had no guns on their vessels, and their towns were virtually defenseless. The capture of a treasure ship nicknamed the *Cacafuego* provided a full cargo of silver and gold for the *Golden Hind.* The capture of another ship, off the coast of Nicaragua, provided him with maps and charts of the Pacific without which the remainder of his voyage to the Spice Islands would have been difficult.

But before heading across the Pacific Drake had another objective. He would discover, if possible, the Strait of Anian. Sailing north, perhaps to 48 degrees latitude, he found no entry that looked promising and came south to careen and repair his vessel. At a point on the coast of California he put into a harbor now believed to be Drake's Bay. There he repaired his ship and claimed the land in the name of the queen, calling it New Albion. Upon a post he nailed up a brass plate with an inscription to certify this claim to all comers. In 1936 a traveling salesman found a brass plate which enthusiastic California historians claimed to be the one Drake left, but later examination has cast suspicion upon its authenticity.

After the repair of the *Golden Hind,* Drake departed for the Spice Islands, which he reached after a three-month voyage. Finding the Sultan of Ternate carrying on a war against the Portuguese, who were then monopolizing the spice trade in the Moluccas, Drake made a treaty with him and loaded as much spice as he could pack into the *Golden Hind.* The overloaded vessel struck a reef and nearly foundered, but after the jettisoning of a few guns and some of the cargo, she floated free. On this occasion the chaplain, the Reverend Francis Fletcher, preached a sermon which Drake apparently thought would endanger morale. Forthwith he called the preacher before the mast and "excommunicated" him. Henceforth poor Fletcher had to wear what the chroniclers of the voyage call a "posy" reading, "Francis Fletcher, the falsest knave that liveth."

The long voyage ended on September 26, 1580, when Drake docked at Plymouth. As he approached his home port he had hailed a fisherman and asked: "Is the queen alive and well?" When assured that she was, he and his crew sailed on with "joyful minds and thankful hearts to God."

News of Drake's raids had long since reached Spain, and the report of his safe return loaded with captured treasure infuriated the Spanish government. Demands were made for its return, and war even threatened. But Queen Elizabeth as usual played a delaying game—and sequestered the treasure, for the lion's share would belong to the Crown. After six months the queen decided that she no longer needed to placate the Spanish ambassador. So she ordered Drake to bring the *Golden Hind* into the Thames and dock her at Deptford, where for many years the ship was an attraction for visitors. The news of Drake's feat and the stories his sailors told made him a popular hero. So the queen on April 4, 1581, on the deck of his own ship, dubbed Francis Drake knight. If Spain needed a signal of a changed attitude in England, the ceremony on the deck of the *Golden Hind* that April day provided it.

The best account of Drake's circumnavigation is found in a volume put together by Drake's nephew who bore his name. It was published in 1628 as *The World Encompassed by Sir Francis Drake . . . Carefully Collected out of the Notes of Master Francis Fletcher . . . and Divers Others His Followers in the Same.* An edition of this work was published by the Hakluyt Society (London, 1854). A later edition was published by Sir Richard Temple (London, 1926). Excerpts from *The World Encompassed* follow:

Drake Claims California for the Queen

From Guatulco we departed the day following, *viz.*, April 16 [1579], setting our course directly into the sea, whereon we sailed 500 leagues in longitude to get a wind, and between that and June 3, 1,400 leagues in all, till we came into 42 degrees of north latitude, where in the night following we found such alteration of heat into extreme and nipping cold that our men in general did grievously complain thereof. . . .

In 38 degrees 30 minutes we fell with a convenient and fit harbor and June 17 came to anchor therein, where we continued till the 23rd day of July following. During all which time, notwithstanding it was in the height of summer and so near the sun, yet were we continually visited with like nipping colds as we had felt before; insomuch that if violent exercises of our bodies and busy employment about our necessary labors had not sometimes compelled us to the contrary, we could very well have been contented to have kept about us still our winter clothes; yea (had our necessities suffered us), to have kept our beds; neither could we at any time, in whole 14 days together, find the air so clear as to be able to take the height of sun or star. . . .

The next day after our coming to anchor in the aforesaid harbor the people of the country showed themselves, sending off a man with great expedition to us in a canoe who, being yet but a little from the shore and a great way from our ship,

spake to us continually as he came rowing on. And at last, at
a reasonable distance staying himself, he began more solemnly
a long and tedious oration after his manner, using in the delivery thereof many gestures and signs, moving his hands,
turning his head and body many ways, and after his oration
ended, with great show of reverence and submission, returned
back to shore again. He shortly came again the second time in
like manner, and so the third time, when he brought with him
(as a present from the rest) a bunch of feathers, much like
the feathers of a black crow, very neatly and artificially gathered
upon a string and drawn together into a round bundle, being
very clean and finely cut and bearing in length an equal proportion one with another, a special cognizance (as we afterwards
observed) which they that guard their king's person wear on
their heads. With this also he brought a little basket made of
rushes and filled with an herb which they called *tabáh* [not
identified as an Indian word of the area; tobacco was not grown
there at the time]; both which, being tied to a short rod, he
cast into our boat. Our general intended to have recompensed
him immediately with many good things he would have bestowed on him, but, entering into the boat to deliver the same,
he could not be drawn to receive them by any means, save one
hat which, being cast into the water out of the ship, he took
up (refusing utterly to meddle with any other thing, though
it were upon a board put off unto him), and so presently made
his return. After which time our boat could row no way but,
wondering at us as at gods, they would follow the same with
admiration.

The third day following, *viz.*, the 21st, our ship, having received a leak at sea, was brought to anchor nearer the shore
that, her goods being landed, she might be repaired; but for
that we were to prevent any danger that might chance against
our safety, our general first of all landed his men with all necessary provision to build tents and make a fort for the defense of
ourselves and goods, and that we might under the shelter of it
with more safety (whatever should befall) end our business.
Which when the people of the country perceived us doing, as
men set on fire to war in defense of their country, in great haste
and companies, with such weapons as they had, they came down
into us, and yet with no hostile meaning or intent to hurt us,

standing, when they drew near, as men ravished in their minds with the sight of such things as they never had seen or heard of before that time, their errand being rather with submission and fear to worship us as gods than to have any war with us as with mortal men. Which thing, as it did partly show itself at that instant, so did it more and more manifest itself afterward during the whole time of our abode amongst them. At this time, being willed by signs to lay from them their bows and arrows, they did as they were directed, and so did all the rest, as they came more and more by companies unto them, growing in a little while to a great number, both of men and women.

To the intent, therefore, that this peace which they themselves so willingly sought might, without any cause of the breach thereof on our part given, be continued, and that we might with more safety and expedition end our business in quiet, our general with all his company used all means possible gently to entreat [treat] them, bestowing upon each of them liberally good and necessary things to cover their nakedness, withal signifying unto them we were no gods but men and had need of such things to cover our own shame; teaching them to use them to the same ends, for which cause also we did eat and drink in their presence, giving them to understand that without that we could not live and therefore were but men as well as they.

Notwithstanding, nothing could persuade them nor remove that opinion which they had conceived of us that we should be gods.

In recompense of those things which they had received of us, as shirts, linen cloth, etc., they bestowed upon our general and divers of our company divers things, as feathers, cauls of network, the quivers of their arrows made of fawn skins, and the very skins of beasts that their women wore upon their bodies. Having thus had their fill of this time's visiting and beholding of us, they departed with joy to their houses, which houses are digged round within the earth and have from the uppermost brims of the circle clefts of wood set up and joined close together at the top like our spires on the steeple of a church, which, being covered with earth, suffer no water to enter and are very warm. The door in the most part of them performs the office also of a chimney to let out the smoke; it's made in bigness and fashion like to an ordinary scuttle in a ship, and standing slopewise. Their beds are the hard ground, only with rushes strewed upon it, and lying round about the house have their fire in the midst, which, by reason that the house is but low vaulted, round, and close, gives a marvelous reflection to their bodies to heat the same.

Their men for the most part go naked; the women take a kind of bulrushes and, combing it after the manner of hemp, make themselves thereof a loose garment which, being knit about their middles, hangs down about their hips and so affords to them a covering of that which Nature teaches should be hidden; about their shoulders they wear also the skin of a deer with the hair upon it. They are very obedient to their husbands and exceedingly ready in all service, yet of themselves offering to do nothing without the consents or being called of the men. . . .

Against the end of three days more (the news having the while spread itself farther and, as it seemed, a great way up into the country) were assembled the greatest number of people which we could reasonably imagine to dwell within any convenient distance round about. Amongst the rest, the king himself, a man of a goodly stature and comely personage, attended with his guard of about 100 tall and warlike men, this day, *viz.*, June 26, came down to see us. . . .

They made signs to our general to have him sit down, unto whom both the king and divers others made several orations, or rather, indeed, if we had understood them, supplications, that he would take the province and kingdom into his hand and become their king and patron, making signs that they would resign unto him their right and title to the whole land and become his vassals in themselves and their posterities; which that they might make us indeed believe that it was their true meaning and intent, the king himself, with all the rest, with one consent and with great reverence, joyfully singing a song, set the crown upon his head, enriched his neck with all their chains, and offering unto him many other things, honored him by the name of *hióh* [possibly *hoípa,* meaning "chief," is intended]. Adding thereunto (as it might seem) a song and dance of triumph, because they were not only visited of the gods (for so they still judged us to be), but the great and chief God was now become their God, their king and patron, and themselves were become the only happy and blessed people in the world.

These things being so freely offered, our general thought not meet to reject or refuse the same, both for that he would not give them any cause of mistrust or disliking of him (that being the only place wherein at this present we were of necessity enforced to seek relief of many things), and chiefly for that he knew not to what good end God had brought this to pass or what honor and profit it might bring to our country in time to come.

Wherefore, in the name and to the use of Her Most Excellent Majesty, he took the scepter, crown, and dignity of the said country into his hand, wishing nothing more than that it had lain so fitly for Her Majesty to enjoy as it was now her proper own, and that the riches and treasures thereof (wherewith in the upland countries it abounds) might with as great conveniency be transported, to the enriching of her kingdom here at home, as it is in plenty to be attained there; and especially that so tractable and loving a people as they showed themselves to be might have means to have manifested their most willing obedience the more unto her, and by her means, as a mother and nurse of the Church of Christ, might by the preaching of the Gospel be brought to the right knowledge and obedience of the true and ever-living God.

The ceremonies of this resigning and receiving of the kingdom being thus performed, the common sort, both of men and women, leaving the king and his guard about him with our general, dispersed themselves among our people, taking a diligent view or survey of every man; and finding such as pleased their fancies (which commonly were the youngest of us), they, presently enclosing them about, offered their sacrifices unto them, crying out with lamentable shrieks and moans, weeping and scratching and tearing their very flesh off their faces with their nails; neither were it the women alone which did this, but even old men, roaring and crying out, were as violent as the women were. . . .

After that our necessary businesses were well dispatched, our general, with his gentlemen and many of his company, made a journey up into the land to see the manner of their dwelling and to be the better acquainted with the nature and commodities of the country. Their houses were all such as we have formerly described and, being many of them in one place, made several villages here and there. The inland we found to be far different from the shore, a goodly country and fruitful soil, stored with many blessings fit for the use of man. Infinite was the company of very large and fat deer which there we saw by thousands, as we supposed, in a herd; besides a multitude of a strange kind of conies by far exceeding them in number. Their heads and bodies, in which they resemble other conies, are but small, his tail, like the tail of a rat, exceeding long, and his feet like the paws of a want or mole. Under his chin, on either side, he hath a bag into which he gathereth his meat when he hath filled his belly abroad, that he may with it either feed his young or feed himself when he lists not to travel from his burrow. The people eat their bodies and make great account of their skins, for their king's holiday's coat was made of them.

This country our general named Albion, and that for two causes: the one in respect of the white banks and cliffs which lie toward the sea; the other that it might have some affinity, even in name also, with our own country, which was sometime so called.

Before we went from thence, our general caused to be set up a monument of our being there, as also of Her Majesty's and successors' right and title to that kingdom; namely, a plate of brass, fast nailed to a great and firm post, whereon is engraven Her Grace's name and the day and year of our arrival there and of the free giving up of the province and kingdom, both by the king and people, into Her Majesty's hands, together with Her Highness' picture and arms in a piece of sixpence current English money, showing itself by a hole made of purpose through the plate. Underneath was likewise engraven the name of our general, etc.

The Spaniards never had any dealing or so much as set a foot in this country, the utmost of their discoveries reaching only to many degrees southward of this place. . . .

Drake Exhorts Sailors and Gentlemen
to Work Together

[*One of the legacies of this remarkable voyage was "Drake's Sermon," preached to the ship's company on a Sunday following the execution of Thomas Doughty. Magellan's Strait lay ahead, and grumbling persisted among the crew over the prospect of a voyage into unknown waters. Drake's words on this occasion have become a classic statement of naval discipline and are indicative of Drake's capacity for leadership. The "sermon" was recorded in the narrative of John Cooke entitled "For Francis Drake." It is printed as Appendix IV of W. S. W. Vaux's edition of* The World Encompassed, *The Hakluyt Society (London, 1854). An excerpt follows:*]

"Nay, soft, Master Fletcher," quoth he, "I must preach this day myself, although I have small skill in preaching. Well, be all the company here, yea or not?" Answer was made that they were all there. Then commanded he every ship's company severally to stand together, which was also done. Then said he:

"My masters, I am a very bad orator, for my bringing up hath not been in learning; but whatso I shall here speak, let any man take good notice of what I shall say, and let him write it down; for I will speak nothing but I will answer it in England, yea, and before Her Majesty; and I have it here already set down." But whether it were in his book, as he made mention of, I know not, but this was the effect of and very near the words:

"Thus it is, my masters, that we are very far from our country and friends; we are compassed in on every side with our enemies; wherefore we are not to make small reckoning of a man, for we cannot have a man if we would give for him £10,000. Wherefore we must have these mutinies and discords that are grown amongst us redressed. For by the life of God it doth even take my wits from me to think on it: here is such controversy between the sailors and the gentlemen, and such stomaching between the gentlemen and sailors that it doth even make me mad to hear it. But, my masters, I must have it left. For I must have the gentleman to haul and draw with the mariner, and the mariner with the gentleman.

"What, let us show ourselves all to be of a company, and let us not give occasion to the enemy to rejoice at our decay and overthrow. I would know him that would refuse to set his hand to a rope, but I know there is not any such here. And as gentlemen are very necessary for government's sake in the voyage, so have I shipped them for that, and to some farther intent. And yet though I know sailors to be the most envious people of the world, and so unruly without government, yet may not I be without them.

"Also, if there be any here willing to return home, let me understand of them and here is the *Marigold,* a ship that I can very well spare. I will furnish her to such as will return with the most credit I can give them, either to my letters or any way else. But let them take heed that they go homeward, for if I find them in my way I will surely sink them. Therefore you shall have time to consider hereof until tomorrow, for by my troth I must needs be plain with you. I have taken that in hand that I know not in the world how to go through withal. It passeth my capacity; it hath even bereaved me of my wits to think on it."

IX

Beginning the Search for the Northwest Passage

DURING the last half of the sixteenth century expansionists in England became increasingly eager to develop
trade with the Orient that might in time rival Portugal's.
Furthermore, knowledge of the immense wealth pouring into
Spain from Mexico and Peru stirred Englishmen to seek a share
of this golden stream. If Cortés and Pizarro had found vast
hoards of gold and silver, who knew but that English explorers
might do the same?

So long as England was nominally at peace with Spain, the
government could not officially encourage English venturers to
poach on Spanish territory. But a region in North America,
discovered by John Cabot and claimed by him for King Henry
VII of England, lay open to exploration and possible exploitation. What might be even more important, a passage by the
northwest might prove a shorter route to China and India than
any yet discovered. A round trip by the Portuguese via the
Cape of Good Hope to India sometimes required three years,
and storms off Africa took a terrible toll of shipping. The
route to Asia by way of the Strait of Magellan was also long
and hazardous. Though the Muscovy Company had tried to
find a northeast passage to Asia around the top of Russia,
Arctic ice had blocked the way. If Englishmen could find the
fabled Northwest Passage, their fortunes would be made. In
the year 1576 a search began that ended only in our own time.

One of the first Englishmen to propagandize for the Northwest Passage was Sir Humphrey Gilbert, better known for his
efforts to found colonies overseas. In 1566 he wrote a treatise to

prove the feasibility of this passage, but the document was not printed until 1576, when it served as publicity for an expedition organized by a London merchant, Michael Lok, and a mariner, Martin Frobisher. Gilbert's treatise was entitled *A Discourse of a Discovery for a New Passage to Cataia* [Cathay, or China] (1576). He argued from logic and from the authority of ancient and modern writers that a passage by the northwest was more reasonable to expect than a passage around Russia to the northeast, though previously geographers had spent much ink trying to show that a northeast passage was feasible.

The Muscovy Company, organized with Sebastian Cabot as its first governor, had sent out in 1553 an expedition commanded by Sir Hugh Willoughby as captain general and Richard Chancellor as chief pilot to discover the northeast passage to Cathay. Willoughby's two ships parted in a storm from Chancellor's vessel, but Willoughby continued his probing of the Arctic seas north of the Russian coast. Anchoring off Murmansk, his vessels froze in the ice during the winter of 1553–54, and Willoughby and all his men perished. Russian fishermen in the succeeding summer found the bodies and retrieved Willoughby's journal. Chancellor with better luck managed to reach a port on the White Sea, not far from Archangel, where he made contact with natives and eventually found his way by sledge to the court of Ivan the Terrible in Moscow. In the summer of 1554 he reached England safely. Encouraged by arrangements that Chancellor had made for trade with Russia, the company applied for a new charter from Queen Mary, which it received in 1555. The Muscovy Company by this charter was given a monopoly of trade in the northern seas.

Although the Muscovy Company had the legal right to pursue the exploration of the Northwest Passage to the exclusion of other venturers, it had shown little interest in that region. Nevertheless it did not welcome a proposal by Lok and Frobisher to fit out an expedition to seek a northwestern route to Asia. It required a letter from the Privy Council, prompted by Lord Burghley, to force the Muscovy Company to grant Frobisher a license for exploration. Not only was Lord Burghley interested, but other men in high place, including Ambrose Dudley, Earl of Warwick, brought pressure on the Muscovy

Company; Michael Lok, a member of the company, devoted full time to the new venture; Dr. John Dee, noted for his knowledge of mathematical, nautical and geographical matters, undertook to instruct Frobisher and his officers in preparation for the voyage.

A useful collection of instruments, maps and books was gathered. And two small but sturdy vessels were procured, the *Gabriel* of perhaps 20 tons, and the *Michael* of some 25 tons. In addition, Frobisher also procured a light-draft pinnace for exploring shallow inlets and rivers. Unlike many exploring expeditions, which were organized at Bristol or Plymouth, Frobisher made his preparations in London.

On June 7, 1576, the expedition sailed down the Thames. As they passed the royal palace at Greenwich, they fired a salvo and Queen Elizabeth waved to them from a window. Frobisher set a course that took him past northern Scotland, the Shetlands and the Faroes to the southern coast of Greenland. In a great storm off Greenland the pinnace was lost, and the *Michael*, which lost contact with Frobisher in the *Gabriel*, decided to return to England. Frobisher sailed on with 18 men.

Frobisher did not know that the land he had sighted, at what we know as Cape Farewell, was Greenland. He called it "Friesland," a mythical island located on one of the maps he carried, published in Venice in 1558 by Nicolo Zeno. This map, which claimed to be derived from discoveries made by two of Zeno's ancestors at the end of the fourteenth century, showed known lands but added other, nonexistent islands including "Friesland" in about the latitude of southern Greenland.

At the end of July Frobisher reached the mainland of North America near Baffin Island, and on August 11 the *Gabriel* entered what Frobisher thought was a strait between North America and Asia. Remembering Magellan's naming the strait in the south after himself, he called the passage "Frobisher's Strait." Actually it was the deep, long fjord we now call "Frobisher's Bay," which has no outlet.

Frobisher and some of his men rowed ashore, where Frobisher climbed a high hill to see if he could discern the western sea, the passage to which he believed he had found. Convinced that the waterway led to the open sea, he returned to his ship. Some trade took place with Eskimos who came out in kayaks. But a boat with five men which rowed to the mainland for further investigation of the natives never returned, and no trace of the five sailors could be found. In the hope of forcing the natives to bring back his crewmen, Frobisher tried to capture hostages, but managed to take only one, an Eskimo who was lifted out of the water, kayak and all. This captive could give no information about the lost men and he was taken back to England.

With only 13 men left and the season growing short, Frobisher decided that he must give up further exploration and return home. So on August 26 he weighed anchor, and on October 2 the *Gabriel* sailed into Harwich harbor. One week later Frobisher brought his vessel into the Thames and docked at London, where he received a rousing welcome. He was convinced that he had found the Northwest Passage, and his backers were soon planning another expedition to confirm the discovery. The Eskimo whom he brought back, a man who ate raw meat, also proved a nine-days' wonder.

By a curious turn of fate, the motivation of Frobisher's ventures now shifted from an effort to find the Northwest Passage to a frenetic search for gold. One of his men had picked up a chunk of rock that Frobisher brought back and turned over to Michael Lok, who jumped to the conclusion that the expedition might have found a gold mine. Although several assayers declared the rock to be only marcasite, that is, crystallized iron pyrites commonly called "fool's gold," Lok was already infected with the virus of gold fever. He found an Italian assayer named Giovanni Agnello who pronounced the rock gold ore and produced some gold dust that he claimed to have extracted from it. That was enough to spread the word of the discovery of a gold mine, and investors swarmed to take stock in the next expedition, though Sir Francis Walsingham remained skeptical and regarded Agnello's finding as a mere "alchemist matter."

As a result of the new enthusiasm, Lok and Frobisher organized a new venture, the Cathay Company, with a charter from the Crown granted on March 17, 1577. Lok was made governor of the company for life and Frobisher was named high admiral of all seas and waters in all countries discovered. Queen Elizabeth herself invested £1,000 in the voyage being planned and lent a royal ship, the *Aid,* of 200 tons. Again, with the *Michael* and the *Gabriel* and the new addition of the queen's ship, Frobisher sailed from London, on May 26, 1577. In addition to miners and gold refiners, he had aboard a few condemned criminals who were to be left on "Friesland" to learn the languages and habits of the natives. His instructions were to sail to the spot where he had picked up the rock supposed to be gold ore and to set the miners at work. He might explore the "strait" for no more than 100 leagues before returning, lest there be too long a delay in bringing the fleet loaded with ore back to England. The investors were eager for profits.

On July 17 the little fleet reached the north side of Frobisher's Bay and landed on an island where the original piece of "ore" had been picked up. Since this spot afforded no more ore, they proceeded to other islands, where they loaded 200 tons which an assayer whom they had brought along declared to be rich. They also captured another Eskimo with his wife and child, whom they took back to England. The first captive had died soon after arrival, and these latest captives lived only about a month in England.

Laden with what Frobisher believed to be riches, the fleet sailed for home on August 23. Though parted in a storm, the three vessels had arrived safely at English ports by September 23. The *Aid* with the precious ore put in at Bristol and deposited a portion of the cargo in Bristol Castle. The rest was taken on to London, where it was placed in the Tower, where the queen commanded that it be kept under lock and key, in fact, under four locks with the keys carried by four individuals. The queen invited Frobisher to court, presented him with a purse of £100 and named the newly discovered lands "Meta Incognita."

But, alas, the ore proved worthless. However, before proof was conclusive, an expedition of 15 vessels sailed under Frobisher with instructions to bring back more, and, it was hoped, better ore. This third expedition sailed from Harwich on May 31, 1578. It reached the "mines" safely, took on a cargo of ore, and the ships returned to various English ports early in October. One positive bit of discovery occurred when Frobisher stumbled into what is now Hudson Strait, which he called

"Mistaken Strait." Because of the pressure of time required for mining, he did not have an opportunity to explore it.

This last cargo of ore proved as valueless as the other, and Lok and Frobisher were ruined. They accused each other of dishonesty and incompetence while the investors complained and the seamen pressed for their wages. Lok wound up in prison for debt. Frobisher eventually returned to favor and to the command of royal ships. During the great Armada fight, he was knighted by the lord admiral at sea for his valor.

Christopher Hall Reports on the First Voyage

[*The only account of Frobisher's first voyage written by an eyewitness was that of Christopher Hall, master of the* Gabriel, *published by Hakluyt in the 1589 edition of* The Principal Navigations. *Primarily a seaman's log, Hall's narrative throws light on the sailing conditions of the time. Excerpts follow:*]

The 7 of June, being Thursday, the two barks, *viz.* the *Gabriel* and the *Michael,* and our pinnace set sail at Ratcliffe [Middlesex] and bare down to Deptford, and there we anchored. The cause was that our pinnace burst her bowsprit and foremast aboard of a ship that rode at Deptford, else we meant to have passed that day by the Court then at Greenwich.

The 8 day, being Friday, about 12 of the clock we weighed at Deptford and set sail, all three of us, and bare down by the Court, where we shot off our ordnance and made the best show we could. Her Majesty, beholding the same, commended it and bade us farewell with shaking her hand at us out of the window. Afterward she sent a gentleman aboard of us who declared that Her Majesty had good liking of our doings and thanked us for it, and also willed our captain to come the next day to the Court to take his leave of her.

The same day toward night M. Secretary Woolly came aboard of us and declared to the company that Her Majesty had appointed him to give them charge to be obedient and diligent to their captain and governors in all things, and wished us happy success.

The 12 day, being over against Gravesend by the castle, or

blockhouse, we observed the latitude, which was 51 degrees 33 min. And in that place the variation of the compass is 11 degrees and a half. . . .

The 25 day, from 4 to 8 a clock in the forenoon, the wind at northwest and by north a fresh gale, I cast about to the westward, the southernmost head of Shetland, called Sumburgh Head, north-northwest from me, and the land of Fair Isle, westsouthwest from me. I sailed directly to the north head of that said land, sounding as I ran in, having 60, 50, and 40 fathoms, and gray red shoals. . . .

The 11 day [of July], at a southeast sun, we had sight of the land of Friesland bearing from us west-northwest 16 leagues and rising like pinnacles of steeples, and all covered with snow. I found myself in 61 degr. of latitude. We sailed to the shore and could find no ground at 150 fathoms. We hoisted out our boat, and the captain with four men rowed to the shore to get on land, but the land lying full of ice, they could not get on land, and so they came aboard again. We had much ado to get clear of the ice by reason of the fog. Yet from Thursday eight a clock in the morning to Friday at noon we sailed southwest 20 leagues.

The 18 day at a southwest sun I found the sun to be elevated 33 deg. And at a south-southeast sun, 40 deg. So I observed it till I found it at the highest, and then it was elevated 52 deg. I judged the variation of the compass to be 2 points and a half to the westward. . . .

The 28 day in the morning was very foggy, but at the clearing up of the fog we had sight of land, which I supposed to be Labrador, with great store of ice about the land. I ran toward it and sounded, but could get no ground at 100 fathom; and the ice being so thick, I could not get to the shore and so lay off. . . . Upon Monday we came within a mile of the shore and sought a harbor. All the sound was full of ice, and our boat, rowing ashore, could get no ground at 100 fathom within a cable's length of the shore. Then we sailed east-northeast along the shore, for so the land lieth, and the current is there great, setting northeast and southwest; and if we could have gotten anchor ground, we would have seen with what force it had run, but I judge a ship may drive a league and a half in one hour with that tide.

This day [July 31] at four of the clock in the morning, being fair and clear, we had sight of a headland, as we judged, bearing from us north and by east, and we sailed northeast and by north to that land; and when we came thither we could not get to the land for ice, for the ice stretched along the coast so that we could not come to the land by five leagues. . . .

The 11 [of August] we found our latitude to be 63 degr. and eight minutes, and this day we entered the strait.

The 12 we set sail toward an island called the Gabriel's Island, which was ten leagues then from us. . . .

The 14 we weighed and ran into another sound where we anchored in eight fathom water, fair sand and black ooze, and there caulked our ship, being weak from the wales upward, and took in fresh water. . . .

The 19 day in the morning, being calm and no wind, the captain and I took our boat, with eight men in her, to row us ashore to see if there were there any people or no; and going to the top of the island we had sight of seven boats which came rowing from the east side toward that island; whereupon we returned aboard again. At length we sent our boat with five men in her to see whither they rowed, and so, with a white cloth, brought one of their boats with their men along the shore, rowing after our boat, till such time as they saw our ship, and then they rowed ashore. Then I went on shore myself . . . and brought one of them aboard of me, where he did eat and drink, and then carried him on shore again. Whereupon all the rest came aboard with their boats, being 19 persons, and they spake, but we understood them not. They be like to Tartars, with long black hair, broad faces and flat noses, and tawny in color, wearing sealskins; and so do the women, not differing in the fashion but the women are marked in the face with blue streaks down the cheeks and round about the eyes. Their boats are made all of sealskins, with a keel of wood within the skin. The proportion of them is like a Spanish shallop, save only they be flat in the bottom and sharp at both ends.

The 20th day we weighed and went to the east side of this island, and I and the captain, with four men more, went on shore and there we saw their houses. And the people, espying us, came rowing toward our boat; whereupon we plied toward our boat; and we being in our boat and they ashore, they called

to us, and we rowed to them; and one of their company came
into our boat, and we carried him aboard and gave him a bell
and a knife. So the captain and I willed [ordered] five of our
men to set him ashore at a rock and not among the company
which they came from; but their willfulness was such that they
would go to them, and so were taken themselves, and our boat
lost.

The next day in the morning we stood in near the shore and
shot off a falconet and sounded our trumpet, but we could hear
nothing of our men. This sound we called the Five Men's
Sound and plied out of it, but anchored again in 30 fathom and
ooze. And riding there all night, in the morning the snow lay
a foot thick upon our hatches.

The 22 day in the morning we weighed and went again to
the place where we lost our men and our boat. We had sight of
14 boats, and some came near to us, but we could learn nothing
of our men. Among the rest, we enticed one boat to our ship's
side with a bell and, in giving him the bell, we took him and
his boat, and so kept him; and so rowed down to Thomas
Williams' Island and there anchored all night.

The 26 day we weighed to come homeward, and by 12 of
the clock at noon we were thwart of Trumpet's Island.

The next day we came thwart of Gabriel's Island, and at eight
of the clock at night we had the Cape Labrador, as we supposed,
west from us ten leagues.

The 28 day we went our course southeast.

We sailed southeast and by east 22 leagues [August 29].

The 1st day of September in the morning we had sight of
the land of Friesland, being eight leagues from us, but we
could not come nearer it for the monstrous ice that lay about it.
From this day till the 6th of this month we ran along island,
and had the south part of it at eight of the clock east from us
ten leagues.

The 7th day of this month we had a very terrible storm,
by force whereof one of our men was blown into the sea out
of our waist, but he caught hold of the foresail sheet and there
held till the captain plucked him again into the ship.

The 25 day of this month we had sight of the island of Ork-
ney, which was then east from us.

The 1st day of October we had sight of the Scheldt, and so

sailed about the coast, and anchored at Yarmouth, and the next day we came into Harwich.

[*The most comprehensive account of Frobisher's three voyages is to be found in a contemporary work by George Best, one of his officers who served in the second and third voyages. In 1578 Best published* A True Discourse of the Late Voyages of Discovery for the Finding of a Passage to Cathay by the Northwest under the Conduct of Martin Frobisher, General. *This was reprinted by Hakluyt in the 1600 edition of* The Principal Navigations. *It has been reprinted several times since. An excellent modern edition of Best and other narratives of Frobisher's voyages is that edited by Vilhjalmur Stefansson,* The Three Voyages of Martin Frobisher (*London: The Argonaut Press, 1938*).

[*Best gives a brief summary of events of the first voyage, including the taking of the Eskimo and his kayak, and fuller details of the second and third voyages. Excerpts follow:*]

The First Voyage

The 20th of July he had sight of an high land, which he called Queen Elizabeth's Foreland [Resolution Island, off Meta Incognita Peninsula, Baffin I.] after Her Majesty's name. And sailing more northerly alongst that coast, he descried another foreland with a great gut, bay, or passage divided as it were two main lands or continents asunder. There he met with store of exceeding great ice all this coast along, and, coveting still to continue his course to the northwards, was always by contrary wind detained overthwart these straits and could not get beyond. Within few days after, he perceived the ice to be well consumed and gone, . . . wherefore he determined to make proof of this place to see how far that gut had continuance and whether he might carry himself through the same into some open sea on the back side, whereof he conceived no small hope; and so entered the same the one-and-twentieth of July [Hall's date was August 11] and passed above 50 leagues therein, as he reported, having upon either hand a great main [land] or continent. And that land upon his right hand as he sailed westward he judged to be the continent of Asia, and there to be divided from the firm of America, which lieth upon the left hand over against the same.

This place he named after his name, Frobisher's Straits, like as Magellanus at the southwest end of the world, having discovered the passage to the South Sea (where America is divided from the continent of that land which lieth under the South Pole) and called the same straits Magellan's Straits.

After he had passed 60 leagues into this foresaid strait, he went ashore and found signs where fire had been made. He saw mighty deer that seemed to be mankind [human?] which ran at him, and hardly he escaped with his life in a narrow way, where he was fain to use defense and policy to save his life.

In this place he saw and perceived sundry tokens of the peoples resorting thither. And being ashore upon the top of a hill, he perceived a number of small things fleeting in the sea afar off which he supposed to be porpoises or seals or some kind of strange fish; but, coming nearer, he discovered them to be men in small boats made of leather. And before he could descend down from the hill certain of those people had almost cut off his boat from him, having stolen secretly behind rocks for that purpose; where he speedily hasted to his boat, and bent himself to his halberd and narrowly escaped the danger, and saved his boat. Afterward he had sundry conferences with them, and they came aboard his ship and brought him salmon and raw flesh and fish, and greedily devoured the same before our men's faces. And to show their agility, they tried many masteries upon the ropes of the ship after our mariners' fashion, and appeared to be very strong of their arms and nimble of their bodies. They exchanged coats of seals' and bears' skins, and suchlike with our men; and received bells, looking glasses, and other toys in recompense thereof again.

After great courtesy and many meetings, our mariners, contrary to their captain's direction, began more easily to trust them; and five of our men going ashore were by them intercepted with their boat and were never since heard of to this day again; so that the captain, being destitute of boat, bark, and all company, had scarcely sufficient number to conduct back his bark again. He could now neither convey himself ashore to rescue his men (if he had been able) for want of a boat; and again the subtle traitors were so wary as they would after that never come within our men's danger.

The captain notwithstanding, desirous to bring some token from thence of his being there, was greatly discontented that he had not before apprehended some of them. And therefore, to deceive the deceivers he wrought a pretty policy: for knowing well how they greatly delighted in our toys, and specially in bells, he rang a pretty lowbell, making signs that he would give him the same that would come and fetch it. And because they would not come within his danger for fear, he flung one bell unto them, which of purpose he threw short that it might fall into the sea and be lost. And to make them more greedy of the matter he rang a louder bell, so that in the end one of them came near the ship side to receive the bell; which when he thought to take at the captain's hand, he was thereby taken himself. For the captain, being readily provided, let the bell fall and caught the man fast and plucked him, with main force, boat and all, into his bark out of the sea. Whereupon, when he found himself in captivity, for very choler and disdain he bit his tongue in twain within his mouth. Notwithstanding, he died not thereof, but lived until he came in England, and then he died of cold which he had taken at sea.

Now with this new prey (which was a sufficient witness of the captain's far and tedious travel toward the unknown parts of the world, as did well appear by this strange infidel whose like was never seen, read, nor heard of before and whose language was neither known nor understood of any) the said Captain Frobisher returned homeward and arrived in England in Harwich the 2 of October following, and thence came to London, 1576, where he was highly commended of all men for his great and notable attempt, but specially famous for the great hope he brought of the passage to Cataya [Cathay].

And it is especially to be remembered that at their first arrival in those parts there lay so great store of ice all the coast along, so thick together, that hardly his boat could pass unto the shore. At length, after divers attempts, he commanded his company, if by any possible means they could get ashore, to bring him whatsoever thing they could first find, whether it were living or dead, stock or stone, in token of Christian possession, which thereby he took in behalf of the queen's most excellent Majesty, thinking that thereby he might justify the having and enjoying of the same things that grew in these unknown parts.

Some of his company brought flowers, some green grass, and one brought a piece of black stone much like to a sea coal in color, which by the weight seemed to be some kind of metal or mineral. This was a thing of no account in the judgment of the captain at the first sight; and yet for novelty it was kept in respect of the place from whence it came.

After his arrival in London, being demanded of sundry his friends what thing he had brought them home out of that country, he had nothing left to present them withal but a piece of this black stone. And it fortuned a gentlewoman, one of the adventurer's wives, to have a piece thereof, which by chance she threw and burned in the fire, so long that, at the length being taken forth and quenched in a little vinegar, it glistered with a bright marcasite of gold. Whereupon, the matter being called in some question, it was brought to certain goldfiners [refiners] in London to make assay thereof, who gave out that it held gold, and that very richly for the quantity. Afterward the same goldfiners promised great matters thereof if there were any store to be found, and offered themselves to adventure for the searching of those parts from whence the same was brought. Some that had great hope of the matter sought secretly to have a lease at Her Majesty's hands of those places, whereby to enjoy the mass of so great a public profit unto their own private gains.

In conclusion, the hope of more of the same gold ore to be found kindled a greater opinion in the hearts of many to advance the voyage again. Whereupon preparation was made for a new voyage against the year following, and the captain more specially directed by commission for the searching more of this gold ore than for the searching any further discovery of the passage.

And being well accompanied with divers resolute and forward gentlemen, Her Majesty then lying at the Right Honorable the Lord of Warwick's house in Essex, he came to take his leave, and, kissing Her Highness' hands, with gracious countenance and comfortable words departed toward his charge.

The Second Voyage

It is a marvelous thing to behold of what great bigness and depth some islands of ice be here, some 70, some 80 fathom under water besides that which is above, seeming islands more than half a mile in circuit. All these ice are in taste fresh, and seem to be bred in the sounds thereabouts or in some land near the Pole, and with the wind and tides are driven alongst the coasts. We found none of these islands of ice salt in taste, whereby it appeareth that they were not congealed of the ocean sea water which is always salt, but of some standing or little-moving lakes or great fresh waters near the shore caused either by melted snow from tops of mountains or by continual access of fresh rivers from the land; and, intermingling with the sea water . . . may cause some part of salt water to freeze so with it and so seem a little brackish; but otherwise the main sea freezeth not, and therefore there is no Mare Glaciale or frozen sea as the opinion hitherto hath been. . . .

On Monday the 6th of August the lieutenant with all the soldiers, for the better guard of the miners and the other things ashore, pitched their tents in the Countess' Island and fortified the place for their better defense as well as they could, and were to the number of 40 persons; when, being all at labor, they might perceive upon the top of a hill over against them a number of the country people wafting with a flag and making great outcries unto them, and were of the same company which had encountered lately our men upon the other shore, being come to complain their late losses and to entreat (as it seemed) for restitution of the woman and child which our men in the late conflict had taken and brought away. Whereupon the general, taking the savage captive with him and setting the woman where they might best perceive her in the highest place of the island, went over to talk with them.

This captive, at his first encounter of his friends, fell so out into tears that he could not speak a word in a great space; but after a while, overcoming his kindness, he talked at full with his companions and bestowed friendly upon them such toys and trifles as we had given him, whereby we noted that they are very kind one to another and greatly sorrowful for the loss of their friends. Our general by signs required his five men which they took captive the last year, and promised them not only to release those which he had taken but also to reward them with great gifts and friendship. Our savage made signs in answer from them that our men should be delivered us, and were yet living, and made signs likewise unto us that we should write our letters unto them, for they knew very well the use we have of writing and received knowledge thereof either of our poor captive countrymen which they betrayed or else by this our new captive who hath seen us daily write, and repeat again, such words of his language as we desired to learn. . . .

I thought the captain's letter well worth the remembering, not for the circumstance of curious inditing but for the substance and good meaning therein contained, and therefore have repeated here the same as by himself it was hastily written:

The form of M. Martin Frobisher's letter to the English captives.

"In the name of God in whom we all believe, who (I trust) hath preserved your bodies and souls amongst these infidels, I commend me unto you. I will be glad to seek by all means you can devise for your deliverance, either with force or with any commodities within my ships, which I will not spare for your sakes, or anything else I can do for you. I have aboard, of theirs, a man, a woman, and a child which I am contented to deliver for you, but the man which I carried away from hence the last year is dead in England. Moreover you may declare unto them that if they deliver you not I will not leave a man alive in their country. And thus, if one of you can come to speak with me they shall have either the man, woman, or child in pawn for you. And thus unto God whom I trust you do serve, in haste I leave you, and to Him we will daily pray for you. This Tuesday morning the seventh of August. *Anno* 1557.

"Yours to the uttermost of my power,
"Martin Frobisher

"[Postscript] I have sent you by these bearers pen, ink, and paper to write back unto me again, if personally you cannot come to certify me of your estate."

Now had the general altered his determination for going any further into the straits at this time for any further discovery of the passage, having taken a man and a woman of that country, which he thought sufficient for the use of language; and having also met with these people here which intercepted his men the last year (as the apparel and English furniture which was found in their tents very well declared), he knew it was but a labor lost to seek them further off when he had found them there at hand. And considering also the short time he had in hand, he thought it best to bend his whole endeavor for the getting of mine, and to leave the passage further to be discovered hereafter. For his commission directed him in this voyage only for the searching of the ore, and to defer the further discovery of the passage until another time. . . .

Saturday the 11th of August the people showed themselves again, and called unto us from the side of a hill over against us. The general (with good hope to hear of his men and to have answer of his letter) went over unto them, where they presented themselves not above three in sight, but were hidden indeed in greater numbers behind the rocks, and, making signs of delay with us to entrap some of us to redeem their own, did only seek advantage to train our boat about a point of land from sight of our company. Whereupon our men, justly suspecting them, kept aloof without their danger, and yet set one of our company ashore which took up a great bladder which one of them offered us and, leaving a looking glass in the place, came into the boat again. In the meanwhile our men which stood in the Countess' Island to behold, who might better discern them than those of the boat by reason they were on higher ground, made a great outcry unto our men in the boat for that they saw divers of the savages creeping behind the rocks toward our men; whereupon the general presently returned without tidings of his men. . . .

Now our work growing to an end, and having, only with five poor miners and the help of a few gentlemen and soldiers, brought aboard almost 200 ton of ore in the space of 20 days, every man, therewithal well comforted, determined lustily . . . to bring our labor to a speedy and happy end. And upon Wednesday at night, being the 21st of August, we fully finished the whole work. And it was now good time to leave, for, as the men were well wearied, so their shoes and clothes were well worn, their baskets' bottoms torn out, their tools broken, and the ships reasonably well filled. Some with overstraining themselves received hurts not a little dangerous, some having their bellies broken, and others their legs made lame. And about this time the ice began to congeal and freeze about our ships' sides a-night, which gave us a good argument of the sun's declining southward, and put us in mind to make more haste homeward. . . .

The 23 of August, having the wind large at west, we set sail from out of the Countess' Sound [i.e., Countess of Warwick's Sound, north shore of Frobisher Bay just above Loks Land] homeward, but, the wind calming, we came to anchor within the point of the same sound again.

The 24 of August about three of the clock in the morning, having the wind large at west, we set sail again, and by nine of the clock at night we left the Queen's Foreland astern of us and, being clear of the straits, we bare further into the main ocean, keeping our course more southerly to bring ourselves the sooner under the latitude of our own climate. The wind was very great at sea so that we lay a-hull all night, and had snow half a foot deep on the hatches. . . .

In this voyage commonly we took the latitude of the place by the height of the sun, because the long day taketh away the light, not only of the Polar but also of all other fixed stars. And here the North Star is so much elevated above the horizon that with the staff it is hardly to be well observed, and the degrees in the astrolabe are too small to observe minutes. Therefore we always used the staff and the sun as fittest instruments for this use. . . .

About one month after our arrival here [Milford Haven, Wales, on or about September 23], by order from the Lords of the Council the ship came up to Bristol, where the ore was committed to keeping in the castle there. Here we found the *Gabriel,* one of the barks, arrived in good safety, who, having never a man within board very sufficient to bring home the ship after the master [William Smith, washed overboard in heavy seas] was lost, by good fortune when she came upon the coast met with a ship of Bristol at sea, who conducted her in safety thither.

Here we heard good tidings also of the arrival of the other

bark, called the *Michael,* in the north parts, which was not a little joyful unto us that it pleased God so to bring us to a safe meeting again, and we lost in all the voyage only one man, besides one that died at sea which was sick before he came aboard and was so desirous to follow this enterprise that he rather chose to die therein than not to be one to attempt so notable a voyage.

The Third Voyage

The general, being returned from the second voyage, immediately after his arrival in England repaired with all haste to the Court, being then at Windsor, to advertise Her Majesty of his prosperous proceeding and good success in this last voyage, and of the plenty of gold ore, with other matters of importance which he had in these septentrional [northern] parts discovered. He was courteously entertained and heartily welcomed of many noblemen, but especially for his great adventure commended of Her Majesty at whose hands he received great thanks and most gracious countenance, according to his deserts. Her Highness also greatly commended the rest of the gentlemen in this service for their great forwardness in this so dangerous attempt; but especially she rejoiced very much that among them there was so good order of government, so good agreement, every man so ready in his calling to do whatsoever the general should command. . . .

And finding that the matter of the gold ore had appearance and made show of great riches and profit, and the hope of the passage to Cataya by this last voyage greatly increased, Her Majesty appointed special commissioners chosen for this purpose, gentlemen of great judgment, art, and skill, to look thoroughly into the cause for the true trial and due examination thereof and for the full handling of all matters thereunto appertaining. And because that place and country hath never heretofore been discovered, and therefore had no special name by which it might be called and known, Her Majesty named it very properly Meta Incognita, as a mark and bound utterly hitherto unknown.

The commissioners, after sufficient trial and proof made of

the ore, and having understood by sundry reasons and substantial grounds the possibility and likelihood of the passage,
advertised Her Highness that the cause was of importance and
the voyage greatly worthy to be advanced again. . . .

It was thought needful, both for the better guard of those
parts already found and for further discovery of the inland
and secrets of those countries, and also for further search of the
passage to Cataya (whereof the hope continually more and more
increaseth) that certain numbers of chosen soldiers and discreet
men for those purposes should be assigned to inhabit there.
Whereupon there was a strong fort or house of timber, artificially
framed and cunningly devised by a notable learned man here at
home, in ships to be carried thither, whereby those men that
were appointed to winter and stay there the whole year might
as well be defended from the danger of the snow and cold air
as also fortified from the force or offense of those country
people which perhaps otherwise with too great multitudes
might oppress them. . . .

The whole number of men which had offered, and were appointed, to inhabit Meta Incognita all the year were 100 persons, whereof 40 should be mariners for the use of ships, 30
miners for gathering the gold ore together for the next year, and
30 soldiers for the better guard of the rest, within which last
number are included the gentlemen, goldfiners, bakers, carpenters, and all necessary persons. To each of the captains was
assigned one ship, as well for the further searching of the coast
and country there as for to return and bring back their companies again if the necessity of the place so urged or, by miscarrying of the fleet the next year, they might be disappointed
of their further provision.

Being therefore thus furnished with all necessaries, there were
ready to depart upon the said voyage 15 sail of good ships,
whereof the whole number was to return again with their loading of gold ore in the end of the summer except those three
ships which should be left for the use of those captains which
should inhabit there the whole year. . . .

The 20th of June, at two of the clock in the morning, the
general descried land and found it to be West Friesland, now
named West England. Here the general and other gentlemen
went ashore, being the first known Christians that we have true

notice of that ever set foot upon that ground. And therefore the general took possession thereof to the use of our Sovereign Lady, the Queen's Majesty, and discovered here a goodly harbor for the ships, where were also certain little boats of that country. And being there landed, they espied certain tents and people of that country which were (as they judge) in all sorts very like those of Meta Incognita, as by their apparel and other things which we found in their tents appeared. . . . Some are of the opinion that this West England is firm land with the northeast parts of Meta Incognita or else with Greenland. And their reason is because the people, apparel, boats, and other things are so like to theirs; and another reason is, the multitude of islands of ice which lay between it and Meta Incognita doth argue that on the north side there is a bay, which cannot be but by conjoining of the two lands together.

And having a fair and large wind, we departed from thence toward Frobisher's Straits the 23rd of June. But first we gave name to a high cliff in West England, the last that was in our sight, and for a certain similitude we called it Charing Cross. . . .

One of our fleet named the *Bark Dennis,* being of 100 ton burden, seeking way in amongst these ice received such a blow with a rock of ice that she sunk down therewith in the sight of the whole fleet. Howbeit, having signified her danger by shooting off a piece of great ordnance, new succor of other ships came so readily unto them that the men were all saved with boats. Within this ship that was drowned there was parcel of our house which was to be erected for them that should stay all the winter in Meta Incognita. . . .

The 7th of July, as men nothing yet dismayed, we cast about toward the inward and had sight of land, which rose in form like the northerland of the straits, which some of the fleet—and those not the worst mariners——judged to be the North Foreland. Howbeit, othersome were of contrary opinion. But the matter was not well to be discerned by reason of the thick fog which a long time hung upon the coast and the new falling snow which yearly altereth the shape of the land and taketh away oftentimes the mariners' marks. And by reason of the dark mists which continued by the space of 20 days together, this doubt grew the greater and the longer perilous. For whereas indeed we thought ourselves to be upon the northeast side of Frobisher's Straits, we were now carried to the southwestward of the Queen's Foreland and, being deceived by a swift current coming from the northeast, were brought to the southwestward of our said course many miles more than we did think possible could come to pass. . . .

Whilst the fleet lay thus doubtful, amongst great store of ice in a place they knew not without sight of sun whereby to take the height and so to know the true elevation of the Pole, and without any clear of light to make perfect the coast, the general with the captains and masters of his ships began doubtfully to question of the matter, and sent his pinnace aboard to hear each man's opinion and specially of James Beare, master of the *Anne Francis,* who was known to be a sufficient and skillful mariner and, having been there the year before, had well observed the place and drawn out cards of the coast. But the rather this matter grew the more doubtful for that Christopher Hall, chief pilot of the voyage, delivered a plain and public opinion in the hearing of the whole fleet that he had never seen the foresaid coast before and that he could not make it for any place of Frobisher's Straits, as some of the fleet supposed, and yet the lands do lie and trend so like that the best mariners therein may be deceived. . . .

The general, albeit with the first perchance [opportunity] he found out the error and that this was not the old straits, yet he persuaded the fleet always that they were in their right course and known straits. Howbeit I suppose he rather dissembled his opinion therein than otherwise, meaning by that policy (being himself led with an honorable desire for further discovery) to induce the fleet to follow him to see a further proof of that place. And as some of the company reported, he hath since confessed that if it had not been for the charge and care he had of the fleet and fraughted [laden with freight] ships, he both would and could have gone through to the South Sea, called Mar del Sur, and dissolved the long doubt of the passage which we seek to find to the rich country of Cataya.

1. Of which mistaken straits, considering the circumstance, we have great cause to confirm our opinion to like and hope well of the passage in this place. For the foresaid bay or sea, the further we sailed therein the wider we found it, with great

likelihood of endless continuance. And where in other places we were much troubled with ice, as in the entrance of the same, so after we had sailed 50 or 60 leagues therein we had no let [hindrance] of ice or other thing at all, as in other places we found.

2. Also this place seemeth to have a marvelous great indraft, and draweth unto it most of the drift ice and other things which do float in the sea, either to the north or eastward of the same, as by good experience we have found.

3. For here also we met with boards, laths, and divers other things driving in the sea which was of the wrack of the ship called the *Bark Dennis* which perished amongst the ice as beforesaid, being lost at the first attempt of the entrance overthwart the Queen's Foreland in the mouth of Frobisher's Straits, which could by no means have been so brought thither, neither by wind nor tide, being lost so many leagues off, if by force of the said current the same had not been violently brought. . . .

And now [August 2] was the whole fleet arrived safely at their port excepting four, besides the ship that was lost, . . . whose absence was some let unto the works and other proceedings, as well for that these ships were furnished with the better sort of miners as with other provision for the habitation.

The 9th of August the general with the captains of his council assembled together and began to consider and take order for the erecting up of the house or fort for them that were to inhabit there the whole year, and that presently the masons and carpenters might go in hand therewith. First therefore they perused the bills of lading—what every man received into his ship—and found that there was arrived only the east side and the south side of the house, and yet not that perfect and entire: for many pieces thereof were used for fenders in many ships, and so broken in pieces whilst they were distressed in the ice. Also, after due examination had and true account taken, there was found want of drink and fuel to serve 100 men, which was the number appointed first to inhabit there, because their greatest store was in the ships which were not yet arrived.

Then Captain Fenton, seeing the scarcity of the necessary things aforesaid, was contented and offered himself to inhabit there with 60 men. Whereupon they caused the carpenters and masons to come before them and demand in what time they would take upon them to erect up a less house for 60 men. They required eight or nine weeks if there were timber sufficient, whereas now they had but six-and-twenty days in all to remain in that country. Wherefore it was fully agreed upon and resolved by the general and his council that no habitation should be there this year. And therefore they willed master Selman, the Register, to set down this decree with all their consents for the better satisfying of Her Majesty, the Lords of the Council, and the adventurers. . . .

The 30th of August the *Anne Francis* was brought aground and had eight great leaks mended which she had received by means of the rocks and ice. This day the masons finished a house which Captain Fenton caused to be made of lime and stone upon the Countess of Warwick's Island to the end we might prove against the next year whether the snow could overwhelm it, the frost break it up, or the people dismember the same. And the better to allure those brutish and uncivil people to courtesy against other times of our coming, we left therein divers of our country's toys, as bells and knives wherein they specially delight, one for the necessary use and the other for the great pleasure thereof. Also pictures of men and women in lead, men on horseback, looking glasses, whistles, and pipes. Also in the house was made an oven, and bread left baked therein for them to see and taste.

We buried the timber of our pretended fort. Also here we sowed peas, corn, and other grain to prove the fruitfulness of the soil against the next year. . . .

Thanks be to God, all the fleet arrived safely in England about the first of October, some in one place and some in another. . . . The *Buss of Bridgewater,* as she came homeward, to the southeastward of Friesland discovered a great island in the latitude of 57 degrees and an half, which was never yet found before, and sailed three days alongst the coast, the land seeming to be fruitful, full of woods, and a champion country [named Buss's Island, it appeared on contemporary maps but was never found again].

There died in the whole fleet in all this voyage not above 40 persons, which number is not great considering how many ships were in the fleet and how strange fortunes we passed.

X

Sir Humphrey Gilbert
Plans Colonies
and Claims Newfoundland

SIR Humphrey Gilbert, elder half-brother of Sir Walter
Raleigh, belonged to the group of expansionists headed by
Sir Francis Walsingham who believed that England's destiny demanded that she occupy a portion of the New World before
Spain seized all of it. He had served as a soldier in Ireland and
in 1567 had been involved in an attempt to settle a colony of
Englishmen in Ulster. This effort may have crystalized his ideas
about colonies overseas. At any rate, on November 6, 1577, he
addressed to Queen Elizabeth a secret memorandum with the
title *A Discourse How Her Majesty May Annoy the King of
Spain*. In this he proposed that the queen might send out a
fleet of warships under the pretext of a voyage of discovery,
but its actual purpose would be to seize Spanish vessels in the
West Indies and Newfoundland and establish English bases
in both places. If the queen took any notice of this suggestion,
no record exists, but it may be significant that a few days after
Gilbert's memorandum Drake sailed on his voyage around the
world.

Gilbert's next step was to obtain a charter, valid for six years,
granting him the right to colonize any heathen lands not already
possessed by any Christian prince. The charter was dated June
11, 1578, and Gilbert immediately set to work to organize an
expedition of 11 ships and 500 men; it sailed on September 23,
1578, but had to put back because of a storm. In the meantime,
captains in the fleet fell to quarreling, and when Gilbert finally

cleared Plymouth on November 19, he had only seven ships. Precisely where he went remains a mystery. He appears to have run into storms and hostile Spanish ships, but he managed to get back to Dartmouth near the end of April 1579 with nothing to show for his pains except debts. Hearing that he proposed to set out again, the Privy Council forbade another voyage unless he gave bond for good behavior, a suggestion that Gilbert and his associates were accused of piracy.

Gilbert's first effort to discover and colonize lands overseas, if, indeed, that is what the expedition of 1578–79 set out to do, was a fiasco. But Gilbert retained his dream of colonization and he continued to make plans for a venture overseas. In 1582 he encouraged a proposal by Sir George Peckham and Sir Thomas Gerrard, two loyal Roman Catholics, to establish a colony where English Catholics who found life difficult at home could settle and live in peace. Although Peckham and Gerrard were unable to launch a strictly Catholic colony under Gilbert's charter, they gave support to his next colonizing voyage, which sailed on June 11, 1583. The fleet consisted of five ships, the *Delight*, the *Bark Raleigh* (owned by Sir Walter Raleigh), the *Golden Hind* (not Drake's ship of this name), the *Swallow*, and the *Squirrel* (a small craft of some ten tons). The fleet had been at sea only two days when the captain of the *Bark Raleigh*, the largest vessel, turned tail and sailed for home, claiming that sickness in the ship forced him to leave the expedition.

Although the four remaining vessels parted on the westward voyage, all managed to rendezvous off Saint John's Harbor, Newfoundland, at the beginning of August, and on August 3 Gilbert entered the harbor and showed his commission to colonize. Thirty-six fishing vessels, English, Spanish, Portuguese and French, were at anchor, for Newfoundland at this time was regarded as an international resort of fishermen, who had their own regulations and appointed from among the ship captains an admiral who adjudicated disputes. On August 5 Gilbert landed, set up a tent and called the fishermen and sailors of the various ships before him. He read the provisions of his charter, claimed the land in the name of the Queen of England and promulgated the first laws under his charter: the religion would be according to the rites of the Church of England; anyone attempting to dispute the queen's rights to the territory would be tried according to the laws of England; and anyone speaking in dishonor of the queen would forfeit his ship and lose his ears. As governor of the new land, Gilbert allotted land to various applicants and leased drying stages to the fishermen on their somewhat vague promises to pay. He then requisitioned fish for his hungry seamen, put up a post with a leaden coat of arms attached and spent the next two weeks exploring his new possession, which pleased him immensely. Some rocks that he discovered gave hope of valuable minerals.

But Gilbert was not content to remain in Newfoundland. His aim was to claim and colonize territory on the mainland. The sailors in his little fleet were grumbling over their short rations and poor equipment, for Gilbert's expedition had been ill-organized from the start. Since some of the men balked at sailing farther westward, Gilbert placed the *Swallow* in charge of the malcontents and let them sail for home. With the other three ships, on August 20 he set a course for what we now call Nova Scotia. Eight days later the *Delight*, with the bulk of supplies for the expedition, ran aground on rocks and was lost with 80 men. Sixteen survivors got away in a pinnace and made a landing in Newfoundland. Disheartened and short of victuals, the crews of the two remaining vessels demanded that Gilbert sail for England, and on August 31 he reluctantly turned eastward. Gilbert chose to remain in the little *Squirrel*, his own vessel, in which he had sailed from Newfoundland. The weather was rough, and Edward Hayes, captain of the *Golden Hind*, urged Gilbert in vain to come aboard the larger ship. On the afternoon of September 9 the *Squirrel* came within hailing distance of the *Golden Hind* and Hayes once more begged Gilbert to leave the *Squirrel*. Sitting on deck, reading a book, Gilbert called back that "we are as near to heaven by sea as by land." That night the crew of the *Golden Hind* saw the lights of the *Squirrel* disappear, and no trace of Gilbert or his vessel was ever found. Thus perished one of the most eager exponents of exploration and colonization—but one who showed little capacity for organization and direction. He nevertheless left a legacy of hope with the expansionists, and his ideas were to be developed by Sir Walter Raleigh and others.

How Her Majesty May Annoy the King of Spain

[*Gilbert's* A Discourse How Her Majesty May Annoy the King of Spain *is preserved in the State Papers, Domestic, Elizabeth, SP 12/118, 12 (1). It has been most recently printed by D. B. Quinn, in* The Voyages and Colonizing Enterprises of Sir Humphrey Gilbert, The Hakluyt Society (London, 1938), I, *170–175. Excerpts follow:*]

The safety of principates, monarchies, and commonwealths rest[s] chiefly on making their enemies weak and poor, and themselves strong and rich, both which God hath specially wrought for Your Majesty's safety, if Your Highness shall not overpass good opportunities for the same when they are offered. . . .

First, Your Highness ought undoubtedly to seek the kingdom of heaven and, upon that foundation, to believe that there can never be constant and firm league of amity between those princes whose division is planted by the worm of their conscience. So that their leagues and fair words ought to be held but as mermaids' songs. . . . Which done, Your Majesty is to think that it is more than time to pare their nails by the stumps that are most ready prest to pluck the crown . . . from Your Highness's head. . . . Then, to foresee by all diligent means that your suspected neighbors may not have opportunity to recover breath whereby to repair their decayed losses; which, for your safety, is principally to be done by the farther weakening of their navies and by preserving and increasing of your own.

And the diminishing of their forces by sea is to be done either by open hostility or by some colorable means: as by giving of license under letters patents to discover and inhabit some strange place, with special proviso for their safeties whom policy requireth to have most annoyed. By which means the doing of the contrary shall be imputed to the executors' fault, Your Highness's letters patents being a manifest show that it was not Your Majesty's pleasure so to have it. After the public notice of which, in fact, Your Majesty is either to avow the same . . . or to dis-

avow both them and the fact as league breakers, leaving them
to pretend it as done without your privity. . . .

This cloak being had for the reign, the way to work the feat
is to set forth under suchlike color of discovery certain ships
of war to the N.L. [New Land] which, with your good
license, I will undertake without Your Majesty's charge. In
which place they shall certainly once in the year meet in effect
all the great shipping of France, Spain, and Portugal; where I
would have take and bring away with these freights and ladings
the best of those ships and to burn the worst. And those that
they take, to carry into Holland or Zeeland or, as pirates, to
shroud themselves for a small time upon Your Majesty's coasts
under the friendship of some certain vice-admiral of this realm;
who may be afterwards committed to prison, as in displeasure
for the same. . . .

The setting forth of shipping for this service will amount to
no great matter, and the return shall certainly be with great
gain. For the N.F. [Newland Fish] is a principal and rich and
everywhere vendible merchandise. And by the gain thereof
shipping, victual, munition, and the transporting of five or six
thousand soldiers may be defrayed.

It may be said that a few ships cannot possibly distress so
many. And that, although by this service you take or destroy
all the shipping you find of theirs in those places, yet are they
but subjects' ships, their own particular navies being nothing
lessened thereby, and therefore their forces shall not so much
be diminshed as it is supposed, whereunto I answer:

There is no doubt to perform it without danger. For although
they may be many in number, and great of burden, yet they
are furnished with men—and munition—but like fishers. And
when they come upon the coasts they do always disperse themselves into sundry ports, and do disbark the most of their people
into small boats for the taking and drying of their fish, leaving
few or none aboard their ships, so that there is as little doubt
of the easy taking and carrying of them away as of the decaying
hereby of those princes' forces by sea. For their own proper
shippings are very few, and of small forces in respect of the
others; and their subjects' shipping, being once destroyed, it
is likely that they will never be repaired, partly through the
decay of the owners and partly through the losses of the trades

whereby they maintained the same. . . . But if they should, it will require a long time to season timber for that purpose. . . .

It may also be objected that although this may be done in act, yet is it not allowable, being against Your Majesty's league. For although by the reach of reason men's eyes may be obscured, yet unto God nothing is hidden, which I answer thus:

I hold it as lawful in Christian policy to prevent a mischief betimes as to revenge it too late, especially seeing that God Himself is a party in the common quarrels now afoot, and His enemy['s] malicious disposition toward Your Highness and His Church manifestly seen, although by God's merciful providence not yet thoroughly felt.

Further it may be said that if this should be done by Englishmen under what color soever they should shroud themselves, yet will that cut us off from all traffic with those that shall be annoyed by such means, and thereby utterly undo the state of merchandise, decay the maintenance of the shipping of this realm, and also greatly diminish Your Majesty's customs. To which I reply thus:

. . . The forces of the Spaniards and Portuguese being there so much decayed as aforesaid, the French of necessity shall be brought under Your Highness' lie. Assuring Your Majesty, the case being as it is, it were better a thousandfold thus to gain the start of them rather than yearly to submit ourselves subject to have all the merchants' ships of this realm stayed in their hands, whereby they shall be armed at our costs to beat us with rods of our own making. . . .

If Your Highness will permit me with my associates either overtly or covertly to perform the aforesaid enterprise, then with the gain thereof there may be easily such a competent company transported to the W.I. [West Indies] as may be able not only to disposses the S. [Spaniards] thereof, but also to possess forever Your Majesty and realm therewith. . . . By which means Your Highness' doubtful friends, or rather apparent enemies, shall not be only made weak and poor, but therewith yourself and realm made strong and rich, both by sea and by land, as well there as here. . . . Then of force this realm, being an island, shall be discharged from all foreign perils if all the monarchies of the world should join against us— so long as Ireland shall be in safekeeping, the league of Scotland maintained, and further amity concluded with the Prince of Orange and the King of Denmark. By which means also Your Majesty shall engraft and glue to your crown, in effect, all the northern and southern voyages of the world, so that none shall be then well able to cross the seas but subject to Your Highness' devotion, considering the great increase of shipping that will grow and be maintained by those long voyages. . . .

And if I may perceive that Your Highness shall like of this enterprise, then will I most willingly express my simple opinion which way the W.I. may without difficulty be more surprised and defended. . . . But if Your Majesty like to do it at all, then would I wish Your Highness to consider that delay doth oftentimes prevent the performance of good things. For the wings of man's life are plumed with the feathers of death.

. . . November 6, 1577.

Your Majesty's most faithful servant and subject.

H. Gilbert

Gilbert's Last Expedition

[*The best account of Gilbert's last voyage, in which he claimed Newfoundland for England, was written by Edward Hayes, captain of the* Golden Hind. *His narrative was printed by Hakluyt in the 1589 edition of* The Principal Navigations *and has been most recently reprinted by Quinn,* Voyages and Colonizing Enterprises, *II, 385–422. Excerpts follow:*]

Orders thus determined, and promises mutually given to be observed, every man withdrew himself unto his charge; the anchors being already weighed and our ships under sail, having a soft gale of wind, we began our voyage upon Tuesday, the eleventh day of June, in the year of Our Lord 1583. . . .

We were in number in all about 260 men, among whom we had of every faculty good choice, as shipwrights, masons, carpenters, smiths, and suchlike, requisite to such an action; also mineral men and refiners. Besides, for solace of our people and allurement of the savages, we were provided of music in good variety, not omitting the least toys, as Morris dancers, hobbyhorse, and May-like conceits to delight the savage people, whom we intended to win by all fair means possible. And to that end we were indifferently furnished of all petty haberdashery wares to barter with those simple people.

In this manner we set forward. . . .

Saturday the 27th of July we might descry not far from us as it were mountains of ice driven upon the sea, being then in 50 degrees, which were carried southward to the weather of us, whereby may be conjectured that some current does set that way from the north.

Before we come to Newfoundland, about 50 leagues on this side, we pass the Bank, which are high grounds rising within the sea and under water, yet deep enough and without danger, being commonly not less than 25 and 30 fathom water upon them: the same (as it were some vein of mountains within the sea) do run along and from the Newfoundland, beginning northward about 52 or 53 degrees of latitude, and do extend into the south infinitely. The breadth of this Bank is somewhere more and somewhere less, but we found the same about ten leagues over, having sounded both on this side thereof and the other toward Newfoundland, but found no ground with almost 200 fathom of line, both before and after we had passed the Bank. The Portugals and French chiefly have a notable trade of fishing upon this bank, where are sometimes an hundred or more sails of ships, who commonly begin the fishing in April and have ended by July. That fish is large, always wet, having no land near to dry, and is called corfish [fish pickled in brine].

During the time of fishing, a man shall know without sounding when he is upon the Bank by the incredible multitude of seafowl hovering over the same, to prey upon the offals and garbage of fish thrown out by fishermen and floating upon the sea.

Upon Tuesday the 11th of June we forsook the coast of England. So again Tuesday the 30th of July (seven weeks after) we got sight of land, being immediately embayed in the Grand Bay, or some other great bay, the certainty whereof we could not judge: so great haze and fog did hang upon the coast as neither we might discern the land well nor take the sun's height. But by our best computation we were then in the 51 degrees of latitude.

Forsaking this bay and uncomfortable coast (nothing appearing unto us but hideous rocks and mountains, bare of trees and void of any green herb), we followed the coast to the south, with weather fair and clear. . . .

. . . After we had met with the *Swallow,* we held on our course southward until we came against the harbor called Saint John's, about five leagues from the former Cape of Saint Francis, where before the entrance into the harbor we found also the frigate or *Squirrel* lying at anchor, whom the English merchants (that were and always be admirals by turns interchangeable over the fleets of fishermen within the same harbor) would not permit to enter into the harbor. Glad of so happy meeting both of the *Swallow* and frigate in one day (being Saturday the 3rd of August), we made ready our fights and prepared to enter the harbor, any resistance to the contrary notwithstanding, there being within of all nations to the number of 36 sails. But first the general dispatched a boat to give them knowledge of his coming for no ill intent, having commission from Her Majesty for his voyage he had in hand. And immediately we followed with a slack gale, and in the very entrance (which is but narrow, not above two butts' length) the admiral fell upon a rock on the larboard side by great oversight, in that the weather was fair, the rock much above water fast by the shore, where neither went any sea-gate. But we found such readiness in the English merchants to help us in that danger that without delay there were brought a number of boats which towed off the ship and cleared her of danger.

Having taken place convenient in the road, we let fall anchors, the captains and masters repairing aboard our admiral, whither also came immediately the masters and owners of the fishing fleet of Englishmen, to understand the general's intent and cause of our arrival there. They were all satisfied when the general had shown his commission and purpose to take possession of those lands to the behalf of the Crown of England and the advancement of Christian religion in those paganish regions, requiring but their lawful aid for repairing of his fleet and supply of some necessaries, so far as conveniently might be afforded him, both out of that and other harbors adjoining. In lieu whereof, he made offer to gratify them with any favor and privilege which upon their better advice [consideration] they should demand, the like being not to be obtained hereafter for greater price. So, craving expedition of his demand, minding to proceed further south without long detention in those parts, he dismissed them after promise given of their best endeavor to satisfy speedily his so reasonable request. The merchants with their masters departed, they caused forthwith to be discharged all the great ordnance of their fleet in token of our welcome.

It was further determined that every ship of our fleet should deliver unto the merchants and masters of that harbor a note of all their wants; which done, the ships as well English as strangers were taxed at an easy rate to make supply. And besides, commissioners were appointed, part of our own company and part of theirs, to go into other harbors adjoining (for our English merchants command all there) to levy our provision; whereunto the Portugals (above other nations) did most willingly and liberally contribute, insomuch as we were presented (above our allowance) with wines, marmalades, most fine rusk or biscuit, sweet oils, and sundry delicacies. Also we wanted not of fresh salmons, trouts, lobsters, and other fresh fish brought daily unto us. Moreover, as the manner is in their fishing every week to choose their admiral anew, or rather they succeed in orderly course and have weekly their admiral's feast solemnized, even so the general, captains, and masters of our fleet were continually invited and feasted. . . .

Monday following the general had his tent set up, who, being accompanied with his own followers, summoned the merchants and masters, both English and strangers, to be present at his taking possession of those countries. Before whom openly was read and interpreted unto the strangers his commission, by virtue whereof he took possession in the same harbor of Saint John's and 200 leagues every way, invested the Queen's Majesty with the title and dignity thereof, had delivered unto him (after the custom of England) a rod and a turf of the same soil, entering possession also for him, his heirs and assigns for ever; and signified unto all men that from that time forward they should take the same land as a territory appertaining to the Queen of England and himself authorized under Her Majesty to possess and enjoy it and to ordain laws for the government thereof, agreeable (so near as conveniently might be) unto the laws of England, under which all people coming thither hereafter, either to inhabit or by way of traffic, should be subjected and governed. And especially at the same time for a beginning he proposed and delivered three laws to be in force immediately, that is to say: the first for religion, which in public exercise should be according to the Church of England; the second for maintenance of Her Majesty's right and possession of those territories, against which if anything were attempted prejudicial, the party or parties offending should be adjudged and executed as in case of high treason according to the laws of England; the third, if any person should utter words sounding to the dishonor of Her Majesty he should lose his ears and have his ship and goods confiscate.

These contents published, obedience was promised by general voice and consent of the multitude, as well of Englishmen as strangers, praying for continuance of this possession and government begun. After this the assembly was dismissed. And afterward were erected not far from that place the arms of England engraven in lead and infixed upon a pillar of wood. Yet further and actually to establish this possession taken in the right of Her Majesty and to the behoof of Sir Humphrey Gilbert, Knight, his heirs and assigns for ever, the general granted in fee farm divers parcels of land lying by the waterside, both in this harbor of Saint John's and elsewhere, which was to the owners a great commodity, being thereby assured (by their proper inheritance) of grounds convenient to dress and to dry their fish, whereof many times before they did fail, being prevented by them that came first into the harbor. For which grounds they did covenant to pay a certain rent and service unto Sir Humphrey Gilbert, his heirs or assigns for ever, and yearly to maintain possession of the same by themselves or their assigns.

Now remained only to take in provision granted according as every ship was taxed which did fish upon the coast adjoining. In the meanwhile the general appointed men unto their charge: some to repair and trim the ships; others to attend in gathering together our supply and provisions; others to search the commodities and singularities of the country to be found by sea or land and to make relation unto the general what either themselves could know by their own travel and experience or by good intelligence of Englishmen or strangers who had longest frequented the same coast. Also some observed the elevation of the Pole and drew plats of the country exactly graded. And by that I could gather by each man's several relation, I have drawn a brief description of the Newfoundland, with the commodities by sea or land already made, and such also as are in possibility and great likelihood to be made. Nevertheless, the cards and plats that were drawing, with the due gradation of the harbors, bays, and capes, did perish with the admiral; wherefore in the description following I must omit the particulars of such things. . . .

While the better sort of us were seriously occupied in repairing our wants and contriving of matters for the commodity of our voyage, others of another sort and disposition were plotting of mischief, some casting to steal away our shipping by night, watching opportunity by the general's and captains' lying on the shore: whose conspiracies discovered, they were prevented. Others drew together in company and carried away out of the harbors adjoining a ship laden with fish, setting the poor men on shore. A great many more of our people stole into the woods to hide themselves, attending time and means to return home by such shipping as daily departed from the coast. Some were sick of fluxes and many dead; and, in brief, by one means or other our company was diminished and many by the general licensed to return home. Insomuch as after we had reviewed our people, resolved to see an end of our voyage, we grew scant of men to furnish all our shipping. It seemed good, therefore, unto the general to leave the *Swallow* with such provision as might be spared for transporting home the sick people.

The captain of the *Delight,* or admiral, returned into England, in whose stead was appointed Captain Maurice Browne, before captain of the *Swallow,* who also brought with him into the *Delight* all his men of the *Swallow,* which before have been noted of outrage perpetrated and committed upon fishermen there met at sea.

The general made choice to go in his frigate, the *Squirrel* (whereof the captain also was among them that returned into England), the same frigate being most convenient to discover upon the coast and to search into every harbor or creek, which a great ship could not do. Therefore the frigate was prepared with her nettings and fights and overcharged with bases [small cannon] and such small ordnance, more to give a show than with judgment to foresee unto the safety of her and the men, which afterward was an occasion also of their overthrow.

Now having made ready our shipping, that is to say, the *Delight,* the *Golden Hind,* and the *Squirrel,* and put aboard our provision, which was wines, bread or rusk, fish wet and dry, sweet oils, besides many other, as marmalades, figs, lemons barrelled, and suchlike. Also we had other necessary provisions for trimming our ships, nets and lines to fish withal, boats or pinnaces fit for discovery. In brief, we were supplied of our wants commodiously, as if we had been in a country or some city populous and plentiful of all things.

We departed from this harbor of Saint John's upon Tuesday the 20th of August, which we found by exact observation to be in 47 degrees 40 minutes. And the next day by night we were at Cape Race 25 leagues from the same harbor. . . .

The Manner How Our Admiral Was Lost

Upon Tuesday, the 27th of August, toward the evening, our general caused them in his frigate to sound, who found white sand at 35 fathom, being then in latitude about 44 degrees.

Wednesday toward night the wind came south, and we bare with the land all the night west-northwest, contrary to the mind of Master Cox; nevertheless we followed the admiral, deprived of power to prevent a mischief, which by no contradiction could be brought to hold other course, alleging they could not make the ship to work better nor to lie otherways.

The evening was fair and pleasant, yet not without token of storm to ensue, and most part of this Wednesday night, like the swan that sings before death, they in the admiral, or *Delight,* continued in sounding of trumpets, with drums and fifes; also winding the cornets, hautboys and, in the end of their jollity, left with the battle and ringing of doleful knells.

Toward the evening also we caught in the *Golden Hind* a very mighty porpoise, with a harping iron, having first stricken divers of them and brought away part of their flesh sticking upon the iron, but could recover only that one. These also, passing through the ocean in herds, did portend storm. I omit

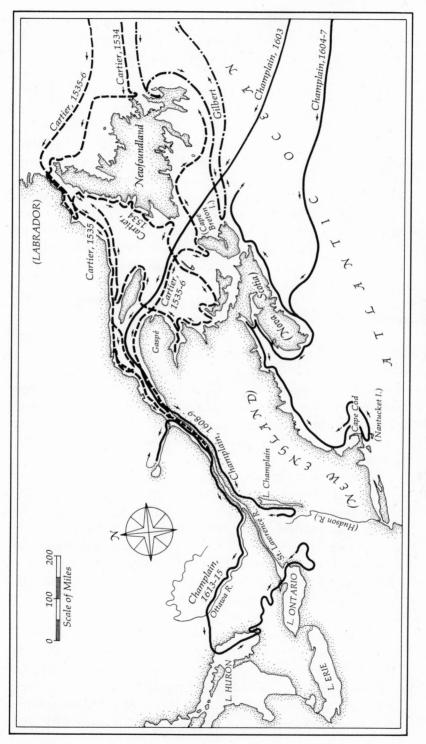

Voyages of Champlain, Cartier, and Gilbert

to recite frivolous reports by them in the frigate of strange voices the same night, which scared some from the helm.

Thursday the 29th of August the wind rose and blew vehemently at south and by east, bringing withal rain and thick mist, so that we could not see a cable length before us. . . .

In this distress we had vigilant eye unto the admiral, whom we saw cast away without power to give the men succor; neither could we espy any of the men that leaped overboard to save themselves, either in the same pinnace or cock, or upon rafters and suchlike means presenting themselves to men in those extremities, for we desired to save the men by every possible means. But all in vain, since God had determined their ruin; yet all that day and part of the next we beat up and down as near unto the wreck as was possible for us, looking out if by good hap we might espy any of them. . . .

Our people lost courage daily after this ill success; the weather continuing thick and blustering with increase of cold, winter drawing on, which took from them all hope of amendment, settling an assurance of worse weather to grow upon us every day. The lee side of us lay full of flats and dangers inevitable if the wind blew hard at south. Some again doubted we were engulfed in the bay of Saint Lawrence, the coast full of dangers and unto us unknown. But above all, provision waxed scant, and hope of supply was gone with loss of our admiral. . . .

So upon Saturday in the afternoon the 31st of August we changed our course and returned back for England, at which very instant, even in the winding about, there passed along between us and toward the land which we now forsook a very lion to our seeming, in shape, hair, and color, not swimming after the manner of a beast by moving of his feet, but rather sliding upon the water with his whole body (excepting the legs) in sight, neither yet diving under and again rising above the water as the manner is of whales, dolphins, tunny, porpoises, and all other fish, but confidently showing himself above water without hiding. Notwithstanding, we presented ourselves in open view and gesture to amaze him, as all creatures will be commonly at a sudden gaze and sight of men. Thus he passed along, turning his head to and fro, yawning and gaping wide, with ugly demonstration of long teeth and glaring eyes, and to bid us a farewell (coming right against the *Hind*) he sent forth a horrible voice, roaring or bellowing as doth a lion, which spectacle we all beheld so far as we were able to discern the same, as men prone to wonder at every strange thing, as this doubtless was, to see a lion in the ocean sea or fish in shape of a lion. What opinion others had thereof, and chiefly the general himself, I forbear to deliver. But he took it for *bonum omen,* rejoicing that he was to war against such an enemy, if it were the Devil. . . .

This Monday the general came aboard the *Hind* to have the surgeon of the *Hind* to dress his foot, which he hurt by treading upon a nail, at what time we comforted each other with hope of hard success [bad luck] to be all past and of the good to come. So, agreeing to carry our lights always by night, that we might keep together, he departed into his frigate, being by no means to be entreated to tarry in the *Hind,* which had been more for his security. Immediately after followed a sharp storm, which we overpassed for that time, praised be God.

The weather fair, the general came aboard the *Hind* again to make merry together with the captain, master, and company, which was the last meeting, and continued there from morning until night. During which time there passed sundry discourses touching affairs past and to come, lamenting greatly the loss of his great ship, more of the men, but most of all of his books and notes, and what else I know not, for which he was out of measure grieved, the same doubtless being some matter of more importance than his books, which I could not draw from him; yet by circumstance I gathered the same to be the ore which Daniel the Saxon had brought unto him in the Newfoundland. Whatsoever it was, the remembrance touched him so deep as, not able to contain himself, he beat his boy in great rage, even at the same time, so long after the miscarrying of the great ship, because upon a fair day when we were calmed upon the coast of the Newfoundland near unto Cape Race he sent his boy aboard the admiral to fetch certain things, amongst which this, being chief, was yet forgotten and left behind. After which time he could never conveniently send again aboard the great ship, much less he doubted her ruin so near at hand. . . .

When he was entreated by the captain, master, and other

his well-willers of the *Hind* not to venture in the frigate, this was his answer: "I will not forsake my little company going homeward, with whom I have passed so many storms and perils." . . .

Seeing he would not bend to reason, he had provision out of the *Hind* such as was wanting aboard his frigate. And so we committed him to God's protection and set him aboard his pinnace, we being more than 300 leagues onward of our way home.

By that time we had brought the islands of Azores south of us; yet we then keeping much to the north until we had got into the height and elevation of England, we met with very foul weather and terrible seas, breaking short and high, pyramid-wise. . . . Howsoever it cometh to pass, men which all their lifetime had occupied the sea never saw more outrageous seas. We had also upon our main yard an apparition of a little fire by night, which seamen do call Castor and Pollux. But we had only one, which they take an evil sign of more tempest; the same is usual in storms.

Monday the 9th of September in the afternoon the frigate was near cast away, oppressed by waves, yet at that time recovered; and, giving forth signs of joy, the general, sitting abaft with a book in his hand, cried out unto us in the *Hind* (so oft as we did approach within hearing), "We are as near to Heaven by sea as by land," reiterating the same speech, well beseeming a soldier resolute in Jesus Christ, as I can testify he was.

The same Monday night, about twelve of the clock or not long after, the frigate being ahead of us in the *Golden Hind,* suddenly her lights were out, whereof, as it were in a moment, we lost the sight, and withal our watch cried the general was cast away, which was too true. For in that moment the frigate was devoured and swallowed up of the sea. Yet still we looked out all that night, and ever after, until we arrived upon the coast of England, omitting no small sail at sea unto which we gave not the tokens between us agreed upon to have perfect knowledge of each other if we should at any time be separated.

In great torment of weather and peril of drowning, it pleased God to send safe home the *Golden Hind,* which arrived in Falmouth the 22nd of September, being Sunday, not without as great danger escaped in a flaw, coming from the southeast with such mist that we could not discern land to put in right with the haven. . . .

Thus have I delivered the contents of the enterprise and last action of Sir Humphrey Gilbert, Knight, faithfully for so much as I thought meet to be published, wherein may always appear (though he be extinguished) some sparks of his virtues, he remaining firm and resolute in a purpose by all pretense honest and godly as was this, to discover, possess, and to reduce unto the service of God and Christian piety those remote and heathen countries of America not actually possessed by Christians and most rightly appertaining unto the Crown of England.

❧ XI ❧

Sir Walter Raleigh's Explorers Report on "Virginia"

SIR Walter Raleigh, a Devonshire gentleman who saw service in Ireland against the rebels and in France as a soldier fighting for the Huguenots during the wars of religion, was an ardent Protestant who looked upon Spain as a dangerous threat to England's security. For all of his active life he was concerned with projects that he hoped would curtail Spain's power and increase England's strength. He became one of the most constant advocates of colonial expansion and devoted much of his personal fortune to exploring expeditions and colonial enterprises.

When Raleigh returned from Ireland in 1581, he came to court and set about making himself agreeable to the queen. His success was such that he quickly became one of her favorite courtiers and in 1585 was knighted and made Lord Warden of the Stannaries, giving him control of the Cornish tin mines. Even more important were various licenses and monopolies that he received as a royal favor, such as the grant of the right to issue licenses for the sale of wine or a license for the free export of cloth. He also was made lord-lieutenant of Cornwall and vice-admiral of Devon and Cornwall. In 1587 Elizabeth made him captain of her guard. These emoluments and offices provided Raleigh with the money, power and influence to implement his expansionist ideas.

When Sir Walter's half-brother, Sir Humphrey Gilbert, was lost at sea and his colonial project collapsed, Raleigh petitioned the queen to transfer to him Gilbert's charter, and on March 25, 1584, he received letters patent that were almost identical with

Gilbert's. One difference was the exclusion from Raleigh's patent of rights to Newfoundland and its fisheries, claimed by Gilbert for the Crown. Raleigh and his heirs forever received the right "to discover, search, find out, and view such remote, heathen, and barbarous lands, countries, and territories not actually possessed of any Christian prince nor inhabited by Christian people." He could "travel thither to inhabit or remain, there to build and fortify at the discretion of the said Walter Raleigh." To settle colonies there he had the right to take "as many of our subjects as shall willingly accompany him" and also "to have, take, and employ and use sufficient shipping and furniture for the transportations and navigations."

With this instrument in hand, Raleigh lost no time in organizing an expedition to seek out a favorable spot for colonies on the unoccupied coast of North America. On April 27 two little ships, one commanded by Arthur Barlow and the other, by Philip Amadas, set sail for America with orders from Raleigh to head for the West Indies and then explore the coastline to the north.

The two vessels reached the West Indies early in June, and a month later they landed on Hatteras; the Outer Banks of the coast of modern North Carolina, one of the worst roadsteads on the entire Atlantic coast, offered no good harbor, but they anchored and went ashore on the narrow sandy island, which they claimed for Queen Elizabeth. Luckily no gale blew up. An exploring party visited Roanoke Island, later to be the site of the first colony. Friendly Indians who came out to trade impressed the explorers with their gentleness, and two, Manteo and Wanchese by name, were persuaded to go on the return voyage to England, which they reached in September. Barlow made an enthusiastic report to Raleigh which was printed by Hakluyt in the 1589 edition of *The Principal Navigations.*

Encouraged by the information gathered by the two captains, Raleigh began immediately to organize an expedition for the colonization of his new land, to which he had given the name Virginia in honor of the Virgin Queen. By the spring of 1585 everything was ready, and on April 9 five ships sailed from Plymouth under the command of Sir Richard Grenville, who followed the same course that Amadas and Barlow had taken by way of the West Indies, where he captured several Spanish

vessels. With the audacity of a Drake, Grenville landed on
Hispaniola and traded for livestock to take to Virginia. At
the end of June he anchored off Ocracoke Island on the Outer
Banks and for some days explored the region. Toward the end
of July the fleet moved to an anchorage which they called "Port
Ferdinando," near what we know as Oregon Inlet. After some
negotiation with the Roanoke Indians, with Manteo acting as
interpreter, Grenville decided to land his colonists on Roanoke
Island. On August 25 Grenville sailed away, leaving 107 men
with Ralph Lane as governor.

As yet there were no women in the colony, and the men
were to serve as a garrison rather than as settlers who would clear
land and establish homes. After all, one purpose of the colony
was to serve as a base where privateers could rendezvous for an
attack on Spanish shipping. Unfortunately the harbors in this
locality were unsuitable for such use.

Two important figures in this garrison were John White,
an artist of considerable skill, and Thomas Hariot, a mathematician and scientific observer. White's drawings of Indians,
as well as of flora and fauna, are the first illustrations made by
an Englishman of North American life. The illustrations have
been published in a handsome format by the University of
North Carolina press. Thomas Hariot made careful observations and wrote a detailed and highly favorable report on the
country in a work which he published in 1588 under the title
of *A Brief and True Report of the New-Found Land of Virginia*.
Ralph Lane also made a report which was printed by Hakluyt
in 1589.

Under Lane's direction, the men explored the back country
and went in search of gold, which was reported to be abundant
in rivers of the interior. They made no effort to sustain themselves by hunting and fishing, and the season was too far advanced to plant crops if they had possessed the skill to do so;
consequently they had to depend on the Roanoke Indians for
corn, fish and game. Eventually they wore out their welcome
and the Indians turned hostile. Lane attacked the Indians with
vigor and killed the chief and some of his principal warriors.
For the moment disaster was averted, but no longer could
Englishmen count the Indians as their friends.

The winter of 1585–86 was hard, and the men on Roanoke

were discouraged and disgruntled. When Sir Francis Drake in the second week of June 1586 sailed up the North Carolina coast and anchored off the Outer Banks, many wanted to go home in his fleet. He had come from a successful raid on the West Indies and had stopped long enough at Saint Augustine to destroy that Spanish base. Now he sent word to Lane that he was prepared to provide him with a ship and boats and men to man them, as well as supplies. Lane gladly accepted the ship *Francis*, of 70 tons, with which he hoped to move his men to a more favorable spot on Chesapeake Bay. But while these plans were being made, a summer storm broke and nearly wrecked the fleet. When it was over, the *Francis* sailed away with some of Lane's men who had gone aboard. The rest of the Roanoke garrison now grew panicky, and Lane decided to accept Drake's invitation to take the whole group back to England. They sailed on June 18 or 19. A short time afterward, a relief ship sent by Raleigh arrived off Roanoke to find the site deserted. A little later Grenville arrived with seven or eight ships, but by this time Raleigh's relief ship had departed and Grenville found only the empty houses of the colonists. He left a token force of 15 men and sailed away.

Although most of Lane's men had little good to say about "Virginia," White, Hariot and Lane himself gave such a good report that Raleigh determined to send out another colony, this time with women and children, to settle and make permanent homes in the new land. The expedition, consisting of 150 prospective settlers, sailed in three ships on May 8, 1587, with John White as governor. The new expedition had planned to settle on the Chesapeake but, after a row with his pilot, White was induced to land his colony at the old site on Roanoke Island, which they reached on June 22. No trace of the 15 men left by Grenville could be found. They had disappeared after an Indian attack.

A month after landing the colonists were already discouraged and begged White to return to England to expedite supplies and equipment that would enable them to remove to a better site. Reluctantly White agreed to go. He left his daughter Eleanor, wife of Ananias Dare, and a granddaughter who had been born to the couple on August 18. She was named Virginia Dare, the first English child born in America.

Before sailing, White arranged that if the colonists had to leave Roanoke, they would carve their destination on a tree, with a cross if they were forced to leave under attack. When he reached England, White persuaded Raleigh to hasten preparations for a relief ship to be sent to Roanoke, but not until the spring of 1588 was an expedition ready, again with Grenville in command. But, because of news of the threatening Spanish Armada, the Privy Council ordered Grenville to remain with his ships in home waters. White finally got permission to embark with two small vessels for Virginia, but their crews took to piracy soon after sailing and finally limped back to port without carrying out their mission. The Spanish Armada arrived off the channel coast in July, and no further aid for Virginia was available until after that crisis had passed. Not until 1590 was White again able to sail for Virginia, this time with a privateering expedition headed for the West Indies. But in August of that year two of the vessels anchored off Port Ferdinando, and White with a boat party went to Roanoke. The colony had disappeared. Carved on a tree were the letters "CRO" and on a post the word "CROATOAN." There was no cross, the signal of distress. What became of the "lost colony" no one knows. They may have put out to sea in boats and have been lost; they may have gone to Croatoan Island and been carried off by Indians. Their disappearance remains one of the mysteries of early American history.

Barlow Praises "Virginia"

[*Arthur Barlow, on his return from the reconnaissance voyage to North America in 1584, wrote an account of the new land and turned it over to Raleigh. Hakluyt received a copy, which he printed. Excerpts follow:*]

The 27th day of April, in the year of our redemption 1584, we departed the west of England with two barks well furnished with men and victuals, having received our last and perfect directions by your letters, confirming the former instructions and commandments delivered by yourself at our leaving the river of Thames. And I think it a matter both unnecessary for

the manifest discovery of the country as also for tediousness'
sake to remember unto you the diurnal [diary] of our course
sailing thither and returning. Only I have presumed to present
unto you this brief discourse by which you may judge how
profitable this land is likely to succeed, as well to yourself
(by whose direction and charge and by whose servants this our
discovery hath been performed), as also to Her Highness and
the commonwealth, in which we hope your wisdom will be
satisfied, considering that as much by us hath been brought to
light as by those small means and number of men we had could
any way have been expected or hoped for. . . .

The 2nd of July we found shoal water, which smelt so sweetly
and was so strong a smell as if we had been in the midst of
some delicate garden, abounding with all kind of odoriferous
flowers, by which we were assured that the land could not be
far distant. And keeping good watch and bearing but slack
sail the fourth of the same month, we arrived upon the coast,
which we supposed to be a continent and firm land, and we
sailed along the same 120 English miles before we could find
any entrance or river issuing into the sea. The first that appeared
unto us we entered, though not without some difficulty, and
cast anchor about three harquebus shot within the haven's
mouth on the left hand of the same. And after thanks given
to God for our safe arrival thither we manned our boats and
went to view the land next adjoining and to "take possession
of the same in the right of the Queen's Most Excellent Majesty
as rightful queen and princess of the same"; and after delivered
the same over to your use, according to Her Majesty's grant
and letters patents under Her Highness' Great Seal. Which
being performed according to the ceremonies used in such
enterprises, we viewed the land about us, being whereas we
first landed very sandy and low toward the waterside, but so
full of grapes as the very beating and surge of the sea overflowed
them, of which we found such plenty, as well there as in all
places else, both on the sand and on the green soil, on the hills
as in the plains, as well on every little shrub as also climbing
toward the tops of the high cedars, that I think in all the world
the like abundance is not to be found, and myself, having seen
those parts of Europe that most abound, find such difference
as were incredible to be written.

We passed from the seaside toward the tops of those hills next
adjoining, being but of mean height, and from thence we beheld the sea on both sides to the north and to the south, finding
no end any of both ways. This land lay stretching itself to the
west, which after[ward] we found to be but an island of 20
leagues long and not above six miles broad. Under the bank
or hill whereon we stood we beheld the valleys replenished with
goodly cedar trees and, having discharged our harquebus shot,
such a flock of cranes (the most part white) arose under us,
with such a cry redoubled by many echoes, as if an army of
men had shouted all together.

This island had many goodly woods full of deer, conies,
hares, and fowl, even in the midst of summer, in incredible
abundance. The woods are not such as you find in Bohemia,
Muscovia [Russia], or Hyrcania [Iran], barren and fruitless,
but the highest and reddest cedars of the world, far bettering
the cedars of the Azores, of the Indies, or of Libanus [Lebanon];
pines, cypress, sassafras, the lentiscus, or the tree that beareth
the mastic, the tree that beareth the rind of black cinnamon
of which Master Winter brought from the Straits of Magellan,
and many other of excellent smell and quality.

We remained by the side of this island two whole days before
we saw any people of the country. The third day we espied one
small boat rowing toward us, having in it three persons. This
boat came to the land's side, four harquebus shot from our
ships, and there, two of the people remaining, the third came
along the shore side toward us, and, we being then all within-
board, he walked up and down upon the point of the land next
unto us. Then the master and the pilot of the admiral, Simon
Ferdinando [Fernandez], and the captain, Philip Amadas, myself, and others rowed to the land, whose coming this fellow
attended, never making any show of fear or doubt.

And after he had spoken of many things not understood by
us, we brought him with his own good liking aboard the ships
and gave him a shirt, a hat, and some other things and made
him taste of our wine and our meat, which he liked very well.
And after having viewed both barks he departed and went to
his own boat again, which he had left in a little cove or creek
adjoining. As soon as he was two bowshots into the water, he
fell to fishing, and in less than half an hour he had laden his

boat as deep as it could swim, with which he came again to
the point of the land, and there he divided his fish into two
parts, pointing [appointing] one part to the ship and the other
to the pinnace, which, after he had (as much as he might) requited the former benefits received, he departed out of our
sight.

The next day there came unto us divers boats and in one of
them the king's brother, accompanied with 40 or 50 men, very
handsome and goodly people and in their behavior as mannerly
and civil as any of Europe. His name was Granganimeo, and
the king is called Wingina, the country Wingandacoa (and now,
by Her Majesty, Virginia). The manner of his coming was in
this sort: he left his boats altogether, as the first man did a little
from the ships by the shore, and came along to the place over
against the ships, followed with 40 men. When he came to the
place, his servants spread a long mat upon the ground on which
he sat down, and at the other end of the mat four others of his
company did the like; the rest of his men stood round about
him, somewhat afar off. When we came to the shore to him
with our weapons, he never moved from his place, nor any of
the other four, nor never mistrusted any harm to be offered
from us, but, sitting still, he beckoned us to come and sit by
him; which we performed, and, being set, he makes all signs
of joy and welcome, striking on his head and his breast and
afterward on ours, to show we were all one, smiling and making
show the best he could of all love and familiarity. After he
had made a long speech unto us, we presented him with divers
things, which he received very joyfully and thankfully. None
of his company durst to speak one word all the time; only the
four which were at the other end spake one in the other's ear
very softly.

The king is greatly obeyed and his brothers and children
reverenced. The king himself in person was at our being there
[while we were there] sore wounded in a fight which he had
with the king of the next country called Wingina [sic] and was
shot in two places through the body and once clean through
the thigh, but yet he recovered; by reason whereof and for that
he lay at the chief town of the country; being six days' journey
off, we saw him not at all.

After we had presented this his brother with such things as

we thought he liked, we likewise gave somewhat to the other[s] that sat with him on the mat. But presently he arose and took all from them and put it into his own basket, making signs and tokens that all things ought to be delivered unto him and the rest were but his servants and followers.

A day or two after this, we fell to trading with them, exchanging some things that we had for chamois, buff[alo], and deerskins. When we showed him all our packet of merchandise, of all things that he saw a bright tin dish most pleased him, which he presently took up and clapped it before his breast and after made a hole in the brim thereof and hung it about his neck, making signs that it would defend him against his enemies' arrows, for those people maintain a deadly and terrible war with the people and king adjoining. We exchanged our tin dish for 20 skins worth 20 crowns or 20 nobles and a copper kettle for 50 skins worth 50 crowns. They offered us very good exchange for our hatchets and axes and for knives, and would have given anything for swords, but we would not depart [part] with any.

After two or three days the king's brother came aboard the ships and drank wine and ate of our meat and of our bread and liked exceedingly thereof. And after a few days overpassed he brought his wife with him to the ships, his daughter, and two or three little children. His wife was very well favored, of mean [medium] stature and very bashful. She had on her back a long cloak of leather with the fur side next to her body and before her a piece of the same. About her forehead she had a broad band of white coral and so had her husband many times. In her ears she had bracelets of pearls, hanging down to her middle (whereof we delivered Your Worship a little bracelet) and those were of the bigness of good peas.

The rest of her women of the better sort had pendants of copper hanging in every ear, and some of the children of the king's brother and other noblemen have five or six in every ear. He himself had upon his head a broad plate of gold or copper, for, being unpolished, we knew not what metal it should be, neither would he by any means suffer us to take it off his head, but, feeling it, it would bow very easily.

His apparel was as his wives', only the women wear their hair long on both sides and the men but on one. They are of color yellowish, and their hair black for the most part, and yet we saw children that had very fine auburn and chestnut-colored hair.

After that these women had been there, there came down from all parts great store of people, bringing with them leather, coral, divers kinds of dyes very excellent, and exchanged with us; but when Granganimeo, the king's brother, was present none durst to trade but himself, except such as wear red pieces of copper on their heads like himself, for that is the difference between the noblemen and governors of countries and the meaner sort. And we both noted there, and you have understood since by these men [Wanchese and Manteo], which we brought home, that no people in the world carry more respect to their king, nobility, and governors than these do. The king's brother's wife, when she came to us, as she did many times, she was followed with 40 or 50 women always, and when she came into the ship, she left them all on land, saving her two daughters, her nurse, and one or two more. The king's brother always kept this order: as many boats as he would come withal to the ships, so many fires would he make on the shore afar off, to the end we might understand with what strength and company he approached.

Their boats are made of one tree, either of pine or of pitch trees, a wood not commonly known to our people nor found growing in England. They have no edge tools to make them withal. If they have any, they are very few and those it seems they had 20 years since, which as those two men declared was out of a wrack which happened upon their coast of some Christian ship, being beaten that way by some storm and outrageous weather, whereof none of the people were saved but only the ship or some part of her, being cast upon the sand, out of whose sides they drew the nails and spikes, and with those they made their best instruments. Their manner of making their boats is this: they burn down some great tree or take such as are wind-fallen, and, putting myrrh and rosin upon one side thereof, they set fire into it, and when it hath burnt it hollow, they cut out the coal with their shells, and everywhere they would burn it deeper or wider they lay on their gums, which burneth away the timber, and by this means they fashion very fine boats and such as will transport 20 men. Their oars are like scoops, and many times they set [push] with long poles, as the depth serveth.

The king's brother had great liking of our armor, a sword, and divers others things which we had, and offered to lay a great box of pearl in gage [deposit] for them, but we refused it for this time, because we would not make them know that we esteemed thereof until we had understood in what places of the country the pearl grew, which now Your Worship doth very well understand.

He was very just of his promise, for many times we delivered him merchandise upon his word, but ever he came within the day and performed his promise. He sent us every day a brace or two of fat bucks, conies, hares, fish, the best of the world. He sent us divers kinds of fruits, melons, walnuts, cucumbers, gourds, peas, and divers roots and fruits very excellent good, and of their country corn, which is very white, fair, and well tasted, and groweth three times in five months. In May they sow, in July they reap; in June they sow, in August they reap; in July they sow, in September they reap. Only they cast the corn into the ground, breaking a little of the soft turf with a wooden mattock or pickaxe. Ourselves proved the soil and put some of our peas into the ground, and in ten days they were of 14 inches high. They have also beans very fair, of divers colors and wonderful plenty, some growing naturally, and some in their gardens, and so have they wheat and oats.

The soil is the most plentiful, sweet, fruitful, and wholesome of all the world. There are above 14 several sweet-smelling timber trees, and the most part of their underwoods are bays and suchlike. They have those oaks that we have, but far greater and better.

After they had been divers times aboard our ships, myself with seven more went 20 mile into the river that runneth toward the city of Skicoake [near the site of Portsmouth, Virginia], which river they call Occam, and the evening following we came to an island which they call Roanoke, distant from the harbor by which we entered seven leagues. And at the north end thereof was a village of nine houses built of cedar and fortified round about with sharp trees to keep out their enemies and the entrance into it made it like a turnpike very artificially.

When we came toward it, standing near unto the water's side, the wife of Granganimeo, the king's brother, came running out to meet us very cheerfully and friendly. Her husband was not then in the village. Some of her people she commanded to draw our boat on the shore for the beating of the billow. Others she appointed to carry us on their backs to the dry ground and others to bring our oars into the house for fear of stealing. When we were come into the utter room, having five rooms in her house, she caused us to sit down by a great fire and after took off our clothes and washed them and dried them again. Some of the women pulled off our stockings and washed them. Some washed our feet in warm water, and she herself took great pains to see all things ordered in the best manner she could, making great haste to dress some meat for us to eat.

After we had thus dried ourselves, she brought us into the inner room, where she set on the board standing along the house some wheatlike frumenty [porridge], sodden [boiled] venison and roasted, fish sodden, boiled, and roasted, melons raw and sodden, roots of divers kinds, and divers fruits. Their drink is commonly water, but while the grape lasteth they drink wine, and, for want of casks to keep it, all the year after they drink water, but it is sodden with ginger in it and black cinnamon, and sometimes sassafras and divers other wholesome and medicinable herbs and trees.

We were entertained with all love and kindness and with as much bounty after their manner as they could possibly devise. We found the people most gentle, loving, and faithful, void of all guile and treason and such as lived after the manner of the Golden Age. The earth bringeth forth all things in abundance as in the first creation, without toil or labor. The people only care to defend themselves from the cold in their short winter and to feed themselves with such meat as the soil affordeth. Their meat is very well sodden, and they make broth very sweet and savory. Their vessels are earthen pots, very large, white, and sweet; their dishes are wooden platters of sweet timber. Within the place where they feed was their lodging and within that their idol which they worship, of which they speak incredible things. . . .

. . . They had our ships in marvelous admiration, and all things else were so strange unto them as it appeared that none of them had ever seen the like. When we discharged any piece, were it but a harquebus, they would tremble thereat for very fear and for the strangeness of the same, for the weapons which themselves use are bows and arrows.

The arrows are but of small canes, headed with a sharp shell or tooth of a fish sufficient enough to kill a naked man. Their swords are of wood hardened; likewise they use wooden breastplates for their defense. The have besides a kind of club in the end whereof they fasten the sharp horns of a stag or other beast. When they go to wars they carry with them their idol, of whom they ask counsel as the Romans were wont of the oracle of Apollo. They sing songs as they march toward the battle, instead of drums and trumpets. Their wars are very cruel and bloody, by reason whereof and of their civil dissensions, which have happened of late years amongst them, the people are marvelously wasted and in some places the country left desolate. . . .

Beyond this island called Roanoke are many islands very plentiful of fruits and other natural increases, together with many towns and villages along the side of the continent, some bounding upon the islands and some stretching up further into the land.

When we first had sight of this country, some thought the first land we saw to be the continent, but after we entered into the haven we saw before us another mighty long sea, for there lieth along the coast a tract of islands 200 miles in length, adjoining to the ocean sea, and between the islands two or three entrances. When you are entered between them (these islands being very narrow for the most part, as in most places six miles broad, in some places less, in few more) then there appeareth another great sea, containing in breadth in some places 40, and in some 50, in some 20 miles over, before you come unto the continent, and in this enclosed sea there are about 100 islands of divers bignesses, whereof one is 16 miles long, at which we were, finding it to be a most pleasant and fertile ground, replenished with goodly cedars and divers other sweet woods full of currants, of flax, and many other notable commodities, which we at that time had no leisure to view. Besides this island, there are many, as I have said, some of two, of three, of four, of five miles, some more, some less, most beautiful and pleasant to behold, replenished with deer, conies, hares, and divers beasts, and about them the goodliest and best fish in the world and in great abundance.

Thus, sir, we have acquainted you with the particulars of our discovery, made this present voyage, as far north as the shortness of the time we there continued would afford to us to take view of. And so contenting ourselves with this service at this time, which we hope hereafter to enlarge as occasion and assistance shall be given, we resolved to leave the country and to apply ourselves to return for England, which we did accordingly and arrived safely in the west of England about the midst of September.

Ralph Lane's Optimistic Account of the New Land

[*Ralph Lane, acting governor of the first colony at Roanoke, wrote a glowing report to Richard Hakluyt the Elder, cousin of Richard Hakluyt, compiler of the voyages. "An extract of M. Lane's letter," first printed in Hakluyt's* Principal Navigations *(1598–1600) follows:*]

In the meanwhile you shall understand that since Sir Richard Grenville's departure from us, as also before, we have discovered the main[land] to be the goodliest soil under the cope of heaven, so abounding with sweet trees that bring such sundry rich and pleasant gums, grapes of such greatness, yet wild, as France, Spain, nor Italy hath no greater, so many sorts of apothecary drugs, such several kinds of flax, and one kind like silk, the same gathered of a grass as common there as grass is here. And now within these few days we have found here a Guinea wheat, whose ear yieldeth corn for bread, 400 upon one ear, and the cane maketh very good and perfect sugar. . . . Besides that, it is the goodliest and most pleasing territory of the world (for the soil is of an huge and unknown greatness, and very well peopled and towned, though savagely) and the climate so wholesome that we had not one sick since we touched the land here. To conclude, if Virginia had but horses and kine in some reasonable proportion, I dare assure myself, being inhabited with English, no realm in Christendom were comparable to it. For this already we find, that what commodities soever Spain, France, Italy, or the East parts do yield unto us in wines of all sorts, in oils, in flax, in rosins, pitch, frankincense, currants, sugars, and suchlike, these parts do abound with the growth of them all, but, being savages that possess the land, they know no use of the same. And sundry other rich commodities that no parts of the world, be they West or East Indies, have, here we find great abundance of. The people naturally are most courteous and very desirous to have clothes, but especially of coarse cloth rather than silk; coarse canvas they also like well of, but copper carrieth the price of all, so it be made red. Thus good M. Hakluyt and Master H., I have joined you both in one letter of remembrance, as two that I love dearly well; and, commending me most heartily to you both, I commit you to the tuition of the Almighty. From the new Fort in Virginia, this 3 September 1585.

Your most assured friend
Rafe Lane

Hariot's "Brief Report"

[*The most famous of the early accounts of Raleigh's colony was Thomas Hariot's* A Brief and True Report of the New-Found Land of Virginia (*1588*). *It was reprinted in 1590 by Theodor de Bry with engravings based on White's drawings. Excerpts follow:*]

To the adventurers, favorers, and well-willers of the enterprise for the inhabiting and planting of Virginia:

Since the first undertaking by Sir Walter Raleigh to deal in the action of discovering of that country which is now called and known by the name of Virginia, many voyages having been thither made at sundry times to his great charge, as first in the year 1584 and afterwards in the years 1585, 1586, and now of late this last year of 1587, there have been divers and variable reports, with some slanderous and shameful speeches, bruited abroad by many that returned from thence. Especially of that discovery which was made by the colony transported by

Sir Richard Grenville in the year 1585, being of all the others
the most principal and as yet of most effect, the time of their
abode in the country being a whole year, whenas in the other
voyage before they stayed but six weeks, and the others after
were only for supply and transportation, nothing more being
discovered than had been before.

Which reports have not done a little wrong to many that
otherwise would have also favored and adventured in the action,
to the honor and benefit of our nation, besides the particular
profit and credit which would redound to themselves, the
dealers therein, as I hope by the sequel of events, to the shame
of those that have avouched the contrary, shall be manifest, if
you, the adventurers, favorers, and well-willers, do but either
increase in number or in opinion continue, or, having been
doubtful, renew your good liking and furtherance to deal
therein according to the worthiness thereof already found and
as you shall understand hereafter to be requisite. Touching
which worthiness, through cause of the diversity of relations
and reports, many of your opinions could not be firm nor the
minds of some that are well disposed be settled in any certainty.

I have therefore thought it good, being one that have been in
the discovery and in dealing with the natural inhabitants
specially employed, and having therefore seen and known more
than the ordinary, to impart so much unto you of the fruits of
our labors as that you may know how injuriously the enterprise
is slandered. . . .

Of our company that returned, some for their misdemeanor
and ill dealing in the country have been there worthily punished, who by reason of their bad natures have maliciously not
only spoken ill of their governors but for their sakes slandered
the country itself. The like also have those done which were
of their consort.

Some, being ignorant of the state thereof, notwithstanding
since their return amongst their friends and acquaintance, and
also others, especially if they were in company where they
might not be gainsaid, would seem to know so much as no
men more and make no men so great travelers as themselves.
They stood so much, as it may seem, upon their credit and
reputation that, having been a twelvemonth in the country, it

would have been a great disgrace unto them, as they thought, if they could not have said much, whether it were true or false. Of which some have spoken of more than ever they saw or otherwise knew to be there; othersome have not been ashamed to make absolute denial of that which, although not by them yet by others, is most certainly and there plentifully known. And othersome make difficulties of those things they have no skill [knowledge] of.

The cause of their ignorance was in that they were of the many that were never out of the island where we were seated, or not far, or at the leastwise in few places else, during the time of our abode in the country; or of that many that, after gold and silver was not so soon found as it was by them looked for, had little or no care of any other thing but to pamper their bellies; or of that many which had little understanding, less discretion, and more tongue than was needful or requisite.

Some, also, were of a nice bringing-up, only in cities or towns, or such as never (as I may say) had seen the world before. Because there were not to be found any English cities, nor such fair houses, nor at their own wish any of their old accustomed dainty food, nor any soft beds of down or feathers, the country was to them miserable and their reports thereof according. . . .

Of the Nature and Manners of the People

It resteth I speak a word or two of the natural inhabitants, their natures and manners, leaving large discourse thereof until time more convenient hereafter: now only so far forth as that you may know how that in respect of troubling our inhabiting and planting [they] are not to be feared, but that they shall have cause both to fear and love us that shall inhabit with them.

They are a people clothed with loose mantles made of deerskins and aprons of the same round about their middles, all else naked; of such a difference of statures only as we in England; having no edge tools or weapons of iron or steel to offend us withal, neither know they how to make any: those weapons that they have are only bows made of witch hazel and arrows of reeds, flat-edged truncheons, also of wood, about a yard long, neither have they anything to defend themselves but targets [shields] made of barks and some armors made of sticks wickered together with thread.

Their towns are but small and near the seacoast but few, some containing but ten or 12 houses, some 20; the greatest that we have seen have been but of 30 houses. If they be walled, it is only done with barks of trees made fast to stakes, or else with poles only fixed upright and close one by another.

Their houses are made of small poles made fast at the tops in round form after the manner as is used in many arbors in our gardens of England, in most towns covered with barks and in some with artificial mats, made of long rushes, from the tops of the houses down to the ground. The length of them is commonly double to the breadth; in some places they are but 12 and 16 yards long, and in othersome we have seen of four and 20.

In some places of the country one only town belongeth to the government of a werowance or chief lord; in othersome two or three; in some six, eight, and more. The greatest werowance that yet we had dealing with had but 18 towns in his government and able to make not above 700 or 800 fighting men at the most. The language of every government is different from any other, and the further they are distant, the greater is the difference.

Their manner of wars amongst themselves is either by sudden surprising one another, most commonly about the dawning of the day or moonlight, or else by ambushes or some subtle devices. Set battles are very rare, except it fall out where there are many trees, where either part may have some hope of defense, after the delivery of every arrow, in leaping behind some or other.

If there fall out any wars between us and them, what their fight is likely to be, we having advantages against them so many manner of ways, as by our discipline, our strange weapons and devices else, especially by ordnance great and small, it may be easily imagined: by the experience we have had in some places, the turning up of their heels against us in running away was their best defense.

In respect of us they are a people poor, and for want of skill and judgment in the knowledge and use of our things do esteem our trifles before things of greater value. Notwithstanding, in their proper manner, considering the want of such means as we have, they seem very ingenious; for although they have no such tools, nor any such crafts, sciences, and arts as we, yet in those things they do they show excellency of wit. And by how much they upon due consideration shall find our manner of knowledges and crafts to exceed theirs in perfection and speed for doing or execution, by so much the more is it probable that they should desire our friendships and love and have the greater respect for pleasing and obeying us. Whereby may be hoped, if means of good government be used, that they may in short time be brought to civility and the embracing of true religion.

Some religion they have already, which although it be far from the truth, yet being as it is, there is hope it may be the easier and sooner reformed.

They believe that there are many gods, which they call *mantóac,* but of different sorts and degrees, one only chief and great god, which hath been from all eternity. Who, as they affirm, when he purposed to make the world, made first other gods of a principal order to be as means and instruments to be used in the creation and government to follow, and after the sun, moon, and stars as petty gods and the instruments of the other order more principal. First, they say, were made waters, out of which by the gods was made all diversity of creatures that are visible or invisible.

For mankind, they say a woman was made first, which by the working of one of the gods conceived and brought forth children; and in such sort they say they had their beginning. . . .

They think that all the gods are of human shape, and therefore they represent them by images in the forms of men, which they call *kewasówok*—one alone is called *kewás;* them they place in houses appropriate, or temples, which they call *machicómuck,* where they worship, play, sing, and make many times offerings unto them. In some *machicómuck* we have seen but one *kewás,* in some two, and in othersome three; the common sort think them to be also gods.

They believe also the immortality of the soul, that after this life, as soon as the soul is departed from the body, according to the works it hath done it is either carried to Heaven, the habitacle of gods, there to enjoy perpetual bliss and happiness, or else to a great pit or hole, which they think to be in the furthest parts of their part of the world toward the sunset, there to burn continually; the place they call *popogusso*. . . .

Most things they saw with us, as mathematical instruments, sea compasses, the virtue of the lodestone in drawing iron, a perspective glass, whereby was showed many strange sights, burning glasses, wildfire works, guns, books (writing and reading), spring clocks that seem to go of themselves, and many other things that we had, were so strange unto them and so far exceeded their capacities to comprehend the reason and means how they should be made and done, that they thought they were rather the works of gods than of men, or at the leastwise they had been given and taught us of the gods. . . .

Many times and in every town where I came, according as I was able, I made declaration of the contents of the Bible: that therein was set forth the true and only God and His mighty works; that therein was contained the true doctrine of salvation through Christ; with many particularities of miracles and chief points of religion, as I was able then to utter and thought fit for the time. And although I told them the book materially and of itself was not of any such virtue as I thought they did conceive, but only the doctrine therein contained, yet would many be glad to touch it, to embrace it, to kiss it, to hold it to their breasts and heads and stroke over all their body with it, to show their hungry desire of that knowledge which was spoken of.

The werowance with whom we dwelt, called Wingina, and many of his people, would be glad many times to be with us at our prayers, and many times call upon us both in his own town as also in others whither he sometimes accompanied us, to pray and sing psalms, hoping thereby to be partaker of the same effects which we by that means also expected. . . .

There was no town where we had any subtle device practiced against us, we leaving it unpunished or not revenged (because we sought by all means possible to win them by gentleness), but that within a few days after our departure from every such town the people began to die very fast, and many in short space: in some towns about 20, in some 40, in some 60, and in one sixscore, which in truth was very many in respect of their numbers. This happened in no place that we could learn but where we had been where they used some practice against us, and after such time. The disease, also, was so strange that they neither knew what it was nor how to cure it; the like, by report of the oldest men in the country, never happened before, time out of mind—a thing specially observed by us, as also by the natural inhabitants themselves.

Insomuch that when some of the inhabitants which were our friends, and especially the werowance Wingina, had observed such effects in four or five towns to follow their wicked practices, they were persuaded that it was the work of our God through our means, and that we by Him might kill and slay whom we would, without weapons, and not come near them.

And thereupon, when it had happened that they had understanding that any of their enemies had abused us in our journeys, hearing that we had wrought no revenge with our weapons and fearing upon some cause the matter should so rest, [they] did come and entreat us that we would be a means to our God that they as others that had dealt ill with us might in like sort die, alleging how much it would be for our credit and profit, as also theirs, and hoping, furthermore, that we would do so much at their requests in respect of the friendship we profess them.

Whose entreaties, although we showed that they were ungodly, affirming that our God would not subject Himself to any such prayers and requests of men; that indeed all things have been and were to be done according to His good pleasure as He had ordained; and that we, to show ourselves His true servants, ought rather to make petition for the contrary, that they with them might live together with us, be made partakers of His truth and serve Him in righteousness; but, notwithstanding, in such sort that we refer that, as all other things, to be done according to His divine will and pleasure and as by His wisdom He had ordained to be best.

Yet because the effect fell out so suddenly and shortly after according to their desires, they thought nevertheless it came to pass by our means, and that we in using such speeches unto them did but dissemble the matter, and therefore came unto us to give us thanks in their manner, that although we satisfied them not in promise, yet in deeds and effect we had fullfilled their desires.

This marvelous accident in all the country wrought so strange opinions of us that some people could not tell whether to think us gods or men, and the rather because that all the space of their sickness there was no man of ours known to die or that was specially sick; they noted also that we had no women amongst us, neither that we did care for any of theirs.

Some, therefore, were of opinion that we were not born of women and therefore not mortal, but that we were men of an old generation many years past, then risen again to immortality. . . .

These their opinions I have set down the more at large that it may appear unto you that there is good hope they may be brought through discreet dealing and government to the embracing of the truth and consequently to honor, obey, fear, and love us.

And although some of our company toward the end of the year showed themselves too fierce, in slaying some of the people in some towns upon causes that on our part might easily have been borne withal, yet notwithstanding, because it was on their part justly deserved, the alteration of their opinions generally and for the most part concerning us is the less to be doubted, and, whatsoever else they may be, by carefulness of ourselves need nothing at all to be feared.

John White Returns to Roanoke as Governor

[John White, appointed governor of the second colony attempted at Roanoke, wrote an account of "The Fourth Voyage Made to Virginia in the Year 1587," which Hakluyt published in 1589. Excerpts follow:]

In the year of Our Lord 1587, Sir Walter Raleigh, intending to persevere in the planting of his country of Virginia, prepared a new colony of 150 men to be sent thither under the charge of John White, whom he appointed governor, and also appointed unto him 12 assistants, unto whom he gave a charter and incorporated them by the name of Governor and Assistants of the city of Raleigh in Virginia. . . .

About the 16th of July we fell with the main of Virginia,

which Simon Fernando took to be the island of Croatoan, where we came to an anchor and rode there two or three days; but, finding himself deceived, he weighed and bare along the coast, where in the night, had not Captain Stafford been more careful in looking out than our Simon Fernando, we had been all cast away upon the beach called the Cape of Fear [modern Cape Lookout], for we were come within two cables' length upon it, such was the carelessness and ignorance of our master.

The 22nd of July we arrived safe at Hatarask [Hatteras], where our ship and pinnace anchored. The governor went aboard the pinnace, accompanied with 40 of his best men, intending to pass up to Roanoke forthwith, hoping there to find those 15 Englishmen which Sir Richard Grenville had left there the year before, with whom he meant to have conference concerning the state of the country and savages; meaning after he had so done to return again to the fleet and pass along the coast to the Bay of Chesapeake, where we intended to make our seat and fort according to the charge given us among other directions in writing under the hand of Sir Walter Raleigh. But as soon as we were put with our pinnace from the ship, a gentleman by the name of Fernando, who was appointed to return for England, called to the sailors in the pinnace, charging them not to bring any of the planters back again but leave them in the island, except the governor and two or three such as he approved, saying that the summer was far spent, wherefore he would land all the planters in no other place. Unto this were all the sailors, both in the pinnace and ship, persuaded by the master; wherefore it booted not the governor to contend with them but passed to Roanoke and the same night at sunset went aland on the island in the place where our 15 men were left; but we found none of them nor any signs that they had been there, saving only we found the bones of one of those 15 which the savages had slain long before.

The 23rd of July, the Governor with divers of his company walked to the north end of the island where Master Ralph Lane had his fort, with sundry necessary and decent dwelling houses, made by his men about it the year before, where we hoped to find some signs or certain knowledge of our 15 men. When we came thither we found the fort razed down but all the houses standing unhurt, saving the nether rooms of them and also of the fort were overgrown with melons of divers sorts, and deer within them feeding on those melons; so we returned to our company without hope of ever seeing any of the 15 men living.

The same day order was given that every man should be employed for the repairing of those houses which we found standing, and also to make other new cottages for such as should need. . . .

The 8th of August, the governor, having long expected the coming of the werowances of Pomeiooc, Aquascogoc, Secotan, and Dasemunkepeuc, seeing that the seven days were past within which they promised to come in or to send their answers by the men of Croatoan and no tidings of them heard, being certainly also informed by those men of Croatoan that the remnant of Wingina his men which were left alive, who dwelt at Dasemunkepeuc, were they which had slain George Howe and were also at the driving of our 11 Englishmen from Roanoke, he thought to defer the revenging thereof no longer. Wherefore the same night about midnight he passed over the water, accompanied with Captain Stafford and 24 men, whereof Manteo was one, whom we took with us to be our guide to the place where those savages dwelt, where he behaved himself toward us as a most faithful Englishman.

The next day, being the 9th of August, in the morning so early that it was yet dark, we landed near the dwelling place of our enemies and very secretly conveyed ourselves through the woods to that side where we had their houses between us and the water; and, having espied their fire and some sitting about it, we presently set on them. The miserable souls, herewith amazed, fled into a place of thick reeds growing fast by, where our men, perceiving them, shot one of them through the body with a bullet, and therewith we entered the reeds, among which we hoped to acquit their evil doing toward us. But we were deceived, for those savages were our friends and were come from Croatoan to gather the corn and fruit of that place, because they understood our enemies were fled immediately after they had slain George Howe and for haste had left all their corn, tobacco, and pompions [pumpkins] standing, in such sort that all had been devoured of the birds and deer if it had not been gathered in time. But they had like to have paid dearly for it; for it was so dark that, they being naked and their men and women appareled all so like others, we knew not but that they were all men; and if that one of them which was a werowance's wife had not had her child at her back, she had been slain instead of a man. And as hap was, another savage knew Master Stafford and ran to him, calling him by his name, whereby he was saved.

Finding ourselves thus disappointed of our purpose, we gathered all the corn, peas, pompions, and tobacco that we found ripe, leaving the rest unspoiled, and took Menatonon his wife, with the young child, and the other savages, with us over the water to Roanoke.

Although the mistaking of these savages somewhat grieved Manteo, yet he imputed their harm to their own folly, saying to them that if their werowances had kept their promise in coming to the governor at the day appointed, they had not known that mischance.

The 13th of August our savage Manteo, by the commandment of Sir Walter Raleigh, was christened in Roanoke and called Lord thereof and of Dasemunkepeuc, in reward of his faithful services.

The 18th, Eleanor, daughter to the governor and wife to Ananias Dare, one of the assistants, was delivered of a daughter in Roanoke, and the same was christened there the Sunday following; and because this child was the first Christian in Virginia, she was named Virginia.

By this time our ships had unladed the goods and victuals of the planters and began to take in wood and fresh water and to new caulk and trim them for England; the planters also prepared their letters and tokens to send back into England. . . .

The 22nd of August the whole company, both of the assistants and planters, came to the governor and with one voice requested him to return himself into England for the better and sooner obtaining of supplies and other necessaries for them; but he refused it and alleged many sufficient causes why he would not. The one was that he could not so suddenly return back again without his great discredit, leaving the action and so

many whom he partly had procured through his persuasions
to leave their native country and undertake that voyage, and
that some enemies to him and the action at his return into England would not spare to slander falsely both him and the action
by saying he went to Virginia but politicly and to no other end
but to lead so many into a country in which he never meant
to stay himself and there to leave them behind him. Also he
alleged that, seeing they intended to remove 50 miles further
up in the main presently, he being then absent, his stuff and
goods might be both spoiled and most of it pilfered away in the
carriage, so that at his return he should be either forced to
provide himself of all such things again or else at his coming
again to Virginia find himself utterly unfurnished, whereof
already he had found some proof, being once from them but
three days. Wherefore he concluded that he would not go
himself. . . .

The governor, being at the last, through their extreme en-
treating, constrained to return into England, having then but
half a day's respite to prepare himself for the same, departed
from Roanoke the seven-and-twentieth of August in the morning.

White's Last Voyage in Search of the Lost Colony

[*In 1590 John White sailed in an expedition of three vessels
headed for the West Indies. Through Raleigh's influence he
obtained a promise that the ships would take him to Virginia
to make a search for the colonists left on Roanoke Island. His
journal of the voyage, telling of his unsuccessful efforts, was
sent to Richard Hakluyt with a covering letter dated February
4, 1593. Excerpts follow:*]

To the Worshipful and my very friend Master Richard Hakluyt, much happiness in the Lord.

Sir, as well for the satisfying of your earnest request as the
performance of my promise made unto you at my last being
with you in England, I have sent you (although in a homely
style, especially for the contentation of a delicate ear) the true

discourse of my last voyage into the West Indies and parts of America called Virginia, taken in hand about the end of February in the year of our redemption 1590. . . .

There were at the time aforesaid three ships absolutely determined to go for the West Indies, at the special charges of M. John Watts of London, merchant. But when they were fully furnished and in readiness to make their departure, a general stay was commanded of all ships throughout England. Which so soon as I heard, I presently (as I thought most requisite) acquainted Sir Walter Raleigh therewith, desiring him that as I had sundry times afore been chargeable and troublesome unto him for the supplies and reliefs of the planters in Virginia, so likewise that by his endeavor it would please him at that instant to procure license for those three ships to proceed on with their determined voyage, that thereby the people in Virginia (if it were God's pleasure) might speedily be comforted and relieved without further charges unto him. Whereupon he, by his good means, obtained license of the Queen's Majesty, and order to be taken, that the owner of the three ships should be bound unto Sir Walter Raleigh or his assigns in 3,000 pounds, that those three ships in consideration of their releasement should take in and transport a convenient number of passengers, with their furnitures and necessaries, to be landed in Virginia.

Nevertheless that order was not observed, neither was the bond taken according to the intention aforesaid. But rather, in contempt of the aforesaid order, I was by the owner and commanders of the ships denied to have any passengers, or anything else transported in any of the said ships saving only myself and my chest; no, not so much as a boy to attend upon me, although I made great suit and earnest entreaty as well to the chief commanders as to the owner of the said ships. Which cross and unkind dealing . . . notwithstanding, the scarcity of time was such that I could have no opportunity to go unto Sir Walter Raleigh with complaint; for the ships, being then all in readiness to go to sea, would have been departed before I could have made my return. Thus both governors, masters, and sailors, regarding very smally the good of their countrymen in Virginia, determined nothing less than to touch at those places, but wholly disposed themselves to seek after purchase and spoils, spending so much time therein that summer was spent before we arrived at Virginia. And when we were come thither, the season was so unfit, and weather so foul, that we were constrained of force to forsake that coast, having not seen any of our planters, with loss of one of our ship-boats and seven of our chiefest men. . . .

Thus committing the relief of my discomfortable company, the planters in Virginia, to the merciful help of the Almighty, whom I most humbly beseech to help and comfort them according to His most holy will and their good desire, I take my leave. From my house at Newtown in Kylmore the 4 of February, 1593.

> Your most well-wishing friend,
> JOHN WHITE

The fifth voyage of M. John White into the West Indies and parts of America called Virginia, in the year 1590.

The 20 of March the three ships, the *Hopewell,* the *John Evangelist,* and the *Little John,* put to sea from Plymouth with two small shallops.

The 25th at midnight both our shallops were sunk being towed at the ships' sterns by the boatswain's negligence. . . .

On the 12 [of August] . . . toward night we came to an anchor at the northeast end of the island of Croatoan by reason of a breach which we perceived to lie out two or three leagues into the sea. Here we rode all that night.

The 13 in the morning, before we weighed our anchors, our boats were sent to sound over this breach. . . . This breach is in 35 degr. and a half and lieth at the very northeast point of Croatoan, whereas goeth a fret [strait] out of the main sea into the inner waters which part the islands and the mainland.

The 15 of August toward evening we came to an anchor at Hatarask, in 36 degr. and one-third, in five fathom water three leagues from the shore. At our first coming to anchor on this shore we saw a great smoke rise in the isle Roanoke near the place where I left our colony in the year 1587, which smoke put us in good hope that some of the colony were there expecting my return out of England.

The 16 and next morning our two boats went ashore, and Captain Cook and Captain Spicer and their company with me,

with intent to pass to the place at Roanoke where our countrymen were left. At our putting from the ship we commanded
our master gunner to make ready two minions and a falcon
well loaden and to shoot them off with reasonable space between every shot, to the end that their reports might be heard to
the place where we hoped to find some of our people. This was
accordingly performed, and our two boats put off unto the shore.
In the admiral's boat we sounded all the way and found from
our ship until we came within a mile of the shore nine, eight,
and seven fathom. But before we were halfway between our
ships and the shore we saw another great smoke to the southwest of Kenricks Mounts [dunes on Hatteras Island]. We
therefore thought good to go to that second smoke first; but it
was much further from the harbor where we landed than we
supposed it to be, so that we were very sore tired before we came
to the smoke. But that which grieved us more was that when we
came to the smoke we found no man nor sign that any had been
there lately, nor yet any fresh water in all this way to drink.
Being thus wearied with this journey we returned to the harbor
where we left our boats, who in our absence had brought
their cask ashore for fresh water, so we deferred our going to
Roanoke until the next morning and caused some of those
sailors to dig in those sandy hills for fresh water, whereof we
found very sufficient. That night we returned aboard with our
boats and our whole company in safety.

The next morning, being the 17 of August, our boats and
company were prepared again to go to Roanoke, but Captain
Spicer had then sent his boat ashore for fresh water, by means
whereof it was ten of the clock aforenoon before we put from
our ships, which were then come to an anchor within two miles
of the shore. The admiral's boat was halfway toward the shore
when Captain Spicer put off from his ship. The admiral's boat
first passed the breach, but not without some danger of sinking,
for we had sea break into our boat which filled us half full
of water; but by the will of God and careful steerage of Captain
Cook we came safe ashore, saving only that our furniture,
victuals, match, and powder were much wet and spoiled. For
at this time the wind blew at northeast and direct into the harbor so great a gale that the sea brake extremely on the bar and
the tide went very forcibly at the entrance.

By that time our admiral's boat was hauled ashore and most of our things taken out to dry, Captain Spicer came to the entrance of the breach with his mast standing up, and was half passed over but, by the rash and undiscreet steerage of Ralph Skinner, his master's mate, a very dangerous sea broke into their boat and overset them quite. The men kept the boat, some in it and some hanging on it, but the next sea set the boat on ground, where it beat so that some of them were forced to let go their hold, hoping to wade ashore. But the sea still beat them down so that they could neither stand nor swim, and the boat twice or thrice was turned the keel upward, whereon Captain Spicer and Skinner hung until they sunk and were seen no more. But four that could swim a little kept themselves in deeper water and were saved by Captain Cook's means, who, so soon as he saw their oversetting, stripped himself and four other that could swim very well and with all haste possible rowed unto them and saved four. There were 11 in all, and seven of the chiefest were drowned. . . .

This mischance did so much discomfort the sailors that they were all of one mind not to go any further to seek the planters. But in the end, by the commandment and persuasion of me and Captain Cook, they prepared the boats; and seeing the captain and me so resolute they seemed much more willing. Our boats and all things fitted again, we put off from Hatarask, being the number of 19 persons in both boats. But before we could get to the place where our planters were left it was so exceeding dark that we overshot the place a quarter of a mile. There we espied toward the north end of the island the light of a great fire through the woods, to which we presently rowed. When we came right over against it we let fall our grapnel near the shore and sounded with a trumpet a call, and afterward many familiar English tunes of songs, and called them friendly; but we had no answer. We therefore landed at daybreak and, coming to the fire, we found the grass and sundry rotten trees burning about the place.

From hence we went through the woods to that part of the island directly over against Dasemunkepeuc, and from thence we returned by the waterside, round about the north point of the island, until we came to the place where I left our colony in the year 1586. In all this way we saw in the sand the print of the savages' feet of two or three sorts, trodden [during] the night; and as we entered up the sandy bank, upon a tree in the very brow thereof were curiously carved these fair Roman letters: "CRO." Which letters presently we knew to signify the place where I should find the planters seated, according to a secret token agreed upon between them and me at my last departure from them, which was that in any ways they should not fail to write or carve on the trees or posts of the doors the name of the place where they should be seated; for at my coming away they were prepared to remove from Roanoke 50 miles into the main. Therefore at my departure from them in *An*[*no*] 1587 I willed them that, if they should happen to be distressed in any of those places, that then they should carve over the letters or name a cross✠ in this form; but we found no such sign of distress.

And having well considered of this, we passed toward the place where they were left in sundry houses, but we found the houses taken down and the place very strongly enclosed with a high palisado of great trees, with curtains and flankers very fort-like. And one of the chief trees or posts at the right side of the entrance had the bark taken off, and five feet from the ground in fair capital letters was graven "CROATOAN," without any cross or sign of distress. This done, we entered into the palisado, where we found many bars of iron, two pigs of lead, four iron fowlers, iron saker shot [shot for large cannon], and suchlike heavy things thrown here and there, almost overgrown with grass and weeds.

From thence we went along by the waterside toward the point of the creek to see if we could find any of their boats or pinnace, but we could perceive no sign of them nor any of the last falcons and small ordnance which were left with them at my departure from them. At our return from the creek some of our sailors meeting us told us that they had found where divers chests had been hidden, and long since digged up again and broken up, and much of the goods in them spoiled and scattered about, but nothing left, of such things as the savages knew any use of, undefaced. Presently Captain Cook and I went to the place, which was in the end of an old trench made two years past by Captain Amadas; where we found five chests that had been carefully hidden of the planters. And of the same

chests three were my own, and about the place many of my
things spoiled and broken, and my books torn from the covers,
the frames of some of my pictures and maps rotten and spoiled
with rain, and my armor almost eaten through with rust. This
could be no other but the deed of the savages our enemies at
Dasemunkepeuc, who had watched the departure of our men
to Croatoan and, as soon as they were departed, digged up every
place where they suspected anything to be buried. But although
it much grieved me to see such spoil of my goods, yet on the
other side I greatly joyed that I had safely found a certain token
of their safe being at Croatoan, which is the place where Manteo was born, and the savages of the island our friends. . . .

The next morning it was agreed by the captain and myself,
with the master and others, to weigh anchor and go for the
place at Croatoan where the planters were, for that then the
wind was good for that place, and also to leave that cask with
fresh water on shore in the island until our return. So then they
brought the cable to the capstan, but when the anchor was
almost apeak, the cable broke, by means whereof we lost another anchor, wherewith we drove so fast into the shore that
we were forced to let fall a third anchor, which came so fast
home that the ship was almost aground by Kenricks Mounts,
so that we were forced to let slip the cable end for end. And
if it had not chanced that we had fallen into a channel of
deeper water, closer by the shore than we accounted of, we
could never have gone clear of the point that lieth to the southward of Kenricks Mounts. Being thus clear of some dangers
and gotten into deeper waters, but not without some loss, for
we had but one cable and anchor left us of four; and the
weather grew to be fouler and fouler; our victuals scarce and
our cask and fresh water lost: it was therefore determined that
we should go for Saint John or some other island to the southward for fresh water. And it was further purposed that, if we
could any ways supply our wants of victuals and other necessaries either at Hispaniola, Saint John, or Trinidad, that then
we should continue in the Indies all the winter following, with
hope to make two rich voyages of one, and at our return to
visit our countrymen at Virginia.

The captain and the whole company in the admiral (with
my earnest petitions) thereunto agreed, so that it rested only

to know what the master of the *Moonlight,* our consort, would do herein. But when we demanded them if they would accompany us in that new determination, they alleged that their weak and leaky ship was not able to continue it; wherefore the same night we parted, leaving the *Moonlight* to go directly for England, and the admiral set his course for Trinidad, which course we kept for two days. . . .

On Wednesday the 30 of September, seeing the wind hang so northerly that we could not attain the island of Saint George, we gave over our purpose to water there and, the next day, framed our due course for England.

≱ XII ≱

Gosnold, Pring, and Weymouth Explore the North American Coastline

THE collapse of the Spanish attempt to invade England in 1588 did not at once free Englishmen of fear that another effort to conquer their island might be attempted. For years a desultory war at sea continued as English seamen raided Spanish shipping or the coast of Spain and Portugal when they could. A build-up of Spanish forces across the English Channel at Brest posed such a menace that Sir Martin Frobisher in 1594 led an expedition that stormed an outlying fortress at Brest and burned it to the ground. The veteran seaman, however, received a wound in his hip that ultimately proved fatal. Spanish sea power was growing rather than diminishing, and Elizabeth's mariners had to remain on the alert. In the summer of 1595 a hit-and-run Spanish raid on three villages in Cornwall showed that Spain remained a potential danger.

Some of Elizabeth's ablest seamen were determined to strike Spain where it would hurt most by cutting the flow of treasure from the New World. Drake and many others had had this dream for two decades, and it would remain a constant hope entertained by Spain's enemies. In the winter of 1594 Drake and Sir John Hawkins decided to make one more attempt to achieve this end and persuaded the queen to authorize an expedition to attempt the seizure of Panama. A fleet of 27 vessels of all types, including six of the queen's ships, and about 3,000 men gathered at Plymouth and finally sailed on August 28, 1595. Drake and Hawkins shared the command. In the meantime news had reached them that a disabled treasure ship lay at anchor off Puerto Rico, toward which they headed. The voyage proved a disaster and both commanders died, Hawkins on November 11, 1595, as the fleet was about to make a vain attack on Puerto Rico, and Drake on January 28, 1596, off Porto Bello. Thus ended the careers of two of Elizabeth's most famous and daring seamen.

In the meantime Sir Walter Raleigh had not been idle. He continued to dream of colonies overseas and of riches to be obtained in America. On February 6, 1595, he himself had sailed in an expedition in search of El Dorado, believed to exist in Guiana, the vast territory of the northern Amazon and Orinoco drainage systems. He returned in August with little except material for a narrative which he published in 1596 describing the "large and beautiful empire of Guiana." By the turn of the century he was again renewing his efforts to explore the coast of Virginia, to seek his lost colonists and perhaps to send others to settle there. In 1602 one of his captains, Samuel Mace, brought back a cargo of sassafras roots, other medicinal materials and cedarwood from the North Carolina coast. Perhaps other vessels of Raleigh's had brought back sassafras, then in great demand as a cure for syphilis, for Raleigh showed great concern about the drop in prices when Bartholomew Gosnold returned in the summer of 1602 from North America with a cargo of sassafras which threatened to bring down the price. Raleigh complained to the authorities that he had a patent for trade with North America and Gosnold had not obtained a license from him. A compromise was reached, however, and an account of Gosnold's voyage written by John Brereton was published, with a dedication to Raleigh, bearing the title *A Brief and True Relation of the Discovery of the North Part of Virginia, Being a Most Pleasant, Fruitful, and Commodious Soil. Made This Present Year, 1602, by Captain Bartholomew Gosnold, Captain Bartholomew Gilbert, and Divers Other Gentlemen Their Asssociates, by the Permission of the Honorable Knight, Sir Walter Raleigh* (1602). For the sake of the publicity for territory to which he still held a patent, Raleigh was willing to connive at the pretense that he had authorized the voyage.

Gosnold, a Devonshire man with important family connections, had organized his voyage for both exploration and colonization. Sailing in the ship *Concord* with a total company of 32 men, Gosnold and 19 others planned to stay on a suitable landing site while the *Concord* with its skeleton crew of 12 returned to England with such cargo as they could load.

The expedition made a landfall at Cape Cod, where Gosnold landed and gave the cape its name because of the abundance of fish. They sailed around Nantucket Island, Martha's Vineyard, which Gosnold also named after his daughter Martha, and traded with Indians who came out to the ship in dugout canoes. The explorers were particularly pleased with the land, and Brereton wrote enthusiastically about the fine trees and the abundance of berries of several sorts. The Indians smoked a tobacco which Brereton maintained was better than any he had used in England. The party finally decided to make a base on Cuttyhunk Island, where they discovered an islet in a lake which offered a safe place for a fort. After a brisk trade with the Indians, who appeared exceedingly friendly, they obtained a cargo of furs, sassafras and timber. As the time approached for the ship's departure, most of the men who had planned to remain on the island with Gosnold wanted to go home, since they had scanty supplies to sustain them. The upshot was that all sailed for England on June 28, 1602, thus ending the first known attempt to settle an English colony in New England.

In addition to Brereton's account of the voyage, another "gentleman in the said voyage," Gabriel Archer, wrote a narrative which Samuel Purchas printed in his collection of voyages, the *Pilgrims* (1625).

Brereton Describes the Goodness of the Land

[*Excerpts from Brereton's* Brief and True Relation *follow:*]

To the Honorable Sir Walter Raleigh, Knight: . . .

On Friday the 14th of May, early in the morning, we made the land [southern coast of Maine]—being full of fair trees, the land somewhat low, certain hummocks or hills lying into the land, the shore full of white sand but very stony or rocky. And, standing fair along by the shore, about twelve of the clock the same day we came to an anchor, where six Indians in a Basque shallop with mast and sail, an iron grapple, and a kettle of copper came boldly aboard us, one of them appareled with a waistcoat and breeches of black serge, made after our sea fashion, hose and shoes on his feet. All the rest (saving one that had a pair of breeches of blue cloth) were all naked. These people are of tall stature, broad and grim visage, of a black swart complexion, their eyebrows painted white; their weapons are bows and arrows. It seemed by some words and signs they made that some Basques, or of Saint-Jean-de-Luz, have fished or traded in this place, being in the latitude of 43 degrees.

But riding here in no very good harbor, and withal doubting the weather, about three of the clock the same day in the afternoon we weighed. Standing southerly off into sea the rest of that day and the night following with a fresh gale of wind, in the morning we found ourselves embayed with a mighty headland [Cape Cod]. But coming to an anchor about nine of the clock the same day within a league of the shore, we hoisted out the one half of our shallop and Captain Bartholomew Gosnold, myself, and three others went ashore, being a white sandy and very bold shore. And marching all that afternoon with our muskets on our necks on the highest hills which we saw (the weather very hot), at length we perceived this headland to be parcel of the main, and sundry islands lying almost round about it. So returning toward evening to our shallop (for by that time the other part was brought ashore and set together), we espied an Indian, a young man of proper stature and of a pleasing countenance. And after some familiarity with him, we left him at the seaside and returned to our ship, where in five or six hours' absence we had pestered [loaded] our ship so with codfish that we threw numbers of them overboard again. And surely I am persuaded that in the months of March, April, and May there is upon this coast better fishing and in as great plenty as in Newfoundland; for the schools of mackerel, herring, cod, and other fish that we daily saw as we went and came from the shore were wonderful; and besides, the places where we took these cod (and might in a few days have laden our ship) were but in seven fathom water and within less than a league of the shore, where in Newfoundland they fish in 40 or 50 fathom water and far off.

From this place we sailed round about this headland almost all the points of the compass, the shore very bold, but as no coast is free from dangers, so I am persuaded this is as free as any—the land somewhat low, full of goodly woods, but in some places plain. At length we were come amongst many fair islands which we had partly discerned at our first landing, all lying within a league or two one of another and the outermost not above six or seven leagues from the main. But coming to an anchor under one of them [Martha's Vineyard] which was about three or four leagues from the main, Captain Gosnold, myself, and some others went ashore, and, going round about it, we found it to be four English miles in compass, without house or inhabitant, saving a little old house made of boughs, covered with bark, an old piece of a weir of the Indians to catch fish, and one or two places where they had made fires. The chiefest trees of this island are beeches and cedars, the outward parts all overgrown with low bushy trees three or four feet in height, which bear some kind of fruits, as appeared by their blossoms; strawberries, red and white, as sweet and much bigger than ours in England, raspberries, gooseberries, hurtleberries [blueberries], and such an incredible store of vines, as well in the woody part of the island, where they run upon every tree, as on the outward parts, that we could not go for treading upon them; also, many springs of excellent sweet water and a great standing lake of fresh water near the seaside, an English mile in compass, which is maintained with the springs running exceeding pleasantly through the woody grounds, which are very rocky.

Here are also in this island great store of deer, which we saw, and other beasts, as appeared by their tracks; as also divers fowls, as cranes, heronshaws, bitterns, geese, mallards, teals, and other fowls, in great plenty, also, great store of peas, which grow in certain plots all the island over. On the north side of this island we found many huge bones and ribs of whales.

This island, as also all the rest of these islands, are full of all sorts of stones fit for building; the seasides all covered with stones, many of them glistering and shining like mineral stones, and very rocky. Also, the rest of these islands are replenished with these commodities and upon some of them inhabitants, as upon an island to the northward and within two leagues of this; yet we found no towns nor many of their houses, although we saw many Indians, which are tall, big-boned men, all naked, saving they cover their privy parts with a black, tewed [tanned] skin, much like a blacksmith's apron, tied about their middle and between their legs behind. They gave us of their fish, ready boiled (which they carried in a basket made of twigs not unlike our osier), whereof we did eat and judged them to be fresh-water fish. They gave us also of their tobacco, which they drink green but dried into powder, very strong and pleasant, and much better than any I have tasted in England. The necks of their pipes are made of clay hard dried (whereof in that island is great store both red and white); the other part is a piece of hollow copper very finely closed and cemented together. We gave unto them certain trifles, as knives, points, and suchlike, which they much esteemed.

From hence we went to another island [Cuttyhunk] to the northwest of this and within a league or two of the main, which we found to be greater than before we imagined, being 16 English miles at the least in compass, for it containeth many pieces or necks of land which differ nothing from several islands, saving that certain banks of small breadth do like bridges join them to this island. On the outsides of this island are many plain places of grass, abundance of strawberries and other berries before mentioned. In mid-May we did sow in this island (as for a trial) in sundry places wheat, barley, oats, and peas, which in 14 days were sprung up nine inches and more. The soil is fat and lusty, the upper crust of gray color, but a foot or less in depth, of the color of our hemp lands in England, and being thus apt for these and the like grains. The sowing or setting (after the ground is cleansed) is no greater labor than if you should set or sow in one of our best prepared gardens in England.

This island is full of high-timbered oaks, their leaves thrice so broad as ours; cedars straight and tall; beech; elm; holly; walnut trees in abundance, the fruit as big as ours, as appeared by those we found under the trees, which had lain all the year ungathered; hazelnut trees; cherry trees, the leaf, bark, and bigness not differing from ours in England, but the stalk beareth the blossoms or fruit at the end thereof like a cluster of grapes, 40 or 50 in a bunch; sassafras trees, great plenty all the island over, a tree of high price and profit; also divers other fruit trees, some of them with strange barks of an orange color, in feeling soft and smooth like velvet. In the thickest parts of these woods you may see a furlong or more round about.

On the northwest side of this island near to the seaside is a standing lake of fresh water almost three English miles in compass, in the midst whereof stands a plot of woody ground an acre in quantity or not above. This lake is full of small tortoises and exceedingly frequented with all sorts of fowls before rehearsed, which breed, some low on the banks and others on low trees, about this lake in great abundance, whose young ones of all sorts we took and ate at our pleasure. But all these fowls are much bigger than ours in England. Also in every island, and almost in every part of every island, are great store of groundnuts, 40 together on a string, some of them as big as hen's eggs; they grow not two inches underground—the which nuts we found to be as good as potatoes. Also, divers sorts of shellfish, as scallops, mussels, cockles, lobsters, crabs, oysters, and whelks exceeding good and very great.

But, not to cloy you with particular rehearsals of such things as God and Nature hath bestowed on these places, in comparison whereof the most fertile part of all England is (of itself) but barren: we went in our light horseman [gig] from this island to the main, right against this island some two leagues off, where, coming ashore, we stood a while like men ravished at the beauty and delicacy of this sweet soil. For besides divers clear lakes of fresh water (whereof we saw no end), meadows very large and full of green grass, even the most woody places (I speak only of such as I saw) do grow so distinct and apart, one tree from another, upon green, grassy ground somewhat higher than the plains, as if Nature would show herself above her power artificial [skillful]. Hard by we espied seven Indians, and, coming up to them, at first they expressed some fear, but, being emboldened by our courteous usage and some trifles which we gave them, they followed us to a neck of land which we imagined had been severed from the main, but, finding it otherwise, we perceived a broad harbor or river's mouth which ran up into the main; but because the day was far spent we were forced to return to the island from whence we came, leaving the discovery of this harbor for a time of better leisure.

Of the goodness of which harbor, as also of many others there-abouts, there is small doubt, considering that all the islands, as also the main (where we were), is all rocky grounds and broken lands.

Now the next day we determined to fortify ourselves in the little plot of ground in the midst of the lake above mentioned, where we built a house and covered it with sedge, which grew about this lake in great abundance; in building whereof we spent three weeks and more. But the second day after our coming from the main we espied nine canoes or boats with 50 Indians in them coming toward us from this part of the main where we, two days before, landed. Being loath they should discover our fortification, we went out on the seaside to meet them; and, coming somewhat near them, they all sat down upon the stones, calling aloud to us (as we rightly guessed) to do the like a little distance from them. Having sat a while in this order, Captain Gosnold willed me to go unto them . . . ; one of them, to whom I had given a knife two days before in the main, knew me (whom I also very well remembered) and, smiling upon me, spake somewhat unto their lord or captain, which sat in the midst of them, who presently rose up and took a large beaver skin from one that stood about him and gave it unto me, which I requited for that time the best I could. But I, pointing toward Captain Gosnold, made signs unto him that he was our captain and desirous to be his friend and enter league with him, which (as I perceived) he understood and made signs of joy. Whereupon Captain Gosnold with the rest of his company, being 20 in all, came up unto them and, after many signs of gratulations [greetings] (Captain Gosnold pre-senting their l[ord] with certain trifles which they wondered at and highly esteemed), we became very great friends, and sent for meat aboard our shallop and gave them such meats as we had then ready dressed, whereof they misliked nothing but our mustard, whereat they made many a sour face. While we were thus merry, one of them had conveyed a target [shield] of ours into one of their canoes, which we suffered only to try whether they were in subjection to this l[ord], to whom we made signs (by showing him another of the same likeness and pointing to the canoe) what one of his company had done; who suddenly expressed some fear and, speaking angrily to one about him (as

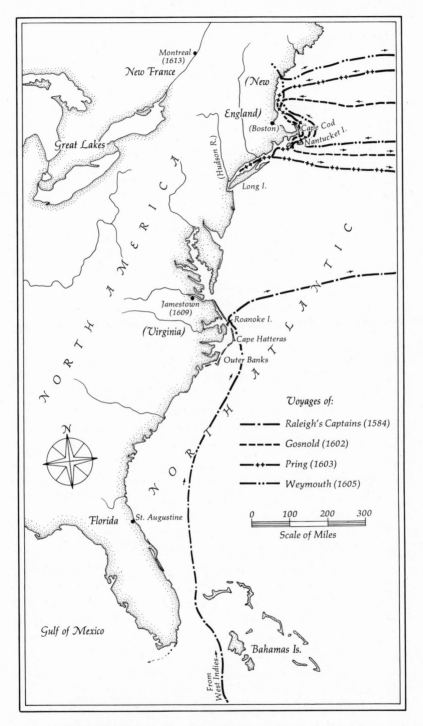

Montreal
(1613)
New France

(New
England)
(Boston)
Cape Cod
Nantucket I.

Great Lakes

(Hudson R.)

Long I.

N O R T H   A M E R I C A

Jamestown
(1609)
(Virginia)
Roanoke I.
Cape Hatteras
Outer Banks

N O R T H   A T L A N T I C

N

Florida   St. Augustine

Gulf of Mexico

From West Indies

Bahamas Is.

Voyages of:

— · — · — Raleigh's Captains (1584)

— — — — Gosnold (1602)

—+—+—+ Pring (1603)

— ·· — ·· — Weymouth (1605)

0   100   200   300
Scale of Miles

Early English exploration of the Atlantic seaboard

we perceived by his countenance), caused it presently to be brought back again. So the rest of the day we spent in trading with them for furs, which are beavers, lucerns, martens, otters, wildcat skins (very large and deep fur), black foxes, cony skins of the color of our hares but somewhat less, deerskins very large, sealskins, and other beasts' skins to us unknown.

They have also great store of copper, some very red and some of a paler color; none of them but have chains, earrings, or collars of this metal. They head some of their arrows herewith much like our broad arrowheads, very workmanly made. Their chains are many hollow pieces cemented together, each piece of the bigness of one of our reeds, a finger in length, ten or 12 of them together on a string, which they wear about their necks. Their collars they wear about their bodies like bandoleers a handful broad, all hollow pieces like the other but somewhat shorter, 400 pieces in a collar, very fine and evenly set together. Besides these, they have large drinking cups made like skulls and other thin plates of copper made much like our boarspear blades, all which they so little esteem as they offered their fairest collars or chains for a knife or suchlike trifle, but we seemed little to regard it. Yet I was desirous to understand where they had such store of this metal and made signs to one of them (with whom I was very familiar), who, taking a piece of copper in his hand, made a hole with his finger in the ground and withal pointed to the main from whence they came.

They strike fire in this manner: every one carrieth about him in a purse of tewed leather a mineral stone (which I take to be their copper), and, with a flat emery stone (wherewith glaziers cut glass and cutlers glaze blades) tied fast to the end of a little stick, gently he striketh upon the mineral stone; and within a stroke or two a spark falleth upon a piece of touchwood (much like our sponge in England) and with the least spark he maketh a fire presently. We had also of their flax, wherewith they make many strings and cords, but it is not so bright of color as ours in England. I am persuaded they have great store growing upon the main, as also mines and many other rich commodities, which we, wanting both time and means, could not possibly discover.

Thus they continued with us three days, every night retiring themselves to the furthermost part of our island two or three miles from our fort. But the fourth day they returned to the main, pointing five or six times to the sun and once to the main, which we understood that within five or six days they would come from the main to us again. But, being in their canoes a little from the shore, they made huge cries and shouts of joy unto us, and we, with our trumpet and cornet and casting up our caps into the air, made them the best farewell we could. Yet six or seven of them remained with us behind, bearing us company every day into the woods, and helped us to cut and carry our sassafras, and some of them lay aboard our ship.

These people, as they are exceeding courteous, gentle of disposition, and well conditioned, excelling all others that we have seen, so for shape of body and lovely favor I think they excel all the people of America: of stature much higher than we; of complexion or color much like a dark olive; their eyebrows and hair black, which they wear long, tied up behind in knots, whereon they prick feathers of fowls in fashion of a crownet. Some of them are black, thin-bearded. They make beards of the hair of beasts, and one of them offered a beard of their making to one of our sailors for his that grew on his face, which, because it was of a red color, they judged to be none of his own. They are quick-eyed and steadfast in their looks; fearless of others' harms, as intending none themselves; some of the meaner sort given to filching, which the very name of savages (not weighing their ignorance in good or evil) may easily excuse. Their garments are of deerskins, and some of them wear furs round and close about their necks. They pronounce our language with great facility, for one of them one day sitting by me, upon occasion I spake smiling to him these words: "How now, sirrah, are you so saucy with my tobacco?" Which words (without any further repetition) he suddenly spoke so plain and distinctly as if he had been a long scholar in the language. Many other such trials we had which are here needless to repeat.

Their women (such as we saw, which were but three in all) were but low of stature, their eyebrows, hair, apparel, and manner of wearing like to the men, fat and very well favored and much delighted in our company. The men are very dutiful toward them. And truly, the wholesomeness and temperature of this climate doth not only argue this people to be answerable to this description but also of a perfect constitution of body, active, strong, healthful, and very witty, as the sundry toys of theirs cunningly wrought may easily witness.

For the agreeing of this climate with us (I speak of myself, and so I may justly do for the rest of our company), that we found our health and strength all the while we remained there so to renew and increase as, notwithstanding our diet and lodging was none of the best, yet not one of our company (God be thanked) felt the least grudging [slight illness] or inclination to any disease or sickness but were much fatter and in better health than when we went out of England.

But after our bark had taken in so much sassafras, cedar, furs, skins, and other commodities as were thought convenient, some of our company that had promised Captain Gosnold to stay, having nothing but a saving [profitable] voyage in their minds, made our company of inhabitants (which was small enough before) much smaller; so as Captain Gosnold, seeing his whole strength to consist but of 12 men, and they but meanly provided, determined to return for England, leaving this island (which he called Elizabeth's Island) with as many true sorrowful eyes as were before desirous to see it. So the 18th of June, being Friday, we weighed and with indifferent fair wind and weather came to anchor the 23rd of July, being also Friday (in all, bare five weeks) before Exmouth.

Your Lordship's to command,
JOHN BRERETON

Martin Pring's Account of "North Virginia"

[Gosnold's report on what was still called "North Virginia" stirred Richard Hakluyt to organize a group of Bristol merchants to send out another exploring expedition under Martin Pring, a daring young Devonshire seaman. This time the venturers took the precaution of getting a license from Sir Walter Raleigh, whose patent for exploring and settling the North American coast was still valid. Pring had command of the Speedwell, a 50-ton vessel with a crew of 30; a second vessel, the Discoverer, with a crew of 13 was commanded by William Brown. The ships, with a supply of trade goods for bartering

with the Indians, were ready to sail on March 20, 1603, but were delayed for two weeks in Milford Haven. While waiting for a fair wind, they heard of the death of Queen Elizabeth. Finally, on April 10 they cleared the coast of England and, sailing by the Azores, reached the Maine coast and Cape Cod Bay in June.

[Following part of Gosnold's route, Pring touched at Martha's Vineyard, probably at Edgartown, and continued his exploration to the south past the site of New Bedford and onward into Long Island Sound. There he conducted a brisk trade with the Indians and, having loaded the Discoverer *with furs and sassafras, he sent it home. Lingering in an excellent harbor, Pring's men went ashore and planted wheat, barley, oats, peas and garden vegetables, "which for the time of our abode there, being about seven weeks, . . . came up very well; giving certain testimony of the goodness of the climate and of the soil." In August Pring was ready to depart, and on October 2 he brought the* Speedwell *into Bristol harbor. He brought back further useful information about the coast of "North Virginia," which had not yet received the name of "New England." He confirmed Gosnold's view of the richness of the soil and the abundance of fish in the sea. He also made further contacts with the Indians and learned something about the prospects for the fur trade.*

[An account of Pring's voyage appeared in Purchas' Pilgrims *and was attributed by Purchas to Pring himself, though apparently someone else had a hand in writing it. Excerpts follow:]*

We set sail from Milford Haven [the port in Wales from which John Cabot sailed in 1497], where the winds had stayed us a fortnight, in which space we heard of Queen Elizabeth's death, the 10th of April, 1603. . . . After we had run some 500 leagues, we fell with a multitude of small islands on the north coast of Virginia in the latitude of 43 degrees [the coast of Maine], the —— of June. Which islands we found very pleasant to behold, adorned with goodly grass and sundry sorts of trees, as cedars, spruce, pine, and fir trees. Here we found an excellent fishing for cod, which are better than those of Newfoundland, and withal we saw good and rocky ground fit to dry them upon; also we see no reason to the contrary but that salt may be made in these parts, a matter of no small importance.

We sailed to the southwest end of these islands and there rode with our ships under one of the greatest. One of them we named Fox Island [still so called] because we found those kind of beasts thereon. So passing through the rest with our boats to the mainland, which lieth for a good space northeast and southwest, we found very safe riding among them in six, seven, eight, ten, and twelve fathoms. At length coming to the main in the latitude of 43 degrees and a half, we ranged the same to the southwest. . . .

In all these places we found no people, but signs of fires where they had been. Howbeit we beheld very goodly groves and woods replenished with tall oaks, beeches, pine trees, fir trees, hazels, witch hazels, and maples. We saw here also sundry sorts of beasts, as stags, deer, bears, wolves, foxes, lucerns [lynx], and dogs with sharp noses. But meeting with no sassafras, we left these places with all the foresaid islands, shaping our course for Savage Rock discovered the year before by Captain Gosnold, where, going upon the main, we found people, with whom we had no long conversation because here also we could find no sassafras. Departing hence we bare into that great gulf which Captain Gosnold overshot the year before, coasting and finding people on the north side thereof. Not yet satisfied in our expectation, we left them and sailed over and came to an anchor on the south side in the latitude of 41 degrees and odd minute; where we went on land in a certain bay [probably Edgartown harbor, Martha's Vineyard] which we called Whitson Bay, by the name of the worshipful Master John Whitson, then mayor of the city of Bristol and one of the chief adventurers. And finding a pleasant hill thereunto adjoining, we called it Mount Aldworth for Master Robert Aldworth's sake [the son of a Bristol merchant who was Hakluyt's patron], a chief furtherer of the voyage as well with his purse as with his travail. Here we had sufficient quantity of sassafras.

At our going on shore, upon view of the people and sight of the place, we thought it convenient to make a small barricado to keep diligent watch and ward in, for the advertisement and succor of our men while they should work in the woods. During our abode on shore, the people of the country came to our men sometimes ten, 20, 40, or threescore, and at one time 120 at once. We used them kindly and gave them divers sorts of our meanest merchandise. They did eat peas and beans with our men. Their own victuals were most of fish.

We had a youth in our company that could play upon a gittern [a type of guitar], in whose homely music they took great delight and would give him many things, as tobacco, tobacco pipes, snakes' skins of six foot long which they use for girdles, fawns' skins, and suchlike; and danced 20 in a ring, and the gittern in the midst of them, using many savage gestures, singing "lo, la, lo, la, la, lo." Him that first brake the ring the rest would knock and cry out upon. Some few of them had plates of brass a foot long and half a foot broad before their breasts. Their weapons are bows of five or six foot long of witch hazel painted black and yellow, the strings of three twists of sinews, bigger than our bowstrings. Their arrows are of a yard and an handful long, not made of reeds but of a fine light wood very smooth and round, with three long and deep black feathers of some eagle, vulture, or kite as closely fastened with some binding matter as any fletcher of ours can glue them on. Their quivers are full a yard long and made of long dried rushes, wrought about two handfuls broad above and one handful beneath, with pretty works and compartments, diamond-wise, of red and other colors.

We carried with us from Bristol two excellent mastiffs, of whom the Indians were more afraid than of 20 of our men. One of these mastiffs would carry a half-pike in his mouth. And one Master Thomas Bridges, a gentleman of our company, accompanied only with one of these dogs . . . passed six miles alone in the country, having lost his fellows, and returned safely. And when we would be rid of the savages' company we would let loose the mastiffs, and suddenly with outcries they would flee away.

These people in color are inclined to a swart, tawny, or chestnut color, not by nature but accidentally, and do wear their hair braided in four parts and trussed up about their heads with a small knot behind; in which hair of theirs they stick many feathers and toys for bravery and pleasure. They cover their privities only with a piece of leather drawn betwixt their twists and fastened to their girdles behind and before, whereunto they hang their bags of tobacco. They seem to be somewhat jealous of their women for we saw not past two of them, who wear aprons of leather skins before them down to the knees and a bear's skin like an Irish mantle over one shoulder. The men are of stature somewhat taller than our ordinary people, strong, swift, well-proportioned, and given to treachery, as in the end we perceived.

Their boats, whereof we brought one to Bristol, were in proportion like a wherry of the River Thames, 17 foot long and four foot broad and made of the bark of a birch tree, far exceeding in bigness those of England; it was sewed together with strong and tough osiers or twigs, and the seams covered over with rosin or turpentine little inferior in sweetness to frankincense, as we made trial by burning a little thereof on the coals at sundry times after our coming home; it was also open like a wherry [small open boat] and sharp at both ends, saving that the beak was a little bending roundly upward. And though it carried nine men standing upright, yet it weighed not at the most above 60 pounds in weight, a thing almost incredible in regard of the largeness and capacity thereof. Their oars were flat at the end like an oven peel [baker's shovel], made of ash or maple very light and strong, about two yards long, wherewith they row very swiftly. Passing up a river we saw certain cottages together, abandoned by the savages, and not far off we beheld their gardens and one among the rest of an acre of ground, and in the same was sown tobacco, pompions, cucumbers, and suchlike; and some of the people had maize or Indian wheat among them. In the fields we found wild peas, strawberries very fair and big, gooseberries, raspberries, hurtleberries, and other wild fruits.

Having spent three weeks upon the coast before we came to this place where we meant to stay and take in our lading, according to our instructions given us in charge before our setting forth, we pared and digged up the earth with shovels and sowed wheat, barley, oats, peas, and sundry sorts of garden seeds, which for the time of our abode there, being about seven weeks, although they were late sown came up very well, giving certain testimony of the goodness of the climate and of the soil. . . .

As for trees, the country yieldeth sassafras, a plant of sovereign virtue for the French pox and, as some of late have learnedly written, good against the plague and many other maladies; vines, cedars, oaks, ashes, beeches, birch trees, cherry trees bearing fruit whereof we did eat, hazels, witch hazels (the best wood of all other to make soap ashes withal), walnut trees, maples, holly to make birdlime with, and a kind of tree bearing a fruit like a small red pear-plum with a crown or knop on the top (a plant whereof, carefully wrapped up in earth, Master Robert Salterne brought to Bristol). We found also low trees bearing fair cherries. There were likewise a white kind of plums which were grown to their perfect ripeness. With divers other sorts of trees to us unknown. . . .

By the end of July we had laded our small bark called the *Discoverer* with as much sassafras as we thought sufficient and sent her home into England before, to give some speedy contentment to the adventurers; who arrived safely in Kingroad [a channel near Bristol] above a fortnight before us. After their departure we so bestirred ourselves that our ship also had gotten in her lading, during which time there fell out this accident: on a day about noontide, while our men which used to cut down sassafras in the woods were asleep, as they used to do for two hours in the heat of the day, there came down about sevenscore savages armed with their bows and arrows and environed our house or barricado, wherein were four of our men alone with their muskets to keep sentinel, whom they sought to have come down unto them, which they utterly refused and stood upon their guard. Our master likewise, being very careful and circumspect, having not past two with him in the ship, put the same in the best defense he could lest they should have invaded the same, and caused a piece of great ordnance to be shot off to give terror to the Indians and warning to our men which were fast asleep in the woods. At the noise of which piece they were a little awaked and began a little to call for Fool and Gallant, their great and fearful mastiffs, and full quietly laid themselves down again. But being quickened up eftsoons again with a second shot, they roused up themselves, betook them to their weapons, and, with their mastiffs—great Fool with an half-pike in his mouth—drew down to their ship. Whom when the Indians beheld afar off, with the mastiff which they most feared, in dissembling manner they turned all to a jest and sport and departed away in friendly manner. Yet not long after, even the day before our departure, they set fire on the woods where we wrought, which we did behold to burn for a mile space, and the very same day that we weighed anchor they came down to the shore in greater number, to wit very near 200 by our estimation, and some of them came in their boats to our ship and would have had us come in again; but we sent them back and would none of their entertainment.

About the 8th or 9th of August we left this excellent haven at the entrance whereof we found 20 fathoms water, and rode at our ease in seven fathoms being landlocked, the haven winding in compass like the shell of a snail, and it is in latitude of one-and-forty degrees and five-and-twenty minutes.

This by the way is not to be forgotten: that our captain fell so much to the northward because he would find high grounds, where commonly the best havens are, which also fell out to his expectation. We also observed that we could find no sassafras but in sandy ground. In our return we brought ourselves into the latitude of 38 degrees about the Azores for certain causes, and within five weeks' space came from our port of Virginia into the soundings of England, but there being long encountered with easterly winds, we came at length into Kingroad the 2nd of October, 1603. The *Discoverer* was out five months and an half. The *Speedwell* was out six months upon the voyage.

Weymouth Investigates the Coast of Maine and Its Inhabitants

[The death of Queen Elizabeth on March 24, 1603 and the accession of James VI of Scotland as James I of England meant the end of Sir Walter Raleigh's influence in the government. His pride and his arrogance had made for him bitter enemies who now connived to bring about his downfall. Accused of plotting to put Arabella Stuart on the throne, he was charged with treason, convicted in November 1603 and, instead of being sent to the block, was confined in the Tower of London at the king's pleasure. His patent for discovery and colonization reverted to the Crown, and future ventures of this sort would

be carried out under new royal licenses or charters. Raleigh's last colonial venture was a voyage sent out under Bartholomew Gilbert in 1603 before he lost his patent. Gilbert landed in what is now Virginia but was killed by the Indians; the voyage was a failure.

[In 1605 a group of Bristol merchants in collaboration with the Earl of Southampton and Lord Arundell of Wardour sent out a ship under Captain George Weymouth to make still another reconnaissance of North Virginia and to trade with the Indians. Weymouth was an experienced navigator who had already made one voyage in search of the Northwest Passage. On Easter Day at the end of March 1605 Weymouth sailed from Dartmouth in the ship Archangel, *equipped with the latest instruments as well as trade goods. He also had aboard two huge mastiffs at which the Indians marveled.*

[By May 7 Weymouth was off the American coast near Nantucket and five days later made a landing on Monhegan Island, off the Maine coast. Examining the islands of this region, he was pleased with the fine trees, the abundance of berries and the vast numbers of fish that these waters afforded. The excellent lobsters especially delighted the crew. On Monhegan the author of the narrative comments that "many of our company wished themselves settled here, not expecting any further hopes or better discovery to be made." Taking the ship's boat, a light shallop made especially for exploring creeks and rivers, Weymouth rowed up Saint George's River and came back with a good report of the land. Indians in canoes came out to trade. Later, continuing their trade on shore, they delighted the Indians with gifts of "sugar candy which after they had tasted they liked and desired more, and raisins which were given them."

[The initial friendliness of the Indians gave way to eventual hostility as the tribesmen made plans to lure the Englishmen into a spot where they could attack them. Avoiding the trap, Weymouth's men captured five Indians, whom they took back to England, where they arrived in mid-July 1605. Three of these Indians Weymouth gave to Sir Ferdinando Gorges, who was planning a colonial venture. Gorges kept the Indians three years and taught them enough English to recommend their country to prospective settlers, certainly a novel method of promotion in that period. One of these Indians was the cele-

brated Squanto (or Tisquantum), who later was of help to the Pilgrims.

[*The account of Weymouth's voyage was written by James Rosier, "a gentleman employed in the voyage," who may have been a priest. His narrative was published in 1605 as* A True Relation of the Most Prosperous Voyage Made This Present Year, 1605, by Captain George Weymouth in the Discovery of the Land of Virginia. *Purchas reprinted it in his* Pilgrims (*1625*).

[*Excerpts from Rosier's* True Relation *follow:*]

Upon Tuesday the 5th of March [1605], about ten o'clock afore noon, we set sail from Ratcliffe and came to an anchor that tide about two o'clock before Gravesend. . . .

Upon Easter Day, being the last of March, the wind coming at north-northeast, about five o'clock afternoon we weighed anchor and put to sea in the name of God, being well victualed and furnished with munition and all necessaries, our whole company being but 29 persons, of whom I may boldly say few voyages have been manned forth with better seamen generally in respect of our small number. . . .

Friday, the 17th of May, about six o'clock at night, we descried the land, which bare from us north-northeast; but because it blew a great gale of wind, the sea very high and near night, not fit to come upon an unknown coast, we stood off till two o'clock in the morning, being Saturday. Then, standing in with it again, we descried it by eight o'clock in the morning, bearing northeast from us. It appeared a mean highland, as we after found it, being but an island of some six miles in compass [Monhegan Island, Maine], but I hope the most fortunate ever yet discovered. About twelve o'clock that day we came to an anchor on the north side of this island, about a league from the shore. About two o'clock our captain with 12 men rowed in his ship-boat to the shore, where we made no long stay but laded our boat with dry wood of old trees upon the shoreside and returned to our ship, where we rode that night.

This island is woody, grown with fir, birch, oak, and beech as far as we saw along the shore, and so likely to be within. On the verge grow gooseberries, strawberries, wild peas, and wild rose bushes. The water issued forth down the rocky cliffs in many places, and much fowl of divers kinds breed upon the shore and rocks.

While we were at shore, our men aboard with a few hooks got above 30 great cods and haddocks, which gave us a taste of the great plenty of fish which we found afterward wheresoever we went upon the coast.

From hence we might discern the mainland from the west-southwest to the east-northeast, and a great way (as it then seemed, and as we after found it) up into the main we might discern very high mountains, though the main seemed but lowland, which gave us a hope it would please God to direct us to the discovery of some good, although we were driven by winds far from that place whither (both by our direction and desire) we ever intended to shape the course of our voyage.

The next day, being Whitsunday, because we rode too much open to the sea and winds, we weighed anchor about twelve o'clock and came along to the other islands [probably Saint George's Islands] more adjoining to the main and in the road directly with the mountains about three leagues from the first island where we had anchored.

When we came near unto them (sounding all along in a good depth), our captain manned his ship-boat and sent her before with Thomas Cam, one of his mates, whom he knew to be of good experience, to sound and search between the islands for a place safe for our ship to ride in. In the meanwhile we kept aloof at sea, having given them in the boat a token to waft in the ship if he found a convenient harbor, which it pleased God to send us far beyond our expectation, in a most safe berth defended from all winds, in an excellent depth of water for ships of any burden in six, seven, eight, nine, and ten fathoms upon a clay ooze very tough.

We all with great joy praised God for His unspeakable goodness, Who had from so apparent danger delivered us and directed us upon this day into so secure an harbor. In remembrance whereof we named it Pentecost Harbor [Saint George's Harbor], we arriving there that day out of our last harbor in England, from whence we set sail upon Easter Day.

About four o'clock, after we were anchored and well moored, our captain with half a dozen of our company went on shore

[Allen's Island] to seek fresh watering and a convenient place to set together a pinnace which we brought in pieces out of England, both which we found very fitting.

Upon this island, as also upon the former, we found (at our first coming to shore) where fire had been made, and about the place were very great eggshells bigger than goose eggs, fish bones, and, as we judged, the bones of some beast.

Here we espied cranes stalking on the shore of a little island adjoining [Benner's Island], where we after saw they used to breed.

Whitmonday, the 20th day of May, very early in the morning, our captain caused the pieces of the pinnace to be carried ashore, where, while some were busied about her, others digged wells to receive the fresh water which we found issuing down out of the land in many places. Here I cannot omit (for foolish fear of imputation of flattery) the painful industry of our captain, who as at sea he is always most careful and vigilant, so at land he refuseth no pains, but his labor was ever as much or rather more than any man's, which not only encourageth others with better content but also effecteth much with great expedition.

In digging we found excellent clay for brick or tile.

The next day we finished a well of good and wholesome clear water in a great empty cask, which we left there. We cut yards, waste trees, and many necessaries for our ship, while our carpenter and cooper labored to fit and furnish forth the shallop.

This day our boat went out about a mile from our ship, and in small time with two or three hooks was fished sufficiently for our whole company three days, with great cod, haddock, and thornback.

And toward night we drew with a small net of 20 fathoms very nigh the shore. We got about 30 very good and great lobsters, many rockfish, some plaice and other small fishes, and fishes called lumps, very pleasant to the taste. And we generally observed that all the fish, of what kind soever we took, were well fed, fat, and sweet in taste.

Wednesday, the 22nd of May, we felled and cut wood for our ship's use, cleansed and scoured our wells, and digged a plot of ground wherein, amongst some garden seeds, we sowed peas and barley, which in 16 days grew eight inches above ground and so continued growing every day half an inch, although this was but the crust of the ground and much inferior to the mould we after found in the main.

Friday, the 24th of May, after we had made an end of cutting wood and carrying water aboard our ship, with 14 shot and pikes we marched about and through part of two of the islands, the bigger of which we judged to be four or five miles in compass and a mile broad.

The profits and fruits which are naturally on these islands are these: all along the shore and some space within, where the wood hindereth not, grow plentifully raspberries, gooseberries, strawberries, roses, currants, wild vines, angelica. Within the islands grow wood of sundry sorts, some very great and all tall: birch, beech, ash, maple, spruce, cherry tree, yew, oak very great and good, fir tree (out of which issueth turpentine in so marvelous plenty and so sweet as our chirurgeon [surgeon] and others affirmed they never saw so good in England). We pulled off much gum congealed on the outside of the bark, which smelled like frankincense. This would be a great benefit for making tar and pitch.

We stayed the longer in this place, not only because of our good harbor (which is an excellent comfort), but because every day we did more and more discover the pleasant fruitfulness, insomuch as many of our company wished themselves settled here, not expecting any further hopes or better discovery to be made.

Here our men found abundance of great mussels among the rocks, and in some of them many pearls; and in one mussel (which we drew up in our net) was found 14 pearls, whereof one of pretty bigness and orient [luster], in another above 50 small pearls, and if we had had a drag, no doubt we had found some of great value, seeing these did certainly show that here they were bred, the shells all glistering with mother of pearl.

Wednesday, the 29th day, our shallop being now finished and our captain and men furnished to depart with her from the ship, we set up a cross on the shoreside upon the rocks.

Thursday, the 30th of May, about ten o'clock afore noon, our captain with 13 men more, in the name of God and with all our prayers for their prosperous discovery and safe return, departed in the shallop, leaving the ship in a good harbor, which before I mentioned, well moored and manned with 14 men.

This day, about five o'clock in the afternoon, we in the ship espied three canoes coming toward us, which went to the island adjoining, where they went ashore and very quickly had made a fire, about which they stood beholding our ship, to whom we made signs with our hands and hats, waving unto them to come unto us, because we had not seen any of the people yet. They sent one canoe with three men, one of which, when they came near unto us, spake in his language very loud and very boldly, seeming as though he would know why we were there, and, by pointing with his oar toward the sea, we conjectured he meant we should be gone. But when we showed them knives and their use by cutting of sticks, and other trifles, as combs and glasses, they came close aboard our ship, as desirous to entertain our friendship. To these we gave such things as we perceived they liked when we showed them the use: bracelets, rings, peacock feathers, which they stuck in their hair, and tobacco pipes. After their departure to their company on the shore, presently came four other in another canoe, to whom we gave as to the former, using them with as much kindness as we could.

The shape of their body is very proportionable, they are well countenanced, not very tall nor big, but in stature like to us. They paint their bodies with black, their faces some with red, some with black, and some with blue.

Their clothing is beavers' skins, or deerskins, cast over them like a mantle and hanging down to their knees, made fast together upon the shoulder with leather. Some of them had sleeves, most had none. Some had buskins of such leather tewed. They have besides a piece of beaver's skin between their legs, made fast about their waist to cover their privities.

They suffered no hair to grow on their faces but on their head very long and very black, which those that have wives bind up behind with a leather string in a long round knot.

They seemed all very civil and merry, showing tokens of much thankfulness for those things we gave them. We found them then (as after) a people of exceeding good invention, quick understanding, and ready capacity.

Their canoes are made, without any iron, of the bark of a birch tree, strengthened within with ribs and hoops of wood, in so good fashion, with such excellent ingenious art, as they are able to bear seven or eight persons, far exceeding any in the Indies. . . .

Our captain had in this small time discovered up a great river, trending alongst into the main about 40 miles. The pleasantness whereof, with the safety of harbor for shipping, together with the fertility of ground and other fruits, which were generally by his whole company related, I omit till I report of the whole discovery therein after performed. For by the breadth, depth, and strong flood imagining it to run far up into the land, he with speed returned, intending to flank his light horseman for arrows, lest it might happen that the further part of the river should be narrow and by that means subject to the volley of savages on either side of the woods.

Until his return our captain left on shore where he landed in a path (which seemed to be frequented) a pipe, a brooch, and a knife, thereby to know if the savages had recourse that way, because they could at that time see none of them, but they were taken away before our return thither.

I return now to our savages, who, according to their appointment, about one o'clock came with four canoes to the shore of the island right over against us, where they had lodged the last night, and sent one canoe to us with two of those savages who had been aboard and another, who then seemed to have command of them. . . . We victualed them and gave them aqua vitae, which they tasted but would by no means drink. Our beverage they liked well. We gave them sugar candy, which after they had tasted they liked and desired more, and raisins which were given them. And some of everything they would reserve to carry to their company. Wherefore, we pitying their being in the rain and therefore not able to get themselves victual (as we thought), we gave them bread and fish.

Thus, because we found the land a place answerable to the intent of our discovery, viz., fit for any nation to inhabit, we used the people with as great kindness as we could devise or found them capable of. . . .

Owen Griffin, which lay on the shore, reported unto me their manner and (as I may term them) the ceremonies of their idolatry, which they perform thus: one among them (the eldest of the company, as he judged) riseth right up; the other, sitting still and looking about, suddenly cried with a loud voice, "Baugh, waugh." Then the women fall down and lie upon the ground, and the men all together, answering the same, fall a-stamping round about the fire with both feet as hard as they can, making the ground shake, with sundry outcries and change of voice and sound. Many take the fire sticks and thrust them into the earth, and then rest awhile. Of a sudden, beginning as before, they continue so stamping till the younger sort fetched from the shore many stones, of which every man took one and first beat upon them with their fire sticks, then with the stones beat the earth with all their strength. And in this manner (as he reported) they continued above two hours.

After this ended, they which have wives take them apart and withdraw themselves severally into the wood all night. . . .

Saturday, the 8th of June, our captain, being desirous to finish all business about this harbor, very early in the morning, with the light horseman, coasted five or six leagues about the islands adjoining and sounded all along wheresoever we went. He likewise diligently searched the mouth of the harbor and about the rocks, which show themselves at all times and are an excellent breach of the water, so as no sea can come in to offend the harbor. This he did to instruct himself, and thereby [be] able to direct others that shall happen to come to this place. For everywhere, both near the rocks and in all soundings about the islands, we never found less water than four and five fathoms, which was seldom. But seven, eight, nine, and ten fathoms is the continual sounding by the shore. In some places much deeper upon clay ooze or soft sand, so that if any bound for this place should be either driven or scanted with winds he shall be able, with his directions, to recover safely his harbor most securely in water enough by four several passages, more than which I think no man of judgment will desire as necessary.

Upon one of the islands (because it had a pleasant, sandy cove for small barks to ride in) we landed and found hard by the shore a pond of fresh water, which flowed over the banks, somewhat overgrown with little shrub trees, and, searching up in the island, we saw it fed with a strong run, which with small labor and little time might be made to drive a mill.

In this island, as in the other, were spruce trees of excellent timber and height, able to mast ships of great burden.

While we thus sounded from one place to another in so good deeps, our captain, to make some trial of the fishing himself, caused a hook or two to be cast out at the mouth of the harbor, not above half a league from our ship, where in small time only, with the baits which they cut from the fish and three hooks, we got fish enough for our whole company (though now augmented) for three days. Which I omit not to report, because it shows how great a profit the fishing would be, they being so plentiful, so great, and so good, with such convenient drying as can be wished near at hand upon the rocks. . . .

Tuesday, the 11th of June, we passed up into the river with our ship about six-and-twenty miles. Of which I had rather not write than by my relation to detract from the worthiness thereof. For the river, besides that it is subject by shipping to bring in all traffics of merchandise—a benefit always accounted the richest treasury to any land, for which cause our Thames hath that due denomination and France by her navigable rivers receiveth her greatest wealth—yet this place of itself from God and nature affordeth as much diversity of good commodities as any reasonable man can wish for present habitation and planting.

The first and chiefest thing required is a bold coast and fair land to fall with; the next, a safe harbor for ships to ride in. The first is a special attribute to this shore, being most free from sands or dangerous rocks, in a continual good depth, with a most excellent landfall, which is the first island we fell with, named by us Saint George's Island [Monhegan Island]. For the second, by judgment of our captain, who knoweth most of the coast of England and most of other countries (having been experienced by employments in discoveries and travels from his childhood), and by opinion of others of good judgment in our ship, here are more good harbors for ships of all burdens than England can afford, and far more secure from all winds and weathers than any in England, Scotland, France, or Spain. For besides, without the river in the channel and sounds about the islands adjoining to the mouth thereof, no better riding can be desired for an infinite number of ships. The river itself [probably Saint George's River, southwest of Penobscot Bay

near Port Clyde] as it runneth up into the main very nigh 40
miles toward the great mountains, beareth in breadth a mile,
sometimes three quarters, and half a mile is the narrowest,
where you shall never have under four and five fathoms water
hard by the shore, but six, seven, eight, nine, and ten fathoms
all along, and on both sides every half mile very gallant coves,
some able to contain almost 100 sail, where the ground is
excellent soft ooze with a tough clay under for anchor hold,
and where ships may lie without either cable or anchor, only
moored to the shore with a hauser.

It floweth, by their judgment, 18 or 20 feet at high water.
Here are made by nature most excellent places as docks to
grave or careen ships of all burdens, secured from all winds,
which is such a necessary, incomparable benefit that in few
places in England or in any parts of Christendom art, with
great charges, can make the like.

Besides, the bordering land is a most rich neighbor, trending
all along on both sides in an equal plain, neither mountainous
nor rocky but, verged with a green border of grass, doth make
tender unto the beholder of her pleasant fertility if, by cleansing
away the woods, she were converted into meadow.

The wood she beareth is not shrubbish, fit only for fuel, but
goodly tall fir, spruce, birch, beech, oak, which in many places
is not so thick but may with small labor be made feeding
ground, being plentiful like the outward islands with fresh
water which streams down in many places.

As we passed with a gentle wind up with our ship in this
river, any man may conceive with what admiration we all
consented [agreed] in joy. Many of our company who had been
travelers in sundry countries and in the most famous rivers
yet affirmed them not comparable to this they now beheld. Some
that were with Sir Walter Raleigh in his voyage to Guiana,
in the discovery of the river Orinoco, which echoed fame to the
world's ears, gave reasons why it was not to be compared with
this, which wanted the dangers of many shoals and broken
ground wherewith that was encumbered; others, before that
notable river in the West Indies called Rio Grande; some, before the river of Loire, the river Seine, and of Bordeaux in
France, which although they be great and goodly rivers, yet it
is no detraction from them to be accounted inferior to this,

which not only yieldeth all the aforesaid pleasant profits but also appeared infallibly to us free from all inconveniences.

I will not prefer it before our river of Thames, because it is England's richest treasure, but we all did wish those excellent harbors, good deeps in a continual convenient breadth, and small tide gates, to be as well therein for our country's good as we found them here beyond our hopes in certain for those to whom it shall please God to grant this land for habitation, which if it had, with the other inseparable adherent commodities here to be found, then I would boldly affirm it to be the most rich, beautiful, large, and secure harboring river that the world affordeth. . . .

The temperature of the climate (albeit a very important matter) I had almost passed without mentioning, because it afforded to us no great alteration from our disposition in England—somewhat hotter up into the main because it lieth open to the south, the air so wholesome as I suppose not any of us found ourselves at any time more healthful, more able to labor, nor with better stomachs to such good fare as we partly brought and partly found. . . .

. . . Our sails being down, Thomas King, boatswain, presently cast out a hook, and before he judged it at ground was fished and hauled up an exceeding great and well-fed cod. Then there were cast out three or four more, and the fish was so plentiful and so great as when our captain would have set sail we all desired him to suffer them to take fish awhile, because we were so delighted to see them catch so great fish so fast as the hook came down. Some, with playing with the hook, they took by the back, and one of the mates, with two hooks at a lead at five draughts together, hauled up ten fishes. All were generally very great, some they measured to be five foot long and three foot about.

This caused our captain not to marvel at the shoaling, for he perceived it was a fish bank, which (for our farewell from the land) it pleased God in continuance of His blessings to give us knowledge of, the abundant profit whereof should be alone sufficient cause to draw men again if there were no other good both in present certain and in hope probable to be discovered. To amplify this with words were to add light to the sun, for every one in the ship could easily account this present commodity—

much more those of judgment which knew what belonged to fishing—would warrant (by the help of God), in a short voyage with few good fishers, to make a more profitable return from hence than from Newfoundland, the fish being so much greater, better fed, and abundant with train, of which some they desired and did bring into England to bestow among their friends and to testify the true report.

After, we kept our course directly for England and, with ordinary winds and sometimes calms, upon Sunday the 14th of July, about six o'clock at night, we were come into sounding in our channel, but with dark weather and contrary winds we were constrained to beat up and down till Tuesday the 16th of July, when by five o'clock in the morning we made [the] Scilly [Islands], from whence, hindered with calms and small winds, upon Thursday the 18th of July, about four o'clock afternoon, we came into Dartmouth, which haven happily (with God's gracious assistance) we made our last and first harbor in England.

❧ XIII ❧

Searching Out Sites for Colonies
in South and North Virginia

ENGLAND'S long but desultory war with Spain ended in
1604 when James I made peace. Although the treaty with
Spain failed to concede English rights to any portion of the New
World, the English from this time onward tacitly assumed rights
to regions in North America not already occupied by any
Christian nation. Two English companies in 1606 were organized to exploit lands overseas. They were both authorized
to make settlements in "Virginia," the land lying between the
Cape Fear River in what is now North Carolina and the forty-
fifth parallel of latitude in Maine. The first of the companies,
the Virginia Company of London, composed of London merchants and a number of noblemen including the Earl of Warwick and the Earl of Southampton received a huge grant
between the thirty-fourth and the thirty-eighth parallels of
latitude. The second company, known as the Plymouth Company, composed of West Country merchants and gentlemen,
headed by Sir John Popham, Lord Chief Justice of England,
and Sir Ferdinando Gorges, received a similar grant between
the forty-first and forty-fifth parallels of latitude. Each company
had a right to make settlements in the intervening territory
provided that such settlements did not encroach within 100 miles
of the other's. In 1609 the Virginia Company of London received a new charter extending its territories to the Great
South Sea (the Pacific).

The Virginia Company of London organized its first colonial
venture in the autumn and early winter of 1606, and at London
late in December embarked its first colonists aboard three ships,

the *Susan Constant,* 100 tons, commanded by Christopher Newport, who was also in general command of the fleet; the *God Speed,* 40 tons, commanded by Bartholomew Gosnold; and the *Discovery,* 20 tons, commanded by John Ratcliffe, sometimes called Sicklemore. The number who sailed is variously estimated at between 80 and 150 souls, some designated gentlemen and the others as soldiers, laborers and members of various trades. The ships sailed down the Thames on December 20, but it took several weeks to clear the English coast. Taking the long route by the Canaries and the West Indies, they did not reach their destination in Virginia until about the middle of May 1607. Their instructions required them to pick a site far enough inland to be reasonably safe from an attack by sea and yet accessible to English ships. The spot the colonists chose on the James River met this requirement. With six fathoms of water under the ships, they could tie up to trees and go ashore. The smell of spring flowers and the odor of strawberries greeted the weary travelers, who thought they had reached the Promised Land.

The colonists set up a ruling council of seven men, but after much quarreling and controversy, Captain John Smith emerged as the dominant leader. A powder explosion injured him, however, and he had to return to England in 1609. Smith's *General History of Virginia,* published in 1624, gives his version of proceedings in Virginia in the first years of the colony and adds accounts by others. In the nineteenth century Henry Adams set out to impugn the accuracy of Smith's narratives, but modern scholarship has rehabilitated Smith's reputation as an accurate observer. Nevertheless, whether his romantic story of his rescue by Pocahontas happened precisely as he relates may be a moot point.

In 1609 the Virginia Company, having received a new charter, sent out a fleet of nine ships with more than 600 men, women and children to settle at Jamestown. Lord Delaware was appointed governor but, since he had to delay his departure, he sent Sir Thomas Gates to rule temporarily in his stead. A great storm scattered the fleet in the south Atlantic, sinking one ship and wrecking Gates' own vessel, the *Sea Venture,* in the Bermudas. Seven ships arrived safely at Jamestown. A year later the survivors of the *Sea Venture,* who had managed to get ashore in Bermuda, reached Jamestown in two pinnaces which they had built on the island. Fortunately the *Sea Venture* had wedged between rocks and the crew and passengers had salvaged food, tools and timbers.

One of the best accounts of the first voyage to Jamestown by Captain Newport's fleet was written by one of the gentlemen in the expedition, George Percy, eighth son of the Earl of Northumberland. This narrative was printed by Samuel Purchas in his *Pilgrims* in 1625. A vivid description of the wreck of the *Sea Venture* was written by William Strachey in a letter which he sent back to an unidentified "noble lady." It was so printed by Purchas and has been reprinted in a modern version, along with Silvester Jourdain's *Discovery of the Bermudas,* edited by Louis B. Wright under the title *A Voyage to Virginia in 1609* (University Press of Virginia, 1964).

George Percy Tells of the Voyage to Virginia in 1606

[*Excerpts from Percy's* Observations Gathered Out of a Discourse of the Plantation of the Southern Colony in Virginia by the English, 1606 *follow:*]

On Saturday the 20th of December in the year 1606 the fleet fell from London, and the 5th of January we anchored in the Downs. But the winds continued contrary so long that we were forced to stay there some time, where we suffered great storms but, by the skillfulness of the captain, we suffered no great loss or danger. . . .

The six-and-twentieth day of April [1607], about four o'clock in the morning, we descried the land of Virginia. The same day we entered into the Bay of Chesupioc [Chesapeake] directly, without any let or hindrance. There we landed and discovered a little way, but we could find nothing worth the speaking of but fair meadows and goodly tall trees, with such fresh waters running through the woods as I was almost ravished at the first sight thereof.

At night, when we were going aboard, there came the savages creeping upon all four from the hills like bears, with their bows in their mouths; charged us very desperately in the faces, hurt Captain Gabriel Archer in both his hands and a sailor in two places of the body very dangerous. After they had spent their arrows and felt the sharpness of our shot they retired into the woods with a great noise and so left us.

The seven-and-twentieth day we began to build up our shallop. The gentlemen and soldiers marched eight miles up into the land. We could not see a savage in all that march. We came to a place where they had made a great fire and had been newly a-roasting oysters; when they perceived our coming they fled away to the mountains and left many of the oysters in the fire. We eat some of the oysters, which were very large and delicate in taste.

The 18th day we launched our shallop. The captain and some gentlemen went in her and discovered up the bay. We found a river on the south side running into the main; we entered it and found it very shoal water, not for any boats to swim. We went further into the bay and saw a plain plot of ground where we went on land and found the place five miles in compass without either bush or tree. We saw nothing there but a canoe which was made out of the whole tree, which was five-and-forty foot long by the rule. Upon this plot of ground we got good store of mussels and oysters which lay on the ground as thick as stones. We opened some and found in many of them pearls. We marched some three or four miles further into the woods where we saw great smokes of fire. We marched to those smokes and found that the savages had been there burning down the grass, as we thought either to make their plantation there or else to give signs to bring their forces together and so to give us battle. We passed through excellent ground full of flowers of divers kinds and colors and as goodly trees as I have seen, as cedar, cypress, and other kinds. Going a little further we came into a little plat of ground full of fine and beautiful strawberries four times bigger and better than ours in England. All this march we could neither see savage nor town. When it grew to be toward night we stood back to our ships. We sounded and found it shallow water for a great way, which put us out of all hopes for getting any higher with our ships which rode at the mouth of the river. We rowed over to a point of land where we found a channel and sounded six, eight, ten, or twelve fathom, which put us in good comfort. Therefore we named that point of land Cape Comfort.

The nine-and-twentieth day we set up a cross at Chesupioc Bay and named that place Cape Henry. Thirtieth day, we came with our ships to Cape Comfort, where we saw five savages running on the shore. Presently the captain caused the shallop to be manned, so, rowing to the shore, the captain called to them in sign of friendship, but they were at first very timorsome until they saw the captain lay his hand on his heart. Upon that they laid down their bows and arrows and came very boldly to us, making signs to come ashore to their town, which is called by the savages Kecoughtan [modern Hampton, Virginia]. We coasted to their town, rowing over a river running into the main where these savages swam over with their bows and arrows in their mouths.

When we came over to the other side there was a many of other savages which directed us to their town, where we were entertained by them very kindly. When we came first aland they made a doleful noise, laying their faces to the ground, scratching the earth with their nails. We did think that they had been at their idolatry. When they had ended their ceremonies they went into their houses and brought out mats and laid upon the ground; the chiefest of them sat all in a rank, the meanest sort brought us such dainties as they had, and of their bread which they make of their maize or Guinea wheat [Indian corn] they would not suffer us to eat unless we sat down, which we did on a mat right against them. After we were well satisfied they gave us of their tobacco, which they took in a pipe made artificially [skillfully] of earth as ours are but far bigger, with the bowl fashioned together with a piece of fine copper. After they had feasted us they showed us, in welcome, their manner of dancing, which was in this fashion: one of the savages standing in the midst singing, beating one hand against another, all the rest dancing about him, shouting, howling, and stamping against the ground, with many antic tricks and faces, making noise like so many wolves or devils. One thing of them I observed: when they were in their dance they kept stroke with their feet just one with another, but with their hands, heads, faces, and bodies every one of them had a several gesture. So they continued for the space of half an hour. When they had ended their dance the captain gave them beads and other trifling jewels. They hang through their ears fowls' legs; they shave the right side of their heads with a shell, the left side they wear of an ell long tied up with an artificial knot, with a many of fowls' feathers sticking in it. They go altogether naked, but their privities are covered with beasts' skins beset commonly with little bones or beasts' teeth; some paint their bodies black, some red, with artificial knots of sundry lively colors, very beautiful and pleasing to the eye, in a braver fashion than they in the West Indies. . . .

The 8th day of May we discovered up the river. We landed in the country of Apamatica [Appomattox]. At our landing there came many stout and able savages to resist us with their bows and arrows in a most warlike manner, with the swords at their backs beset with sharp stones and pieces of iron able to cleave a man in sunder. Amongst the rest, one of the chiefest standing before them cross-legged, with his arrow ready in his bow in one hand and taking a pipe of tobacco in the other, with a bold uttering of his speech demanded of us our being there, willing us to be gone. We made signs of peace, which they perceived in the end and let us land in quietness. . . .

We found store of turkey nests and many eggs. If it had not been disliked because the ship could not ride near the shore, we had settled there to all the colony's contentment.

The 13th day we came to our seating place in Paspiha's country, some eight miles from the point of land which I made mention before, where our ships do lie so near the shore that they are moored to the trees in six fathom water.

The 14th day we landed all our men, which were set to work about the fortification, and othersome to watch and ward as it was convenient. The first night of our landing, about midnight, there came some savages sailing close to our quarter; presently there was an alarum given; upon that the savages ran away and we not troubled any more by them that night. Not long after there came two savages that seemed to be commanders, bravely dressed with crowns of colored hair upon their heads, which came as messengers from the werowance of Paspiha telling us that their werowance was coming and would be merry with us with a fat deer.

The 18th day the werowance of Paspiha came himself to our

quarter with 100 savages armed, which guarded him in a very warlike manner with bows and arrows, thinking at that time to execute their villainy. Paspiha made great signs to us to lay our arms away, but we would not trust him so far. He, seeing he could not have convenient time to work his will, at length made signs that he would give us as much land as we would desire to take. As the savages were in a throng in the fort, one of them stole a hatchet from one of our company, which spied him doing the deed. Whereupon he took it from him by force and also struck him over the arm. Presently another savage, seeing that, came fiercely at our man with a wooden sword thinking to beat out his brains. The werowance of Paspiha saw us take to our arms, went suddenly away with all his company in great anger. . . .

This river [the James] which we have discovered is one of the famousest rivers that ever was found by any Christian; it ebbs and flows 100 and threescore miles where ships of great burden may harbor in safety. Wheresoever we landed upon this river we saw the goodliest woods, as beech, oak, cedar, cypress, walnuts, sassafras, and vines in great abundance which hang in great clusters on many trees, and other trees unknown; and all the grounds bespread with many sweet and delicate flowers of divers colors and kinds. There are also many fruits, as strawberries, mulberries, raspberries, and fruits unknown. There are many branches of this river which run flowing through the woods with great plenty of fish of all kinds; as for sturgeon, all the world cannot be compared to it. In this country I have seen many great and large meadows having excellent good pasture for any cattle. There is also great store of deer, both red and fallow. There are bears, foxes, otters, beavers, muskrats, and wild beasts unknown.

The four-and-twentieth day we set up a cross at the head of this river, naming it King's River, where we proclaimed James, King of England, to have the most right unto it. When we had finished and set up our cross, we shipped our men and made for James Fort. By the way we came to Powhatan's Tower, where the captain went on shore suffering none to go with him. He presented the commander of this place with a hatchet, which he took joyfully and was well pleased.

But yet the savages murmured at our planting in the country, whereupon this werowance made answer again very wisely of a savage: "Why should you be offended with them as long as they hurt you not, nor take anything away by force? They take but a little waste ground which doth you nor any of us any good."

I saw bread made by their women, which do all their drudgery. The men take their pleasure in hunting and their wars, which they are in continually, one kingdom against another. The manner of baking of bread is thus: after they pound their wheat into flour with hot water, they make it into paste and work it into round balls and cakes; then they put it into a pot of seething water; when it is sod [boiled] thoroughly they lay it on a smooth stone; there they harden it as well as in an oven.

There is notice to be taken to know married women from maids: the maids you shall always see the fore part of their head and sides shaven close, the hinder part very long, which they tie in a plait hanging down to their hips. The married women wear their hair all of a length and is tied of that fashion that the maids' are. The womenkind in this country doth pounce [abrade] and race [scratch] their bodies, legs, thighs, arms, and faces with a sharp iron which makes a stamp in curious knots and draws the proportion of fowls, fish, or beasts; then with paintings of sundry lively colors they rub it into the stamp, which will never be taken away because it is dried into the flesh where it is seared.

The savages bear their years well, for when we were at Pamunkey's we saw a savage by their report was above eight-score years of age. His eyes were sunk into his head, having never a tooth in his mouth, his hair all gray, with a reasonable big beard which was as white as any snow. It is a miracle to see a savage have any hair on their faces; I never saw, read, nor heard any have the like before. This savage was as lusty and went as fast as any of us, which was strange to behold.

The 15th day of June we had built and finished our fort, which was triangle-wise, having three bulwarks at every corner like a half-moon and four or five pieces of artillery mounted in them. We had made ourselves sufficiently strong for these savages. We had also sown most of our corn on two mountains; it sprang a man's height from the ground. This country is a fruitful soil bearing many goodly and fruitful trees, as mulberries, cherries, walnuts, cedars, cypress, sassafras, and vines in great abundance.

Monday the two-and-twentieth of June in the morning Captain Newport in the admiral departed from James Port for England. . . .

The two-and-twentieth day of August there died Captain Bartholomew Gosnold, one of our Council. He was honorably buried, having all the ordnance in the fort shot off with many volleys of small shot. After Captain Gosnold's death the Council could hardly agree, by the dissension of Captain Kendall, which afterward was committed about heinous matters which was proved against him. . . .

The 4th day of September died Thomas Jacob, sergeant. The 5th day, there died Benjamin Beast. Our men were destroyed with cruel diseases, as swellings, fluxes, burning fevers, and by wars; and some departed suddenly; but for the most part they died of mere famine. There were never Englishmen left in a foreign country in such misery as we were in this new-discovered Virginia. We watched every three nights, lying on the bare cold ground what weather soever came; warded all the next day, which brought our men to be most feeble wretches; our food was but a small can of barley sod in water to five men a day, our drink, cold water taken out of the river, which was at a flood very salt, at a low tide, full of slime and filth, which was the destruction of many of our men. Thus we lived for the space of five months in this miserable distress, not having five able men to man our bulwarks upon any occasion. If it had not pleased God to have put a terror in the savages' hearts, we had all perished by those vile and cruel pagans, being in that weak estate as we were. Our men night and day groaning in every corner of the fort most pitiful to hear; if there were any conscience in men, it would make their hearts to bleed to hear the pitiful murmurings and outcries of our sick men, without relief every night and day for the space of six weeks—some departing out of the world, many times three or four in a night; in the morning their bodies trailed out of their cabins like dogs to be buried. In this sort did I see the mortality of divers of our people.

It pleased God, after a while, to send those people which were our mortal enemies to relieve us with victuals, as bread, corn, fish, and flesh in great plenty; which was the setting up of our feeble men, otherwise we had all perished. Also we were frequented by divers kings in the country, bringing us store of provision to our great comfort.

The 11th day there was certain articles laid against Master Wingfield, which was then president. Thereupon he was not only displaced out of his presidentship, but also from being of the Council. Afterward Captain John Ratcliffe was chosen president.

The 18th day, died one Ellis Kinistone, which was starved to death with cold. The same day at night died one Richard Simmons. The 19th day there died one Thomas Mouton. . . .

[*"The rest is omitted, being more fully set down in Captain Smith's Relations."*]

The Wreck of the *Sea Venture* in Bermuda

[*Excerpts from William Strachey's* A True Reportory of the Wreck and Redemption of Sir Thomas Gates, Knight, upon and from the Islands of the Bermudas . . . *follow:*]

Excellent Lady, know that upon Friday late in the evening we brake ground out of the sound of Plymouth, our whole fleet then consisting of seven good ships and two pinnaces, all of which from the said 2nd of June unto the 23rd of July kept in friendly consort together, not a whole watch at any time losing the sight each of other. Our course, when we came about the height of between 26 and 27 degrees, we declined to the northward and, according to our governor's instructions, altered the trade and ordinary way used heretofore by Dominica and Nevis in the West Indies and found the wind to this course indeed as friendly as in the judgment of all seamen it is upon a more direct line and by Sir George Somers our admiral had been likewise in former time sailed, being a gentleman of approved assuredness and ready knowledge in seafaring actions, having often carried command and chief charge in many ships royal of Her Majesty's and in sundry voyages made many defeats and attempts in the time of the Spaniard's quarreling with us upon the islands and Indies, etc.

We had followed this course so long as now we were within seven or eight days at the most, by Captain Newport's reckoning, of making Cape Henry upon the coast of Virginia, when on St. James his day, July 24, being Monday (preparing for no less all the black night before), the clouds gathering thick upon us and the winds singing and whistling most unusually (which made us to cast off our pinnace, towing the same until then astern), a dreadful storm and hideous began to blow from out the northeast, which, swelling and roaring as it were by fits, some hours with more violence than others, at length did beat all light from Heaven; which, like an hell of darkness, turned black upon us, so much the more fuller of horror as in such cases horror and fear use to overrun the troubled and overmastered senses of all, which taken up with amazement, the ears lay so sensible to the terrible cries and murmurs of the winds and distraction of our company as who was most armed and best prepared was not a little shaken. . . .

For 24 hours the storm in a restless tumult had blown so exceedingly as we could not apprehend in our imaginations any possibility of greater violence; yet did we still find it not only more terrible but more constant, fury added to fury, and one storm urging a second more outrageous than the former, whether it so wrought upon our fears or indeed met with new forces. Sometimes strikes [? shrieks] in our ship amongst women and passengers not used to such hurly [confusion] and discomforts made us look one upon the other with troubled hearts and panting bosoms, our clamors drowned in the winds and the winds in thunder. Prayers might well be in the heart and lips but drowned in the outcries of the officers; nothing heard that could give comfort, nothing seen that might encourage hope. It is impossible for me, had I the voice of Stentor and expression of as many tongues as his throat of voices, to express the outcries and miseries, not languishing but wasting his spirits, and art constant to his own principles but not prevailing.

Our sails wound up lay without their use, and if at any time we bore but a hullock [scrap of sail] or half forecourse, to guide her before the sea, six and sometimes eight men were not enough to hold the whipstaff in the steerage and the tiller below in the gunner room: by which may be imagined the strength of the storm, in which the sea swelled above the clouds and gave battle unto Heaven. It could not be said to rain: the waters like whole rivers did flood in the air. And this I did still observe: that whereas upon the land when a storm hath poured itself forth once in drifts of rain, the wind, as beaten down and vanquished therewith, not long after endureth; here the glut of water (as if throttling the wind erewhile) was no sooner a little emptied and qualified but instantly the winds (as having gotten their mouths now free and at liberty) spake more loud and grew more tumultuous and malignant. What shall I say? Winds and seas were as mad as fury and rage could make them. For my own part, I had been in some storms before, as well upon the coast of Barbary and Algiers, in the Levant, and one, more distressful, in the Adriatic gulf in a bottom of Candy [ship of Crete]. . . .

Yet all that I had ever suffered gathered together might not hold comparison with this: there was not a moment in which the sudden splitting or instant oversetting of the ship was not expected. . . .

Our governor, upon the Tuesday morning (at what time, by such who had been below in the hold, the leak was first discovered) had caused the whole company, about 140, besides women, to be equally divided into three parts and, opening the ship in three places (under the forecastle, in the waist, and hard by the bittacle [binnacle]), appointed each man where to attend; and thereunto every man came duly upon his watch, took the bucket or pump for one hour, and rested another. Then men might be seen to labor, I may well say, for life; and the better sort, even our governor and admiral themselves, not refusing their turn and to spell each the other, to give example to other. The common sort, stripped naked as men in galleys, the easier both to hold out and to shrink from under the salt water which continually leapt in among them, kept their eyes waking and their thoughts and hands working with tired bodies and wasted spirits three days and four nights, destitute of outward comfort and desperate of any deliverance, testifying how mutually willing they were yet by labor to keep each other from drowning, albeit each one drowned whilst he labored.

Once so huge a sea brake upon the poop and quarter upon us as it covered our ship from stern to stem like a garment or a vast cloud; it filled her brim full for a while within, from the hatches up to the spardeck. The source or confluence of water was so violent as it rushed and carried the helm-man from the helm and wrested the whipstaff out of his hand, which so flew from side to side that when he would have seized the same again it so tossed him from starboard to larboard as it was God's mercy it had not split him. . . .

During all this time the heavens looked so black upon us that it was not possible the elevation of the Pole might be observed; nor a star by night nor sunbeam by day was to be seen. Only upon the Thursday night Sir George Somers, being upon the watch, had an apparition of a little, round light, like a faint star, trembling and streaming along with a sparkling blaze, half the height upon the main mast and shooting sometimes from shroud to shroud, 'tempting to settle, as it were, upon any of the four shrouds. And for three or four hours together, or rather more, half the night, it kept with us, running sometimes along the main yard to the very end and then returning; at which Sir George Somers called divers about him and showed them the same, who observed it with much wonder and carefulness. But upon a sudden, toward the morning watch, they lost the sight of it and knew not what way it made.

The superstitious seamen make many constructions of this sea fire, which nevertheless is usual in storms, the same (it may be) which the Grecians were wont in the Mediterranean to call Castor and Pollux, of which if one only appeared without the other they took it for an evil sign of great tempest. The Italians and such who lie open to the Adriatic and Tyrrhenian Sea call it (a sacred body) *corpo sancto;* the Spaniards call it Saint Elmo and have an authentic and miraculous legend for it. Be it what it will, we laid other foundations of safety or ruin than in the rising or falling of it. . . .

. . . And it being now Friday, the fourth morning, it wanted little but that there had been a general determination to have shut up hatches and, commending our sinful souls to God, committed the ship to the mercy of the gale. Surely, that night we must have done it, and that night had we then perished. But see the goodness and sweet introduction of better hope by our merciful God given unto us: Sir George Somers, when no man dreamed of such happiness, had discovered and cried land. . . .

. . . But having no hope to save her by coming to an anchor in the same, we were enforced to run her ashore as near the land as we could, which brought us within three quarters of a mile of shore; and by the mercy of God unto us, making out our boats, we had ere night brought all our men, women, and children, about the number of 150, safe into the island. . . .

About the last of April [1610] Sir George Somers launched his pinnace and brought her from his building bay in the main island into the channel where ours did ride; and she was by the keel nine-and-twenty foot, at the beam 15 foot and an half, at the luff 14, at the transom nine; and she was eight foot deep and drew six foot water, and he called her the *Patience*.

From this time we only awaited a favorable westerly wind to carry us forth, which longer than usual now kept at the east and southeast, the way which we were to go. The 10th of May early, Sir George Somers and Captain Newport went off with their longboats and with two canoes buoyed the channel which we were to lead it out in and which was no broader from shoals on the one side and rocks on the other than about three times the length of our pinnace. About ten of the clock, that day being Thursday, we set sail an easy gale, the wind at south. . . .

The 17th of May we saw change of water and had much rubbish swim by our ship side, whereby we knew we were not far from land. The 18th about midnight we sounded with the dipsey [deep-sea] lead and found 37 fathom. The 19th in the morning we sounded and had 19 and an half fathom, stony and sandy ground. The 20th about midnight we had a marvelous sweet smell from the shore (as from the coast of Spain short of the straits), strong and pleasant, which did not a little glad us. In the morning by daybreak (so soon as one might well see from the foretop) one of the sailors descried land; about an hour after I went up and might discover two hummocks to the southward, from which (northward all along) lay the land which we were to coast to Cape Henry. About seven of the clock we cast forth an anchor, because the tide (by reason of the freshet that set into the bay) made a strong ebb there and the wind was but easy, so as, not being able to stem the tide, we purposed to lie at an anchor until the next flood; but the wind coming southwest a loom [moderate] gale about eleven, we set sail again and, having got over the bar, bore in for the cape.

This is the famous Chesapeake Bay, which we have called (in honor of our young Prince) Cape Henry, over against which within the bay lieth another headland, which we called, in honor of our princely Duke of York, Cape Charles; and these lie northeast and by east and southwest and by west, and they may be distant each from the other in breadth seven leagues, between which the sea runs in as broad as between Queenborough [in Kent] and Leigh [in Essex]. Indeed it is a goodly bay and a fairer not easily to be found.

The one-and-twentieth, being Monday in the morning, we came up within two miles of Point Comfort, when the captain of the fort discharged a warning piece at us, whereupon we came to an anchor and sent off our longboat to the fort to certify who we were. By reason of the shoals which lie on the south side, this fort easily commands the mouth of the river, albeit it is as broad as between Greenwich and the Isle of Dogs. . . .

. . . When our skiff came up again the good news of our ships' and men's arrival the last year did not a little glad our governor, who went soon ashore and as soon (contrary to all our fair hopes) had new, unexpected, uncomfortable, and heavy news of a worse condition of our people above at Jamestown.

Upon Point Comfort our men did the last year (as you have heard) raise a little fortification, which since hath been better perfected and is likely to prove a strong fort and is now kept by Captain James Davies with 40 men, and hath to name Algernon Fort, so called by Captain George Percy, whom we found at our arrival president of the colony and at this time likewise in the fort when we got into the Point, which was the one-and-twentieth of May, being Monday about noon; where, riding before an Indian town called Kecoughtan, a mighty storm of thunder, lightning, and rain gave us a shrewd [sharp] and fearful welcome.

From hence in two days (only by the help of tides, no wind stirring) we plied it sadly up the river, and the three-and-twentieth of May we cast anchor before Jamestown, where we landed, and our much grieved governor, first visiting the church, caused the bell to be rung, at which all such as were able to come forth of their houses repaired to church, where our minister, Master Bucke, made a zealous and sorrowful prayer, finding all things so contrary to our expectations, so full of misery and misgovernment.

After service our governor caused me to read his commission and Captain Percy (then president) delivered up unto him his commission, the old patent, and the council seal. Viewing the fort, we found the palisades torn down, the ports open, the gates from off the hinges, and empty houses (which owners' death had taken from them) rent up and burnt, rather than the dwellers would step into the woods a stone's cast off from them to fetch other firewood. And it is true, the Indian killed as fast without, if our men stirred but beyond the bounds of their blockhouse, as famine and pestilence did within; with many more particularities of their sufferances (brought upon them by their own disorders the last year) than I have heart to express.

In this desolation and misery our governor found the condition and state of the colony and (which added more to his grief) no hope how to amend it or save his own company and those yet remaining alive from falling into the like necessities. For we had brought from the Bermudas no greater store of provision (fearing no such accidents possible to befall the colony here) than might well serve 150 for a sea voyage. And it was not possible at this time of the year to amend it by any help from the Indian; for besides that they (at their best) have little more than from hand to mouth, it was now likewise but their seedtime and all their corn scarce put into the ground. Nor was there at the fort (as they whom we found related unto us) any means to take fish, neither sufficient seine nor other convenient net, and yet if there had, there was not one eye of sturgeon yet come into the river. All which considered, it pleased our governor to make a speech unto the company, giving them to understand that what provision he had they should equally share with him, and if he should find it not possible and easy to supply them with something from the country by the endeavors of his able men, he would make ready and transport them all into their native country (accommodating them the best that he could); at which there was a general acclamation and shout of joy on both sides, for even our own men began to be disheartened and faint when they saw this misery amongst the others and no less threatened unto themselves. In the meanwhile, our governor published certain orders and instructions which he enjoined them strictly to observe, the time that he should stay amongst them, which, being written out fair, were set up upon a post in the church for everyone to take notice of. . . .

Unto such calamity can sloth, riot, and vanity bring the most settled and plentiful estate. Indeed (right noble Lady) no story can remember unto us more woes and anguishes than these people, thus governed, have both suffered and pulled upon their own heads. . . .

. . . And with this idleness, when something was in store, all wasteful courses exercised to the heighth, and the headless multitude (some neither of quality nor religion) not employed to the end for which they were sent hither—no, not compelled (since in themselves unwilling) to sow corn for their own bellies, nor to put a root, herb, etc., for their own particular good in their gardens or elsewhere—I say, in this neglect and sensual surfeit, all things suffered to run on, to lie sick and languish, must it be expected that health, plenty, and all the goodness of a well-ordered state, of necessity for all this, to flow in this country? You have a right and noble heart (worthy Lady), be judge of the truth herein.

Then suffer it not be concluded unto you, nor believe, I beseech you, that the wants and wretchedness which they have endured ascend out of the poverty and vileness of the country, whether be respected the land or rivers. . . .

From the three-and-twentieth of May unto the seventh of June our governor attempted and made trial of all the ways that both his own judgment could prompt him in and the advice of Captain George Percy and those gentlemen whom he found of the council when he came in, as of others whom he caused to deliver their knowledges concerning the state and condition of the country. But after much debating it could not appear how possibly they might preserve themselves (reserving that little which we brought from the Bermudas in our ships and was upon all occasions to stand good by us) ten days from starving. For besides that the Indians were of themselves poor, they were forbidden likewise (by their subtle King

Powhatan) at all to trade with us; and not only so, but to endanger and assault any boat upon the river or straggler out of the fort by land, by which (not long before our arrival) our people had a large boat cut off and divers of our men killed, even within command of our blockhouse; as, likewise, they shot two of our people to death after we had been four and five days come in. And yet would they dare then to enter our ports and truck with us (as they counterfeited underhand) when, indeed, they came but as spies to discover our strength, trucking with us upon such hard conditions that our governor might very well see their subtlety and therefore neither could well endure nor would continue it. And I may truly say beside, so had our men abased and to such a contempt had they brought the value of our copper that a piece which would have bought a bushel of their corn in former time would not now buy a little cade or basket of a pottle [half gallon]. And for this misgovernment chiefly our colony is much bound to the mariners, who never yet in any voyage hither but have made a prey of our poor people in want; insomuch as unless they might advance four or five for one (how assured soever of the payments of their bills of exchange) they would not spare them a dust of corn nor a pint of beer to give unto them the least comfort or relief, although that beer purloined and stolen perhaps, either from some particular supply or from the general store: so uncharitable a parcel of people they be and ill conditioned. . . .

It soon, then, appeared most fit, by a general approbation, that to preserve and save all from starving there could be no readier course thought on than to abandon the country and, accommodating themselves the best that they might in the present pinnaces then in the road, namely, in the *Discovery* and the *Virginia* and in the two brought from and builded at the Bermudas, the *Deliverance* and the *Patience,* with all speed convenient to make for the Newfoundland, where (being the fishing time) they might meet with many English ships into which happily they might disperse most of the company.

This consultation taking effect, our governor, having caused to be carried aboard all the arms and all the best things in the store which might to the adventurers make some commodity upon the sale thereof at home, and burying our ordnances before the fort gate which looked into the river, the seventh of June, having appointed to every pinnace, likewise, his complement and number, also delivered thereunto a proportionable rate of provision, he commanded every man at the beating of the drum to repair aboard. And because he would preserve the town (albeit now to be quitted) unburned, which some intemperate and malicious people threatened, his own company he caused to be last ashore and was himself the last of them when about noon, giving a farewell with a peal of small shot, we set sail and that night, with the tide, fell down to an island in the river, which our people have called Hog Island; and the morning tide brought us to another island, which we have called Mulberry Island, where, lying at an anchor in the afternoon stemming the tide, we discovered a longboat making toward us from Point Comfort. Much descant we made thereof! About an hour it came up, by which, to our no little joys, we had intelligence of the Honorable My Lord La Warr his arrival before Algernon Fort the 6th of June, at what time, true it is, His Lordship, having understood of our governor's resolution to depart the country, with all expedition caused his skiff to be manned and in it dispatched his letters by Captain Edward Bruster (who commandeth His Lordship's company) to our governor, which preventing us before the aforesaid Mulberry Island (the 8th of June afore said), upon the receipt of His Honor's letters, our governor bore up the helm with the wind coming easterly and that night (the wind so favorable) relanded all his men at the fort again. Before which (the 10th of June, being Sunday) His Lordship had likewise brought his ships and in the afternoon came ashore with Sir Ferdinando Wainman and all His Lordship's followers. . . .

True it is, I may not excuse this our fort, or Jamestown, as yet seated in somewhat an unwholesome and sickly air, by reason it is in a marish [marshy] ground, low, flat to the river, and hath no freshwater springs serving the town but what we drew from a well six or seven fathom deep, fed by the brackish river oozing into it; from whence I verily believe the chief causes have proceeded of many diseases and sicknesses which have happened to our people, who are indeed strangely afflicted with fluxes and agues, and every particular infirmity too: all which, if it had been our fortunes to have seated upon some hill, accommodated with fresh springs and clear air, as do the natives of the country, we might have, I believe, well escaped. . . .

Upon His Lordship's landing at the south gate of the palisade (which looks into the river), our governor caused his company in arms to stand in order and make a guard. It pleased him that I should bear his colors for that time. His Lordship, landing, fell upon his knees and before us all made a long and silent prayer to himself, and after marched up into the town, where at the gate I bowed with the colors and let them fall at His Lordship's feet, who passed on into the chapel, where he heard a sermon by Master Bucke, our governor's preacher, and after that caused a gentleman, one of his own followers, Master Anthony Scot, his ancient, to read his commission, which entitled him lord governor and captain general during his life of the colony and plantation in Virginia (Sir Thomas Gates, our governor hitherto, being now styled therein lieutenant general).

After the reading of His Lordship's commission, Sir Thomas Gates rendered up unto His Lordship his own commission, both patents, and the council seal. After which the lord governor and captain general delivered some few words unto the company, laying many blames upon them for many vanities and their idleness, earnestly wishing that he might no more find it so lest he should be compelled to draw the sword of justice to cut off such delinquents, which he had much rather, he protested, draw in their defense to protect them from injuries; heartening them with the knowledge of what store of provisions he had brought for them, *viz.,* sufficient to serve 400 men for one whole year.

The Colony on the Kennebec

[*The charter that the Virginia Company of London received in 1606, under which the Jamestown settlement was made, provided for two companies, one of London and one of Plymouth. The Plymouth Company in the spring of 1607 fitted out two ships and sent them to establish a colony in "North Virginia"—somewhere on the Maine coast. The descriptions that Gosnold, Pring and Weymouth had brought back gave assurances of a benign climate and a fertile land. The expedition, under the command of George Popham, brother of Chief Justice Sir John Popham, and Raleigh Gilbert, son of Sir Humphrey Gilbert, took out 120 prospective colonists. The ships, named the* Mary and John *and the* Gift of God, *reached the North Atlantic coast at the very end of July and, after exploring islands and inlets along the shore, on August 19 decided upon a site for a settlement at the mouth of the Kennebec River, which they called the River Sagadahoc. There they built a fort and settled down. Short of supplies and suffering from the bitter cold, they passed a miserable winter in 1607–08. George Popham, the governor, proved incompetent and could not keep the little group from constant quarrels. Before the winter was over he was dead and the survivors were discouraged and eager to return to England. They had contrived, however, to build a pinnace which they named the* Virginia *and had loaded it with furs and timber. In the summer of 1608 Gilbert sailed for home with the disheartened colonists. The expedition had failed, but it had succeeded in confirming the observations about the possibilities of the fur trade and the fisheries in that region.*

An anonymous writer composed a brief description of the voyage made by Popham and Gilbert and their colony on the Kennebec. The manuscript, mutilated and incomplete, was discovered in 1875 in the Lambeth Palace Library. It has been several times printed. William Strachey had access to it before its mutilation and included an account of the colony in his History of Travel into Virginia Britannia *(1612), which was printed by the Hakluyt Society in 1849 and reprinted in a newly edited version by Louis B. Wright and Virginia Freund (London: Hakluyt Society, 1953). Brief excerpts from both the anonymous manuscript and Strachey follow:]*

The Relation of a Voyage unto New England. Began from the Lizard, the 1st of June, 1607, by Captain Popham in the ship the *Gift* and Captain Gilbert in the *Mary and John.*

Written by ———— and found amongst the papers of the truly Worshipful Sir Ferdinando Gorges, Knight, by me William Griffith.

Departed from the Lizard the 1st day of June *Anno Domini* 1607, being Monday, about six of the clock in the afternoon; and it bore off me then northeast and by north eight leagues off. From thence directed our course for the Islands of Flowers [Flores] and Corvo [islands of the Azores], in the which we were 24 days attaining of it. All which time we still kept the sea and never saw but one sail, being a ship of Salcombe [Devon] bound for the Newfoundland. . . .

Saturday, being the 15th of August, the storm ended and the wind came fair for us to go for Sagadahoc. So we weighed our anchors and set sail and stood to the eastward and came to the island of Sutquin, which was two leagues from those islands we rode at anchor before. And here we anchored under the island of Sutquin in the eastern side of it; for that the wind was off the shore that we could not get into the river of Sagadahoc. And here Captain Popham's ship's boat came aboard of us and gave us 20 fresh cods that they had taken, being sent out a-fishing. . . .

Monday, being the 17th of August, Captain Popham in his shallop with 30 others and Captain Gilbert in his ship's boat with 18 other persons departed early in the morning from their ships and sailed up the river of Sagadahoc for to view the river and also to see where they might find the most convenient place for their plantation, myself being with Captain Gilbert. So we sailed up into this river near 14 leagues and found it to be a most gallant river, very broad and of a good depth. We never had less water than three fathom when we had least, and abundance of great fish [sturgeon] in it leaping above the water on each side of us as we sailed. So, the night approaching, after a while we had refreshed ourselves upon the shore, about nine of the clock we set backward to return and came aboard our ships the next day following about two of the clock in the afternoon. We find this river to be very pleasant, with many goodly islands in it, and to be both large and deep water, having many branches in it. That which we took bendeth itself toward the northeast.

Tuesday, being the 18th, after our return we all went to the shore and there made choice of a place for our plantation, which is at the very mouth or entry of the river of Sagadahoc on the west side of the river, being almost an island of a good bigness. Whilst we were upon the shore there came in three canoes by us, but they would not come near us but rowed up the river and so passed away.

Wednesday, being the 19th August, we all went to the shore where we made choice for our plantation, and there we had a sermon delivered unto us by our preacher, and after the sermon our patent was read with the orders and laws therein prescribed, and then we returned aboard our ships again.

Thursday, being the 20th of August, all our companies landed and there began to fortify. Our president, Captain Popham, set the first spit of ground unto it, and after him all the rest followed and labored hard in the trenches about it.

Friday, the 21st of August, all hands labored hard about the fort, some in the trench, some for fagots, and our ship carpenters about the building of a small pinnace or shallop. . . .

The 16th, 17th, 18th, 19th, 20th, 21st, 22d [of September] nothing happened but all labored hard about the fort and the storehouse for to land our victuals.

The 23d, being Wednesday, Captain Gilbert accompanied with 19 others, myself one of them, departed from the fort to go for the head of the river of Sagadahoc. We sailed all this day. So did we the like the 24th until the evening. Then we landed there to remain that night. Here we found a gallant champion land and exceeding fertile. So here we remained all night.

The 25th, being Friday, early in the morning we departed from hence and sailed up the river about eight leagues farther until we came unto an island [no longer extant; it was near the site of Augusta], being low land and flat. At this island is a great downfall of water, the which runneth by both sides of this island very swift and shallow. In this island we found great store of grapes, exceeding good and sweet, of two sorts, both red but the one of them is a marvelous deep red. By both the sides of this river the grapes grow in abundance, and also very good hops and also chibols [onions] and garlic. And for the goodness of the land, it doth so far abound that I cannot, almost, express the same. Here we all went ashore and, with a strong rope made fast to our boat and one man in her to guide her against the swift stream, we plucked her up through it perforce. After we had passed this downfall we all went into our boat again and rowed near a league farther up into the river; and, night being at hand, we here stayed all night. And in the first of the night about ten of the clock there came on the farther side of the river certain savages calling unto us in broken English. We answered them again. So for this time they departed.

The 26th, being Saturday, there came a canoe unto us and in her four savages—those that had spoken unto us in the night before. His name that came unto us is Sabenoa. He makes himself unto us to be lord of the river of Sagadahoc.

[*The anonymous manuscript has the following conclusion added in a later hand, possibly Griffith's: "End: The relation of Whole Voyage to Virginia, New England, 1607." Strachey continues the story in his* History of Travel into Virginia Britannia, *Book II, as follows:*]

26 [September], in the morning there came a canoe unto them and in her a sagamore and four savages, some of those which spoke to them the night before. The sagamore called his name Sabenoa and told us how he was lord of the river of Sagadahoc. They entertained him friendly and took him into their boat and presented him with some trifling things which he accepted. Howbeit, he desired some one of our men to be put into his canoe as a pawn of his safety, whereupon Captain Gilbert sent in a man of his, when presently the canoe rowed away from them with all the speed they could make up the river. They followed with the shallop, having great care that the sagamore should not leap overboard. The canoe quickly rowed from them and landed, and the men made to their houses, being near a league in on the land from the riverside, and carried our man with them. The shallop, making good way, at length came unto another downfall which was so shallow and so swift that by no means they could pass any further; for which Captain Gilbert, with nine others, landed

and took their fare, the savage sagamore, with them and went in search after those other savages whose houses, the sagamore told Captain Gilbert, were not far off. And after a good tedious march they came (indeed) at length unto those savages' houses, where they found near 50 able men, very strong and tall such as their like they had not seen, all new painted and armed with their bows and arrows. Howbeit, after that the sagamore had talked with them they delivered back again the man and used all the rest very friendly, as did ours the like by them, who showed them their commodities of beads, knives, and some copper, of which they seemed very fond; and by way of trade, made show that they would come down to the boat and there bring such things as they had to exchange them for ours. So Captain Gilbert departed from them, and, within half an hour after he had gotten to his boat, there came three canoes down unto them, and in them some 16 savages, and brought with them some tobacco and certain small skins which were of no value. Which Captain Gilbert perceiving, and that they had nothing else wherewith to trade, he caused all his men to come aboard; and as he would have put from the shore, the savages, perceiving so much, subtly devised how they might put out the fire in the shallop—by which means they saw they should be free from the danger of our men's pieces. And to perform the same one of the savages came into the shallop and, taking the firebrand which one of our company held in his hand thereby to light the matches, as if he would light a pipe of tobacco, as soon as he had gotten it in his hand he presently threw it into the water and leaped out of the shallop. Captain Gilbert, seeing that, suddenly commanded his men to betake them to their muskets and the targetiers too, from the head of the boat; and bade one of the men before, with his target on his arm, to step on the shore for more fire. The savages resisted him and would not suffer him to take any, and some others holding fast the boat rope that the shallop could not put off. Captain Gilbert caused the musketeers to present their pieces, the which the savages seeing, presently let go the boat rope and betook them to their bows and arrows and ran into the bushes nocking their arrows, but did not shoot, neither did ours at them. So the shallop departed from them to the further side of the river, where one of the canoes came unto them and would have excused the fault of the others. Captain Gilbert made show as if he were still friends and entertained them kindly and so left them, returning to the place where he had lodged the night before and there came to an anchor for that night. The head of this river standeth in 45 degrees and odd minutes. Upon the continent they found abundance of spruce trees such as are able to mast the greatest ship His Majesty hath, and many other trees: oak, walnut, pineapple [a type of pine probably with cones shaped like pineapples]; fish, abundance; great store of grapes, hops, chibols; also they found certain cods [pods] in which they supposed the cotton wool to grow, and also upon the banks many shells of pearl.

27. Here they set up a cross and then returned homeward, in the way seeking the by-river of some note called Sasanoa [the tidal river connecting the Kennebec with Sheepscot Bay]. This day and the next they sought it; when the weather turned foul and full of fog and rain they made all haste to the fort, before which, the 29, they arrived.

30, and 1 and 2 of October, all busy about the fort.

3 [October]. There came a canoe unto some of the people of the fort as they were fishing on the sand, in which was Skidwares who bade them tell their president that Nahanada, with the Bashaba's brother and others, were on the further side of the river and the next day would come and visit him.

4. There came two canoes to the fort in which were Nahanada and his wife and Skidwares and the Bashaba's brother and one other called Amenquin, a sagamore; all whom the president feasted and entertained with all kindness both that day and the next, which being Sunday, the president carried them with him to the place of public prayers, which they were at both morning and evening, attending it with great reverence and silence.

6. The savages departed all except Amenquin the sagamore, who would needs stay amongst our people a longer time. Upon the departure of the others, the president gave unto every one of them copper, beads, or knives, which contented them not a little; as also delivered a present unto the Bashaba's brother to be presented unto the Bashaba and another for his wife,

giving him to understand that he would come unto his court in the river of Penobscot and see him very shortly, bringing many suchlike of his country commodities with him.

You may please to understand how, whilst this business was thus followed here soon after their first arrival, that [there] had [been] dispatched away Captain Robert Davies in the *Mary and John* to advertise both of their safe arrival and forwardness [progress] of their plantation within this river of Sagadahoc, with letters to the Lord Chief Justice importuning a supply for the most necessariest wants to the subsisting of a colony to be sent unto them betimes [early] the next year.

After Captain Davies' departure they fully finished the fort, trenched and fortified it with 12 pieces of ordnance, and built 50 houses [probably an error] therein, besides a church and a storehouse; and the carpenters framed a pretty pinnace of about some 30 ton which they called the *Virginia,* the chief shipwright being one Digby of London.

Many discoveries likewise had [would have] been made both to the main[land] and unto the neighbor rivers, and the frontier nations fully discovered, by the diligence of Captain Gilbert had not the winter proved so extreme unseasonable and frosty. For, it being in the year 1607, when the extraordinary frost was felt in most parts of Europe, it was here likewise as vehement, by which no boat could stir upon any business. Howbeit, as time and occasion gave leave, there was nothing omitted which could add unto the benefit or knowledge of the planters; for which, when Captain Davies arrived there in the year following (set out from Topsam, the port town of Exeter, with a ship laden full of victuals, arms, instruments, and tools, etc.), albeit he found Mr. George Popham, the president, and some other dead, yet he found all things in good forwardness and many kinds of furs obtained from the Indians by way of trade; good store of sarsaparilla gathered; and the new pinnace all finished. But by reason that Captain Gilbert received letters that his brother was newly dead [Sir John Gilbert died July 8, 1608] and a fair portion of land fallen unto his share which required his repair home; and no mines discovered nor hope thereof, being the main intended benefit expected to uphold the charge of this plantation; and the fear that all other winters would prove like the first: the company by no means would stay any longer in the country, especially Captain Gilbert being to leave them and Mr. Popham, as aforesaid, dead. Wherefore they all embarked in this new-arrived ship and in the new pinnace, the *Virginia,* and set sail for England. And this was the end of that northern colony upon the river of Sagadahoc.

XIV

Champlain Explores Canada and Lays the Foundation for an Empire

EVER since Jacques Cartier's explorations of the Saint Lawrence in 1535, French mariners had made periodic visits to North Atlantic shores in search of furs and fish. French fishing vessels swarmed to Newfoundland each summer and some of them continued onward to the mainland, where they made contacts with the Indians and gathered valuable cargoes of furs. How many unrecorded voyages were made by Frenchmen to this region in the period after Cartier, no man can tell.

This traffic attracted the attention of shrewd observers in Brittany and Normandy, and in 1603 Aymar de Chastes, the governor of Dieppe, petitioned Henry IV for a monopoly of the fur trade, with the promise that he would establish colonies in North America. To keep peace with merchants and mariners on the French coast who had made a good thing of the fur trade and did not want their trade taken over by a monopolist, de Chastes enlisted some of these under his banner. One who joined him was du Pont Gravé, a merchant of Saint-Malo already experienced in the fur trade. He also obtained the services of Samuel de Champlain, a soldier and sailor under Henry IV. The king appointed Champlain Geographer Royal and instructed him to bring back from the projected expedition a full report of the land.

Champlain had made a voyage in the Spanish service to the West Indies and Mexico in 1599 and upon his return had

written a "Brief Discourse" of what he had observed, a document that evidently had impressed the king. A translation was
published by the Hakluyt Society in 1859. In this document
Champlain suggested a canal across the Isthmus of Panama
to save the immense journey required to reach the South Sea.

In March of 1603 began the first of Champlain's expeditions
to what we now call Canada. Two ships sailed from Honfleur,
one commanded by du Pont Gravé and the other by Sieur
Prevert of Saint-Malo. Champlain went along as geographer.
The two vessels sailed up the Saint Lawrence as far as the
site of Montreal but found no trace of the Indian town of
Hochelaga, which had so impressed Cartier. After trading for
furs, the expedition returned to Le Havre on September 20.
They were greeted by the news that the patentee for the fur
trade, de Chastes, was dead.

Pierre de Guast, Sieur de Monts, a Huguenot, next obtained
from the king not only a ten years' monopoly for the fur trade
but a grant of authority over the whole territory from the
fortieth to the forty-sixth degree of latitude, or roughly from
Philadelphia to a region north of Montreal. Realizing that the
experience of du Pont Gravé and Champlain would be in-
valuable, de Monts enlisted them in his enterprise and organized a voyage that sailed from Le Havre in April 1604. This
expedition established a colony at the mouth of the Saint Croix
River on the boundary between Maine and New Brunswick,
but when that site proved inhospitable, the colony moved
to Port Royal in Nova Scotia (now Annapolis Royal).

During the next three years Champlain explored the coast
of New England and made the best maps yet devised of this
area. His voyages took him as far south as Cape Cod and
Plymouth. For the rest of his life Champlain busied himself
with the exploration and development of Canada, and he is
properly called "the father of New France." His explorations
took him into the interior of the country as far as the Great
Lakes, and he, more than any other explorer in this early period, provided accurate information to his own country and the
world about the northern portion of America. After his first
voyage of 1603 he made a report to the king which was published as Des Sauvages: ou Voyage de Samuel Champlain . . .
(1604). In 1613 he published in Paris an account of his voyages

up to that time with a title which translates as *A Most Faithful Journal of Observations Made in the Exploration of New France. . . .*

Some Account of Champlain's Voyages

[*Brief excerpts from Champlain's* Faithful Journal of Observations *follow. The translation is from* Voyages *of Samuel de Champlain, 1604–1618, edited by W. L. Grant, Original Narratives of Early American History (New York, 1907).*]

Book I CHAPTER 1

The benefits of commerce have induced several princes to seek an easier route for traffic with the people of the East. Several unsuccessful voyages. Determination of the French for this purpose. Undertaking of Sieur de Monts: his commission and its revocation. New commission to Sieur de Monts to enable him to continue his undertaking.

The inclinations of men differ according to their varied dispositions; and each one in his calling has his particular end in view. Some aim at gain, some at glory, some at the public weal. The greater number are engaged in trade, and especially that which is transacted on the sea. Hence arise the principal support of the people, the opulence and honor of states. This is what raised ancient Rome to the sovereignty and mastery over the entire world, and the Venetians to a grandeur equal to that of powerful kings. It has in all times caused maritime towns to abound in riches, among which Alexandria and Tyre are distinguished, and numerous others, which fill up the regions of the interior with the objects of beauty and rarity obtained from foreign nations. For this reason, many princes have striven to find a northerly route to China, in order to facilitate commerce with the Orientals, in the belief that this route would be shorter and less dangerous. . . .

So many voyages and discoveries without result, and attended with so much hardship and expense, have caused us French in late years to attempt a permanent settlement in those lands which we call New France, in the hope of thus realizing more easily this object; since the voyage in search of the desired passage commences on the other side of the ocean, and is made along the coast of this region. . . .

CHAPTER 2

Description of Sable Island; Cape Breton; La Hève; Port au Mouton; Port Cape Nègre; Sable Bay and Cape; Cormorant Island; Cape Fourchu; Long Island; Bay of Saint Mary; Port Saint Margaret; and of all noteworthy objects along this coast.

Sieur de Monts, by virtue of his commission having published in all the ports and harbors of this kingdom the prohibition against the violation of the monopoly of the fur trade accorded him by His Majesty, gathered together about 120 artisans, whom he embarked in two vessels: one of 120 tons, commanded by Sieur de Pont Gravé; another, of 150 tons, in which he embarked himself, together with several noblemen.

We set out from Havre de Grâce April 7, 1604, and Pont Gravé April 10, to rendezvous at Canseau, 20 leagues from Cape Breton. But, after we were in mid-ocean, Sieur de Monts changed his plan, and directed his course toward Port Mouton, it being more southerly and also more favorable for landing than Canseau.

On May 1, we sighted Sable Island, where we ran a risk of being lost in consequence of the error of our pilots, who were deceived in their calculation, which they made 40 leagues ahead of where we were. . . .

On the 12th of May, we entered another port, five leagues from Cap de la Hève, where we captured a vessel engaged in the fur trade in violation of the king's prohibition. The master's name was Rossignol, whose name the port retained [now Liverpool], which is in latitude 44° 15′.

On the 13th of May, we arrived at a very fine harbor, where there are two little streams, called Port au Mouton, which is seven leagues distant from that of Rossignol. The land is very stony, and covered with copse and heath. There are a great many rabbits, and a quantity of game in consequence of the ponds there.

As soon as we had disembarked, each one commenced making
huts after his fashion, on a point at the entrance of the harbor
near two freshwater ponds. Sieur de Monts at the same time
dispatched a shallop, in which he sent one of us, with some
savages as guides, as bearers of letters, along the coast of La
Cadie, to search for Pont Gravé, who had a portion of the
necessary supplies for our winter sojourn. The latter was
found at the Bay of All-Isles, very anxious about us (for he
knew nothing of the change of plan); and the letters were
handed to him. As soon as he had read them, he returned to
his ship at Canseau, where he seized some Basque vessels
engaged in the fur trade, notwithstanding the prohibition of
His Majesty, and sent their masters to Sieur de Monts, who
meanwhile charged me to reconnoitre the coast and the harbors
suitable for the secure reception of our vessel. . . .

After having explored as particularly as I could the coasts,
ports, and harbors, I returned, without advancing any farther,
to Long Island passage, whence I went back outside of all the
islands in order to observe whether there was any danger at
all on the water side. But we found none whatever, except
there were some rocks about half a league from Sea-Wolf
Islands, which, however, can be easily avoided, since the sea
breaks over them. Continuing our voyage, we were overtaken
by a violent wind, which obliged us to run our barque ashore,
where we were in danger of losing her, which would have
caused us extreme perplexity. The tempest having ceased,
we resumed the sea, and the next day reached Port Mouton,
where Sieur de Monts was awaiting us from day to day, thinking
only of our long stay, and whether some accident had not
befallen us. I made a report to him of our voyage and where
our vessels might go in safety. Meanwhile, I observed very
particularly that place which is in latitude 44°.

The next day Sieur de Monts gave orders to weigh anchor
and proceed to the Bay of Saint Mary, a place which we
had found to be suitable for our vessel to remain in, until we
should be able to find one more advantageous. Coasting along,
we passed near Cape Sable and the Sea-Wolf Islands, whither
Sieur de Monts decided to go in a shallop, and see some islands
of which we had made a report to him, as also of the countless
number of birds found there. Accordingly he set out, accom-

panied by Sieur de Poutrincourt and several other noblemen, with the intention of going to Penguin Island, where we had previously killed with sticks a large number of these birds [auks]. Being somewhat distant from our ship, it was not in our power to reach it, and still less to reach our vessel; for the tide was so strong that we were compelled to put in at a little island to pass the night, where there was much game. I killed there some river birds, which were very acceptable to us, especially as we had taken only a few biscuit, expecting to return the same day. The next day we reached Cape Fourchu, distant half a league from there. Coasting along, we found our vessel in the Bay of Saint Mary. Our company were very anxious about us for two days, fearing lest some misfortune had befallen us; but, when they saw us all safe, they were much rejoiced.

Two or three days after our arrival one of our priests, named Messire Aubry, from Paris, got lost so completely in the woods while going after his sword, which he had forgotten, that he could not find the vessel. And he was thus 17 days without anything to subsist upon except some sour and bitter plants like the sorrel, and some small fruit of little substance large as currants [partridge berry] which creep upon the ground. Being at his wits' end, without hope of ever seeing us again, weak and feeble, he found himself on the shore of Baye Françoise, thus named by Sieur de Monts, near Long Island, where his strength gave out, when one of our shallops out fishing discovered him. Not being able to shout to them, he made a sign with a pole, on the end of which he had put his hat, that they should go and get him. This they did at once, and brought him off. Sieur de Monts had caused a search to be made not only by his own men, but also by the savages of those parts, who scoured all the woods, but brought back no intelligence of him. Believing him to be dead, they all saw him coming back in the shallop to their great delight. A long time was needed to restore him to his usual strength. . . .

CHAPTER 4

Sieur de Monts, finding no other place better adapted for a permanent settlement than the island of Saint Croix, fortifies it and builds dwellings. Return of the vessels to France, and of

Ralleau, secretary of Sieur de Monts, for the sake of arranging some business affairs.

Not finding any more suitable place than this island, we commenced making a barricade on a little islet a short distance from the main island, which served as a station for placing our cannon. All worked so energetically that in a little while it was put in a state of defense, although the mosquitoes (which are little flies) annoyed us excessively in our work. For there were several of our men whose faces were so swollen by their bites that they could scarcely see. The barricade being finished, Sieur de Monts sent his barque to notify the rest of our party, who were with our vessel in the bay of Saint Mary, to come to Saint Croix. This was promptly done, and while awaiting them we spent our time very pleasantly.

Some days after, our vessels having arrived and anchored, all disembarked. Then, without losing time, Sieur de Monts proceeded to employ the workmen in building houses for our abode, and allowed me to determine the arrangement of our settlement. After Sieur de Monts had determined the place for the storehouse, which is nine fathoms long, three wide, and 12 feet high, he adopted the plan for his own house, which he had promptly built by good workmen, and then assigned to each one his location. Straightway, the men began to gather together by fives and sixes, each according to his desire. Then all set to work to clear up the island, to go to the woods, to make the framework, to carry earth and other things necessary for the buildings.

While we were building our houses, Sieur de Monts dispatched Captain Fouques in the vessel of Rossignol to find Pont Gravé at Canseau, in order to obtain for our settlement what supplies remained. . . . Meanwhile, work on the houses went on vigorously and without cessation; the carpenters engaged on the storehouse and dwelling of Sieur de Monts, and the others each on his own house, as I was on mine, which I built with the assistance of some servants belonging to Sieur d'Orville and myself. It was forthwith completed, and Sieur de Monts lodged in it until his own was finished. An oven was also made, and a handmill for grinding our wheat, the working of which involved much trouble and labor to the most of us,

since it was a toilsome operation. Some gardens were afterwards
laid out, on the mainland as well as on the island. Here many
kinds of seeds were planted, which flourished very well on the
mainland but not on the island, since there was only sand here,
and the whole were burned up when the sun shone, although
special pains were taken to water them.

Some days after, Sieur de Monts determined to ascertain
where the mine of pure copper was which we had searched for
so much. With this object in view, he dispatched me together
with a savage named Messamoüet, who asserted that he knew
the place well. I set out in a small barque of five or six tons,
with nine sailors. Some eight leagues from the island, toward
the river Saint John, we found a mine of copper which was not
pure, yet good according to the report of the miner, who said
that it would yield 18 percent. Farther on we found others
inferior to this. When we reached the place where we supposed that was which we were hunting for, the savage could
not find it, so that it was necessary to come back, leaving the
search for another time.

Upon my return from this trip, Sieur de Monts resolved to
send his vessels back to France, and also Sieur de Poutrincourt,
who had come only for his pleasure and to explore countries
and places suitable for a colony, which he desired to found; for
which reason he asked Sieur de Monts for Port Royal, which he
gave him in accordance with the power and directions he had
received from the king. He sent back also Ralleau, his secretary, to arrange some matters concerning the voyage. They
set out from the island of Saint Croix the last day of August,
1604. . . .

CHAPTER 6

Of the Mal de la Terre, a very desperate malady. How the
savages, men and women, spend their time in winter. And all
that occurred at the settlement while we were passing the
winter.

When we arrived at the island of Saint Croix, each one had
finished his place of abode. Winter came upon us sooner than
we expected, and prevented us from doing many things which

we had proposed. Nevertheless, Sieur de Monts did not fail
to have some gardens made on the island. Many began to clear
up the ground, each his own. I also did so with mine, which
was very large, where I planted a quantity of seeds, as also
did the others who had any, and they came up very well. But
since the island was all sandy, everything dried up almost as
soon as the sun shone upon it, and we had no water for irriga-
tion except from the rain, which was infrequent.

Sieur de Monts caused also clearings to be made on the
mainland for making gardens, and at the falls three leagues
from our settlement he had work done and some wheat sown,
which came up very well and ripened. Around our habitation
there is, at low tide, a large number of shellfish, such as cockles,
mussels, sea urchins, and sea snails, which were very acceptable
to all.

The snows began on the 6th of October. On the 3d of
December, we saw ice pass which came from some frozen river.
The cold was sharp, more severe than in France, and of much
longer duration; and it scarcely rained at all the entire winter.
I suppose that is owing to the north and northwest winds
passing over high mountains always covered with snow. The
latter was from three to four feet deep up to the end of the
month of April; lasting much longer, I suppose, than it would
if the country were cultivated.

During the winter many of our company were attacked by
a certain malady called the *mal de la terre;* otherwise scurvy,
as I have since heard from learned men. There were produced,
in the mouth of those who had it, great pieces of superfluous
and driveling flesh (causing extensive putrefaction), which got
the upper hand to such an extent that scarcely any thing but
liquid could be taken. Their teeth became very loose, and
could be pulled out with the fingers without its causing them
pain. The superfluous flesh was often cut out, which caused
them to eject much blood through the mouth. Afterward, a
violent pain seized their arms and legs, which remained swollen
and very hard, all spotted as if with fleabites; and they could
not walk on account of the contraction of the muscles, so that
they were almost without strength, and suffered intolerable
pains. They experienced pain also in the loins, stomach, and
bowels, had a very bad cough, and short breath. In a word,

they were in such a condition that the majority of them could not rise nor move, and could not even be raised up on their feet without falling down in a swoon. So that out of 79, who composed our party, 35 died, and more than 20 were on the point of death. The majority of those who remained well also complained of slight pains and short breath. We were unable to find any remedy for these maladies. A *post mortem* examination of several was made to investigate the cause of their disease. . . .

Our surgeons could not help suffering themselves in the same manner as the rest. Those who continued sick were healed by spring, which commences in this country in May. That led us to believe that the change of season restored their health rather than the remedies prescribed.

During this winter all our liquors froze, except the Spanish wine [sherry]. Cider was dispensed by the pound. The cause of this loss was that there were no cellars to our storehouse, and that the air which entered by the cracks was sharper than that outside. We were obliged to use very bad water, and drink melted snow, as there were no springs nor brooks; for it was not possible to go to the mainland in consequence of the great pieces of ice drifted by the tide, which varies three fathoms between low and high water. Work on the handmill was very fatiguing, since the most of us, having slept poorly, and suffering from insufficiency of fuel, which we could not obtain on account of the ice, had scarcely any strength, and also because we ate only salt meat and vegetables during the winter, which produce bad blood. The latter circumstance was, in my opinion, a partial cause of these dreadful maladies. All this produced discontent in Sieur de Monts and others of the settlement.

It would be very difficult to ascertain the character of this region without spending a winter in it; for, on arriving here in summer, everything is very agreeable, in consequence of the woods, fine country, and the many varieties of good fish which are found there. There are six months of winter in this country.

The savages who dwell here are few in number. During the winter, in the deepest snows, they hunt elks and other animals, on which they live most of the time. And, unless the snow is deep, they scarcely get rewarded for their pains, since they cannot capture anything except by a very great effort, which is the reason for their enduring and suffering much. When they do not hunt, they live on a shellfish called the cockle. They clothe themselves in winter with good furs of beaver and elk. The women make all the garments, but not so exactly but that you can see the flesh under the armpits, because they have not ingenuity enough to fit them better. When they go a-hunting, they use a kind of snowshoe twice as large as those hereabouts, which they attach to the soles of their feet, and walk thus over the snow without sinking in, the women and children as well as the men. They search for the track of animals, which, having found, they follow until they get sight of the creature, when they shoot at it with their bows, or kill it by means of daggers attached to the end of a short pike, which is very easily done, as the animals cannot walk on the snow without sinking in. Then the women and children come up, erect a hut, and they give themselves to feasting. Afterward, they return in search of other animals, and thus they pass the winter. In the month of March following, some savages came and gave us a portion of their game in exchange for bread and other things which we gave them. This is the mode of life in winter of these people, which seems to me a very miserable one.

We looked for our vessels at the end of April; but, as this passed without their arriving, all began to have an ill boding, fearing that some accident had befallen them. For this reason, on the 15th of May, Sieur de Monts decided to have a barque of 15 tons and another of seven fitted up, so that we might go at the end of the month of June to Gaspé in quest of vessels in which to return to France, in case our own should not meanwhile arrive. But God helped us better than we hoped; for, on the 15th of June ensuing, while on guard about 11 o'clock at night, Pont Gravé, captain of one of the vessels of Sieur de Monts, arriving in a shallop, informed us that his ship was anchored six leagues from our settlement, and he was welcomed amid the great joy of all.

The next day the vessel arrived, and anchored near our habitation. Pont Gravé informed us that a vessel from Saint-Malo, called the *Saint Éstienne,* was following him, bringing us provisions and supplies.

On the 17th of the month, Sieur de Monts decided to go in

quest of a place better adapted for an abode, and with a better temperature than our own. With this view, he had the barque made ready, in which he had purposed to go to Gaspé. . . .

Book II CHAPTER 1

Determination of Sieur de Monts to make explorations in the interior; his commission, and its infringement by the Basques, who disarmed the vessel of Pont Gravé; and the agreement between them which they subsequently made.

Having returned to France after a stay of three years in New France, I proceeded to Sieur de Monts, and related to him the principal events of which I had been a witness since his departure, and gave him the map and plan of the most re-markable coasts and harbors there.

Some time afterward, Sieur de Monts determined to con-tinue his undertaking and complete the exploration of the interior along the great river Saint Lawrence, where I had been by order of the late King Henry the Great [Henry IV, who was assassinated May 14, 1610] in the year 1603, for a distance of some 180 leagues, commencing in latitude 48° 40', that is, at Gaspé, at the entrance of the river, as far as the great fall, which is in latitude 45° and some minutes, where our exploration ended and where boats could not pass as we then thought, since we had not made a careful examination of it as we have since done.

Now after Sieur de Monts had conferred with me several times in regard to his purposes concerning the exploration, he resolved to continue so noble and meritorious an undertaking, notwithstanding the hardships and labors of the past. He honored me with his lieutenancy for the voyage; and, in order to carry out his purpose, he had two vessels equipped, one commanded by Pont Gravé, who was commissioned to trade with the savages of the country and bring back the vessels, while I was to winter in the country.

Sieur de Monts, for the purpose of defraying the expenses of the expedition, obtained letters from His Majesty for one year, by which all persons were forbidden to traffic in peltry with the savages. . . .

I proceeded to Honfleur for embarkation, where I found the vessel of Pont Gravé in readiness. He left port on the 5th of April [1608]; I did so on the 13th, arriving at the Grand Bank on the 15th of May, in latitude 45° 15′. On the 26th we sighted Cape Saint Mary, in latitude 46° 45′, on the Island of Newfoundland. On the 27th of the month we sighted Cape Saint Lawrence [Cape North] on Cape Breton, and also the Island of Saint Paul, distant 83 leagues from Cape Saint Mary. On the 30th we sighted Isle Percée and Gaspé, in latitude 48° 40′, distant from Cape Saint Lawrence from 70 to 75 leagues.

On the 3d of June we arrived before Tadoussac, distant from Gaspé from 80 to 90 leagues; and we anchored in the roadstead of Tadoussac, a league distant from the harbor, which latter is a kind of cove at the mouth of the river Saguenay, where the tide is very remarkable on account of its rapidity, and where there are sometimes violent winds, bringing severe cold. . . .

. . . The winds from the south-southeast strike the harbor, which are not to be feared; but those, however, from the Saguenay are. The two points above mentioned are dry at low tide; our vessel was unable to enter the harbor, as the wind and tide were unfavorable. I at once had the boat lowered, in order to go to the port and ascertain whether Pont Gravé had arrived. While on the way, I met a shallop with the pilot of Pont Gravé and a Basque, who came to inform me of what had happened to them because they attempted to hinder the Basque vessels from trading, according to the commission obtained by Sieur de Monts from His Majesty that no vessels should trade without permission of Sieur de Monts, as was expressed in it; and that, notwithstanding the notifications which Pont Gravé made in behalf of His Majesty, they did not desist from forcibly carrying on their traffic; and that they had used their arms and maintained themselves so well in their vessel that, discharging all their cannon upon that of Pont Gravé, and letting off many musket shots, he was severely wounded, together with three of his men, one of whom died, Pont Gravé meanwhile making no resistance; for at the first shower of musketry he was struck down. The Basques came on board of the vessel and took away all the cannon and arms, declaring that they would trade, notwithstanding the prohibition of the king, and that when they were ready to set out for France they would restore to him his cannon and ammunition, and that they were keeping them in order to be in a state of security. Upon hearing all these particulars, I was greatly annoyed at such a beginning, which we might have easily avoided.

Now, after hearing from the pilot all these things I asked him why the Basque had come on board of our vessel. He told me that he came in behalf of their master, named Darache, and his companions, to obtain assurance from me that I would do them no harm when our vessel entered the harbor.

I replied that I could not give any until I had seen Pont Gravé. The Basque said that, if I had need of anything in their power, they would assist me accordingly. What led them to use this language was simply their recognition of having done wrong, as they confessed, and the fear that they would not be permitted to engage in the whale fishery. After talking at length, I went ashore to see Pont Gravé, in order to deliberate as to what was to be done. I found him very ill. He related to me in detail all that had happened. We concluded that we could only enter the harbor by force, and that the settlement must not be given up for this year, so that we considered it best, in order not to make a bad cause out of a just one and thus work our ruin, to give them assurances on my part so long as I should remain there, and that Pont Gravé should undertake nothing against them, but that justice should be done in France, and their differences should be settled there.

Darache, master of the vessel, begged me to go on board, where he gave me a cordial reception. After a long conference I secured an agreement between Pont Gravé and him, and required him to promise that he would undertake nothing against Pont Gravé, or what would be prejudicial to the king and Sieur de Monts; that, if he did the contrary, I should regard my promise as null and void. This was agreed to and signed by each.

In this place were a number of savages who had come for traffic in furs, several of whom came to our vessel with their canoes, which are from eight to nine paces long and about a pace or pace and a half broad in the middle, growing narrower toward the two ends. They are very apt to turn over, in case one does not understand managing them, and are made of birch bark, strengthened on the inside by little ribs of white cedar very neatly arranged; they are so light that a man can easily carry one. Each can carry a weight equal to that of a pipe [cask]. When they want to go overland to a river where they have business, they carry them with them. From Choüacoet along the coast as far as the harbor of Tadoussac, they are all alike.

CHAPTER 2

Of the River Saguenay, and the savages who visited us there. Of the Island of Orleans, and all that we observed there worthy of note.

After this agreement, I had some carpenters set to work to fit up a little barque of 12 or 14 tons for carrying all that was needed for our settlement, which, however, could not be got ready before the last of June.

Meanwhile, I managed to visit some parts of the river Saguenay, a fine river, which has the incredible depth of some 150 to 200 fathoms. About 50 leagues from the mouth of the harbor, there is, as is said, a great waterfall, descending from a very high elevation with great impetuosity. There are some islands in this river, very barren, being only rocks covered with small firs and heathers. . . .

The savages told me that, after passing the first fall, they meet with eight others, when they go a day's journey without finding any. Then they pass ten others, and enter a lake [Lake Saint John], which they are three days in crossing, and they are easily able to make ten leagues a day upstream. At the end of the lake there dwells a migratory people. . . .

These people of the north report to our savages that they see the salt sea; and, if that is true, as I think it certainly is, it can be nothing but a gulf entering the interior on the north [Hudson's Bay, discovered by Henry Hudson in 1610]. The savages say that the distance from the north sea to the port of Tadoussac is perhaps 45 or 50 days' journey, in consequence of the difficulties presented by the roads, rivers, and country, which is very mountainous, and where there is snow for the most part of the year. This is what I have definitely ascertained in regard to this river. I have often wished to explore it, but

could not do so without the savages, who were unwilling that
I or any of our party should accompany them. Nevertheless,
they have promised that I shall do so. This exploration would
be desirable, in order to remove the doubts of many persons in
regard to the existence of this sea on the north, where it is
maintained that the English have gone in these latter years
to find a way to China.

I set out from Tadoussac the last day of the month to go to
Quebec. . . .

CHAPTER 3

Arrival at Quebec, where we constructed our place of abode;
its situation. Conspiracy against the service of the king and
my life by some of our men. Punishment of them, and all that
transpired in the affair.

From the Island of Orleans to Quebec [Cartier's Stadacona]
the distance is a league. I arrived there on the 3d of July, when
I searched for a place suitable for our settlement, but I could
find none more convenient or better situated than the point
of Quebec, so called by the savages, which was covered with
nut trees. I at once employed a portion of our workmen in
cutting them down, that we might construct our habitation there:
one I set to sawing boards, another to making a cellar and digging ditches, another I sent to Tadoussac with the barque to get
supplies. The first thing we made was the storehouse for keeping
under cover our supplies, which was promptly accomplished
through the zeal of all, and my attention to the work.

Some days after my arrival at Quebec, a locksmith conspired
against the service of the king. His plan was to put me to death,
and, getting possession of our fort, to put it into the hands
of the Basques or Spaniards, then at Tadoussac, beyond which
vessels cannot go from not having a knowledge of the route, nor
of the banks and rocks on the way.

In order to execute his wretched plan, by which he hoped to
make his fortune, he suborned four of the worst characters,
as he supposed, telling them a thousand falsehoods and pre-
senting to them prospects of acquiring riches.

These four men, having been won over, all promised to act

in such a manner as to gain the rest over to their side; so that, for the time being, I had no one with me in whom I could put confidence, which gave them still more hope of making their plan succeed: for four or five of my companions, in whom they knew that I put confidence, were on board of the barques, for the purpose of protecting the provisions and supplies necessary for our settlement.

In a word, they were so skillful in carrying out their intrigues with those who remained that they were on the point of gaining all over to their cause, even my lackey, promising them many things which they could not have fulfilled.

Being now all agreed, they made daily different plans as to how they should put me to death, so as not to be accused of it, which they found to be a difficult thing. But the devil blindfolding them all and taking away their reason and every possible difficulty, they determined to take me while unarmed and strangle me; or to give a false alarm at night, and shoot me as I went out, in which manner they judged that they would accomplish their work sooner than otherwise. They made a mutual promise not to betray each other, on penalty that the first one who opened his mouth should be poniarded. They were to execute their plan in four days, before the arrival of our barques, otherwise they would have been unable to carry out their scheme.

On this very day, one of our barques arrived, with our pilot, Captain Testu, a very discreet man. After the barque was unloaded and ready to return to Tadoussac, there came to him a locksmith, named Natel, an associate of Jean du Val, the head of the conspiracy, who told him that he had promised the rest to do just as they did; but that he did not in fact desire the execution of the plot, yet did not dare to make a disclosure in regard to it, from fear of being poniarded.

Antoine Natel made the pilot promise that he would make no disclosure in regard to what he should say, since, if his companions should discover it, they would put him to death. The pilot gave him his assurance in all particulars, and asked him to state the character of the plot which they wished to carry out. This Natel did at length, when the pilot said to him: "My friend, you have done well to disclose such a malicious design, and you show that you are an upright man, and under the

guidance of the Holy Spirit. But these things cannot be passed
by without bringing them to the knowledge of Sieur de
Champlain, that he may make provision against them; and I
promise you that I will prevail upon him to pardon you and
the rest. And I will at once," said the pilot, "go to him without
exciting any suspicion; and do you go about your business,
listening to all they may say, and not troubling yourself about
the rest."

The pilot came at once to me, in a garden which I was
having prepared, and said that he wished to speak to me in a
private place, where we could be alone. I readily assented, and
we went into the wood, where he related to me the whole affair.
I asked who had told it to him. He begged me to pardon him
who had made the disclosure, which I consented to do, although
he ought to have addressed himself to me. He was afraid, he
replied, that you would become angry, and harm him. I told
him that I was able to govern myself better than that, in such
a matter; and desired him to have the man come to me, that I
might hear his statement. He went and brought him all
trembling with fear lest I should do him some harm. I reassured him, telling him not to be afraid; that he was in a place
of safety and that I should pardon him for all that he had done,
together with the others, provided he would tell me in full the
truth in regard to the whole matter and the motive which
had impelled them to it. Nothing, he said, had impelled them,
except that they had imagined that, by giving up the place
into the hands of the Basques or Spaniards, they might all
become rich, and that they did not want to go back to France.
He also related to me the remaining particulars in regard to
their conspiracy.

After having heard and questioned him, I directed him to
go about his work. Meanwhile, I ordered the pilot to bring
up his shallop, which he did. Then I gave two bottles of wine
to a young man, directing him to say to these four worthies,
the leaders of the conspiracy, that it was a present of wine,
which his friends at Tadoussac had given him, and that he
wished to share it with them. This they did not decline, and at
evening were on board the barque where he was to give them
the entertainment. I lost no time in going there shortly after,
and caused them to be seized and held until the next day.

Then were my worthies astonished indeed. I at once had all get up, for it was about ten o'clock in the evening, and pardoned them all, on condition that they would disclose to me the truth in regard to all that had occurred; which they did, when I had them retire.

The next day I took the depositions of all, one after the other, in the presence of the pilot and sailors of the vessel, which I had put down in writing; and they were well pleased, as they said, since they had lived only in fear of each other, especially of the four knaves who had ensnared them. But now they lived in peace, satisfied, as they declared, with the treatment which they had received.

The same day I had six pairs of handcuffs made for the authors of the conspiracy: one for our surgeon, named Bonnerme, one for another, named La Taille, whom the four conspirators had accused, which, however, proved false, and consequently they were given their liberty.

This being done, I took my worthies to Tadoussac, begging Pont Gravé to do me the favor of guarding them, since I had as yet no secure place for keeping them, and as we were occupied in constructing our places of abode. Another object was to consult with him, and others on the ship, as to what should be done in the premises. We suggested that, after he had finished his work at Tadoussac, he should come to Quebec with the prisoners, where he should have them confronted with their witnesses, and, after giving them a hearing, order justice to be done according to the offense which they had committed.

I went back the next day to Quebec, to hasten the completion of our storehouse, so as to secure our provisions, which had been misused by all those scoundrels, who spared nothing, without reflecting how they could find more when these failed; for I could not obviate the difficulty until the storehouse should be completed and shut up.

Pont Gravé arrived some time after me, with the prisoners, which caused uneasiness to the workmen who remained, since they feared that I should pardon them, and that they would avenge themselves upon them for revealing their wicked design.

We had them brought face to face, and they affirmed before them all [that] which they had stated in their depositions, the prisoners not denying it, but admitting that they had acted in a wicked manner and should be punished, unless mercy might be exercised toward them; accusing, above all, Jean du Val, who had been trying to lead them into such a conspiracy from the time of their departure from France. Du Val knew not what to say, except that he deserved death, that all stated in the depositions was true, and that he begged for mercy upon himself and the others, who had given in their adherence to his pernicious purposes.

After Pont Gravé and I, the captain of the vessel, surgeon, mate, second mate, and other sailors, had heard their depositions and face-to-face statements, we adjudged that it would be enough to put to death Du Val, as the instigator of the conspiracy; and that he might serve as an example to those who remained, leading them to deport themselves correctly in future, in the discharge of their duty; and that the Spaniards and Basques, of whom there were large numbers in the country, might not glory in the event. We adjudged that the three others be condemned to be hung, but that they should be taken to France and put into the hands of Sieur de Monts, that such ample justice might be done them as he should recommend; that they should be sent with all the evidence and their sentence, as well as that of Jean du Val, who was strangled and hung at Quebec, and his head was put on the end of a pike, to be set up in the most conspicuous place on our fort. . . .

CHAPTER 9

Departure from the fall of the Iroquois River. Description of a large lake. Encounter with the enemy at this lake; their manner of attacking the Iroquois and their behavior in battle.

I set out accordingly from the fall of the Iroquois River on the 2d of July. All the savages set to carrying their canoes, arms, and baggage overland, some half a league, in order to pass by the violence and strength of the fall, which was speedily accomplished. Then they put them all in the water again, two men in each with the baggage; and they caused one of the men of each canoe to go by land some three leagues, the extent of the fall, which is not, however, so violent here as at the mouth, except in some places, where rocks obstruct the river, which is not broader than 300 or 400 paces. After we had passed the fall, which was attended with difficulty, all the savages, who had gone by land over a good path and level country, although there are a great many trees, reembarked in their canoes. My men went also by land; but I went in a canoe. The savages made a review of all their followers, finding that there were 24 canoes, with 60 men. After the review was completed, we continued our course to an ,island three leagues long, filled with the finest pines I had ever seen. Here they went hunting and captured some wild animals. Proceeding about three leagues farther on, we made a halt, in order to rest the coming night.

They all at once set to work, some to cut wood, and others to obtain the bark of trees for covering their cabins, for the sake of sheltering themselves, others to fell large trees for constructing a barricade on the riverbank around their cabins, which they do so quickly that in less than two hours so much is accomplished that 500 of their enemies would find it very difficult to dislodge them without killing large numbers. They make no barricade on the riverbank where their canoes are drawn up, in order that they may be able to embark if occasion requires. After they were established in their cabins, they dispatched three canoes, with nine good men, according to their custom in all their encampments, to reconnoiter for a distance of two or three leagues to see if they can perceive anything, after which they return. They rest the entire night, depending upon the observation of these scouts, which is a very bad custom among them; for they are sometimes while sleeping surprised by their enemies, who slaughter them before they have time to get up and prepare for defense. Noticing this, I remonstrated with them on the mistake they made, and told them that they ought to keep watch, as they had seen us do every night, and have men on the lookout, in order to listen and see whether they perceived anything, and that they should not live in such a manner like beasts. They replied that they could not keep watch and that they worked enough in the daytime in the chase, since, when engaged in war, they divide their troops into three parts: namely, a part for hunting scattered in several places; another to constitute the main body of their army, which is always under arms; and the third to act as *avant-coureurs* [scouts], to look out along the rivers and observe whether they can see any mark or signal showing where their enemies or friends have passed. This they ascertain by certain marks which the chiefs of different tribes make known to each other; but, these not continuing always the same, they inform themselves from time to time of changes, by which means they ascertain whether they are enemies or friends who have passed. The hunters never hunt in advance of the main body, or *avant-coureurs,* so as not to excite alarm or produce disorder, but in the rear and in the direction from which they do not anticipate their enemy. Thus they advance until they are within two or three days' march of their enemies, when they proceed by night stealthily and all in a body, except the *avant-coureurs.* By day they withdraw into the interior of the woods, where they rest, without straying off, neither making any noise nor any fire, even for the sake of cooking, so as not to be noticed in case their enemies should by accident pass by. They make no fire, except in smoking, which amounts to almost nothing. They eat baked Indian meal, which they soak in water, when it becomes a kind of porridge. They provide themselves with such meal to meet their wants when they are near their enemies or when retreating after a charge, in which case they are not inclined to hunt, retreating immediately.

In all their encampments, they have their Pilotois, or Ostemoy, a class of persons who play the part of soothsayers, in whom these people have faith. One of these builds a cabin, surrounds it with small pieces of wood, and covers it with his robe; after it is built, he places himself inside, so as not to be seen at all, when he seizes and shakes one of the posts of his cabin, muttering some words between his teeth, by which he says he invokes the devil, who appears to him in the form of a stone and tells him whether they will meet their enemies and kill many of them. This Pilotois lies prostrate on the ground, motionless, only speaking with the devil: on a sudden, he rises to his feet, talking, and tormenting himself in such a manner that, although naked, he is all of a perspiration. All the people surround the cabin, seated on their buttocks like apes. They frequently told me that the shaking of the cabin, which I saw, proceeded from the devil, who made it move, and not the man inside, although I could see the contrary;

for, as I have stated above, it was the Pilotois who took one
of the supports of the cabin and made it move in this manner.
They told me also that I should see fire come out from the
top, which I did not see at all. These rogues counterfeit also
their voice, so that it is heavy and clear, and speak in a language unknown to the other savages. And, when they represent it as broken, the savages think that the devil is speaking
and telling them what is to happen in their war, and what they
must do.

But all these scapegraces, who play the soothsayer, out of a
hundred words do not speak two that are true, and impose
upon these poor people. There are enough like them in the
world, who take food from the mouths of the people by their
impostures, as these worthies do. I often remonstrated with
the people, telling them that all they did was sheer nonsense
and that they ought not to put confidence in them.

Now, after ascertaining from their soothsayers what is to be
their fortune, the chiefs take sticks a foot long and as many
as there are soldiers. They take others, somewhat larger, to
indicate the chiefs. Then they go into the wood and seek out
a level place, five or six feet square, where the chief, as sergeant-
major, puts all the sticks in such order as seems to him best.
Then he calls all his companions, who come all armed; and
he indicates to them the rank and order they are to observe
in battle with their enemies. All the savages watch carefully
this proceeding, observing attentively the outline which their
chief has made with the sticks. Then they go away and set to
placing themselves in such order as the sticks were in, when
they mingle with each other, and return again to their proper
order, which maneuver they repeat two or three times, and at
all their encampments, without needing a sergeant to keep them
in the proper order, which they are able to keep accurately
without any confusion. This is their rule in war.

We set out on the next day, continuing our course in the
river as far as the entrance of the lake. There are many
pretty islands here, low, and containing very fine woods and
meadows, with abundance of fowl and such animals of the
chase as stags, fallow deer, fawns, roebucks, bears, and others,
which go from the mainland to these islands. We captured a
large number of these animals. There are also many beavers,
not only in this river but also in numerous other little ones

that flow into it. These regions, although they are pleasant, are not inhabited by any savages on account of their wars; but they withdraw as far as possible from the rivers into the interior, in order not to be suddenly surprised.

The next day we entered the lake, which is of great extent, say 80 or 100 leagues long, where I saw four fine islands, ten, 12, and 15 leagues long, which were formerly inhabited by the savages, like the River of the Iroquois; but they have been abandoned since the wars of the savages with one another prevail. There are also many rivers falling into the lake, bordered by many fine trees of the same kinds as those we have in France, with many vines finer than any I have seen in any other place; also many chestnut trees on the border of this lake, which I had not seen before. There is also a great abundance of fish of many varieties. . . .

Continuing our course over this lake on the western side, I noticed, while observing the country, some very high mountains on the eastern side, on the top of which there was snow [the Green Mountains of Vermont, the "snow," in July, was probably white limestone]. I made inquiry of the savages whether these localities were inhabited, when they told me that the Iroquois dwelt there, and that there were beautiful valleys in these places, with plains productive in grain such as I had eaten in this country, together with many kinds of fruit without limit. They said also that the lake extended near mountains, some 25 leagues distant from us, as I judge. I saw, on the south, other mountains, no less high than the first, but without any snow [the Adirondacks]. The savages told me that these mountains were thickly settled, and that it was there we were to find their enemies; but that it was necessary to pass a fall [Ticonderoga] in order to go there (which I afterward saw), when we should enter another lake [Lake George] nine or ten leagues long. After reaching the end of the lake, we should have to go, they said, two leagues by land and pass through a river [the Hudson] flowing into the sea on the Norumbega coast, near that of Florida, whither it took them only two days to go by canoe, as I have since ascertained from some prisoners we captured, who gave me minute information in regard to all they had personal knowledge of through some Algonquin interpreters, who understood the Iroquois language.

Now, as we began to approach within two or three days' journey of the abode of their enemies, we advanced only at night, resting during the day. But they did not fail to practice constantly their accustomed superstitions, in order to ascertain what was to be the result of their undertaking; and they often asked me if I had had a dream and seen their enemies, to which I replied in the negative. Yet I did not cease to encourage them and inspire in them hope. When night came, we set out on the journey until the next day, when we withdrew into the interior of the forest and spent the rest of the day there. About ten or eleven o'clock, after taking a little walk about our encampment, I retired. While sleeping, I dreamed that I saw our enemies, the Iroquois, drowning in the lake near a mountain, within sight. When I expressed a wish to help them, our allies, the savages, told me we must let them all die and that they were of no importance. When I awoke, they did not fail to ask me, as usual, if I had had a dream. I told them that I had, in fact, had a dream. This, upon being related, gave them so much confidence that they did not doubt any longer that good was to happen to them.

When it was evening, we embarked in our canoes to continue our course; and, as we advanced very quietly and without making any noise, we met on the 29th of the month the Iroquois, about ten o'clock at evening, at the extremity of a cape [Crown Point] which extends into the lake on the western bank. They had come to fight. We both began to utter loud cries, all getting their arms in readiness. We withdrew out on the water, and the Iroquois went on shore, where they drew up all their canoes close to each other and began to fell trees with poor axes, which they acquire in war sometimes, using also others of stone. Thus they barricaded themselves very well.

Our forces also passed the entire night, their canoes being drawn up close to each other and fastened to poles, so that they might not get separated and that they might be all in readiness to fight, if occasion required. We were out upon the water, within arrow range of their barricades. When they were armed and in array, they dispatched two canoes by themselves to the enemy to inquire if they wished to fight, to which the latter replied that they wanted nothing else; but they said that, at present, there was not much light and that

it would be necessary to wait for daylight, so as to be able to
recognize each other; and that, as soon as the sun rose, they
would offer us battle. This was agreed to by our side. Meanwhile, the entire night was spent in dancing and singing,
on both sides, with endless insults and other talk; as, how little
courage we had, how feeble a resistance we should make against
their arms, and that, when day came, we should realize it
to our ruin. Ours also were not slow in retorting, telling
them they would see such execution of arms as never before,
together with an abundance of such talk as is not unusual in
the siege of a town. After this singing, dancing, and bandy-
ing words on both sides to the fill, when day came, my companions and myself continued under cover, for fear that the
enemy would see us. We arranged our arms in the best manner possible, being, however, separated, each in one of the
canoes of the savage Montagnais. After arming ourselves with
light armor, we each took an harquebus and went on shore.
I saw the enemy go out of their barricade, nearly 200 in number, stout and rugged. in appearance. They came at a slow
pace toward us, with a dignity and assurance which greatly
amused me, having three chiefs at their head. Our men also
advanced in the same order, telling me that those who had
three large plumes were the chiefs, and that they had only
these three, and that they could be distinguished by these
plumes, which were much larger than those of their companions, and that I should do what I could to kill them. I
promised to do all in my power, and said that I was very
sorry they could not understand me, so that I might give
order and shape to their mode of attacking their enemies, and
then we should, without doubt, defeat them all; but that this
could not now be obviated, and that I should be very glad to
show them my courage and good will when we should engage
in the fight.

As soon as we had landed, they began to run for some 200
paces toward their enemies, who stood firmly, not having as
yet noticed my companions, who went into the woods with
some savages. Our men began to call me with loud cries; and,
in order to give me a passageway, they opened in two parts,
and put me at their head, where I marched some 20 paces in
advance of the rest until I was within about 30 paces of the

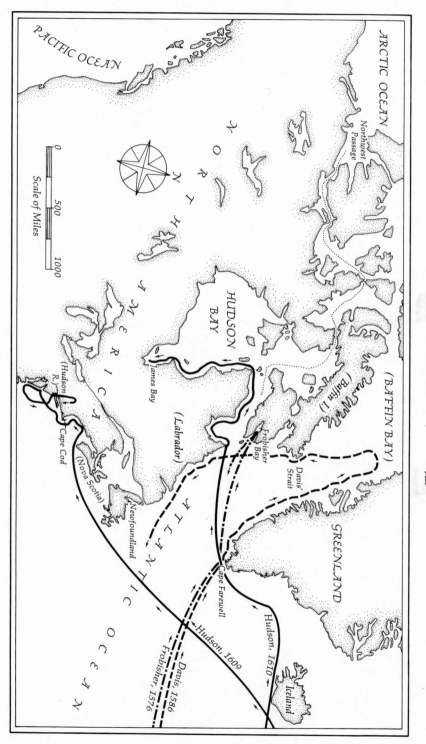

The search for the Northwest Passage

enemy, who at once noticed me, and, halting, gazed at me, as I did also at them. When I saw them making a move to fire at us, I rested my musket against my cheek, and aimed directly at one of the three chiefs. With the same shot, two fell to the ground; and one of their men was so wounded that he died some time after. I had loaded my musket with four balls. When our side saw this shot so favorable for them, they began to raise such loud cries that one could not have heard it thunder. Meanwhile, the arrows flew on both sides. The Iroquois were greatly astonished that two men had been so quickly killed, although they were equipped with armor woven from cotton thread and with wood which was proof against their arrows. This caused great alarm among them. As I was loading again, one of my companions fired a shot from the woods, which astonished them anew to such a degree that, seeing their chiefs dead, they lost courage and took to flight, abandoning their camp and fort, and fleeing into the woods, whither I pursued them, killing still more of them. Our savages also killed several of them, and took ten or 12 prisoners. The remainder escaped with the wounded. Fifteen or 16 were wounded on our side with arrow shots; but they were soon healed.

After gaining the victory, our men amused themselves by taking a great quantity of Indian corn and some meal from their enemies, also their armor, which they had left behind that they might run better. After feasting sumptuously, dancing and singing, we returned three hours after with the prisoners. The spot where this attack took place is in latitude 43° and some minutes [near Ticonderoga] and the lake was called Lake Champlain.

CHAPTER 10

Return from the battle, and what took place on the way.

After going some eight leagues, toward evening they took one of the prisoners, to whom they made a harangue, enumerating the cruelties which he and his men had already practiced toward them without any mercy, and that, in like manner, he ought to make up his mind to receive as much. They commanded him to sing, if he had courage, which he did; but it was a very sad song.

Meanwhile our men kindled a fire; and, when it was well burning, they each took a brand and burned this poor creature gradually, so as to make him suffer greater torment. Sometimes they stopped, and threw water on his back. Then they tore out his nails, and applied fire to the extremities of his fingers and private member. Afterward, they flayed the top of his head and had a kind of gum poured all hot upon it; then they pierced his arms near the wrists, and, drawing up the sinews with sticks, they tore them out by force; but, seeing that they could not get them, they cut them. This poor wretch uttered terrible cries, and it excited my pity to see him treated in this manner, and yet showing such firmness that one would have said, at times, that he suffered hardly any pain at all. I remonstrated with them, saying that we practiced no such cruelties, but killed them at once; and that, if they wished me to fire a musket shot at him, I should be willing to do so. They refused, saying that he would not in that case suffer any pain. I went away from them, pained to see such cruelties as they practiced upon his body. When they saw that I was displeased, they called me and told me to fire a musket shot at him. This I did without his seeing it, and thus put an end, by a single shot, to all the torments he would have suffered, rather than see him tyrannized over. After his death, they were not yet satisfied, but opened him and threw his entrails into the lake. Then they cut off his head, arms, and legs, which they scattered in different directions; keeping the scalp, which they had flayed off, as they had done in the case of all the rest whom they had killed in the contest. They were guilty also of another monstrosity in taking his heart, cutting it into several pieces, and giving it to a brother of his to eat, as also to others of his companions who were prisoners; they took it into their mouths, but would not swallow it. Some Algonquin savages, who were guarding them, made some of them spit it out, when they threw it into the water. This is the manner in which these people behave toward those whom they capture in war, for whom it would be better to die fighting or to kill themselves on the spur of the moment, as many do, rather than fall into the hands of their enemies. After this execution, we set out on our return with the rest of the prisoners, who kept singing as they went along, with no better hopes for the future than he had had who was so wretchedly treated.

XV

Henry Hudson Finds a
Great River, a Bay—and Death

THE discovery of a northern passage to Asia was a hope that the English and Dutch did not relinquish. Many navigators from Frobisher's time onward continued the search in the cold seas to the north, hoping to find a way either to the east or the west that would lead them through the ice to Cathay and the wealth of the Indies.

One of the most competent of the Elizabethan navigators was John Davis (sometimes spelled Davys) of Sandridge, who, beginning in 1589, made three voyages to the northwest and on the third voyage went slightly beyond 72 degrees north latitude through what we now call Davis Strait into Baffin Bay His observations made him believe that the whole north part of America was composed of islands. After an earlier voyage in 1585, he wrote to Sir Francis Walsingham: "I am hereby, according to my duty, to signify unto your honor that the northwest passage is a matter nothing doubtful but at any time almost to be passed, the sea navigable, void of ice, the air tolerable, and the waters very deep." [1]

Subsidized by wealthy London and West Country merchants, the principal one being William Sanderson, Davis between 1585 and 1587 explored and mapped the northern seas but failed to penetrate the ice packs in passages that might lead to the Pacific. He did, however, maintain that four openings that he discovered would lead to the desired passage to the Pacific; but choking ice prevented the penetration of any of

[1] Quoted in Albert H. Markham, *The Voyages and Works of John Davis, the Navigator* (London: The Hakluyt Society, 1880), p. xix.

these passages. Davis made an important contribution in accurately charting the coasts along which he sailed and in proving that Greenland was not part of North America.

The creation of the East India Company by charter granted on December 31, 1600, gave a renewed impetus to the search for a shorter route to the Indies. The company sent out George Weymouth to explore in the northwest in 1602, before his better-known voyage to the coast of New England in 1605, but Weymouth merely covered areas previously visited by earlier navigators.

One of the most important explorers of the early seventeenth century was Henry Hudson, who sailed for both the English and the Dutch and discovered not only the river that now bears his name but the great bay in Canada of the same name. After him came other explorers in search of the elusive Northwest Passage. In 1612 a group known as the Company of Merchants of London, Discoverers of the North West Passage, was chartered, with Sir Thomas Smith, a great merchant and promoter, as governor. The company subsidized expeditions to try to open the way to China by the northwest. In 1615 the company sent out Robert Bylot and William Baffin to make a further exploration of these northern seas. They explored Hudson Bay, which navigators had come to believe led to the Northwest Passage, and concluded that it had no opening to the Pacific. The next year Baffin and Bylot again sailed to the northwest and proceeded into what is now called Baffin Bay as far as 78 degrees, where ice stopped further progress. For seventeenth-century navigators the Northwest Passage would remain blocked by ice.

Henry Hudson's first voyage of discovery was made in 1607 for the Muscovy Company, which sent him out in the ship *Hopewell* to see if he could find his way over the North Pole to the Spice Islands. Ever since the days of Robert Thorne in the early years of the sixteenth century the belief had persisted that the polar seas were open and that a passage could be found thence to Asia. Hudson sailed along the east coast of Greenland and continued northward until he struck barriers of ice that forced him eastward along the coast of Spitzbergen. Finding no opening through the ice, he returned to England in September.

Again in 1608 the Muscovy Company sent him out to see if he could find a passage to the northeast, a route that Richard Chancellor and Sir Hugh Willoughby in 1552 had tried in vain to discover. Hudson sailed in April and made his way around the North Cape with the hope of sailing to the north of Novaya Zemlya into seas that would lead him to Asia. Once more ice packs blocked his progress and he had to sail for home, which he reached at the end of August.

The next year, 1609, Hudson was approached by officers of the Dutch East India Company, which had been organized in 1602, with a proposal that he lead a voyage of discovery for them, for, like the English, the Dutch were eager to find a quick route to the Spice Islands. On April 6, 1609, Hudson sailed from Amsterdam in the ship *Half-Moon* with a mixed crew of English and Dutch. He had an accompanying ship, the *Good Hope*, but it turned back and returned to Holland after encountering ice and storms in a northeasterly voyage. For Hudson, and his Dutch masters, continued to believe that a northeast passage to Asia was possible. In the *Half-Moon* Hudson again probed the seas off the bleak and barren coast of Novaya Zemlya until his crew threatened mutiny. With some persuasion, he got them to agree to turn westward to search for a northwest passage, and in mid-July they reached the North American coast somewhere on the coast of Maine, where they went ashore to cut a new mast for the *Half-Moon*. They also fished and traded with the natives for furs. Fearing attacks from the Indians, Hudson stood out to sea and sailed south until he reached the Chesapeake Bay region. He made no exploration of the Chesapeake, but turned north and sailed into the mouth of Delaware Bay; after deciding that it was not the passage that he sought, he turned north and reached on September 2 the mouth of the great river that we now call the Hudson. Pleased with the prospect of the land as he sailed up the river, Hudson continued in the *Half-Moon* as far as the site of Albany, where the water grew too shallow to risk further sailing. Nevertheless he sent out some of his crew in the ship's boat to see if further navigation would be possible. When they brought a negative report, Hudson turned back.

On the voyage up the river and back they traded with the natives for furs and foodstuffs, maize, pumpkins, grapes and other native commodities. But on October 2, as they neared Manhattan island, the Indians became hostile and Hudson turned his guns on them, killing several. The tribesmen were to remember this encounter 15 years later, when the Dutch in 1624 settled on Manhattan. On October 4 they sailed out of the river and set their course for England, which they reached on November 7 and docked at Dartmouth.

Hudson and the English members of the crew were restrained from going on to Holland in the *Half-Moon,* though they were legitimately in the employ of the Dutch East India Company. Apparently Hudson's papers were also sequestered. At long last, in July of 1610, the *Half-Moon* was permitted to return to Amsterdam.

Hudson made one more voyage in search of the Northwest Passage, for the London merchants continued to hope for a quick and easy route to the Far East. In 1610 a group of wealthy Londoners financed a voyage that Hudson undertook in the ship *Discovery*. This time he sailed directly to the northwest via Iceland and entered Hudson Strait. He sailed on into what we now call Hudson Bay, and by the end of October the *Discovery* was caught in the ice in James Bay. Through the long winter the men suffered and quarreled. When the ice broke up in the spring, under the leadership of Robert Juet, who had been a mate, and a malcontent named Henry Greene, the crew mutinied and cast Hudson, his son and the sick men adrift in an open boat. They then sailed away and left them to die. Greene and three other mutineers were killed by Eskimos and Juet died before reaching England. With Robert Bylot as captain, the remnant of the crew reached home with lame excuses, but the record does not reveal their punishments. Bylot, however, recovered his reputation sufficiently to take part in another expedition in 1615, in search once more of the Northwest Passage.

Henry Hudson is particularly remembered by Americans for the exploration of New York harbor and the Hudson River. He was not the first to visit the region, however, for Verrazano and others had been in New York harbor before him, but he was the first to explore the great river as far as Albany, and his discoveries stirred the Dutch to make a settlement in 1624 on Manhattan.

Van Meteren's Account of Hudson's Voyage in the *Half-Moon*

[*Emanuel van Meteren included in his* Historie der Neder-landscher [*History of the Netherlanders*] (*edition printed in Utrecht in 1611*) *a brief account of Hudson's voyage in the* Half-Moon. *A translation of this account, taken from* Narratives of New Netherland, 1609–1664, Original Narratives of Early American History, *edited by J. Franklin Jameson (New York, 1909), follows:*]

We have observed in our last book that the directors of the East India Company in Holland had sent out in March last [1609], on purpose to seek a passage to China by northeast or northwest, as skillful English pilot named Herry Hutson [*sic*], in a Vlie boat [a flat-bottomed vessel designed to navigate the shoals at the Vlie; the *Half-Moon* was not technically a Vlie boat as she had a topsail], having a crew of 18 or 20 men, partly English, partly Dutch, well provided.

This Henry Hutson left the Texel on the 6th of April, 1609, doubled the Cape of Norway the 5th of May, and directed his course along the northern coasts toward Nova Zembla; but he there found the sea as full of ice as he had found it in the preceding year, so that they lost the hope of effecting anything during the season. This circumstance and the cold, which some of his men, who had been in the East Indies, could not bear, caused quarrels among the crew, they being partly English, partly Dutch, upon which Captain Hutson laid before them two propositions. The first of these was to go to the coast of America, to the latitude of 40°, moved thereto mostly by letters and maps which a certain Captain Smith had sent him from Virginia, and by which he indicated to him a sea leading into the western ocean by the north of the southern English colony. Had this information been true (experience goes as yet to the contrary), it would have been of great advantage, as indicating a short way to India. The other proposition was to direct their search through Davis' Straits. This meeting with general approval, they sailed thitherward on the 14th of May, and arrived on the last day of May with a good wind at the Faeroe Islands, where they stopped but 24 hours to supply themselves with fresh water. After leaving these islands they sailed on till on the 18th of July they reached the coast of Nova Francia [New France], under 44°, where they were obliged to run in, in order to get a new foremast, having lost theirs. They found one, and set it up. They found this a good place for cod fishing, as also for traffic in good skins and furs, which were to be got there at a very low price. But the crew behaved badly toward the people of the country, taking their property by force, out of which there arose quarrels among themselves. The English, fearing that between the two they would be outnumbered and worsted, were therefore afraid to pursue the matter further. So they left that place on the 26th of July, and kept out at sea till the 3d of August, when they came near the coast in 42° of latitude. Thence they sailed on till on the 12th of August they again reached the shore, under 37° 45'. Thence they sailed along the shore until they reached 40° 45', where they found a good entrance between two headlands, and entered on the 12th of September into as fine a river as can be found, wide and deep, with good anchoring ground on both sides.

Their ship finally sailed up the river as far as 42° 40'. But their boat went higher up. In the lower part of the river they found strong and warlike people; but in the upper part they found friendly and polite people, who had an abundance of provisions, skins, and furs of martens and foxes, and many other commodities, as birds and fruit, even white and red grapes, and they traded amicably with the people. And of all the above-mentioned commodities they brought some home. When they had thus been about 50 leagues up the river, they returned on the 4th of October and went again to sea. More could have been done if there had been good will among the crew and if the want of some necessary provisions had not prevented it. While at sea, they held counsel together, but were of different opinions. The mate, a Dutchman, advised to winter in Newfoundland and to search the northwestern passage of Davis throughout. This was opposed by Skipper Hutson. He was afraid of his mutinous crew, who had sometimes savagely threatened him; and he feared that during the cold season they would entirely consume their provisions and would then be obliged to return, [with] many of the crew ill and sickly. Nobody, however, spoke of returning home to Holland, which circumstance made the captain still more suspicious. He proposed therefore to sail to Ireland and winter there, which they all agreed to. At last they arrived at Dartmouth, in England, the 7th of November, whence they informed their employers, the directors in Holland, of their voyage. They proposed to them to go out again for a search in the northwest, and that, besides the pay and what they already had in the ship, 1,500 florins should be laid out for an additional supply of provisions. He [Hudson] also wanted six or seven of his crew exchanged for others, and their number raised to 20. He would then sail from Dartmouth about the 1st of March, so as to be in the northwest toward the end of that month, and there to spend the whole of April and the first half of May in killing whales and other animals in the neighborhood of Panar Island [unidentified], then to sail to the northwest and there to pass the time till the middle of September, and then to return to Holland around the northeastern coast of Scotland. Thus this voyage ended.

A long time elapsed, through contrary winds, before the company could be informed of the arrival of the ship in England. Then they ordered the ship and crew to return as soon as possible. But, when this was about to be done, Skipper Herry Hutson and the other Englishmen of the ship were commanded by the government there not to leave [England], but to serve their own country. Many persons thought it strange that captains should thus be prevented from laying their accounts and reports before their employers, having been sent out for the benefit of navigation in general. This took place in January [1610], and it was thought probable that the English themselves would send ships to Virginia, to explore further the aforesaid river.

Juet's Report on the Third Voyage

[A detailed account of the third voyage, kept log-fashion by Robert Juet, one of Hudson's crew on the voyage for the Dutch,

*gives a day-by-day chronicle of events. Excerpts from Juet's
journal, printed in* Henry Hudson the Navigator, *edited by
G. M. Asher (London: Hakluyt Society, 1860) follow:]*

On Saturday the five-and-twentieth of March, 1609, after the
old account [i.e., April 4 by the Gregorian calendar], we set
sail from Amsterdam, and by the seven-and-twentieth day we
were down at the Texel; and by twelve of the clock we were
off the land, it being east of us two leagues off. And because it
is a journey usually known, I omit to put down what passed
till we came to the height of the North Cape of Finnmark
[northern Norway], which we did perform by the 5th of May
(*stilo novo* [new style, i.e., Gregorian]), being Tuesday. On
which day we observed the height of the pole and found it to be
71 degrees and 46 minutes. . . .

After much trouble, with fogs sometimes and more dangerous
[*sic*] of ice, the 19th, being Tuesday, was close stormy weather,
with much wind and snow, and very cold; the wind variable
between the north-northwest and northeast. We made our way
west and by north till noon. . . .

The 4th [of September] in the morning, as soon as the day
was light, we saw that it was good riding farther up. So we
sent our boat to sound, and found that it was a very good
harbor and four and five fathoms two cables' length from the
shore. Then we weighed and went in with our ship. Then our
boat went on land [possibly Coney Island] with our net to fish
and caught ten great mullets of a foot and a half long apiece,
and a ray as great as four men could hale [haul] into the
ship. . . . This day the people of the country came aboard of
us, seeming very glad of our coming, and brought green tobacco
and gave us of it for knives and beads. They go in deerskins,
loose [and] well dressed. They have yellow copper. They desire
clothes and are very civil. They have great store of maize, or
Indian wheat, whereof they make good bread. The country is
full of great and tall oaks.

The 5th in the morning, as soon as the day was light, the
wind ceased and the flood came. So we heaved off our ship
again into five fathoms water and sent our boat to sound the
bay. . . . This day many of the people came aboard, some in
mantles of feathers and some in skins of divers sorts of good

furs. Some women also came to us with hemp. They had red copper tobacco pipes and other things of copper they did wear about their necks. At night they went on land again, so we rode very quiet but durst not trust them. . . .

The 9th, fair weather. In the morning two great canoes came aboard full of men; the one with their bow and arrows, and the other in show of buying of knives to betray us. But we perceived their intent. We took two of them to have kept them, and put red coats on them, and would not suffer the other to come near us. So they went on land, and two others came aboard in a canoe; we took the one and let the other go. But he which we had taken got up and leapt overboard. Then we weighed [anchor] and went off into the channel of the river and anchored there all night. . . .

The 14th, in the morning, being very fair weather, the wind southeast, we sailed up the river 12 leagues. . . . The river is a mile broad; there is very high land on both sides. Then we went up northwest a league and an half, deep water. Then northeast by north five miles; then northwest by north two leagues, and anchored. The land grew very high and mountainous [the neighborhood of present-day West Point]. The river is full of fish.

The 15th, in the morning, was misty until the sun arose; then it cleared. So we weighed with the wind at south and ran up into the river 20 leagues, passing by high mountains [the Catskills]. We had a very good depth, as six, seven, eight, nine, ten, 12, and 13 fathoms, and great store of salmons in the river. This morning our two savages got out of a port and swam away. After we were under sail, they called to us in scorn. At night we came to other mountains, which lie from the river's side. There we found very loving people, and very old men; where we were well used. Our boat went to fish and caught great store of very good fish. . . .

The 19th was fair and hot weather. At the flood, being near eleven of the clock, we weighed, and ran higher up two leagues above the shoals, and had no less water than five fathoms. We anchored and rode in eight fathoms. The people of the country came flocking aboard and brought us grapes and pompions, which we bought for trifles. And many brought us beavers' skins and otters' skins, which we bought for beads, knives and hatchets. So we rode there all night [near the site of Albany]. . . .

The 1st of October, fair weather, the wind variable between the west and the north. In the morning we weighed at seven of the clock with the ebb, and got down below the mountains, which was seven leagues. Then it fell calm and the flood was come, and we anchored at twelve of the clock. The people of the mountains came aboard us, wondering at our ship and weapons. We bought some small skins of them for trifles. This afternoon one canoe kept hanging under our stern with one man in it, which we could not keep from thence, who got up by our rudder to the cabin window, and stole out my pillow and two shirts and two bandoleers. Our master's mate shot at him and struck him on the breast and killed him. Whereupon all the rest fled away, some in their canoes, and some leapt out of them into the water. We manned our boat and got our things again. Then one of them that swam got hold of our boat, thinking to overthrow it. But our cook took a sword and cut off one of his hands, and he was drowned. By this time the ebb was come, and we weighed and got down two leagues. By that time it was dark. So we anchored in four fathoms water and rode well.

The 2nd, fair weather. At break of day we weighed, the wind being at northwest, and got down seven leagues. Then the flood was come strong, so we anchored. Then came one of the savages that swam away from us at our going up the river, with many other, thinking to betray us. But we perceived their intent and suffered none of them to enter our ship. Whereupon two canoes full of men, with their bows and arrows, shot at us after our stern. In recompense whereof we discharged six muskets and killed two or three of them. Then above 100 of them came to a point of land to shoot at us. There I shot a falcon at them and killed two of them. Whereupon the rest fled into the woods. Yet they manned off another canoe with nine or ten men, which came to meet us. So I shot at it also a falcon, and shot it through and killed one of them. Then our men with their muskets killed three or four more of them. So they went their way.

Within a while after, we got down two leagues beyond that place and anchored in a bay—clear from all danger of them on the other side of the river—where we saw a very good piece of ground. And hard by it was a cliff that looked of the color of a white green, as though it were either copper or silver mine. And I think it to be one of them by the trees that grow upon it; for they be all burned, and the other places are green as grass. It is on that side of the river that is called Manna-hata [Manhattan]. There we saw no people to trouble us. . . .

The 4th was fair weather, and the wind at north-northwest. We weighed and came out of the river [the Hudson] into which we had run so far. Within a while after, we came out also of the great mouth of the great river, that runneth up to the northwest [the mouth of the Hudson trends to the northwest]. . . . And by twelve of the clock we were clear of all the inlet. Then we took in our boat, and set our mainsail and spritsail and our topsails, and steered away east-southeast and southeast by east off into the main sea. . . .

We continued our course toward England, without seeing any land by the way, all the rest of this month of October. And on the 7th day of November, . . . being Saturday, by the grace of God we safely arrived in the range of Dartmouth, in Devonshire, in the year 1609.

XVI

Captain John Smith Observes the Fisheries and the Profits from Furs

THE most colorful figure in the Jamestown colony during its first two years was Captain John Smith, who after many quarrels emerged as a leader of genuine ability.[1] He was an explorer of skill, with keen powers of observation, and he developed into an enthusiastic advocate of colonization and trade. To John Smith we owe the change of the name of "North Virginia" to "New England." He was also one of the first to realize that prosperity might be achieved in the New World from fishing, the fur trade and forest products rather than from the discovery of gold mines.

During his stay in Virginia from 1607 to September 1609 Smith engaged in two extensive exploring expeditions that took him up the Potomac River to the fall line beyond the present District of Columbia and later into Chesapeake Bay to the fall line of the Susquehanna River. In his shallop he poked about in various bays, inlets, creeks and rivers and encountered a variety of Indian tribesmen, some friendly and others hostile. Surprisingly, he and his handful of men contrived to bluff attacking Indians and survived. His account of the back country of the Chesapeake Bay region gave Englishmen their first accurate report of the river system of this amazing country.

Injured in an explosion of gunpowder, Smith sailed from Virginia in September 1609. Back in England with his health

[1] A detailed discussion of Smith's career will be found in Philip L. Barbour, *The Three Worlds of Captain John Smith* (Boston, 1964).

recovered, he began planning other expeditions to the New World. In the meantime, two pieces from his pen about Virginia had got into print, the beginning of a long literary career for Smith. These were *A True Relation of Such Occurrences and Accidents of Note as Hath Happened in Virginia . . .* (1608) and *A Map of Virginia* (1612), which contained a description of the country written by Smith and incorporated in this composite work.

In 1614 Smith managed to enlist the interest of a rich young merchant of London, Marmaduke Rawdon, who hired him to lead a curious voyage to the North Atlantic in search of fish and whales. The expedition consisted of two ships, one commanded by Smith and another by one Thomas Hunt, who turned out to be a rogue who kidnapped 24 Indians and sold them into slavery in Spain. Smith and Hunt not only were to fish and trade with the Indians, but they were also instructed to search for possible gold mines, for the gold delusion still plagued English explorers.

The two ships arrived off Monhegan Island on the coast of Maine in late April 1614. They had poor luck catching whales, but they caught fish, which they cured, and they traded with the Indians for furs. Smith soon realized that the likelihood of discovering gold mines was slight, but he was impressed by the possibilities of the fisheries and the fur trade. And, inveterate explorer and map maker that he was, he was fascinated with the coastline, which he set out to examine closely in his shallop.

From Penobscot Bay Smith sailed south, mapping as he went, trading with the Indians and picking up such information as he could. He explored the mouth of the Kennebec River, Massachusetts Bay, Cape Cod and Plymouth Harbor. To many of the points that he passed he gave names that stuck, though some were too fanciful. For example, the point we now know as "Cape Ann," Smith named "Cape Tragabigzanda," after a Greek girl in Istanbul whose memory he cherished. Smith's careful observations were incorporated in a book that he published on his return to England with the title *A Description of New England; Or, The Observations and Discoveries of Captain John Smith (Admiral of That Country) in the North of America in the Year of Our Lord 1614* (1616). The work was designed as propaganda for colonization and Smith himself planned to lead a colonial venture to New England, as he had christened the land. Unluckily his efforts at colonization failed, and, after hair-raising adventures in 1616 in an effort to get back to America, he had to resign himself to becoming a fireside explorer. In 1624 he published *The General History of Virginia, the Somer Isles, and New England,* which influenced his own and others' writings on the subject.

Smith's Report on the Prospects in New England

[*Excerpts from Smith's* A Description of New England (*1616*) *follow:*]

In the month of April 1614 with two ships from London of a few merchants, I chanced to arrive in New England, a part of America, at the isle of Monhegan in 43½ of northerly latitude. Our plot was there to take whales and make trials of a mine of gold and copper. If those failed, fish and furs was then our refuge, to make ourselves savers howsoever. We found this whale fishing a costly conclusion; we saw many and spent much time in chasing them, but could not kill any, they being a kind of jubartes [gibbartas, a finback whale] and not the whale that yields fins and oil as we expected. For our gold, it was rather the master's device to get a voyage that projected it than any knowledge he had at all of any such matter.

Fish and furs was now our guard, and by our late arrival and long lingering about the whale, the prime of both those seasons were past ere we perceived it, we thinking that their seasons served at all times, but we found it otherwise; for by the midst of June the fishing failed. Yet in July and August some was taken, but not sufficient to defray so great a charge as our stay required. Of dry fish we made about 40,000, of cor [pickled] fish about 7,000. Whilst the sailors fished, myself with eight or nine others of them [that] might best be spared, ranging the coast in a small boat, we got for trifles near 1,100 beaver skins, 100 martens, and near as many otters; and the most of them within the distance of 20 leagues. We ranged the coast both east and west much further; but eastward our commodities were not esteemed, they were so near the French who affords

them better; and right against us in the main was a ship of Sir
Francis Popham's [son of Sir John Popham of the Plymouth
Company] that had there such acquaintance, having many
years used only that port, that the most part there was had by
him. And 40 leagues westward were two French ships that had
made there a great voyage by trade during the time we tried
those conclusions, no knowing the coast nor savages' habitation.
With these furs, the train [oil], and cor fish I returned for
England in the bark, where within six months after our departure from the Downs we safe arrived back. The best of this
fish was sold for five pound the hundred, the rest by ill usage
betwixt three pound and 50 shillings. The other ship stayed
to fit herself for Spain with the dry fish which was sold, by the
sailors' report that returned, at 40 ryals the quintal, each
hundred weighing two quintals and a half.

New England is that part of America in the Ocean Sea
opposite to Nova Albion in the South Sea, discovered by the
most memorable Sir Francis Drake in his voyage about the
world. In regard whereto this is styled New England, being
in the same latitude. New France, off it, is northward. Southward is Virginia and all the adjoining continent, with New
Granada, New Spain, New Andalusia, and the West Indies.
Now because I have been so oft asked such strange questions
of the goodness and greatness of those spacious tracts of land,
how they can be thus long unknown, or not possessed by the
Spaniard, and many suchlike demands: I entreat your pardons
if I chance to be too plain or tedious in relating my knowledge
for plain men's satisfaction.

Florida is the next adjoining to the Indies, which unpros-
perously was attempted to be planted by the French. A country
far bigger than England, Scotland, France, and Ireland, yet
little known to any Christian but by the wonderful endeavors
of Ferdinando de Soto, a valiant Spaniard, whose writings in
this age is the best guide known to search those parts.

Virginia is no isle (as many do imagine) but part of the
continent adjoining to Florida, whose bounds may be stretched
to the magnitude thereof without offense to any Christian
inhabitant. For from the degrees of 30 to 45 His Majesty hath
granted his letters patents, the coast extending southwest and
northeast about 1,500 miles. But to follow it aboard, the shore

may well be 2,000 at the least, of which 20 miles is the most [that] gives entrance into the Bay of Chesapeake, where is the London plantation; within which is a country (as you may perceive by the description in a book and map printed in my name of that little I there discovered) may well suffice 300,000 people to inhabit. And southward adjoineth that part discovered at the charge of Sir Walter Raleigh by Sir Ralph Lane and that learned mathematician Mr. Thomas Hariot. Northward six or seven degrees is the River Sagadahoc [Kennebec], where was planted the western colony by that honorable patron of virtue Sir John Popham, Lord Chief Justice of England. There is also a relation printed by Captain Bartholomew Gosnold of Elizabeth's Isles, and another by Captain Weymouth of Pemaquid. From all these diligent observers posterity may be bettered by the fruits of their labors. . . .

I have had six or seven several plots of those northern parts so unlike each to other, and most so differing from any true proportion or resemblance of the country, as they did me no more good than so much waste paper, though they cost me more. It may be it was not my chance to see the best, but, lest others may be deceived as I was, or through dangerous ignorance hazard themselves as I did, I have drawn a map from point to point, isle to isle, and harbor to harbor, with the soundings, sands, rocks, and landmarks as I passed close aboard the shore in a little boat. Although there be many things to be observed which the haste of other affairs did cause me to omit— for, being sent more to get present commodities than knowledge by discoveries for any future good, I had not power to search as I would—yet it will serve to direct any shall go that ways to safe harbors and the savages' habitations. What merchandise and commodities for their labor they may find, this following discourse shall plainly demonstrate. . . .

That part we call New England is betwixt the degrees of 41 and 45; but that part this discourse speaketh of stretcheth but from Penobscot to Cape Cod, some 75 leagues by a right line distant each from other; within which bounds I have seen at least 40 several habitations upon the seacoast and sounded about 25 excellent good harbors. In many whereof there is anchorage for 500 sail of ships of any burden; in some of them for 5,000; and more than 200 isles overgrown with good timber of divers sorts of wood, which do make so many harbors as requireth a longer time than I had to be well discovered. . . .

The coast of the Massachusetts is so indifferently mixed with high clayey or sandy cliffs in one place, and then tracts of large long ledges of divers sorts and quarries of stones in other places so strangely divided with tinctured veins of divers colors as: free stone for building, slate for tiling, smooth stone to make furnaces and forges for glass or iron, and iron ore sufficient conveniently to melt in them. But the most part so resembleth the coast of Devonshire I think most of the cliffs would make such limestone. If they be not of these qualities, they are so like they may deceive a better judgment than mine. All which are so near adjoining to those other advantages I observed in these parts that, if the ore prove as good iron and steel in those parts as I know it is within the bounds of the country, I dare engage my head (having but men skillful to work the simples there growing) to have all things belonging to the building, the rigging of ships of any proportion, and good merchandise for the freight, within a square of ten or 14 leagues. And were it for a good reward, I would not fear to procure it in a less limitation.

And surely by reason of those sandy cliffs and cliffs of rocks, both which we saw so planted with gardens and corn fields and so well inhabited with a goodly, strong, and well-proportioned people; besides the greatness of the timber growing on them, the greatness of the fish, and moderate temper of the air (for of 25, not any was sick but two that were many years diseased before they went, notwithstanding our bad lodging and accidental diet); who can but approve this a most excellent place both for health and fertility? And of all the four parts of the world that I have yet seen not inhabited, could I have but means to transport a colony, I would rather live here than anywhere. And if it did not maintain itself, were we but once indifferently well fitted, let us starve.

The main staple from hence to be extracted, for the present to produce the rest, is fish; which, however it may seem a mean and a base commodity, yet who will but truly take the pains and consider the sequel, I think will allow it well worth the labor. It is strange to see what great adventures the hopes of setting forth men-of-war to rob the industrious innocent would

procure, or such massy [solid] promises in gross, though more
are choked than well fed with such hasty hopes. But who doth
not know that the poor Hollanders, chiefly by fishing—at a
great charge and labor in all weathers in the open sea—are
made a people so hardy and industrious? And by the venting
[selling] this poor commodity to the Easterlings [Baltic mer-
chants] for as mean, which is wood, flax, pitch, tar, rosin, cord-
age, and suchlike (which they exchange again to the French,
Spaniards, Portugales, and English, etc. for what they want),
are made so mighty, strong, and rich as no state but Venice,
of twice their magnitude, is so well furnished with so many
fair cities, goodly towns, strong fortresses, and that abundance
of shipping and all sorts of merchandise, as well of gold, silver,
pearls, diamonds, precious stones, silks, velvets, and cloth-of-
gold as [of] fish, pitch, wood, or such gross commodities? What
voyages and discoveries, east and west, north and south, yea
about the world, make they? What an army by sea and land
have they long maintained in despite of one of the greatest
princes of the world? And never could the Spaniard with all
his mines of gold and silver pay his debts, his friends, and army
half so truly as the Hollanders still have done by this con-
temptible trade of fish. Divers [many] (I know) may allege
many other assistances, but this is their mine, and the sea the
source of those silvered streams of all their virtue, which hath
made them now the very miracle of industry, the pattern of
perfection for these affairs; and the benefit of fishing is that
primum mobile [prime mover] that turns all their spheres to
this height of plenty, strength, honor, and admiration. . . .

If from all those parts such pains is taken for this poor gains
of fish, and by them [that] hath neither meat, drink, nor clothes,
wood, iron, nor steel, pitch, tar, nets, leads, salt, hooks, nor
lines for shipping, fishing, nor provision but at the second,
third, fourth, or fifth hand, drawn from so many several parts
of the world ere they come together to be used in this voyage:
if these, I say, can gain, and the sailors live going for shares,
less than the third part of their labors, and yet spend as much
time going and coming as in staying there (so short is the
season of fishing), why should we more doubt . . . but to do
much better than they where there is victual to feed us, wood
of all sorts to build boats, ships, or barks, the fish at our doors,

pitch, tar, masts, yards, and most of other necessaries only for making? And here are no hard landlords to rack us with high rents, or extorted fines to consume us; no tedious pleas in law to consume us with their many years' disputations for justice; no multitudes to occasion such impediments to good orders as in popular states. So freely hath God and His Majesty bestowed those blessings on them that will attempt to obtain them as here every man may be master and own labor and land— or the greatest part—in a small time. If he have nothing but his hands, he may set up this trade and by industry quickly grow rich, spending but half that time well which in England we abuse in idleness, worse or as ill. Here is ground also as good as any lieth in the height of 41, 42, 43, etc., which is as temperate and as fruitful as any other parallel in the world. . . .

The ground is so fertile that questionless it is capable of producing any grain, fruits, or seeds you will sow or plant, growing in the regions aforenamed, but it may be not every kind to that perfection of delicacy; or some tender plants may miscarry because the summer is not so hot and the winter is more cold in those parts we have yet tried near the seaside than we find in the same height in Europe or Asia. Yet I made a garden upon the top of a rocky isle in 43½, four leagues from the main, in May that grew so well as it served for sallets [salads] in June and July. All sorts of cattle may here be bred and fed in the isles, or peninsulas, securely for nothing. In the interim till they increase, if need be (observing the seasons), I durst undertake to have corn enough from the savages for 300 men, for a few trifles. And if they should be untoward (as it is most certain they are), 30 or 40 good men will be sufficient to bring them all in subjection and make this provision, if they understand what they do; 200 whereof may nine months in the year be employed in making merchantable fish till the rest provide other necessaries fit to furnish us with other commodities.

In March, April, May, and half June here is cod in abundance; in May, June, July, and August, mullet and sturgeon, whose roes do make caviar and botargo. Herring, if any desire them, I have taken many out of the bellies of cods, some in nets; but the savages compare their store in the sea to the hairs of their heads, and surely there are an incredible abundance upon this coast. In the end of August, September, October, and November you have cod again to make cor fish, or Poor John [dried salted fish]. And each hundred is as good as 200 or 300 in the New-found Land, so that half the labor in hooking, splitting, and turning is saved, and you may have your fish at what market you will before they can have any in Newfound Land, where their fishing is chiefly but in June and July whereas it is here in March, April, May, September, October, and November, as is said. So that by reason of this plantation the merchants may have freight both out and home, which yields an advantage worth consideration. . . .

Now, young boys and girls, savages, or any other, be they never such idlers, may turn, carry, and return fish without either shame or any great pain. He is very idle that is past twelve years of age and cannot do so much, and she is very old that cannot spin a thread to make engines to catch them.

For their transportation, the ships that go there to fish may transport the first, who, for their passage, will spare the charge of double-manning their ships, which they must do in New-found Land to get their freight; but one-third part of that company are only but proper to serve a stage, carry a barrow, and turn Poor John. Notwithstanding, they must have meat, drink, clothes, and passage as well as the rest. Now all I desire is but this: that those that voluntarily will send shipping should make here the best choice they can, or accept such as are presented them, to serve them at that rate. And their ships, returning, leave such with me, with the value of that they should receive coming home in such provisions and necessary tools, arms, bedding and apparel, salt, hooks, nets, lines, and suchlike as they spare of the remainings; who till the next return may keep their boats and do them many other profitable offices, provided I have men of ability to teach them their functions and a company fit for soldiers to be ready upon an occasion; because of the abuses which have been offered the poor savages and the liberty both French or any that will hath to deal with them as they please; whose disorders will be hard to reform, and the longer the worse. . . .

Salt upon salt may assuredly be made, if not at the first in ponds, yet till they be provided this may be used; then the ships may transport kine, horse, goats, coarse cloth, and such commodities as we want; by whose arrival may be made that provision of fish to freight the ships that they stay not; and then if the sailors go for wages it matters not. It is hard if this return defray not the charge, but care must be had they arrive in the spring, or else provision be made for them against the winter. . . .

Of beavers, otters, martens, black foxes, and furs of price, may yearly be had 6,[ooo] or 7,000. And if the trade of the French were prevented, many more: 25,000 this year were brought from those northern parts into France, of which trade we may have as good part as the French if we take good courses.

Of mines of gold and silver, copper, and probabilities of lead, crystal, and alum I could say much if relations were good assurances. It is true indeed I made many trials according to those instructions I had, which do persuade me I need not despair but there are metals in the country. But I am no alchemist, nor will promise more than I know, which is: who will undertake the rectifying of an iron forge—if those that buy meat, drink, coals, ore, and all necessaries at a dear rate, gain—where all these things are to be had for the taking up, in my opinion cannot lose.

✤ XVII ✤

The Other Side of
the Continent

WITH the publication of Captain John Smith's *A De-scription of New England* in 1616, describing his voyage of two years before, the main outlines of the east coast of what would one day be the United States were fairly well defined. Both French and English explorers had also gained a comprehensive knowledge of Canadian waters; Frenchmen had even penetrated to the sources of the Saint Lawrence River and the Great Lakes. The Northwest Passage, shrouded in fog and blocked with ice, would continue to tantalize explorers for generations to come, but at least navigators were aware of the land masses in northern Canada and the possible sea routes to the west if they could get past the ice barriers. The most significant exploration during the next century would involve the discovery of the interior of North America, and the exploitation of land where Englishmen, Frenchmen and Dutchmen had gained a precarious foothold on the Eastern Seaboard.

The enormous extent of the continent remained a mystery to most settlers on the East Coast. For a long time men believed that they might find a water route to the western ocean. By traveling up some of the broad rivers they discovered on the Atlantic side, they thought they might eventually reach a point where a short portage across a continental divide would lead to another great river down which they could float to the Pacific. That was one of Thomas Jefferson's dreams when he sent out the Lewis and Clark Expedition of 1803–06.

The seventeenth century knew little about the West Coast of the North American continent. Francis Drake, it is true, had touched upon the coast of California on his circumnavigation of the globe and had claimed New Albion for England, but England had not developed its claim. Captain John Smith had mentioned Drake's New Albion, thus showing England's continued awareness of the western reaches of empire, but the land remained merely a vague geographical expression. Spanish explorers, of course, had learned more about the West Coast, but the northern reaches of the western region remained neglected and little known.

When Peter the Great of Russia visited England to learn about shipbuilding and other developments, he was stimulated by stories of European explorations and the new lands beyond the seas that western Europeans were exploiting. He knew that Cossacks from southwestern Russia had pushed across Siberia and had reached the great peninsula of Kamchatka on the Pacific. What lay beyond interested Peter the Great, and he determined to send explorers to find out. If western Europeans had found new worlds across the Atlantic to exploit, Russians might find lands on the other side of the Pacific. Futhermore, scientists whom Peter invited to Russia were interested in exploration for the scientific information that might be revealed. A new day of scientific investigation was dawning as men grew more concerned about the flora, fauna, and human races in the unexplored regions of the earth.

The penetration of Siberia had shown that the fur trade with the interior would be profitable, and traders reaped a rich harvest of marten, ermine, sable, and other furs as well as fossil ivory left by long extinct mammoths in the Siberian wastes. Though the Siberian land was hostile to man, the tough Cossacks and others whom Peter the Great sent eastward brought back goods and reports that stimulated further investigation.

Peter the Great had long been curious about the geography of northeastern Siberia, particularly whether it joined the American continent, for as yet the Arctic seas had not been explored. In 1719 he sent two Russian navigators to sail from Kamchatka in an effort to determine this fact, but they floundered about in the foggy seas without coming to any definite conclusion. Six months before his death in 1725, Peter once more outlined a plan for the exploration of the northern Pacific and appointed a Dane, Vitus Bering, to lead the expedition. Bering had served for some 20 years in the Russian navy and had had experience in the Pacific. Peter ordered him to take as assistants Martin Spanberg, another Dane, and Alexei Chirikov, a Russian. They were to build two ships on the coast of Kamchatka or some other place convenient for their operations, to sail north, to determine whether the two continents were joined, and to try to make contact with some European settlement on the American side—if any such existed.

The task facing Bering and his colleagues was stupendous, for they had to take supplies across Russia and Siberia to a base on the Pacific. Leaving Saint Petersburg in January 1725, they spent more than six months on the overland journey as far as Yakutsk, which was still 700 miles from Okhotsk on the coast opposite the Kamchatka peninsula. Winter closed in before the men and supplies reached Okhotsk, but eventually a surviving remnant struggled into the Siberian port town with equipment sufficient to build one ship, the *Fortune,* completed by the summer of 1727. Another year went by before the second ship, the *Saint Gabriel,* was launched.[1]

During the summer of 1728 Bering cautiously probed the northern coast of Siberia and went as far as the strait that now bears his name, but fog so enveloped the sea that he never saw the mainland of Alaska nor did he actually ascertain that the sea in which he found himself was a strait separating the two continents. Fearful of being caught in the ice with the approach of winter, he turned back to Kamchatka. Native Chukchi told of a great island to the east—meaning, probably, the mainland of America. On his voyage Bering had noted and named the Diomede Islands and Saint Lawrence Island.

After wintering on Kamchatka, Bering took advantage of summer weather in 1729 to sail the *Saint Gabriel* eastward, but again fog prevented his discovering land supposed to lie in that direction, and he turned back and sailed to Okhotsk, whence he set out overland for Saint Petersburg to report on his tentative conclusions to the Empress of Russia. Bering's timidity and his vague report displeased both the empress and the Admiralty College, which had general oversight of the exploration.

[1] Jeannette Mirsky, *To the Arctic! The Story of Northern Exploration from Earliest Times to the Present* (New York, 1948), gives a succinct account of Bering's misadventures.

During the summer of 1730 the *Saint Gabriel,* which had been left at Okhotsk, was ordered to sail eastward under the command of a pilot named Federov and a scientist named Michael Gvosdev. They actually touched land in Alaska, but Federov died and Gvosdev's log book was long lost. Though they were the first Russians known to have reached the mainland of America from across the Pacific, their feat remained clouded in obscurity like the very fogs that kept Bering from knowing where he was.

Despite Bering's failure to find anything tangible on his first two voyages into the Arctic, he was given command of another expedition to be organized at Okhotsk. In 1733 he again left Saint Petersburg, and for seven long years he labored at Okhotsk to get ships built for his next explorations. Finally, in the summer of 1740 two vessels, the *Saint Peter,* commanded by Bering, and the *Saint Paul,* commanded by Chirikov, were ready. They sailed eastward in June but in the fog the two vessels lost contact and never met again.

Chirikov made a landfall on a heavily wooded shore and sent a boat with ten men to explore. When they did not return, he sent another boat with four armed men to investigate. They, too, disappeared without a trace. With the rest of the sailors on board in a panic at the mysterious disappearances through witchcraft or treachery of natives hidden in the forests, Chirikov had no choice but to sail away. Without water and with dwindling food supplies, the *Saint Paul* managed at last to get back to Kamchatka with nothing to show for its troubles.

In the meantime, Bering in the *Saint Peter* was having no better luck. Sailing eastward, the men at last glimpsed the wooded land of Alaska in clear weather. This was the country they had come to find. But Bering himself was already too ill with scurvy to appreciate the magnitude of his discovery. A German scientist whom he had brought with him, Wilhelm Steller, wanted to land and investigate the terrain. But the season was far advanced and Bering was fearful of wintering on a strange shore. He ordered the water casks filled and sailed away. Soon the *Saint Peter* ran into storms, and for 40 days the ship wallowed in the seas off Kamchatka. Finally, battered and near shipwreck, the *Saint Peter* was beached in an island harbor and the men went ashore. Bering died on December 19, 1741,

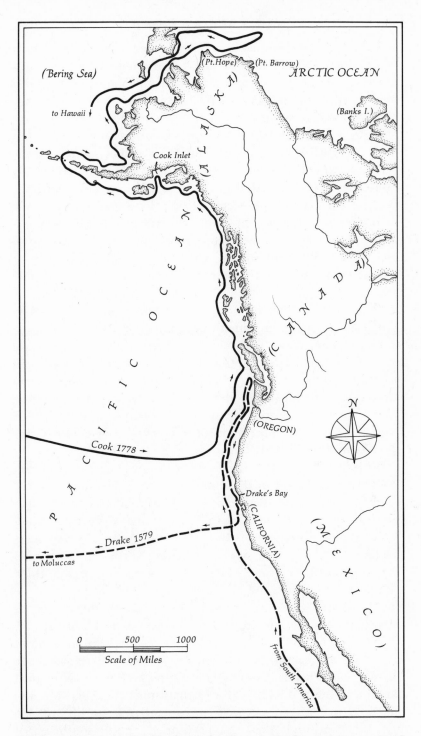

Exploration of the Pacific Coast by Francis Drake and James Cook

and Steller took command. Though beset by droves of blue foxes, a majority of the crew survived the winter and managed to build a smaller craft from timbers of the *Saint Peter*. In this they sailed in the spring to Kamchatka. The island where they had wintered now bears the name of Bering.

Though Bering's voyages were all plagued with disaster, these expeditions served to stir further Russian interest in the fur trade with the islands of the North Pacific and eventually to arouse interest in Alaska. Later expeditions discovered the Pribilof Islands and the Aleutians and developed the fur trade with natives of this region. The demand for sealskins and sea-otter fur in time became a consuming passion almost equivalent to the gold mania of an earlier period as the Russians attempted to supply the insatiable demand of the Chinese for fine furs.

The Russians had discovered that the continents of Asia and America were not joined in the north, but it remained for Captain James Cook, with better luck than had been the fate of Vitus Bering, to map the region and give the world an accurate conception of its geography. Cook made three voyages around the world between the years 1768 and 1779. On his last voyage he made a search for the western entrance of the fabled Northwest Passage, which had been a concern of explorers for the past two and a half centuries.

With two ships, the *Discovery* and the *Resolution,* Cook sailed from England in the summer of 1776. His dramatic discoveries in the South Pacific had made him famous, and he had disposed once and for all of the notion that a great continent lay in the southern ocean. But when the Admiralty wanted a leader to search for a passage around North America from the west, Cook once more offered his services. On this third voyage he sailed around the Cape of Good Hope, across the Indian Ocean to Australia and New Zealand, thence to the Hawaiian Islands, and from there to the coast of what is now Oregon, which he reached on March 7, 1778. From a point about 44 degrees 55 minutes north latitude he slowly made his way northward, mapping the coast as he went. Not until August 29 did he turn back, for by that time he had encountered an ice barrier that prevented further progress northward. He had sailed around Alaska to Icy Cape, a point southwest of

Point Barrow (the northernmost spot in Alaska). Furthermore, Cook, unlike Bering, had been favored with enough clear weather to get a visual understanding of the country, which he and his log keepers dutifully described.

Cook had not discovered the entrance to the Northwest Passage, but he planned to winter in the Hawaiian Islands and return for a further search. On the way south he skirted the Siberian coast and mapped that region. In January of 1779 the two vessels reached the Hawaiian Islands, where they planned to refit. On February 14, as they were planning to sail, a hostile crowd of natives attacked Cook and his landing party. Cook himself received a blow on the head and was finally stabbed to death. Later his body was partially burned, but his remains were recovered and buried a few days later.

The second in command, Captain Charles Clarke (or Clerke), took over and the two ships returned to the Pacific Northwest to search for the elusive passage. He, too, had to turn back and died in Avatcha Bay on August 22, 1779. If the expeditions had not found the Northwest Passage, they had accumulated a great store of accurate geographical information about the Pacific Northwest.

Rickman Tells of Cook's Explorations in the Pacific Northwest

[*One of the most popular accounts of Cook's third voyage was John Rickman's* Journal of Captain Cook's Last Voyage to the Pacific Ocean on Discovery Performed in the Years 1776, 1777, 1778, 1779, *first published in London in 1781. The authorship of the narrative was long a mystery and it was once attributed to John Ledyard, an American in the expedition.*

[*Excerpts from Rickman's* Journal *follow:*]

Having taken in our guns at the Galleons, and what stores were wanting,

On the 14th of June 1776, both ships came to an anchor at the Nore; but our fresh provisions being nearly exhausted, we weighed next day, and left the *Resolution* waiting for her commander.

On the 16th, came to off Deal, and received on board a great quantity of beef and mutton for the ship's company, and a boat for the captain's use. It blew hard in the night and all the next day.

On the 18th we weighed anchor and sailed; but we had no sooner entered the channel than a storm arose, by which we were driven into Portland Roads, where we received considerable damage. We had blowing weather till

The 26th, when we arrived at Plymouth. There we found a large fleet of men-of-war and transports with troops on board for America, and saluted the admiral with 11 guns. They had been driven in by stress of weather, several of them much damaged. About twelve at noon we came to moorings in the Sound.

On the 30th the *Resolution* arrived, saluted the admiral, and came to and moored close by us.

It was now found necessary to go into harbor to repair the damages our ship had received in the storm of the 18th, and the *Resolution* proposed to wait till we were in readiness; but it was with difficulty that an order was obtained for the carpenters to proceed, and when it was obtained it was some time before it could be carried into execution. The repairs of the fleet for America being judged of greater consequence than the repairs of a single ship.

The *Resolution,* tired with delay, when the day came that she set sail on her former voyage, which was

On the 12th of July, the impatience of the ship's company and the notion they had entertained of its being a lucky day induced Captain Cook to comply with their importunities, and he accordingly set sail, leaving orders with Captain Clarke to follow him to Santiago, one of the Cape Verde Islands, and if he should there miss of him, to pursue his course directly for the Cape of Good Hope.

This was unwelcome news to the ship's company of the *Discovery,* who were equally impatient to be gone and who were not without their prognostics, their omens and fancies, any more than their neighbors; but necessity, that irresistible conqueror to whose power all human passions must submit, compelled their acquiescence, though it could not remove their scruples. . . .

On the 1st of August we weighed, and proceeded, with all sails set, to join the *Resolution*. While our ship was repairing, it was observable that those who had never been employed on discovery before were more impatient to depart than those who had already experienced the severities of a southern navigation near and within the polar circle; and it was diverting enough to listen to the ludicrous remarks of these last, on their freshwater brethren, as they called them, whom they ventured to foretell, would, like the Jews in the wilderness, be the first to murmur and cry out for "the leeks and the onions of Egypt"; intimating thereby that when these raw sailors came among the islands of ice in the frozen regions, to *feel* the effects of scanty fare and hard duty, they would then be the first to repent their impetuosity, and to sigh for the beef and the beer of the land they were now so desirous to leave.

We proceeded with a brisk gale till the 7th, when in sight of Cape Finisterre the clouds began to darken and the ocean to swell and to threaten by every appearance an approaching tempest. Several ships were then in sight, and we could clearly discern that they were preparing, as well as ourselves, to meet the storm. For 24 hours it blowed and rained incessantly; but on the 9th a calm succeeded which, however, was not of long continuance; for in the evening of the same day it thundered, lightened, and the rain poured down in torrents. The drops were such as no man on board had seen the like. To prevent the effects of the lightning, it was thought necessary to let fall the chain from the masthead, a precaution which Captain Clerke never omitted when there was danger from an accumulation of electricity in the atmosphere to be apprehended.

On the 20th, seeing a ship to windward bearing down very fast, and suspecting her to be an American privateer, all hands were ordered to quarters to be in readiness to engage. She proved to be a Lisbon trader, who by the violence of the gale the day before had been driven many leagues to the westward of her course, and was in some distress. We spared her those things of which she stood most in need, and pursued our voyage. . . .

Nothing worth notice till the 17th [of September], when we crossed the line [the Equator]. The weather being squally, the usual ceremony of keelhauling the sailors who had never crossed it before was omitted. This ceremony is so well known that it were needless to describe it.

On the 20th the weather became moderate, when upon examination, the starboard main trestletree was found to be sprung.

On the 20th George Harrison, Corporal of Marines, sitting carelessly on the bowsprit diverting himself with the sporting of the fishes, fell overboard. He was seen to fall, and the ship was instantly hove to, and the boats got out with all possible expedition; but he was never again seen to rise. His Dutch cap was taken up at the ship's stern; and, as it was known that he could swim as well as any man on board, the boats made a large circuit round the ship in hopes to recover him, but in vain. It is remarkable that in Captain Cook's former voyage one Henry Smock, one the carpenter's mates, sitting on the scuttle, fell overboard about the same place, and much in the same manner, and shared the same fate. Both these were young men, sober, and of good characters. Their loss was regretted by the officers, but more particularly so by their comrades among the crew. It is more than probable that both were instantly swallowed up by sharks that constantly attend the ships.

On the 1st of August we caught a large shark, ten feet long, with several young dolphins in her belly; part of the entrails, when cleansed and dressed, were eaten in the great cabin, and the body given to those by whom it was caught. When fried it is tolerable meat; but the fat is very loathsome. . . .

October 1st, having now been at sea just two months without once setting foot on land, those who were unaccustomed to such long voyages began to put on a very different aspect to that they wore at first setting out. They were, indeed, somewhat comforted by the cheerfulness and vivacity which they observed to prevail in almost every countenance except their own; from whence they concluded that many days could not elapse before the painful sensations of a solitary sea life would be recompensed by the pleasurable enjoyments they would find when they came on shore. Such, perhaps, were the feelings, at that time, of the writer of this journal. . . .

On the 7th, at six in the morning, the man at the masthead called out land; and at eight we could all see it involved in a misty cloud. It proved to be Table Land, bearing southwest, at the distance of about ten leagues, which induced us to change our course from east-southeast; to south-southwest.

On the 10th we entered Table Bay, and

On the 11th, came to and anchored in six fathom water, where, to our great joy, we found the *Resolution*.

We saluted the garrison with 13 guns, and were answered by the same number. Captain Cook, with the principal officers and gentlemen belonging to the ship, came on board to bid us welcome. By them we learned that they had been at the cape near three weeks; that they had stopped at Vera Cruz only three days, and had taken on board some wine, of which they very kindly offered us a part, and that they made no stay at Port Praia except to purchase some goats as presents to the chiefs of the Southern Isles.

On our landing our captain was met by the officers of the garrison and the gentlemen belonging to the Dutch East India Company, who received him very politely and gave him a general invitation to share with them the entertainments of the place.

The subordinate officers on board were met by another class of inferior gentry belonging to the same company, with a like invitation but on different terms. Almost every officer in the pay of the Dutch Company entertain strangers, who lodge and board with them on moderate terms, from two shillings a day to five.

Nothing in nature can make a more horrid appearance than the rugged mountains that form the bay. One would almost be tempted to think that the Dutch had made choice of the barrenest spot upon earth to shew what may be effected by slow industry and continued perseverance; for besides the craggy cliffs that render the open country almost inaccessible, the soil is so sandy and poor that, except some vineyards, there is scarce a shrub or a tree to be seen within any walking distance from the place; insomuch that the vast profusion of all sorts of provisions of beef, mutton, poultry, flour, butter, cheese and every other necessary, is brought from four- to five-and-twenty days' journey from Capetown, where the governor and company have their residence.

This town has already been so fully described by Captain Cook in his former voyage, and by other writers before him, that little remains to be added. The town is neatly built and, ac-

cording to the natural character of the Dutch, as neatly kept
in order. It has the advantage of a small rivulet, by means of
which there are canals in all the principal streets of the town;
on both sides of which are planted rows of stately oaks. The
town is situated below the mountains and, when seen from their
summits, appears, with the gardens and plantations that run
along the shore, exceedingly picturesque: nothing can be more
romantic, nor any prospect more pleasing to the eye.

The ship was no sooner moored than all hands were employed to strip off the rigging and to unload the stores; places
proper for repairing the one and for airing and examining the
other being prepared beforehand by Captain Cook; and the
utmost dispatch was made to shorten our stay, as the time for
navigating the high latitudes through which we were to pass
was advancing apace, and the *Resolution* was already in a state
fit to undertake the voyage.

What remained for Captain Cook to do when we arrived was
chiefly to purchase live cattle for presents to Arees in the South
Sea; likewise livestock for the ships' use; these are always the
last things provided, because it is found necessary to shorten,
as much as possible, their continuance on board. He had already
laid in sufficient store of beef, mutton, poultry, and greens for
present use, and had contracted for a good quantity of salted
beef to save what we had brought from England, as that is found
to keep better than the beef salted at the cape, though this
last is preferred for present use.

Among the cattle purchased were four horses and mares
of a delicate breed, for Omai, several bulls and cows of the buf-
falo kind, as more suitable to the tropical climates than any
brought from Europe; likewise some African rams and ewes;
dogs of the she kind, some with and some without puppies;
cats we had plenty on board; and goats Captain Cook had
purchased at Santiago.

Stored with these, the *Resolution* resembled the Ark, in
which all the animals that were to stock the earth were collected; and with their provender, they occupied no small part
of the ship's stowage.

While the riggers, sailmakers, carpenters, caulkers, smiths,
coopers, and storekeepers, were busily employed in their several
stations, the astronomers were not idle, nor the surgeons; the

former were engaged in making observations; the latter in attending the sick, of whom there were not many, and those, on being carried on shore, very soon recovered. The dry soft air of the African mountains proved a restorative superior to all the physic in the world. Of the efficacy of this salubrious air, the Dutch East Indiamen have experience every voyage, both in going to and returning from their settlements in India.

While we remained at the cape two of their ships arrived full of sick soldiers, who had been enlisted in Holland and who were in a miserable condition both as to health and want of common necessaries. They had been near five months on their voyage from Amsterdam, and had lost on the passage more men than the compliments of both our ships amounted to, owing to nastiness and close confinement. It is remarkable that no ships have the appearance of being neater kept than those of the Dutch; nor any more slovenly where they are not exposed to open view. . . .

On the 1st of December at three in the morning we took our departure, after saluting the fort with 11 guns, which they returned with the same number. At this time we observed that luminous appearance about our ships which different voyagers have attributed to different causes; but which Dr. Franklin has endeavored to account for on the principles of electricity. About five in the afternoon we met with one of those terrible gusts so frequently experienced by voyagers in doubling the Cape of Good Hope, in which our mainsail was split, but fortunately we received no other damage; the southernmost land then bearing south by east distance nine or ten leagues, both ships in company.

On the 24th in the morning it blew a hurricane and split the jib. About two in the afternoon, unbent and bent another. . . .

On the 25th at four in the morning the boats were sent out to reconnoiter the coast, and, if possible, to discover a more convenient harbor for taking in water. About seven they returned, having found a bottle with a letter enclosed importing that in January 1772 this island was discovered by M. de Kerguelen; that it contained plenty of water, but no wood; that it was barren and without inhabitants; but that the shores abounded with fish, and the land with seals, sea lions, and penguins. The harbor where this bottle was deposited being more commodious than that where the ships were anchored, and Captain Cook, intending to keep Christmas here and refresh his men, gave orders to weigh, and the ships to change their station; which orders were instantly obeyed.

The contents of the letter enclosed in the bottle were in every respect found to be true. . . .

On the 27th our repairs being nearly completed and a great part of our water on board, Christmas was proclaimed; a double quantity of grog served out to each common man; and a certain proportion of wine and spirits to every petty officer. Leave was likewise given to such as were ailing to go ashore for the benefit of the land air; and the officers of both ships reciprocally met in compliment to each other. Past dangers were forgotten, and the day was spent by the common sailors with as much mirth and unconcern as if safely moored in Portsmouth harbor.

On the 28th parties were sent out to procure what vegetables the island produced by way of refreshment; but none were found for culinary purposes except a kind of wild cabbage, and that in small quantities and gathered with much labor among the cliffs of the rocks. Mr. Nelson, a gentleman whom Mr. Banks sent out to collect such varieties as he should find indigenous to the islands and climates through which he should pass, found growing among those cliffs a kind of yellow moss of a silky softness, which he had not yet discovered in any of his former researches.

On the 29th the *Resolution* weighed, with orders to surround the island, in order to explore the opposite side, which, however, upon examination, was found equally barren, craggy, steep, and desolate with that we had just left. Penguins and sea lions were its chief inhabitants, among which our people made great havoc; of the former for the sake of provision, penguins having been found tolerable eating when fresh, or just salted; and of the latter for blubber, which was afterward boiled and converted into oil on our arrival at New Zealand.

On the 30th at nine in the morning we weighed and took leave of this island, which we found by observation to lie in lat. 49° 30′ south 78° 10′ long. At 12 the southernmost part of the land bore south-southwest to south distant about five leagues. We now pursued our course for Van Diemen's Land [Australia], and, having no discoveries in view, took every advantage of the weather to carry sail. . . .

March the 1st [1778] the wind died away, and being in lat. 45 deg. 95 min. and long. 225 deg. 14 min. we sounded with 180 fathom, but found no bottom. We now began to feel the effects of an alteration in the climate. From intense heat it became piercing cold; and our men, who despised their Magellan jackets while within the temperate climates, now first began to find the comfort of them in these northern regions.

On the 5th, being moderate weather, we sounded and at 56 fathom found bottom, loamy sand and shells. At six in the evening we shortened sail, and stood all night south to west with the water as white as milk.

On the 6th both ships wore and stood north by east shortening sail in the evening, and standing all night to the southward.

On the 7th we made the land. Cape Blanco, the westernmost known point of California, bearing east-northeast then distant about eight or nine leagues. It appeared mountainous and covered with snow. This day the gentlemen in the gunroom dined on a fricassee of rats, which they accounted a venison feast, and it was a high treat to the sailors, whenever they could be lucky enough to catch a number sufficient to make a meal.

On the 8th we wore ship, and stood northeast by east. We had heavy squalls, with snow and rain for a whole week, and after a series of the most tempestuous weather that ever blew, and in which the *Resolution* most miraculously escaped perishing upon a sunken rock, it was the 28th before we could get sight of a bay wherein we could anchor; at length we discovered an inlet, the mouth of which was not more than two miles over, in which we entered and found it a sound which narrowed as we advanced, tho' it still continued of a considerable depth. About seven in the evening we anchored 97 fathom water, and was presently joined by the *Resolution*. We made signs for some of the natives to come on board; but this they declined, though some hundreds soon came about the ships, to which they appeared to be no strangers as they gave us to understand that iron was what they valued most. We observed likewise that their weapons were headed with copper and their arrows with iron, which they could obtain only from the Russians or from trade with the Hudson's Bay Company. Though they declined coming on board, they were nevertheless very civil, and when they took their leave saluted us with a war song. We were now so far advanced to the northward and eastward as to be far beyond the limits of European geography, and to have reached that void space in our maps which is marked as a country unknown.

Early on the morning of the 30th the boats were armed and manned, and both captains proceeded to examine the sound, in order to find a convenient place to refit the ships which had suffered materially in the violent gales which for the last 20 days they had been combating, at the hazard of being hourly dashed to pieces about the rocks, or stranded upon the sands of this inhospitable coast.

In their progress they were fortunate enough to discover a cove the most convenient that could be wished, the entrance of which was about two cables' length, bounded by high land on each side, and furnished with wood and water (now much wanted) so conveniently situated that both could be taken on board at less than a cable's length from the shore; but, tho' now within the distance of four miles, it was four o'clock in the evening before we could get the ships properly moored, owing to the uncertainty of the weather and the violent gusts to which this coast is subject. All this while the Indians behaved peaceably and apparently with much friendship. They brought, after a short acquaintance, a great variety of valuable skins, such as beaver, foxes, raccoons, squirrels, reindeer, bears, and several others with which we were but little acquainted, but what they chiefly desired in exchange were cutlery wares of all sorts, edge tools, copper, pewter, iron, brass, or any kind of metal, with the use of which they were not unacquainted. All our people were now employed in the necessary repairs of the ships and in cutting wood and getting water on board, while the gentlemen diverted themselves in shooting and botanizing; when,

On the 1st of April, about four in the evening, there entered the cove a large canoe in which were 30 armed Indians, who, on their first appearance, began a war song, and when they had finished, took to their paddles and rowed round the ships, having first stripped themselves of their clothing, except one man, who stood upright in the vessel delivering an oration of which not a man on board could understand a word. They paddled round the ships several times as if led by curiosity, but did not offer to molest any of the workmen, nor did they offer to trade. All hands were instantly ordered under arms; when these new visitors were seen to clothe themselves before and to make toward the ships. The orator made not the least hesitation, but mounted the ship's side and accosted the captain with much civility, and, after receiving some presents and stopping a little while to observe the artificers, he took a very polite leave, descended to his boat, and was landed on the opposite shore of the sound.

On the 3d a large body of Indians were seen paddling along the sound, mostly armed with spears from 20 to 30 feet long and with bows and arrows very neatly made. On their nearer approach they too were heard to tune up their war song and to brandish their weapons, as if in defiance of an enemy. Their number was alarming, there being not less than 300 and 400 of them in their war canoes, who we apprehended were come to attack us; but we afterward understood they were come to attack a body of their enemies on the opposite shore, whom they afterward engaged, and returned victorious. We were frequently visited by such parties, who appeared always in arms; but never offered the least violence. They brought, besides skins, great quantities of fish, with plenty of game, which we purchased of them for glass bowls, looking glasses, nails, hatchets, or whatever utensils or toys were either useful or ornamental.

The men were of an athletic make, very rough to appearance, but more civilized than from their aspect there was reason to expect. To iron they gave the name of *ten-tum-miné*, and to other metals *che-à-poté*.

On the 5th the water, which was excellent, was so handily situated that by erecting a stage and constructing a spout, we could convey it into casks in the ship without farther trouble. This facilitated the labor of the waterers, and shortened our stay, as wood was conveyed on board with very little more trouble.

On the 6th it blew a storm, and the tide came rolling in at an alarming rate; it presently rose eight or nine feet higher than usual, and drifted several of our materials from the shore, which we never could recover; and at nine in the morning the *Discovery* drifted very near the *Resolution* and very narrowly escaped being bilged.

On the 7th the artificers again resumed their labor. The

natives continued their visits, and besides fish, furs and venison, brought bladders of oil, which were greedily purchased by the men. With this they made sauce for their salt fish, and no butter in England was ever thought half so good. . . .

On the 1st of June in the afternoon we set sail. We were now in lat. 61 deg. 15 min. north and in long. 209 deg. 55 min. east many leagues within land, and it was not till the 6th that we cleared the channel.

On the 4th, being His Majesty's birthday, we kept as a day of rejoicing.

On the 5th we passed the burning mountains.

The 6th we cleared the strait, to the unspeakable joy of the sailors who, during the whole time from our entrance till our return, worked with incredible labor, anchoring and weighing as the winds and the tide afforded opportunity. During our passage we had frequent interviews with the natives, who, the nearer we approached the shore, were better clothed, and shewed some manufactures of their own and other nations; and were in possession of a greater variety of skins than those within land, which were strong indications of a foreign trade, but by what conveyance carried on, all our endeavors at this time could not discover. On this day our course was southeast.

On the 7th we stood south by east to east and about two P.M. we passed two very large islands, having passed several small ones before. We continued this course with very little variation till the 10th, when the *Resolution,* in coasting along the main, ran foul of a dangerous reef that appeared just above water close under her lee bow. Her good fortune still accompanied her, for she slid off without damage.

On the 11th we were alarmed by the clashing of the waves, as if some great building was tumbling in, and, looking round the ship, we saw ourselves involved among shoals of seals and sea lions, who presently set up the most frightful howlings that possibly can be conceived; at the same time we observed a large whale to pass along, at which we fired a swivel, but without effect. We this day stood to the northeast as the land trended.

On the 12th we pursued the same course, and saw the land bear northeast to a great distance. The extreme of the eastward point bore east-southeast.

On the 13th at two P.M. we altered our course, and stood to the south.

On the 14th in the morning we saw the eastward point distant seven or eight leagues, lat. 56 deg. 23 min. long. 205 deg. 16 min. We directed our course along shore.

On the 15th, the weather hazy, we lost sight of land, sounded and found no ground at 100 fathom. A storm came on, and both ships stood to sea.

On the 16th it abated, the weather clear, stood west-southwest with a stiff breeze. . . .

About two in the afternoon [June 21] we came again in sight of the two burning mountains which we had before seen, but at a great distance, bearing northwest by west. Our course during the night was south-southwest. During the course of this day, the weather being fair and but little wind, the men were employed in fishing, and in less than four hours caught more than three ton weight of cod and halibut, some of the latter more than a 100 pounds weight.

On the 22d our men were employed in salting and barrelling up, for future use, what the ship's company could not consume while fresh, which proved a most acceptable supply. All this day we kept our course southwest by south.

On the 23d in the evening we shaped our course more to the westward, the weather thick and hazy.

On the 24th, little wind and hazy. Saw no land; but, looking over the ship's side, observed the water to change color to a milky white. Sounded, and found ground at 47 fathom. About four P.M. we saw two very high islands bearing northwest distance about five leagues, and could discern the mainland contiguous. We bore away under the lee of the westernmost, and continued steering all night south by east.

On the 25th in the morning we changed our course, steering southwest as the land trended. At ten the same morning we had a full view of the land for many miles but saw no signs of houses or inhabitants; but doubtless, tho' the country appeared rugged and barren and in many places white with snow, there were many people in the inland parts. About seven in the evening we could see land at a great distance, bearing due south, which had the appearance of a large island. Hitherto we had been exploring the coasts of an unknown continent, un-

known at least to our European geographers; though we shall
see by the sequel that it was not wholly unexplored by the
Asiatic Russians. Toward night, tho' it had been perfectly clear
all day, the air began to thicken, and by ten at night, the fog
was so thick that we could not see the ship's length. We
kept firing guns, burning false fires, and standing off land all
night, as did the *Resolution,* and in the morning of the

26th, when the fog dispersed, we found ourselves in a deep
bay, surrounded by high lands, and almost ashore under a high
mountain which we had not before discovered. Both ships
instantly dropped anchor in 24 fathom water, blue muddy
bottom within two cables' length of the shore and among shoals
and breakers, from which we most miraculously escaped. For
some time we stood in amazement how we could possibly get
into such a frightful situation. But being in it, for our own
safety we moored both ships; and happy it was we used that
precaution; for a gale came on, when our whole existence
depended upon the goodness of our cables.

On the 27th, at three A.M. it ceased blowing, and the weather
began to clear. At six we unmoored, and sailed under close
reefed topsails, directing our course northwest for an opening
we saw at about a league distance, but at nine, the wind dying
away, we anchored again in 25 fathom water, loamy sand. It
being a dead calm, our boats were ordered out, and some
gentlemen went on shore to examine the land. In their search
they found something like an Indian mansion, being a deep pit
sunk in the earth, with some poles placed across it after their
manner, and covered with sods and a hole to creep into it
about two feet square. In it they found the bones of dried fish
and of birds, and near it a place where there had been a fire,
but all had the appearance of being long deserted. They also
found the rib of a whale about eight feet long, which it was not
easy to account how it could come there. About noon the
gentlemen returned on board, and, a breeze springing up from
the eastward, we weighed and took leave of this dangerous bay,
to which Captain Cook gave the name of Providence Bay as it
was owing to providence that we were here miraculously preserved from perishing. . . .

On the 10th [of August] we had fine weather and a calm sea
and were proceeding at a great rate when, unexpectedly, we

opened into a deep bay, where we saw at the distance of a few leagues a large Indian town, of which, probably, our commodore was in search, as the Russians in their late discoveries had found a town upon the extremity of the Asiatic coast to which they had given the name of Heleneski. . . . This bay, by observation, lies in lat. 66 deg. 27 min. north and in long. 188 deg. 3 min. east near which the Russians have fixed the northeasternmost point of the Asiatic continent, and which we have now proved to join the main continent of America, having traced that continent from Cape Blanco, the westernmost known cape of California, to the present bay, without being able to find any communication with Hudson's Bay or any other sea whatever. But of this more hereafter.

Here we cast anchor, and both captains, attended by a proper guard of marines, went on shore and were met by an old Indian at the head of a numerous body of his countrymen, all dressed in the skins of beasts. He had in his right hand a spear 12 feet long, and over his left shoulder hung his bow and shaft of arrows. He addressed the strangers in a speech of half an hour, at the conclusion of which he displayed a cloak of white feathers, as a signal of peace, which Captain Cook answered by waving his white handkerchief. These preliminaries over, the Indian made signs to his followers to ground their arms, and set them the example by laying down his own, and making his submission. The parties then approached each other, and Captain Cook presented the Indian with a few European trifles, such as knives, scissors, needles, pins, beads, and small looking glasses, which were found more acceptable here than iron or more costly merchandise, with which the Indian was so pleased that he stripped himself of the garment which he wore and presented it with his weapons of war to the captain in return, making signs at the same time to the company to accompany him to the town, where we should meet with things more worthy our acceptance. This invitation both captains, with their train, accepted, and, after walking little more than two miles, we came to the town of which the old Indian appeared to be chief. Here was trafficked for furs of various sorts, sables, martens, foxes, beaver, and some deerskins dressed in a particular manner, on both sides, two of which we purchased for drum heads. They had dogs in abundance of a large breed, but we saw no other domestic animal. Their houses, or rather holes, were built much like those we had seen all along the coast. After staying about two hours, the company returned to the ships, the Indians accompanying us to the shore, where they took their leave, kneeling when we parted. We were no sooner embarked than the signal was made to weigh and get under way, shaping our course north-northeast. . . .

On the 12th we altered our course and stood to the northwest till noon, when we again stood to the east leaving several islands on our starboard bow. In the evening we crossed the Arctic Circle, and stood all night west by south as the land trended.

In the morning of the 13th we stood once more to the eastward. We were now in lat. 66 deg. 35 min. long 189, the weather warm and fine.

On the 15th, finding ourselves near land on a shallow and rocky coast, we stood off west-southwest, when presently we were attacked by a heavy storm of wind, attended with rain, which lasted the whole day. At night we stood again north-northeast and so continued till morning.

On the 16th at noon we found ourselves in lat. 69 deg. 46 min. long. 192 east. We then stood from north-northeast to northeast, sounding from 22 to 23 fathom water.

On the 17th the weather began to grow piercing cold. The frost set in and froze so hard that the running rigging was soon loaded with ice, and rendered almost impossible to make the sheafs or blocks traverse without the assistance of six men to do the work of one. But what is most remarkable, the sudden transition from heat to such severe cold. The day before was warm and pleasant, but in the evening of this day the ice was seen hanging at our hair, our noses, and even at the men's fingers' ends, if they did but expose them to the air for five or six minutes: And still the farther they ran to the eastward, the colder it grew, and the ice the more connected.

On the 18th hot victuals froze while we were at table; and this weather continued for some days. We were now advanced as far as lat. 69 deg. 46 min. north, and in long. 192 east and involved among islands of ice, some of which hung over our heads as we passed them and excited very frightful apprehensions. On some of these islands many sea morse [walruses] and other sea animals were seen. Being now well in with the ice, and having lost sight of land, we stood on to the northward till

The 19th, when looking round in the morning, as soon as the fog cleared away, we saw nothing but fields of ice covered over with whole herds of sea lions, sea horses, and other amphibious animals to the number, as it was thought, of some thousands. Thus surrounded, a signal was made from the *Resolution* to bring to and to load the great guns while the boats were getting ready to attack these hideous-looking creatures with muskets. This by the sailors from both ships was accounted sport; and they went to the attack with as much alacrity as if to a match at football. Orders were given, as soon as the great guns were discharged, to quicken the attack with the musketry as fast as possible. In a few minutes not a creature was to be seen upon the ice but such as were killed or so severely wounded as not to be able to crawl to the open sea. Some lay growling on the ice not quite dead, with two or three balls through their heads, and others tumbling about with horrible vindictive looks, threatening destruction to whoever should approach them. All hands were employed to collect the carcasses and to carry them on board; but what was thought an ill reward for their labor, orders were next day given by Captain Cook to substitute the flesh of these sea monsters in the room of all other provisions, flour only excepted. This was strongly opposed by the crew of the *Resolution,* and Captain Clarke remonstrated against it. He was told by Captain Cook that he might do what he pleased on board his own ship; but the state of the provisions on board the *Resolution* made it necessary; and that he himself should set the example. Captain Clarke endeavored, but in vain, to enforce the order, and the matter passed on without any serious consequences.

On the 20th we tacked ship and stood to the westward, the wind much against us. We tacked every two hours, still working over to the Asiatic shore with a view to examine the coasts on both sides before we returned to the southward. We were now in lat. 70 deg. 9 min. long. 194 deg. 55 min.

We continued laboring among the ice till the 25th, when a storm came on which made it dangerous for us to proceed; a consultation was therefore held on board the *Resolution* as soon as

the violence of the gale abated, when it was unanimously resolved that, as this passage was impracticable for any useful
purpose of navigation, which was the great object of the voyage,
to pursue it no farther, especially in the condition the ships were
in, the winter approaching, and the distance from any known
place of refreshment great. On observation being had at noon,
we found we were in lat. 71, and long. 197 when the ships put
about.

About two in the morning of the 26th we observed a great
body of ice nearing us very fast, and in a few hours after, we
saw the ice all closed as far as the eye could carry. Bearing from
northeast to southwest we continued to sail west-southwest.

On the 28th several pieces of loose ice passed us, one of which
came foul of the *Discovery* and shook her whole frame; it was
feared she had received considerable damage, but upon the
carpenter's examining her fore and aft, nothing was found
amiss. We now took leave of the ice for this season, directing
our course south-southwest.

On the 29th we saw land in the morning, which bore from
north-northwest to southwest very high and covered with snow.
In the evening we were in with the land; not a shrub to be
seen, but birds innumerable.

On the 31st we came in sight of the eastern cape, bearing
south-southeast very high and covered with snow; at three in
the afternoon we saw two small but very high islands, bearing
from north-northeast to northwest. We were then in lat. 68
deg. 10 min. and long. 182 deg. 2 min.

Sept. 1 we continued coasting to the southward.

On the 3d we opened into the great bay, where we anchored
the 10th of last month, lat. 66 deg. 31 min. long. 188 deg. 17
min. east.

On the 5th we lost sight of the main continent of Asia,
which we left the day before.

On the 6th we saw land from west-northwest to east-northeast
very woody, and covered with snow in the valleys. Here we
found the continent of America and the Asiatic shore not above
six leagues distant, lat. 63 deg. 58 min. long. 192 deg. 10
min. . . .

On the 13th, while the cutters were on this service, the boats
were busy in wooding and watering, and before the return of

the former, the latter had got more than 20 tons of water on board the *Discovery,* and near double that quantity on board the *Resolution,* with a proportionable quantity of wood. The men had then leave to go ashore, by turns, to gather berries, which they now found ripe and in great abundance, such as raspberries, blueberries, black and red currants, huckleberries, with various other sorts, all in full perfection. A party was likewise sent out to cut spruce to brew into beer for both ships. Of this liquor, however, the men were not very fond in this cold climate, especially when they were given to understand that their grog was to be stopped and this beer substituted in the room of it. This occasioned great murmuring, and it was found necessary to give it alternately, spruce one day and grog another.

On these excursions the parties were always well armed and had marines to attend them, and their orders were never to go out of hearing of the ships' guns, but to repair instantly on board on the proper signals. These precautions, however, seemed unnecessary as they never met with any molestation from the natives, who were not numerous upon the coast.

On the 17th, the party that were sent out to survey the bay returned, after a diligent examination of two days and two nights. Their report was that it extended within land above 40 leagues, that they coasted it round, sounding as they went, that they found the soundings regular from 5 to 3½ fathom; that it had no communication with any other sea nor any current that indicated a passage to any other continent whatever. This report being confirmed by the officers who commanded the cutters from both ships, the boats were all taken on board and secured, and

On the 18th we weighed and sailed, retracing the coasts we had before explored without making any material discovery.

Conclusion:
From Vancouver to the *Manhattan*

Captain James Cook's explorations of the Pacific Northwest cleared up many of the mysteries of that region but not all. To try once more to see whether a water passage eastward might be found, Captain George Vancouver was ordered by the Admiralty to sail from England in the *Discovery* on April 1, 1791, to explore the Pacific area previously visited by Cook. Vancouver had been one of Cook's junior officers on both his second and third voyages and was already a mariner with excellent experience in these waters.

Following Cook's route around the Cape of Good Hope to Australia, New Zealand and Tahiti, Vancouver sailed across the Pacific and sighted the northern coast of California on April 18, 1792, at latitude 39 degrees 27 minutes, not far from the present little coast town of Westport. Proceeding north, he sailed around the great island off British Columbia that now bears his name and continued onward to latitude 52 degrees 18 minutes before returning to the Hawaiian Islands to winter and refit.

In April 1793 Vancouver was again on the west coast of North America exploring from latitude 35 degrees to 56 degrees, or roughly from Pismo Beach, California, to Heceta Island in southern Alaska. After mapping the coast, he once more went to the Hawaiian Islands to winter. The spring of 1794 found him again exploring in the Northwest. From Kodiak Island off southern Alaska he sailed into Cook's Inlet, once believed to be a river, and determined that it was not an outlet to the east. After mapping the southern Alaskan coast he again explored the coast of California north of San Francisco and mapped the region. In October 1794 he at last sailed for England by way of Cape Horn and arrived in the Thames on October 20, 1795. While still preparing an extensive report of his expeditions, he died on May 10, 1798.

Vancouver had performed an enormous task in mapping the Pacific Northwest, but he had missed one important feature. Not only had he failed to find a western entrance to the Northwest Passage, but he had missed a great river that emptied into the Pacific somewhere in the north. Reports of the Great River of the West had reached fur traders, but Vancouver was skeptical.

It remained for Americans to discover this river. In 1787 a group of Boston merchants sent out two ships to trade for sea-otter skins on the West Coast. One vessel, the *Columbia*, was commanded by Robert Gray, and the other, the *Washington*, had as captain John Kendrick. Gray searched the northwest coast for the fabled river in 1788 but, failing to find it, obtained a cargo of furs and went on to China. Kendrick, following his instructions, erected a fort to serve as a trading post on Nootka Sound, negotiated with the Indians for the purchase of large tracts of land and sailed for Boston. He and his ship were lost on the homeward voyage.

Gray, however, returned to the Northwest in 1792. The sea-otter trade with China had proved profitable, and he prepared to continue the plans for a trading post that Kendrick had started. On May 11, 1792, he brought his ship, the *Columbia*, through breakers over a sandbar into the mouth of a great river, where he anchored. He had found the river that he had sought and he named it after his vessel. More than that, his discovery of the Columbia River gave the United States a claim to the whole drainage system of this stream and helped to establish its possession of Oregon and Washington. Robert Gray's persistence in searching for the mouth of the Columbia River paid vast dividends. The next year, 1793, a British officer of the Northwest Fur Company, Alexander Mackenzie, made an epochal overland journey to the West Coast, but his discoveries fall into the category of land explorations, a theme full of fascination for another volume.

By the time of Robert Gray's discovery of the mouth of the Columbia River, the main outlines of both the east and west coasts of the North American continent were fairly well known and mapped. Men would continue to search for the Northwest Passage for many years to come and it would remain for courageous mariners and scientists in our own time to accomplish what seamen for more than four centuries had dreamed of doing. From 1903 to 1906 Roald Amundsen in the ship *Gjoa* struggled to get through the ice-packed Northwest Passage and finally made it, the first to complete the journey entirely by ship. In 1918–20 he also sailed the *Maud* through the Northeast Passage to Asia, thus becoming the first man to negotiate both of these perilous passages by ship. Earlier, Nils Adolf Erik Nordenskjold in 1879–80 had reached China and returned to Sweden by way of the Northeast Passage.

In our time modern icebreakers can crash through the frozen packs where earlier wooden ships left their broken ribs.

Submarines can cruise below the ice and break through floes above. Modern knowledge of food and vitamins have long since removed the danger of scurvy which afflicted explorers until Captain Cook learned to carry along lime juice for his sailors.[2] But the Northwest Passage is still not a journey that one would take for pleasure.

The most recent voyage of exploration was made by the tanker *Manhattan* to see if the shipping of oil from Alaska's North Slope across the top of the world to the East Coast is feasible—and profitable. The *Manhattan,* a powerful tanker, left the Delaware Capes on August 25, 1969, headed for the Arctic. Accompanied by the Canadian icebreaker, the *John A. MacDonald,* she sailed through Baffin Bay, south of Devon Island and south of Banks Island to anchor on September 19 in Prudhoe Bay in northern Alaska. There she took on a symbolic barrel of oil before continuing to Point Barrow, the most northerly point in Alaska. From there she started her return journey, bucking immense ice floes and dodging sea ice as she went. She reached Halifax, Nova Scotia, early in November and made a quick run down the coast to New York by November 12. She had covered more than 10,000 miles in less than three months and had conquered ice packs that had turned back mariners through the centuries. Whether the Northwest Passage will prove as profitable as men have dreamed remains yet to be seen. But the route that daring seamen sought for so long is known and it may at last become an artery of commerce.

2 According to *A Dictionary of Americanisms* (Chicago, 1951), the American slang term "limey," meaning a Britisher, originally was applied to British sailors because they regularly received a ration of lime or lemon juice.

Index

THIS BOOK WAS SET IN

BASKERVILLE AND PERPETUA TYPES BY

BROWN BROS. LINOTYPERS, INC.

IT WAS PRINTED BY

HALLIDAY LITHOGRAPH CORPORATION

AND BOUND BY

MONTAUK BOOK MANUFACTURING CO., INC.

TYPOGRAPHY IS BY

BARBARA COHEN.